ISLANDS OF RAINFOREST

Islands of Rainforest

Agroforestry, logging and eco-tourism in Solomon Islands

EDVARD HVIDING
University of Bergen

TIM BAYLISS-SMITH
University of Cambridge

Ashgate

Aldershot • Burlington USA • Singapore • Sydney

Published by
Ashgate Publishing Ltd
Gower House
Croft Road
Aldershot
Hants GU11 3HR
England

Ashgate Publishing Company
131 Main Street
Burlington
Vermont 05401
USA

Ashgate website: http://www.ashgate.com

British Library Cataloguing in Publication Data
Hviding, Edvard
    Islands of rainforest : agroforestry, logging and
    eco-tourism in Solomon Islands. - (SOAS studies in
    development geography)
    1. Rain forests - Solomon Islands 2. Agroforestry - Solomon
    Islands 3. Ecotourism - Solomon Islands 4. Sustainable
    forestry - Solomon Islands
    I. Title II. Bayliss-Smith, Timothy P. III. University of
    London. School of Oriental and African Studies
    333.7'5'099593

Library of Congress Catalog Card Number: 00-131249

ISBN 0 7546 1233 3

Printed and bound by Athenaeum Press, Ltd.,
Gateshead, Tyne & Wear.

Contents

List of Illustrations

Figures

Plates (following page 326)

Preface

This is a book about tropical forests, but it offers a rather different view from other books in this genre. Our geographical focus is Island Melanesia, in the southwest Pacific. Our methodology is simultaneously social-anthropological and ecological, while our perspective is historical and local rather than futuristic and global. We aim to provide an ethnographically grounded analysis of continuities and disjunctures in the pre-colonial, colonial and post-colonial ways of using the forests of Marovo Lagoon in New Georgia, Solomon Islands. We see the uses of the rainforest in Marovo as something rooted in indigenous knowledge and in Melanesian cultural practice, but also as something firmly connected to modern realities. The book stands at the intersection of anthropology, historical geography, and the human ecology of the tropical rainforest, and also at the interface of the local and the global. We begin with a reconstruction of Marovo agroforestry circa 1840, and we end with the confusion of competing rainforest narratives that characterises the millennium.

Islands of Rainforest is the outcome of collaborative work by two authors over more than ten years. The book evolved as the situation "in the field" itself became transformed in the 1990s, with an expanding cast of actors, local and global, involved in complex situations of collaboration, co-operation and confrontation. Our cast includes Marovo chiefs, big-men and ordinary forest users, Solomon Islands politicians, New Zealand conservationists, UNESCO bureaucrats and Anglo-American eco-tourists. In seeking to understand their various interactions, we need to construct a new kind of ethnography which encompasses the present-day reality of a rainforest in which the local/ traditional and the global/modern are both present, as ideologies and as agencies. We need to appreciate the wide range of rainforest narratives that now co-exist, many of them contradictory, and each with the power to explain and to legitimate a set of decisions and actions. For Marovo men and women it is not a straightforward binary choice between "conservation" and "exploitation", so we cannot construct a simple story about rainforest friends and enemies, vulnerable natives and intrusive foreigners, goodies and baddies. Instead we believe the 21st century will see the emergence of a new Melanesian modernity in places like the Marovo Lagoon, as the islands of rainforest – large and small, actual and metaphorical – become contested between local big-men, chiefs, tradition-alists and entrepreneurs, between capitalists and conservationists, and be-tween insiders and outsiders of new and different kinds.

The two authors can justly claim to have studied rather thoroughly, and over an extended period, the full range of rainforest-related activities in the Marovo Lagoon region. Moreover we have done this primarily through field research, although we have approached the field situation from quite diffe-rent standpoints. Edvard Hviding, a social anthropologist, has carried out altogether thirty-two months of anthropological fieldwork in the Marovo area (eighteen months in 1986-87, then in 1989, 1990, 1991-92, 1994 and 1996) with a focus on material and symbolic practice and on the social, political and ideological dimensions of resource use on the lands and reefs of Marovo Lagoon, as well as on ethnobiology and ethnobotany, languages and history (e.g. Hviding, 1988, 1993a,b, 1995a,b,c, 1996a,b, 1998a,b; Hviding and Baines, 1994). His main approach has been one of prolonged residence and participant observation in a range of Marovo communities (in particular the villages of Chea, on Marovo Island in the central lagoon, and Tamaneke in the northern lagoon), with an emphasis on taking part in maritime practice but also with considerable engagement in agricultural and hunting and gathering activities in all types of forest. This has enabled him to interpret the decision-making processes involved in the day-to-day management of resources, how these management practices have changed during the life times of present-day elders, and how they interact with an increasing presen-ce of foreign agents also interested in appropriating resources for their own ends. This knowledge is supplemented by information from oral history, not least dealing with the complex, large-scale sociopolitical relationships and production systems of pre-colonial Marovo, and by detailed and up-to-date information on the extralocal contexts for present-day developments (notab-ly logging). Hviding speaks the Marovo language fluently and has sufficient knowledge of the other languages of the area (particularly Hoava) to allow for comparative analysis.

Tim Bayliss-Smith, a human geographer with an interest in population, resources and development (and with many years of research experience on agricultural systems in the New Guinea highlands, in Fiji and on the Poly-nesian outlier of Ontong Java in the Solomons), quantified in July-August 1986 many aspects of time use, land use and diet in Marovo Lagoon, via a sample survey in four contrasted communities (Bayliss-Smith, 1987, 1993). This work included detailed surveys of cultivated land, mapped for sample households in these four communities. He also has made observations and plant collections so that a descriptive model can be constructed of the eco-logical succession which, in some instances, allows cultivated land in

Marovo to return to secondary forest and thereby to regenerate successfully its nutrient status. Bayliss-Smith visited the Marovo Lagoon briefly again in 1996 and 1997, which provided opportunities to reexamine some of the areas surveyed ten years previously, and to follow up recent developments in New Georgia concerning such topics as logging, reforestation and eco-tourism. Most of our work has been independent, but in both 1986 and 1996 we were able to carry out joint fieldwork.

Examination of archival material in collections and libraries in Sydney, Cambridge, London, Honiara and elsewhere has shed light on precolonial New Georgia and on the colonial period. Consistent collecting of contemporary written material in the form of unpublished reports and mass media articles (including an increasing number of items found on the World Wide Web) has contributed to insights into the present-day scene in Solomon Islands. Both of us can also provide comparative perspectives drawn from the wider Melanesian and Oceanic region. Taken together, we believe that our joint work provides a firm basis for appreciating the continuity and the adaptation of Marovo worldviews and ways of life, and for interpreting the tensions generated by economic development and sociocultural transformations.

Meetings in mid-1986 during fieldwork and in June 1989 in Cambridge enabled us to achieve some preliminary integration. In 1990, the joint planning and teaching in Cambridge of a course on the human ecology of Melanesia was an opportunity for further work, and meetings since then in Bergen, Cambridge and Marovo Lagoon itself have allowed a fuller integration over the years of our separate but complementary empirical data and analytical insights. On this background the present book constitutes an ethnographically-based yet interdisciplinary study of the Marovo agro-forestry system viewed in anthropological, ecological, ethnobotanical and historical terms, and of the system's capacity to satisfy the people's needs for sustainable agricultural development. Simultaneously, the book is on a more general level a longitudinal study of a Melanesian people's relations to wider worlds. In this we wish to follow the programmatic call from elsewhere in Melanesian anthropology for using the particular strengths of the anthropological, fieldwork-based perspective to do "some justice to the complexity and significance of change in colonial and postcolonial situations" (Errington and Gewertz, 1995:1).

Whereas we share responsibility for all chapters of the book, Hviding assumes responsibility as senior author from the basis of a long-term association with, practical engagement in and detailed knowledge of most fields of Marovo practice, as well as command of vernacular language, continuing observation of many exogenous processes directly affecting life in Marovo, and intimate day-to-day experience from any manner of Malinowskian "imponderabilia of actual life" (Malinowski, 1922:18).

Thematically, this book should serve to extend significantly the very limited literature on local uses of rainforest and land in Solomon Islands. It also produces some insights into the interaction of social and ecological processes that should be of wider interest. The contextualisation provided in the two introductory chapters should make clear the urgent need for detailed localised case studies – from Island Melanesia and elsewhere – of changing agroforestry practices and the associated technical knowledge, in circumstances of population growth, commodification, intensified resource development and other corollaries of potentially profound sociocultural transformation. There is indeed a need for emphasising the long-term dynamics of specific production systems and material realities of everyday lives in places like Marovo Lagoon, and an analysis of the Marovo people and their land is of interest in comparative terms, as an example of the "local-in-the-global" through trajectories of world history, and as a pointed illustration that lives in faraway tropical islands are not only constituted locally. In this perspective the present study addresses the issue of what is rhetorically "traditional" or "indigenous" from the basic theoretical premise that social life and cultu-ral beliefs have always been undergoing change, while acknowledging that some events, processes and times of change are certainly more momentous than others. Thus we depart from any dualist opposition between "traditional" and "modern".

The book also has another, parallel, non-dualist vein. In our special attention to the ostensibly "ecological" dimensions of past and present life in Marovo we follow Gísli Pálsson (1997) in his recent call for integrating human ecology and social theory by drawing on pragmatism and phenomenology, thereby departing from inherently dualist thinking of "nature" as something separate from "culture". Yet for our analysis of the wider ecological and demographic ramifications of agroforestry we insist on approaching the material world through certain structured methodologies of human ecological and archaeologically reconstructive analysis. The latter approaches contribute importantly to our analysis of agroforestry and its transformations in present-day Marovo, and to our reconstruction of a pre-colonial regional system founded on large-scale irrigated taro cultivation, ranked chiefdoms, internal distribution through barter and tribute, and overseas warfare, exchange and alliance (for the latter, see also Hviding, 1996a:79-101). This documentation of large-scale irrigated agriculture (interacting with swiddens) in a context of hierarchical polities should serve to locate the New Georgian part of Melanesia more firmly in a debate that dissolves the now-obsolete (and ill-founded, cf. Thomas, 1989b) but long-lived dichotomies between "Melanesian" and "Polynesian" types of sociopolitical organisation.

This book will hopefully be a resource to the Marovo people themselves as they enter yet another new phase of rapid and accelerating change. The onset of this phase has seen the large-scale logging of what would otherwise be reserve lands, and an increasing shortage of good garden land in relative proximity to village settlements. There is now the prospect, as expressed by a concerned Marovo leader, that

> People will soon have to go back to the old life again, by returning into the bush to settle in hamlets there and to take up intensified agriculture. Maybe we should revive the old methods like **ruta** [irrigated taro pondfields]. We must see to it that we still remember how to make the most out of the bush in the future, because there will not be enough coastal garden land, nor fish and shells, for all.

In Marovo, as elsewhere in the tropical world, the fate of the forest depends in part on what alternative benefits present generations believe they can get from forest lands kept off-limits to bulldozers – relative to the short-term benefits of (outrageously low) royalties paid for round logs by transnational companies to owners of land and trees. The future of the Marovo forests also depends on what is going to happen to the rather large areas that have already had the majority of large trees removed by loggers.

It would seem to be a fundamental Melanesian axiom that many trees have to be felled and land has to be somehow cleared before one can make intensive use of it for agricultural purposes. The modification history and present-day state of Marovo forests certainly attests to such an observation. But experience in the 1990s shows that large-scale logging may not be the most beneficial means of 'taming' (in Marovo, **va manavasia**) the forest. There are more ways of rainforest modification – other ways to transform 'wild' forest into cultivated land – as will be demonstrated by this long-term study of the place of agroforestry in the past and present lives of the people whose lives depend on the islands of rainforest and coral reefs around the Marovo Lagoon.

Acknowledgements

This book has evolved slowly over a rather long period, but unlike many research monographs we cannot claim that our work represents the outcome of a particular project, research programme or line of sponsorship. In Solomon Islands the field research that enabled us to write this book was the outcome of consistent and rather open-ended support from the various authorities. No obstacles were put in our path by those who could have queried our presence – rather the reverse: at all levels there seemed to be a consensus that the tangle of events in Marovo's past, present and future was an important topic for concern. In the outside world, however, we never sought nor received official sponsorship from any institution. Nor did we require funding for the fieldwork on a scale much beyond the occasional airfare to and from Europe. Throughout the period of the book's gradual emergence both of us were fortunate enough to be securely salaried by our respective universities, and we were under no particular pressure to pursue a "rainforest project" rather than some other programme of research and teaching.

Yet we both felt impelled to see the project through to its final conclusion (namely, this book) despite the lack of institutional pressure or any need to justify ourselves to financial sponsors. A strong reason was the hidden hand of an increasing obligation that we have felt towards the Marovo people, who themselves never had any difficulty in understanding the relevance of our task, and who well appreciated its increasing urgency. Secondly there has been the rising tide of rainforest rhetoric in the wider world, as voiced by our students, by the media, by web sites on the Internet, and not least by our friends and colleagues. Ever since the mid-1980s "the tropical rainforest" has seemed like an increasingly important topic for research, for an interesting set of cultural reasons that themselves demand attention (see Chapter 1). For us, the various conflicting "narratives" about the rainforest became focussed largely on our fieldwork experiences in Marovo, and increasingly it was the contradictions between them that demanded some sort of intellectual resolution. This book can be seen, therefore, as an attempt to resolve these rainforest contradictions, and to place on record some of the knowledge that we have been able to document from the guardians of one small section of the global rainforest – the Marovo people.

There is therefore a large and varied set of persons who have given freely of their time and knowledge, and whose contribution demands more than the usual polite listing of sponsors, facilitators and local "counterparts". Yet these people belong in very different categories: in the terms that we develop in this book's final chapter, these people have informed us about very different and sometimes quite contradictory "narratives" of the rainforest. Some persons might even object to seeing their names in the same list alongside certain other names! We therefore simply organise our thanks in terms of people's proximity to the geographical centre of our enquiry, thus moving from the ostensibly more local to the apparently more global sphere – but not forgetting that increasingly many people move easily between spheres.

In Marovo Lagoon itself we are especially grateful to the Marovo Area Council and its President Allan Pulepae and Secretary Eddison Kotomae, to Harold Jimuru and his wife Wendy, to Vincent Vaguni and his wife Amina Kada, to Eddie Moses and his wife Aedalin; and (in alphabetical order) to Erik and Vivian Andersen, Tena Baketi, Letipiko Bale, Hon. Tenapiko Barora, Gloria Dennie, Jonathan Evu, Freeman Hite, the late D.K. Jimuru, Mapeli Jino, the late Pastor Julias, David Livingstone Kavusu, Aivin Kerovo, Lawrence Kilivisi, Billy Kioto, Nicolas Kwate'ana, Jessie and Dennie Loni, Ezekiel Mateni, Frank Mulvey, Romulus Paoni of Lagoon Lodge, the late Pastor Kata Ragoso and his wife Elizabeth, Frank Riqeo, Piko Riringi and the staff of Ropiko Lodge, the late Philip Ronu, Kurt and Susan Sjoberg, Piali Tivuru, Stanley Vaka and the staff of Vanua Rapita, Hon. Stephen Veno, Billy Vinajama, Luten Watts of Tibarene Lodge, and John Wayne.

Secondly we would like to thank some participants in the wider sphere of New Georgia affairs: in Gizo, the administration of Western Province especially John Nige and Kenneth Roga of the Cultural Affairs Division, Seri Hite, Jully Makini, Ellen Woodley and Brent Tegler; In Munda Sam Patavaqara, Marius Willem Quist, Jaap Schep, Nixon Dennie, and Peter Paulsen; and in Ringgi Moray Iles, Paul Speed and Eric Havea.

In the kaleidoscope world of the Solomon Islands capital, Honiara, we were helped by a bewildering range of people in the fields of national politics, administration, NGOs and the business community, as well as those elected to represent the interests of Marovo and New Georgia. They include: the Solomon Islands Museum and its Director Lawrence Foana'ota, the National Research Officer Audrey Rusa, and (in alphabetical order) Hon. Christopher Columbus Abe, Tony Hughes, Beraki Jino, Max Jino, Lulu Laejama, Wilson Liligeto, Wilson Maelaua, Paul Miles, John Naitoro, Hon. Danny Philip, John Preece, Yalu Revo, Rhys Richards, John Roughan, Hon.

Snyder Rini, Hon. Job Dudley Tausinga, Elspeth Wingham, and Ronald Ziru and the staff of Pakoe Lodge.

While assistance from people in Solomon Islands has been so wide and varied that we have only been able to list a selection of names, acknowledging support and collaboration from academic colleagues is a simpler task. Europe is a long way from Solomon Islands, and necessarily in this continent there has been less opportunity for dialogue concerning Marovo Lagoon and its complexities. But special thanks are due to Graham Baines (now in Brisbane), whose inspired leadership as environmental adviser to Western Province and the Solomon Islands government paved the way for our initial involvement with Marovo Lagoon in 1986. His presence in our project cannot be underestimated. Secondly, in Cambridge, we have valued enormously the interest and support of Tim Whitmore, whose knowledge and commitment to Solomon Islands forestry deserves far more than this brief acknowledgement. In Cambridge and England we also wish to thank Mike Young and Philip Stickler for their cartographic skills; and Bill Adams, Ben Burt, Paul Sillitoe, Marilyn Strathern, and Liz Watson; and in Norway Fredrik Barth, Cato Berg, Reidar Grønhaug, Karen Leivestad, and Arve Sørum. Friends and loved ones were also part of this project and its fieldwork over the years. They include Patrizia Gaudenzio, Tom and James Bayliss-Smith, Inga-Maria Mulk, Karen Leivestad and Nina Shilpa Hviding.

Finally, we gratefully acknowledge financial and logistic support from St John's College, Cambridge, the Smuts Fund of the University of Cambridge, the University of Bergen, the Research Council of Norway, Ájtte Museum in Jokkmokk, Sweden, and the Commonwealth Science Council in London.

Edvard Hviding
Tim Bayliss-Smith

St John's College, Cambridge
August 1999

Conventions

Bold type and italics

Many Latin binomials – scientific names mainly of important agroforestry plants – occur in the text, and are set in *italics*. The text also contains a substantial number of terms from the Marovo language and other vernaculars of New Georgia. For maximum distinctiveness these vernacular terms are set in **bold type**. There are five languages in the Marovo area: Marovo, Bareke, Vangunu, Hoava and Kusaghe. Unless stated (such as in cases of linguistic comparison), the words given are in the Marovo language. This is for the sake of clarity and consistency, and also in recognition of the role of the 'coastal' Marovo language as the lingua franca of the entire Marovo Lagoon area. It is to be noted, though, that a significant number of plant names and terms for agroforestry activities are different in the four additional 'bush' languages of the area. A comprehensive Marovo-and-English environmental dictionary published by one of the authors (Hviding 1995b) contains rather exhaustive additional lists of plant (and animal) names in the two 'bush' languages of Hoava and Vangunu, with corresponding Marovo equivalents. Whereas Hoava is closely related to the Kusaghe language of northern New Georgia, Vangunu is even more closely related to the Bareke language (both are languages of Vangunu Island), and so the dictionary effectively bridges the five languages of the Marovo area.

Spelling and pronunciation of vernacular terms

The spelling followed in this book for the Marovo language follows the conventions set out in the Marovo Bible translation, accomplished in the 1950s mainly by first-generation Seventh-day Adventist converts from Marovo Island in the central lagoon. Details concerning this system of spelling and pronunciation and its relations to Marovo phonetics have been published by Hviding (1996a:xxvii-xxix); here is a brief summary.

In Marovo, as in the four other related languages, vowels – represented as **a, e, i, o, u** – are pronounced roughly as they would be in Italian. Diphthongs are abundant. For the consonants, several distinctive features stand out: (1) The voiced stops represented as **b, d** and **j** are "pre-nasalised", thus usually being pronounced rather like **mb**, **nd** and **nj** (the **j** being approximately like in English "Joe", though pre-nasalised as noted). (2) Two distinct pre-nasalised velar stops and one velar fricative have representations centred on "g". They are: **g**, pronounced as in English "finger"; **ng**, pronounced as in English "singer"; and **gh**, pronounced like the Greek *gamma* and exemplified by the "soft g" occurring between vowels in Spanish, e.g. as in *agua* "water". (3) The voiceless palatal/alveo-palatal fricative represented as **ch** is pronounced like in English "child". (4) The Hoava bush language utilises a different spelling, based on the Bible translation accomplished by Methodists in the neighbouring Roviana language. The only significant differences for the purposes of this book are: the Marovo **g** is represented as **q** in Hoava, the Marovo **ng** becomes Hoava **n̠**, and the Marovo **gh** becomes Hoava **g**.

Quotation marks

For English glosses of words and concepts in the Marovo language, single inverted commas are used. Otherwise, normal quotation marks are given as double inverted commas.

Exchange rates

The Solomon Islands Dollar (SI$) as of April 1999: SI$1.00 = US$0.20; US$1.00 = SI$5.00. Its value has been consistently falling over the last decade.

1 Conceptualising the Rainforest

The tropical rainforest in global discourse

We begin with a question – how to account for the rising importance of the tropical rainforest in the global agenda? The tropical rainforest has emerged as one of the most potent symbols in North-South discourse, but yet its prominence cannot be easily explained. For example, its geographical extent is not particularly impressive. Even before the recent wave of clearance the tropical rainforest only covered about 3% of the earth's surface. Its proportion of the world's forested areas is not overwhelming – the tropical rainforest makes up only about 30% of the world's forest cover (Whittaker and Likens, 1975). Moreover these forests are all located within a handful of mostly poor tropical countries that are bystanders in the deadly geopolitical struggles of the great powers. Until recently tropical rainforests seemed to be almost cut off from the mainstream of world history.

The change in perception has been rather dramatic. Only one hundred years ago the tropical rainforest was constructed in the Western imagination as a place that was simultaneously alluring, mysterious and hostile, while being also seen as a wilderness that was essentially without use and without value. The knowledge of its inhabitants was despised or disregarded, even though Western knowledge of this environment was extremely limited. When Paul Richards published his book *The Tropical Rain Forest* in 1952, the totality of scientific knowledge about rainforest ecology from English, French and German sources was contained within a volume of only 407 pages. As late as the 1950s it was widely assumed in the West that the rainforest could achieve value in the age of global capitalism only if the disease problems endemic to these tropical regions could be overcome and only if the soils could be made more productive by a transformation in land use (e.g. Gourou, 1947).

Yet today school children in Western Europe organise fund-raising schemes to help to "save the rainforest". The fate of the tropical rainforest has become part of the political agenda in North-South relations, with concerns ranging widely across the rights of indigenous peoples, wildlife conservation, eco-timber, biodiversity prospecting, smoke pollution from forest fires, global

1

climate change, and more. The tropical rainforest has become an icon for the environmental movement, and its fate is a form of moral discourse with the power to unite or divide the peoples of the planet. In the mass media and across the World Wide Web, the forest is again being discussed in terms of wonder and mystery. Once forgotten corners of Brazil, Zaire or Borneo are being "discovered" as treasure houses of values that we – the "people of the planet" – cannot and should not translate into material terms. Plane loads of eco-tourists from the rich countries are setting out to discover for themselves some of these natural wonders. Meanwhile, even as we complete this book, the efforts of loggers, plantation companies and impoverished slash-and-burn farmers to "destroy" the rainforest are being amplified by huge forest fires across Indonesia and as far as New Guinea, and in the Brazilian Amazon. The image on television screens of thousands of square kilometres shrouded in smoke evokes looming disaster, with global implications for climate change, the extinction of species and human welfare. Rather than discouraging interest these images of disaster probably stimulate the eco-tourism industry, with its promise of providing easy access to the wonders of nature before they disappear for ever.

The rediscovery of the magic and mystery of the tropical rainforest takes us back to an earlier and more innocent phase of globalisation. Modern eco-tourists are following in the footsteps of earlier travellers such as Alfred Russel Wallace and Charles Darwin, who in retrospect look almost like pioneers of this cultural phenomenon. Even Darwin's intellectual curiosity was initially submerged by a much more emotional response. When he stepped ashore in Bahia after a two-month journey across the Atlantic by sailing ship, he wrote as follows in his diary:

> February 29th 1832 ... Delight is a weak term to express the feelings of a naturalist who, for the first time, has wandered by himself in a Brazilian forest. The elegance of the grasses, the novelty of the parasitical plants, the beauty of the flowers, but above all the general luxuriance of the vegetation has filled me with admiration. (Darwin, 1839:10)

Our book is also written in a spirit of admiration, but it is admiration for the people who inhabit the rainforest as much as for the forest ecosystem itself. Our focus is not Brazil, Zaire or Borneo, but the Solomon Islands, within the region of Melanesia in the southwest Pacific. As elsewhere globalisation and its effects have become an inescapable feature of the lives of rainforest peoples in this region, even though only a generation ago they would have been classified as among the least "globalised" people on the planet.

Inevitably the present-day concerns in the West have also influenced our choice to work among the people who depend on Solomon Islands rainforests, and certainly this upsurge in interest on environment-development interfaces has facilitated the funding of our research. However, we have chosen as our starting point not the global rhetoric of rainforest conservation and eco-tourism, nor the global reality of an uncontrolled scramble for tropical hardwoods by the logging companies. Of course these new external pressures do influence how Solomon Islanders are now using their forests, but we would argue that global processes do not provide a good starting point. Indeed, these processes are part of the cultural baggage of pre-conceptions and stereotypes that any Westerner must jettison before attempting the task of understanding the forest through the eyes of its inhabitants rather than through the optic of global discourse.

Instead of starting at the present day and with the "global" concerns of environmentalism and logging that now dominate perceptions of the rainforest in the West, we therefore begin our analysis with the past and with the local. We examine the meanings and uses of forests by the men and women who live in small village communities on the shores of the Marovo Lagoon, situated in the New Georgia archipelago in the Western Solomons, and we approach these topics initially through a reconstruction of historical change. The assumed *un*-changing character of rainforest peoples has been part of the mythology of Western observers ever since this zone of the world came under the gaze of the agents of Western imperialism. It is a particularly unhelpful stereotype when we come to consider the long-term interactions between local culture and global process. Like so many others seemingly left on the periphery of the "world system", tropical rainforest peoples are far from being "people without history" (Wolf, 1982; and see Tsing, 1993). Nor have the Pacific islanders of New Georgia been the victims of any "fatal impact" from "the West" along the lines of widespread popular assertions (e.g. Moorehead, 1968).

From an analysis of historical change it is possible to argue that the Marovo people have been successfully (according to their own criteria) confronting the challenges and opportunities offered by remote worlds for more than 150 years, ever since first contact with Europeans in the pre-colonial era. Since whaling ships started calling in the New Georgia islands around 1790 to replenish their stores and to weather the cyclone season, most contacts of Marovo people with faraway worlds have been dominated by the miscellaneous outsiders' aspirations to reap benefits, in one way or another, from the resources of Marovo's lands, reefs and seas (Hviding, 1996a). Only by piecing together this story of encounters and confrontations with, and adaptation to, the outside world can we appreciate the present-day pattern of response in Marovo to outsiders in their various forms. Today's outsiders include Malaysian, Indonesian and Korean loggers, North American and European eco-tourists, and New Zealand and Australian conservationists – as well as Melanesians from neighbouring islands of the Solomons, more interested in access to cultivation in the Marovo forest than in its commodification to meet global needs.

Beyond historical ethnography

The story we are about to tell contains many strands leading towards more general statements about people's relationships to their environments and about the comparative study of social and ecological systems. On the surface this book may well be seen by some to fall under the very topical umbrella of "rainforest studies". If that helps to spread our messages to audiences concerned with tropical rainforests in particular, that is fine. But in the realm of scholarship we would prefer to situate the book somewhat differently. Acknowledging other recent contributions from Melanesian anthropology (such as those of Frederick Errington and Deborah Gewertz) towards understanding Melanesian lives in relation to worlds beyond, we follow their ambition to "make *grounded* sense of how [local] people have actually lived with and engaged in some of the rather large and compelling issues of our time" (Errington and Gewertz, 1995:1, italics in original). From a starting point in ethnographic analysis we attempt in this book to establish a truly holistic viewpoint, with a focus on the local in relation to the global and on the complexities of colonial and post-colonial situations. In order to understand the interactions of the various agents, local and global, who are currently operating in and near the forests of Marovo, we have been forced to extend our time horizon back into the past beyond the reach of ethnographic observation.

Our overall objective has been to remain ethnographically well-informed while also pursuing general theoretical perspectives and comparative debates. Thus, despite working in a time and age of intensified specialisation within subdisciplines, in this book we draw on concepts, approaches and published and unpublished material from a diverse number of disciplines such as anthropology, geography, history, archaeology, linguistics, ecology and botany. We set out to define the basic parameters of forest utilisation in Marovo, while also considering how the environment is perceived, experienced and known by the Marovo people themselves. Our approach to understanding the shifting nature of Marovo people's relationships to their rainforests, then, has aspirations extending beyond those of specialised "cultural ecology" or "human ecology" and far beyond the more nebulous gaze of the fashionable but ill-defined realm of "environmental studies".

Although being based in two different disciplines, we are both field ethnographers who give analytical priority to detailed knowledge of what unfolds on the ground, understood not only through general more or less objectivist languages but also – and in many respects more significantly – through the cosmological frameworks and epistemological evaluations of "the people" themselves. But our attempts to reconstruct and analyse the structures and dynamics of Marovo people's involvement with their lands and forests range over some 150 years, and this time scale dictates that this can be no syn-chronic work built up from glimpses of events and activities that were all observed by us in the field. In theoretical and methodological terms we feel compelled, therefore, to attempt yet another expansion of recent historical-anthropological approaches of general bearing but developed with particular reference to Oceania (cf. Sahlins, 1985; Thomas, 1989a). Our perspective inte-grates the general with the particular, for example general archaeological infe-rences about land-people interactions in prehistoric Melanesia with highly specific information – obtained first-hand through recent fieldwork – on Marovo people's perceptions of the forest and their utilisation of its potentials.

In this respect we recognise the magnificent recent contribution on Hawaiian "historical ethnography" and "archaeology of history" by the two distinguished scholars Patrick Kirch and Marshall Sahlins (1992). Yet, for our analysis of long-term developments in Marovo we need to add further dimensions to the ethnography-history-archaeology axis. Those additional dimensions are not limited to the views of conventional political economy on colonial subjugation of the peripheral, nor to the more recent ones of globali-sation theory. The multiple discourses that shape today's uses of the Marovo rainforest – the "ethnographic present" employed in parts of this book – are not to be defined only, not even mainly, from a basis of local knowledge and practice, but from dialogues between micro- and macro-levels, wherein "micro" (for which read: the "local") as often as not appears to modify incur-sions by "macro" (for which read: the "global"). In analysing these dialogues we wish to emphasise the cultural and historical specificities of events – as well as similarities and convergences in encounters between Marovo people and other people from elsewhere. These others include such disparate actors as British colonial officers pursuing land alienation, representatives of European and Asian logging companies, and conservationists from Austra-lia, New Zealand and the USA, as well as any number and variety of past and present visitors – friends and foes – from other islands in the Solomons.

Although the second half of the book to a large degree deals with events of today that may well be seen to form a core of an emerging "Melanesian modernity", we wish to avoid an overly great insistence – in search of "radi-cal alterity" (Keesing, 1994) – on deep and fundamental cultural differences between Melanesian and Western approaches. In that sense this book does not rest easily within the anthropological genre called by some recent com-mentators "New Melanesian Ethnography" (Foster, 1995; after Josephides, 1991). In this genre, disparities between Melanesian and Western views of social reality are highlighted, and the diversity of the "Melanesian Other" is explored, by means of a consistent methodological reliance on an Us/ Them divide (exemplified most brilliantly by Strathern, 1988). While we recogni-

['

se, and highlight where needed, significant differences between past and present New Georgian and European approaches to New Georgian people, lands, forests and lagoons, we build the analysis from a general premise that involvement between – and entanglements of – people of disparate backgrounds and agendas, yet still somehow oftentimes with shared projects, are a rule rather than an exception in world history. The approach followed in this book is to be seen as "ethnography with time and transformation built into it" (Sahlins, 1993:1), and the colonial and post-colonial trajectories we address through an ethnographically founded view in many ways become the shared histories of Solomon Islanders and Europeans and Asians; the two latter categories having various old and new colonial agendas with respect to the resources of the former.

Ultimately, Marovo "tradition" (or, in Melanesian terms, **kastom**) and ways of life are to be seen as influenced and transformed by circumstances over which the villagers around the lagoon appear to have little control, yet in their own way – quite consistent with widespread Melanesian approaches to the unexpected (cf. Strathern, 1992) – the Marovo people transform and partly subvert these challenges by subjecting issues and protagonists to Marovo agendas of social and political process. Ecologically oriented adventure tourists, timber-hungry logging companies and other arrivals of recent years are not altogether new for the villagers of Marovo.

From pre-colonial to post-colonial: the *longue durée* in New Georgia

With the above in mind, a general lesson may be learnt from analysing the past 150 years of Marovo people's involvement with their rainforest. We propose that, in the time frame and fields of practice analysed here, the firmly "colonial" condition (comprising the period 1893-1978, during which the Solomon Islands was a British colony) has been rather more stable, even tranquil, than both "pre-" and "post-colonial" stages. We do not thereby intend to minimise the suffering the centuries of imperialism and colonialism imposed on other colonised peoples all over the world, nor to undercommunicate the ways in which colonialism in the Solomons paved the way for certain new uses, and abuses, of power. And granted, the imposition of Pax Britannica in New Georgia around the turn of the century did coincide with the cessation of headhunting and warfare and the breakdown of the material and spiritual bases of regional polities, including the irrigated cultivation of large surpluses of taro. But long before that, the people of Marovo and the wider New Georgia Group had been operating their own exchange and trade enterprises in regular contact with representatives of global systems, as often

as not in ways that forced the European traders to conform to New Georgia standards of exchange and general conduct. By 1840 New Georgians had acquired a reputation for sharp trade practices and exclusive tastes concerning the European objects bartered for their turtle shell and bêche-de-mer (see Hviding, 1996a; Somerville, 1897; Jackson, 1978; McKinnon, 1975; as well as Thomas, 1991 for general perspectives on this era in the Pacific).

In this light the established colonial age (from around 1900) was in many respects a rather quiet interlude for Marovo people, characterised by firm, identifiable principles and procedures, not least concerning land use which was gradually geared towards "rural development" and the ultimate colonial project of land alienation. That period's steady expansion of a mono-crop copra economy with its associated "overlay" of coconut groves on prime agricultural land had an aura, also to Marovo people themselves, of predictable, unidirectional change. The establishment of colonial moral certainties (cf. Thomas, 1997:23) in this period was facilitated initially by the intense activities of Christian missions in the sudden void left by the breakdown of religion and regional systems – and colonial "stability", most notably characterised by supreme powers wielded by expatriate agents of colonial administration and churches, was interrupted only by the sudden, brief cataclysm of World War II. This long period of calm and of little contact with overseas worlds (enhanced by British restrictions on interisland travel and inter-village migration) was truly different from the dizzying and unpredictable blend of logging, mining, conservation, tourism, agricultural diversification and general instability of more recent years – as well as from the perhaps no less lively and complicated mix of large-scale taro irrigation, migrations, trading-and-warfare-based regional politics and interisland travel of past centuries, connecting back to (and beyond) the distant past of Austronesian migrations and expansions. With this in mind we give less emphasis in this book to colonial times proper and instead devote considerably more pages to "old" and "present" Marovo, respectively. It is an emphasis consistent with our proposal that the pre-colonial past and immediate present deserve more attention in studies of the history/anthropology interface where the focus is on "colonial transformation" in Melanesia, or indeed elsewhere.

Certainly, the far-ranging social and cultural transformations seen around the turn of the century – when headhunting, human sacrifice and prestige-goods economies gave way to Christianity and cash cropping – can only be understood from a reconstructive historical ethnography of what went on in preceding decades (and centuries). The amalgamations of old and new, of local and global, of Melanesian and Western that took place around 1900 were truly momentous, yet they represented no uniquely new challenge and were indeed but one stage in a continuum, as evidenced by the intense mixing – again of ostensibly "new" and "old", the latter now being referred to by the pan-Melanesian, self-referential concept of **kastom** (e.g., White and Lindstrom, 1993) – in the 1990s.

Landscapes of memory

In the section which follows we give a brief introductory sketch – in the ethnographic present – of an everyday life in Marovo which is grounded above all in an interrelatedness of land and sea, of root crops and fish, of dry and wet (physically and metaphorically). Our introductory sketch exemplifies an ideational, practice-oriented analytical stance which has been pursued in already published works on Marovo (cf. Hviding, 1995a, 1996a, 1996b). Such an experience-oriented, phenomenological approach – dependent on ethnographic fieldwork – aims to convey local points of view and also emphasises what Tim Ingold (e.g., 1992) has termed a "mutualism" between people and their environment(s) – in contrast to the separation implied by an analysis grounded in the pursuit of objective circumstances of "nature" upon which people(s) are seen to impose their subjective grid(s) of "culture(s)". In Chapters 3 and 4 we demonstrate that the rainforest-related practices carried out in present-day Marovo unfold in a landscape in which complex histories of social and ecological relationships are "inscribed". The rainforest is thus a cultural landscape in which so-called management practices always convey meanings to those concerned which go far beyond the immediate and tangible material levels.

We therefore include within our notion of the Marovo landscape the cultural meanings associated with the rainforest, and the metaphors, symbols and artefacts through which these meanings are expressed (cf. Hviding, 1996a, ch. 6). In terms of a well-known framework in ecological anthropology, this cultural landscape includes the "cognized environment" described by Roy Rappaport (1968:237-241, 1979) in his account of the Tsembaga Maring's use of the montane rainforest in New Guinea (and proposed for people/environment relations more generally). Rappaport's cognized environment co-exists with an "operational environment", the domain which is defined by a (Western) scientific understanding of the world in which people engage with the environment through their everyday activities. But in theoretical terms this proposed coexistence is an uneasy one, insofar as it appears ontologically grounded in a dualist notion of seeing an "objective" nature through "subjective" cultural images (cf. Ellen, 1982:206), whereby locally specific cultural meaning is seen as interacting with the general "laws" that regulate nature. Marovo people do not subscribe to such a universalist notion, and certainly classify their environment in ways different from those of Western science.

Moreover their everyday engagement with rainforest and reefs is informed by notions about linkages between people and environment that transcend "natural laws" and defy simple separations of "nature" from "culture" (Hviding, 1996b).

Nevertheless, we do not advocate an extreme relativism claiming that "nature" and "culture" and similar dualist frameworks are entirely inapplicable as analytical concepts for understanding the relations between people and rainforest in time and space. Our position is more of an intermediate one where we wish to open up the Marovo case for further comparison; not only in the sense of relating the "local" as it appears in Marovo to "local" worlds elsewhere, but also in the more immediate sense of comparing and analytically relating the "local" to beliefs held and strategies followed by more and more agents of the "global" as they appear on the Marovo scene. For Western conservationists and eco-tourists, "nature" and "culture" certainly do exist as distinct realms for them to encounter in Marovo. The lack of such a dichotomy in Marovo people's own approach to the environment (cf. Hviding, 1996b, 1996a:25-28, 365-370) plays little, if any, part in the overall schemes through which these "global" actors meet with the Marovo Lagoon and its inhabitants. In order to attain an ethnographically grounded understanding of the epistemological processes at work in current encounters between Marovo people and agents of "global" movements, the dualist beliefs underlying many a Western visitor's approach to Marovo have to be taken explicitly into account, and the potential of these beliefs for converging with or diverging from Marovo views has to be addressed.

On a conceptual level, Rappaport's "cognized" and "operational" environments can be kept apart in an attempt to understand people/environment relations in a given locality, but as the historian Simon Schama (1995) argues in *Landscape and Memory*, they are in fact inseparable:

> Although we are accustomed to separate nature and culture perception into two realms, they are, in fact, indivisible. Before it can ever be a repose for the senses, landscape is the work of the mind. Its scenery is built up as much from strata of memory as from layers of rock .... Landscapes are culture before they are nature; constructs of the imagination projected on to wood and water and rock. (Schama, 1995:6-7, 61)

In Europe, Schama shows how an historian can trace some continuities in the cultural meanings associated with forests, rivers and mountains over a period of 2,000 years.

With fewer written sources, our own analysis of the Marovo forests can only extend back over a couple of centuries, but in the minds of the Marovo people the longer-term continuities are not only obvious, they are essentially timeless. Some of the oral histories collected by Hviding (1995c, 1996a:234-

243) can connect us to this timeless world of 'the people of old'. Western science talks of culture change, agricultural origins, and migrations. The underlying message of an archaeological study from New Guinea, "40,000 years of taming the rainforest" (Groube, 1989), suggests it is possible to put time limits on the cultural landscapes of Melanesia, but the Marovo people may not share this view. They know, and they have shown us, that their rainforest landscape can be approached from the material traces that exist today, in boundary markers, old settlements, shrines and irrigated terraces, the trees planted by ancestors, and present-day cultivation and forest clearance. They also know that such knowledge is only a beginning: ultimately the meanings of these physical features reside in the minds and the memories of those who use the forests today. Such meanings cannot be constructed from the outside looking in.

From the points of view of methodology in general and of "rainforest studies" in particular, our book can therefore be read as a plea for rainforest management to be approached from the bottom up, and from the recent past forwards to the present, rather than adopting the prevailing top-down, future-focussed and outwards-looking approach. There is an interesting convergence between the analytical approach that we have found useful and the new approaches in the study of rainforest ecology. The scientific understanding of the forest as an ecosystem has been revolutionised since the days of Paul Richards' (1952) classic account. There is a new focus on the dynamic regeneration cycle at local scale following a "gap phase" (Whitmore, 1990) in which openings in the canopy caused by fallen trees allow pioneers or suppressed seedlings to occupy the space. The maintenance of biodiversity in the forest is now seen as depending upon processes of regeneration within small stands of trees, and over time periods extending from a few decades up to one or two hundred years. An appreciation of local history and the detailed monitoring of individual trees has been the key to this insight, which contrasts with the more deductive top-down approach and the assumption of timelessness that characterised the earlier work.

We believe that an understanding of the management of forests by local communities also should be approached in the same way. The rainforests of Solomon Islands are not an empty and timeless wilderness, a sort of blank sheet of paper upon which ideal schemes of exploitation or conservation can be worked out. We know that in the Solomon Islands the "taming of the rainforest" is a process which has been going on for at least 40,000 years (cf. Spriggs, 1997), so that the ways the forest has been used and given cultural meanings have been developing over a very long period. We see the modern forest as a cultural landscape that has been shaped to meet the changing needs of its inhabitants, and in that process the forest becomes further "inscribed" with those people's history, as represented by place names, narratives about localities and settlement, and so forth.

Our understanding of what is happening now needs to begin at "grass-roots" level (although tree-roots would be a better metaphor for this region of little grassland), and through an explicit consideration of the historical origins of the present-day people/forest relationship. The local and the historical are valuable tools of explanation. We believe firmly that in today's tropics they need to be linked more closely with scholarly attempts to grapple with current affairs, particularly logging and eco-tourism – affairs that up to now have been overwhelmingly the subject of ahistorical, generalist and technical approaches, tainted by partisan NGO rhetoric and a moral, rather than a scholarly form of discourse. There is currently an astounding scarcity of ethnographically-based studies of the local manifestations of such global affairs. In relation to one small corner of Melanesia, we therefore hope that we can demonstrate, by building outwards from the local while maintaining an ethnographic approach to the wider worlds with which the local engages, a general model of explanation which has relevance to "rainforest discourse" and wider debates on "political ecology" (cf. Escobar, 1999) in other parts of the world.

Into the local

Those who depend on the forests of the southeastern New Georgia islands – the Marovo people – today constitute a population of somewhat more than 10,000 living in small and large coastal settlements on the shores of the Marovo Lagoon and its adjacent weather coasts. This is an ecologically diverse area of high, densely forested volcanic islands, whose mountain ridges and peaks in places reach more than 1,000m, fringed by more than 700 square kilometres of extensive mangrove, lagoon and coral reef systems. The Marovo people base their day-to-day subsistence on root crop agriculture and reef fishing, supplemented by hunting and gathering in rainforest and mangroves and on coral reefs, and by a great range of intermittent cash income sources.

Practically every day of the year the men, women and children of Marovo leave their village homes and 'go to the bush' or 'go to the sea' according to a gender-based though rather flexible division of labour. Their purpose is to obtain the ingredients for the main meal, taken by the households around sunset, and to maintain the subsistence basis by monitoring the state of the environment and tending its cultivated components. We think it worthwhile, here at the outset, to indicate the cultural notions around which each day's main meal, and consequently so many fields of everyday life, are organised. In the Marovo language, 'food' (**nginongo**) basically equals root crop staples, but a balanced meal also requires **binaso**, 'that which is eaten with [staple] food'. This important category provides the required 'wet' **(mohu)** and 'fat, greasy' **(deana)** supplement to the 'dry' **(popa)** root crops.[1]

The opposition between the 'wet/fat' and the 'dry', and its inherent scenario of necessary complementarity, are all-pervasive schema that fundamentally inform and organise Marovo thought and practice. Indeed **binaso** covers all animal protein (whether from the sea or the forest, the former being predominant), wild and cultivated nuts (most notably of *Canarium* trees), leafy greens (also referred to as **kinudu**, 'edible leaves and shoots picked off growing plants') and, in situations of improvised eating, even such modest and simple relishes as grated coconut meat. Mediating between the realms of **nginongo** and **binaso** are a large variety of ceremonial and more mundane puddings made from pounded or grated root crops mixed with coconut cream and/or smoked and pounded *Canarium* nuts. These puddings, subsumed generically as **ruja** (from the verb 'to pound'), are simultaneously 'wet', 'greasy' and 'dry'. They may fill the roles of both **nginongo** – such as when eaten with protein food, mainly fish, pork and turtle meat – and **binaso** – when eaten with 'dry' root crops (cf. Leivestad, 1995, nd).

Through their day-to-day agricultural work and forest walks for hunting and gathering, Marovo people encounter a multitude of significant stone constructions as well as rocks, trees and more general areas with special meaning, all of which are 'signs' and mediators of history and of the basics of group-territory relationships, relationality or "relatedness" itself, and person-hood (cf. Hviding, 1996a, chapter 6).[2] In an important sense, this book is precisely about aspects of those histories and relationships and their long-term dynamics, seen from the vantage point of how the forest is used.

The maritime practices and traditions of the rather strongly sea-oriented people of the Marovo Lagoon are complex in character and regionally remarkable, and worthy of a study in their own right. Such a study, which includes the bearings of maritime traditions and practices on Marovo identity, and the diachronic dynamics of the customary marine tenure system, has been carried out by one of the present authors (e.g., Hviding, 1988, 1995a, 1996a). Specifically, the book *Guardians of Marovo Lagoon* (Hviding, 1996a) is a comprehensive monograph that also gives detailed cultural, historical and social background analysis relevant to this study. The reader may consult that monograph for further detail on general topics, including details about cosmology and kinship, about history and about Marovo relationships to wider worlds. Considering the overall interrelatedness of sea and land in Marovo thought and practice, the present book is, then, in many senses a companion piece to the already published maritime-oriented work. However it also has a number of aims beyond filling out the ethnographic, historical and cultural-ecological information on the Marovo Lagoon and its people.

We believe that the complex agricultural system represented by the Marovo case, as well as the fortunate circumstances that have permitted us to carry out periods of joint fieldwork and to develop long-term collaborative research and writing, may provide an extension of, indeed also perhaps a corrective to, many notions about shifting or swidden tropical agriculture and its potential role in sustainable development. With its past history of large-scale irrigation systems and ranked societies, and its continuing close integration of cultivation forms and forest types, the Marovo case should serve to amply illustrate that these types of tropical agriculture may constitute far more than the much-maligned and allegedly unsophisticated "slash-and-burn" practices which are often given much of the blame for the imminent demise of tropical rainforests. Accordingly, we believe that the potential significance of the present study ranges beyond a reappraisal of received wisdom about Melanesian agriculture, to overall Oceanic contexts and to the wider tropical world.

And finally, beyond the fields of agricultural practice, the present-day picture wherein a multitude of logging companies have descended on Marovo – in a brew of rapid resource extraction, environmental damage, bribery, ephemeral economic wealth, conflict, and government involvement – merits close attention. It is a complex example of a much-lamented Melanesia-wide pattern (cf. Barlow and Winduo, 1997) with precedents, parallels and contrasts from most parts of the tropical world. The "logging scene" in Marovo in many ways is the core organisational focus of local politics in the 1990s. Logging and related conflicts in and beyond Marovo also constitute an important field for cultural and social transformation of wider relevance and, indeed, appear as the generative mechanism for a distinctive brand of "Melanesian modernity" in a part of the world where the local-global interfaces appear temporally "compressed" and exhibit an "axiomatically condensed form" (Knauft, 1999:243, with reference to Gewertz and Errington, 1997). In the Marovo Lagoon of the 1990s very much happens very quickly, engaging farflung connections, but with surprisingly few participants actually present on the ground. Moreover, logging in Marovo has its own history of ups and downs through several decades, and shares today's scene with a disparate set of additional outside actors such as conservationist organisations, developers of "eco-tourism", and "eco-timber" enterprises. This book thus seeks to fill a noticeable void in Melanesian ethnography by providing up-to-date and ethnographically rich analysis of these processes as observed from the strikingly eventful vantage point of Marovo in the 1990s.

Present, past and future: outline of the book

The local needs to find its intellectual context in the global. In this introductory chapter we have situated forest-related practices of Marovo in relation to some ongoing theoretical debates. In the one that follows (Chapter 2) we contextualise Marovo practices within the global concept of "agroforestry". Marovo people's agroforestry is one variant of a more widespread form of rainforest management in Melanesia, and all these practices can be fitted into the terms provided by the wider agroforestry literature – but how well do they fit? And what does the degree of mismatch tell us about the persistent tendency of Western science to iron out the particularities of local practices? By privileging global models of rainforest management and by dismissing the implied awkwardness of local practice, Western science creates its own illusion of homogeneity and of logical incompatibility with the "vagaries" of the local. At the end of the day, it is implied, these rather "simple" rainforest societies all have agroforestry practices which are basically variations on a single theme. Marovo, we believe, provides an excellent starting point for a critical assessment of this bland assumption.

Chapter 3 then introduces the Marovo Lagoon area in closer detail, with particular attention to the interactions of environment, resources and people seen in an ethnographic present largely representative of the decade 1986-1996. The cultural and ecological diversity of the area is described, and close attention is given to the dynamics of customary tenure over territories and resources, conceptually and practically revolving around the twin components of **butubutu** ('corporate, localised kin-based group') and **puava** ('defined territory of land and/or sea held as ancestral estate by a **butubutu**'). This generalised perspective sets the stage for the subsequent focus on land, forest and agricultural practices. A detailed overview is given (mainly in tabular form) of Marovo concepts concerning plant communities and the 'lives' of plants, and of the ways in which different forest zones – from cloudy mountain ridges through the agroforestry zones of lower hills to seaside mangroves and the unique forests on the barrier reef islands – are used locally.

Chapter 4 examines in some detail Marovo perspectives on land use practice. The chapter builds on the ethnobotanical overview given in chapter 3 and gives a synchronic overview of present-day agroforestry in Marovo, centred on a stage-by-stage description of the shorter-term dynamics of 'gardening' practices and on the close interactions between shifting cultivation and the surrounding forest in its different stages. This presentation is given partly in schematised form. The chapter also provides information on general principles and everyday practice concerning land tenure and land availability. Finally, the chapter examines Marovo soil classification and the relationships between soil types and agricultural potential, as well as the everyday activities carried out in gardens and forest including the associated tools and technologies.

Chapter 5 shifts to a diachronic, long-term view of Marovo agroforestry and uses archival material and oral history in an attempt to re-construct the Marovo agroforestry system around the time of intensified European contact – around 1840. We give special emphasis to large-scale irrigated taro cultivation (predominantly by inland-dwelling 'bush' people) and its role in regional systems of exchange and warfare (controlled by 'coastal' sea-oriented people), the importance of *Canarium* nut harvests, and the introduction of new crops and technologies. This chapter also examines intriguing evidence for a very early establishment of the sweet potato as a crop in the New Georgia islands.

Chapter 6 analyses some rather far-ranging transformations in the Marovo Lagoon of the early colonial period (ca. 1880-1910), entailing major demographic changes, colonial pacification, missionisation and breakdown of warfare-based polities, a gradual population movement to all-coastal settlement with a concurrent abandonment of irrigated taro cultivation inland, major readjustments in land distribution, and the rise of the sweet potato as an important swidden crop.

Chapter 7 analyses the relatively quiet agricultural interlude of most of the colonial period, with a gradual but marked spread of coconut plantations to the best coastal land (the coconut overlay), disruptions during World War II, a general expansion of cash-cropping and establishment of infrastructure by missions and colonial government, and – towards the late colonial period – a complete dependence on sweet potato and cassava as epidemics of virus disease virtually wiped out taro. The chapter then introduces the complex topic of logging through a comparative analysis of "objective" views of the Marovo forests (as represented by late-colonial land surveys) and local perspectives on the uses of trees targeted as commercial timber. Finally chapter 7 sets the stage for the next part of the book by outlining five options for the Marovo lands and forests in 21st century, ranging from modified local agroforestry through several forms of logging to conservation and eco-tourism.

The accelerated pace of post-independence economic development is taken up in Chapter 8, which first provides a detailed comparative examination of agroforestry in four Marovo villages in the late- to post-colonial era of "rural development". The chapter then deals with some main facets of the agricultural diversification brought on during the 1980s and into the 1990s by the decline of copra as a cash crop, increased local marketing of garden crops, minor but locally significant demographic shifts, and a greatly expanded range of external inputs such as from agricultural extension work.

Chapter 9 examines the recent boom in large-scale logging operations in the Marovo area, and analyses the commodification of the forest from a diverse set of perspectives. Circumstances surrounding the late-colonial government's purchases of customary land for transformation into "forest estates", in effect a prelude to the large-scale logging of later decades, are examined, as are the present-day Marovo contexts of logging "on the ground", in the rather enigmatic political economy of the nation-state. This chapter provides detailed analysis of logging's recent, still evolving history in three contrasting main localities of the greater Marovo area.

Chapter 10 takes off from present-day logging activities and addresses the immediate future. The topic of reforestation is discussed and a range of post-logging scenarios is considered, starting from the basic premise that Melanesian forests such as those of Marovo do have a future even after they have been logged. Drawing on comparative information from areas of the New Georgia islands that were "logged out" more than twenty years ago, various strategies for re-using logged areas, ranging from institutional plantation-type reforestation to local agricultural entrepreneurship, are examined. This leads on to a discussion of a similarly wide range of present-day initiatives for the Marovo area.

Chapter 11 examines the notion of "sustainable forestry" as an organised alternative to rapid large-scale logging, represented by initiatives by non-governmental organisations (NGOs) towards community-based sawmilling and eco-timber production as well as the promotion of non-timber usages of the forest. NGO enthusiasm and local support in many parts of Marovo notwithstanding, such alternatives have so far had little involvement by government agencies and their future remains uncertain.

Scenarios of environmental conservation, involving a rather Utopian moral discourse as well as more concerted efforts to promote village-level income generation by eco-tourism, are examined in Chapter 12. The long-standing but still pending proposal that Marovo Lagoon should be enlisted as a UNESCO World Heritage Site forms an important backdrop for this discussion.

Finally, an Epilogue (Chapter 13) forms a metadiscussion of sorts of the book and its interrelated themes concerning the present, past and future uses of Marovo's forests, including general theoretical issues pertaining to the book's analytical emphasis on the many linkages, tangible and not so tangible, between local realities and global connections, and to the ethnographically founded analysis of such a complexity of histories and "narratives". An Appendix provides a glossary of the many Marovo terms and concepts used in the text.

2 Conceptualising Melanesian Agroforestry

Questions of terminology

For the purposes of this book we have chosen to apply the term "agroforestry" to the land use systems of the Marovo Lagoon. We favour the agroforestry term because it suggests a functional integration between cultivation practices (including the cultivation of tree crops) and the management of the forest itself. This integration not only matches the practice of food production from the land in Marovo and how it is conceptualised locally; it also conforms to current scientific understanding of how these systems of production are sustained (cf. Clarke and Thaman, 1993). "Agroforestry" describes agricultural practices which achieve an integration of trees with food plants, either through inter-cropping (crops grown in close juxtaposition to trees) or through shifting cultivation (crops grown after a tree fallow). The agricultural activities of the Marovo people, although at first glance dominated by the latter practice, rely firmly on both. Indeed the secondary growth of old and recent fallows itself forms part of the continuous crops harvested in Marovo. In this Marovo shares features in common with other more well-documented Oceanic production systems, such as those on the island of Yap in Micronesia (Falanruw, 1989) and on various islands in Polynesia (Kirch, 1994).

The ecological rationale for agroforestry is well demonstrated by the ubiquitous nature of these practices, but it now receives further support from science. There is clear evidence that in the humid tropics some form of agroforestry is almost essential for the nutrient cycle to permit sustained cropping, at least for those agricultural systems that are not transformed by water management (such as wet rice and taro) or by high use of inputs (e.g. fertilisers). On the institutional (and international) level, the Commonwealth Science Council, London, has since the 1980s recognised the importance of agroforestry in a research programme entitled "The Amelioration of Soil by Trees". Such dedicated support is also represented by the activities of the International Council for Research in Agroforestry (ICRAF) in Nairobi, by CATIE in Costa Rica, by UNEP, and by many other organisations.

Accordingly, new "institutional" agroforestry systems are being devised, for example the technique of alley cropping (maize between *Leucaena* hedges) developed at IITA in Ibadan, Nigeria. Alley cropping is now being extended for smallholder use in Latin America (e.g. Costa Rica), Southeast Asia (e.g. the Philippines) and elsewhere. However, it is increasingly being recognised that there is also much to be learnt from existing indigenous agroforestry practices, which have emerged in many parts of the tropics as a successful form of rainforest management. These practices have usually been described as variants of "swidden" or "shifting cultivation" systems (Hands et.al., 1995).

Some forms of shifting cultivation do lead to forest destruction, because there is no attempt by the farmer to encourage the re-establishment of trees after abandonment of the plot, or alternatively because the bush fallow periods are progressively shortened following population pressure (Nye and Greenland, 1960; Boserup, 1965). But in other cases shifting cultivation is managed to be ecologically sustainable, by means of the re-establishment of a tree cover after the abandonment of agricultural sites. Indeed the forest fallow may itself be greatly valued for its products, gained by the gathering of fruits, nuts, edible herbs and medicinal leaves, through hunting, and through the collecting of firewood (Clay, 1987; Denslow and Padoch, 1988).

Ecologically sustainable methods for agricultural production are urgently needed. In that light, there is hardly a need for stressing the wider reasons for wishing to further understand the economics and cultural ecology of indigenous agroforestry systems. Only through an appreciation of what systems exist already, and of the extent to which they are functioning successfully, can sound proposals be formulated for changing, or alternatively for reinforcing, existing systems. Indigenous technical knowledge of agroforestry has often accumulated empirically and gradually over long periods of management. Some of this knowledge is of wide significance, yet its perpetuation is jeopardised by the impact of modernisation and "development". Rural populations switch to new opportunities and adopt new sources of livelihood, including cash crops. These crops may be grown in ways that are incompatible with traditional subsistence agriculture, so that agroforestry-related knowledge is no longer transmitted to the new generation of "modern" farmers – whose aspirations and activities may, moreover, be strongly influenced by mono-crop-oriented policy-makers from the field of "rural development".

At the same time there may also be valuable insights to be gained from the adaptations of such "modern" farmers, who are often very creative in incorporating new practices and new crops into old agroforestry systems. These indigenous systems clearly function successfully in cultural and social terms as well as being successful from an economic and an ecological perspective. The same may not be true for invented, "institutional" systems such as alley cropping. However successful such systems may appear under experimental conditions they are often not compatible with local sociocultural circumstances and with smallholder economies as they exist away from the agricultural research stations and beyond the gaze of the development experts. Let us now shift our perspective on agroforestry to a regional level; to the Melanesian archipelagoes of the southwestern tropical Pacific (Figure 2.1).

Melanesian agroforestry: old wine in new bottles

In fact none of the English words used to describe Melanesian cultivation practices are altogether satisfactory. The 1980s term "agroforestry" seems useful especially if we restrict its use to indigenous rather than institutional forms. However, it can be argued that agroforestry would not strictly include the irrigated taro pondfields (**ruta**) that were formerly cultivated in the New Georgia islands, as their functional integration with the surrounding forest is rather limited. In relation to Marovo people's cultivation of the rainforest we shall also use the old Anglo-Saxon word "swidden", which was rescued from obscurity by geographers in the 1960s and was applied to tropical "slash-and-burn", and to bush-fallowing practices generally. Nevertheless "swidden" does seem inappropriate to some situations in the Solomon Islands archipelago, where fire plays a rather limited role, and where a more accurate term might be "slash-and-mulch". Some writers also use the terms 'horticulture' and 'gardening' in the context of Melanesia, perhaps because the word **gaden** (or its derivatives, from English "garden") is so widely used in the Pidgin languages of the region (cf. Leach, 1999). These terms are correct in implying the cultivation of individual plants rather than undifferentiated populations of plants, but they also have an unfortunate association with fences and proximity to houses.

A further problem for fitting the everyday practices of the Melanesian into the constraints of the English language is the importance in Oceania of cultivated trees. It is for this reason that Yen (1974b, 1982) adopted the word 'arboriculture', to describe the many tree species in Melanesia that have been at least semi-domesticated (i.e. genetically selected), and which are found in the vicinity of settlements, swiddens and also growing semi-wild in the secondary forest. Yen noted that arboriculture was particularly well developed in the eastern Solomons (where breadfruit is a staple), but it is prominent also in Marovo particularly in connection with *Canarium* nut trees, coconuts and sago palms.

In each of these cases the English language is imposing new words on to very old Melanesian practices – truly a case of new bottles to present very old wine. The terms are unsatisfactory because of their origin in the agricultural activities of farmers in temperate latitudes who manipulate nature in quite different ways from those found in Oceania. In Melanesia the origins of cultivation

Figure 2.1   Map of Melanesia

(to use perhaps the most neutral English word of all) are now traced back to the management of wild plants, such as aroids, wild yams, palms and fruiting trees. It is thought that these resources first came into cultivation some time in the Pleistocene, perhaps as far back as 30-40,000 years ago as is suggested by such evidence as artefacts suited for forest clearance and starch residues on stone flake tools (Groube, 1989; Loy et.al., 1992). Early cultivation techniques must have included vegetation clearance by ringbarking or fire, tillage of the soil, and the selection for transplanting of varieties of yams or aroids that were non-spiny or less acrid. In relation to trees such as coconuts, sago and *Canarium*, the necessary interventions must have included canopy clearance, the protection of seedlings and the transplanting of cuttings of selected varieties. Over very long periods these practices led to genetic changes and the creation of an enhanced resource base, including seemingly "natural" forests full of particularly useful plants (Yen, 1982; Henderson and Hancock, 1988; Spriggs, 1996).

Alongside the cultivation and in some cases the domestication of these wild plants, the archaeologists infer a continued commitment to fishing, hunting and collecting. The overall impact on the rainforest was so small as to leave no trace of deforestation in the pollen record, and no impact on slope stability such as to cause soil erosion (Allen et.al., 1989; Gosden et.al., 1989). For this reason the term "agriculture" seems inappropriate to describe Melanesian cultivation practices over this long prehistoric period. Matthew Spriggs (1996, 1997) suggests that full-scale agriculture did not begin until post-Lapita times, i.e. until after the spread of Austronesian languages and the introduction of the taro-yams-bananas complex along with the pig, dog and fowl. Lapita culture is the name given to the agricultural (yet also maritime-oriented) settlements that first appeared in the islands adjacent to New Guinea about 3,900 years before present (cf. Kirch, 1997; Spriggs, 1997). One Lapita settlement site was recorded by Reeve (1989) in Roviana Lagoon along the southern side of New Georgia Island, and several potential sites (where pottery fragments have already been found in the coastal zone) are presently under investigation in central Marovo by Western Province archaeological staff. Archaeological evidence from a number of Lapita sites in Island (or "Seaboard") Melanesia indicates that the new agricultural practices introduced by these people may have contributed to a serious increase of environmental instability from about 3,500 years ago onwards, owing not least to accelerated forest clearance (Spriggs, 1997).

From this point onwards Melanesian cultivation can be described as including practices that are fully "agricultural", although on most sites agriculture was still dependent on forest regeneration to achieve a sustainable nutrient cycle (hence our preference for the term "agroforestry"). Alongside this full-scale cultivation of fully domesticated crops we see the continuation of pre-

Austronesian arboriculture and wild plant cultivation, as well as the persistence of still more ancient practices including the gathering of wild plants from the forests. One example of a fully "agricultural" practice in Marovo is the cultivation in intensive monocultures of irrigated *Colocasia* taro, in the system locally known as **ruta**. This type of cultivation is now practically extinct in the western Solomons, but our reconstruction of the 19th-century situation in New Georgia indicates that **ruta** were formerly of great importance. This system is elsewhere in the Pacific called "inundated pondfields" (Spriggs, 1985; Kirch, 1984), and it consists of irrigated terraces with walls of stone (and sometimes wood) and built canals that divert water from streams on to fields. Such systems can be found scattered throughout Austronesian speaking areas of Island Melanesia, and are possibly a variation of the type of pondfield system now used for rice in insular southeast Asia (Spriggs, 1982).

In his seminal comparative studies of Melanesian agriculture Jacques Barrau (1958, 1965) pointed to a persistent and widespread division in land use, labour and gender ideology between "the wet" and "the dry". These are generally the wet (irrigated) taro and the dry (swidden) yams, and Barrau stressed that to varying degrees almost all Melanesian agricultural systems include elements of both practices. Through a variable emphasis on yam cultivation in dryland sites, taro cultivation in wetlands, and arboriculture, Melanesians were able to utilise all the potentially productive sites in their island environments. The wet/dry dichotomy is not everywhere a simple taro/yams correlation. As Yen (1982) has pointed out, taro is not necessarily restricted to wetland sites since it can successfully be grown in dryland swiddens in fertile, high rainfall areas – such as the island of New Georgia. Conversely, even in lowlying swamp land small "islands" of yam cultivation can be created by elaborate mounding techniques, as on Kolepom island off the coast of Irian Jaya (Serpenti, 1965).

In the Solomon Islands most studies (e.g., Oliver, 1955, on Bougainville; Ross, 1973, on Malaita; and the brief accounts on Guadalcanal, Malaita and the southeastern Solomons in Clarke and Thaman, 1993) have focused on the 'dry' – whether yams or taro – rather than the 'wet' because wetland management is, at least today, so much less prominent. In terms of its ethnographic visibility wet taro is associated with the Polynesian outliers such as Ontong Java and Sikaiana (Bayliss-Smith, 1974, 1977), Anuta (Yen 1973) and Tikopia (Kirch and Yen 1982). There are only few examples of irrigated taro being still prominent in some parts of Papua New Guinea, for example in parts of Milne Bay (Kahn, 1984, 1986).

Of the detailed ethnographic works from Island Melanesia, the monumental study by Malinowski (1935) of agriculture in the Trobriands stands out for its emphasis on the minute day-to-day practicalities – and magical correlates – of yam gardening. We wonder if the "coral gardens" so thoroughly dealt with by Malinowski may have helped – despite Malinowski's own observation (1935, II:18) that the term "garden" corresponded to no Trobriand word – to foster the notion that Melanesians are preoccupied above all with "horticulture" carried out in small circumscribed "gardens" apparently carved out of the surrounding rainforest, or alternatively nourished on "barren" coral. It is our argument that this "horticultural" view of the Melanesians as "gardeners" may have dominated the overall ethnographic view of Island Melanesian agriculture and obscured the complex and finely-tuned, short- and long-term inter-relationships between root crop gardens under cultivation and the surrounding fallows and forests.

On a more indirect level, researchers' emphasis on "gardens" and their neglect of existing irrigation in Melanesia have surely contributed to the deeply entrenched ethnological dichotomy between the apparently simple and egalitarian polities of the "small-scale" sociopolitical systems of Melanesian shifting cultivators and the hierarchical "hydraulic" systems of regional redistribution underpinned by the complex irrigated agriculture of Polynesia (e.g., the influential contribution by Sahlins, 1963). More recent discussions (e.g. Thomas, 1989b, on a general level; and Kirch, 1984, 1994, on irrigated agriculture and political systems) have done much to complicate this over-simplistic picture of a Melanesia/Polynesia division with inherent unilinear evolutionary schemes. The present book documents in empirical detail that the Marovo area – located in the "heart of Melanesia" – has a history characterised firmly by complex irrigation systems, hierarchical chiefly polities, ranked societies and large-scale regional exchange throughout much of the Solomons archipelago (see also Hviding, 1996a, nd a). Thus, in the spirit of widely comparative Austronesian studies, this book should serve to further dissolve now-obsolete dichotomies between Melanesia and Polynesia.

At the same time, while highlighting social stratification and irrigated taro cultivation in the Island Melanesian "heartland", we do not wish to imply any simple correlation with Wittfogel's (1957) well-known "hydraulic hypothesis" that the administrative requirements of irrigation necessitated centralised "government". As noted by Spriggs (1982) and Kirch (1984) the relationships between irrigation and politically stratified Oceanic societies are complex and many-sided and involve regional feasting systems and large-scale food prestations as well as the incentive to surplus production provided by the perennial nature of irrigated taro and the relative permanence of terraces and canal systems.

Although we employ "Melanesia" as a term in this book we do it only with reference to a certain geographical area of western Oceania, characterised by dense archipelagoes of relatively large high islands and by extraordinary linguistic diversity. In this we aim to contribute to a developing regional view of "Island Melanesia" (cf. Spriggs, 1997), in many ways distinct from mainland

Papua New Guinea and in some ways tied in with the greater, predominantly Austronesian world of the Pacific Islands. It is also with the above-mentioned problems in mind that we insist on viewing the past and present agricultural systems of Marovo holistically, as garden-fallow-forest interaction in many combinations – as "agroforestry" in which harvests are derived simultaneously from root crops, planted trees and "wilder" forest. This notwithstanding the fact that Marovo people, as most Melanesians, consistently use a modification of the English term "garden" when speaking of their own agricultural activities in Melanesian Pidgin (in this case the variant called Solomon Islands Pijin [cf. Keesing, 1988]) – as in "**go long gaden**" ('go to [work in] the garden'). Closer examination in the next chapter will show that the closest apparent Marovo equivalent to 'garden' – **chigo** – refers to far more than a small site of horticultural activity somehow opposed to the forest. So, too, does our use – for lack of a better term – of "garden" throughout the following chapters.

Taming Solomon Islands rainforests over 40,000 years

The Solomon Islands, as a chain of high volcanic islands stretching southeast from the Bismarck archipelago (Figure 2.2), is a core area of the Island Melanesian region not just in a purely spatio-geographical sense, but also in profound cultural-historical terms. The Solomons are likely to have been a major scene for interaction between Austronesian sea-oriented yet agricultural colonists and long-established pre-agricultural hunter-gatherer populations, in the Lapita period ca. 3,500-2,000 years before present. The ultimate outcome was the present-day cultural and linguistic mosaic. Within the national political boundaries of Solomon Islands (i.e. excluding Bougainville and adjacent areas within Papua New Guinea) some 60 to 70 related Austronesian languages coexist with 15 non-Austronesian or "Papuan" languages (Tryon and Hackman, 1983). Thus more than 80 distinct languages are spoken among a population of slightly more than 400,000 (as of 1997).

In the absence of extensive archaeological work we can only speculate on the encounters, migrations and assimilations that resulted from the Austronesian incursion into islands already populated by speakers of non-Austronesian languages of the "East Papuan" phylum. The inland-coastal dichotomies still prevailing in Island Melanesia in and beyond the Solomons are only a fragment of this picture, often not even systematically related to Austronesian/non-Austronesian linguistic patterns. But in any event, the tropical rainforests that constitute the natural vegetation of all parts of the humid equatorial Solomons do exhibit convincing signs of a long prehistory of human-induced modification, as discussed above. Archaeological research is sorely needed to develop these clues.

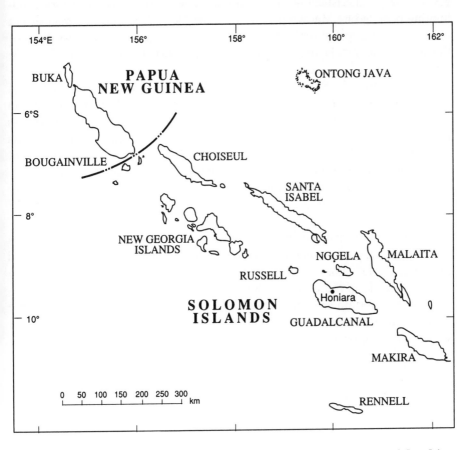

Figure 2.2   Map of Solomon Islands (excluding the eastern outer islands)

On a somewhat shorter and better-documented time scale, the rainforests of the Marovo area, as well as of most major islands of the Solomons, may (even in their relatively "pristine" state of colonial times before logging escalated) contain very little primary or "virgin" forest at all. The uninhabited forest interiors of the large islands that border the lagoon of Marovo (Figure 2.3) contain ample indicators of past modification and management in the form of taro terraces, old settlement sites, and groves of ageing *Canarium* nut trees. An even closer look at the vegetation, from either a Marovo or a western-botanical perspective, reveals forest areas with a tree composition indicative of extensive disturbance, even clearance, of the canopy within the past 100 years or so – the probable sites of old yam swiddens and irrigated taro pondfields. These signs all point to a not-too-distant past when intensive agricultural production was a pivot in large interisland networks of exchange, warfare and predatory head-hunting operated by Marovo people and other New Georgians in a manner not unlike, but on a spatial scale far exceeding, the **kula** and associated systems of the Massim archipelagoes (Hviding, 1995a, 1996a, nd a; see also Thomas, 1991:45).

Throughout the Solomon Islands, and coexisting with the production of root crop staples, there is a range of ancient Oceanic food plants still in extensive cultivation. For some of these plants there is a continuing process of diversification through people's intensive pursuit of good cultivars. This continuing search for new cultivars, often along pathways offered by old interisland exchange networks, is also characteristic of Solomon Islanders' approaches to more recently introduced crops such as sweet potato (already in widespread cultivation before European contact) and cassava (introduced in the 20th century).

The long history of rainforest modification in the Solomon Islands does not imply that past ecological relationships have necessarily been balanced or "sustainable". For example, in some areas of poorer soils (such as the Nggela Islands in the central Solomons) or pronounced seasonality of rain-fall (such as certain areas of Guadalcanal), environmental degradation of the rather distant past is evident in the form of permanent loss of forest cover with well-developed, irreversible grasslands. They have been created by repeated burning and are dominated by the tall, hardy *Imperata* grasses. A few such patches, possibly man-made, of *Imperata* and the fern *Gleichenia linearis* are also found in Marovo, namely on the upper lagoon-facing northern slopes of the volcanic island of Gatokae, although in this case other explanations may apply.[1]

The widespread evidence for agricultural intensification in the Solo-mons of the past, such as yam mounds and – not least – irrigated taro terra-cing, has not been well studied and its interpretation remains uncertain. The lack of attention given to Melanesian irrigation plays a major role in this knowledge gap. Thus there are many aspects of the long- and short-term historical dynamics of Solomon Islands agroforestry that remain poorly understood. These aspects include the complex interactions between "the wet and the dry" in terms of co-existing irrigation systems and swiddens (Barrau, 1965; Kirch, 1994), and between short-term fallows and arboricul-ture, so typical of the larger islands of Melanesia. But most importantly, given the increased appreciation of the present and future potential of indigenous agroforestry systems such as those of Melanesia, far too little attention has been given to the effects on indigenous systems of the new opportunities, constraints and challenges experienced in colonial and post-colonial times. These impacts include:

- a new technology for clearing fallow vegetation based on steel tools (available since intermittent contact with European ships started ca. 1800), as well as, more recently, spades, hoes and picks supplementing the ubiquitous digging stick for soil tillage (particularly important for sweet potato mounds);
- the expansion of coconut plantations, often to areas with the best access and the highest soil fertility; initially this was associated with European traders and planters; later it occurred in the name of local economic development, instigated by churches and the colonial administration;
- the decline in traditional staples like yams and taro, partly because these crops are labour intensive and demand prime sites, and partly (in the case of taro) because of devastation throughout the Solomons from the 1950s onwards by introduced plant disease;
- the conversion of ritually important tree crops (in the Solomon Islands notably *Canarium* nuts) into significant commodities, and thus their maintenance as key items of intergroup and interisland trade, but nowadays tied to a cash economy;
- the incorporation through longer and shorter time spans of numerous introduced cultivars, including fruits like papaya and pineapple, vegetables like beans and onions, and – most importantly – two new root crops, sweet potato and cassava, which in more recent times have replaced yams and (particularly) taro;
- social and demographic changes including movement to the coast and the abandoning of inland settlement, which have modified and partly transformed former settlement patterns, land tenure arrangements, work organisation and gender-based divisions;
- more recently, a rapid population growth which is leading to an intensification of agriculture, and is further escalated by overall commercialisation and more or less planned "rural development";
- a Melanesia-wide pattern of accelerating large-scale commercial logging by foreign companies of previously only lightly disturbed rainforest.

The latter process is indeed a focus for major present-day transformations; not just of an ecological kind but also – and not least – with fundamental consequences for social, political and cultural dimensions of life in Melanesia. It is tempting to say that the logging boom of the 1990s is where a unique Solomon Islands version of "modernity" – globalised yet distinctively Melanesian – is being made.

Agroforestry in the Marovo Lagoon

All the above general Melanesian trends in the agriculture-arboriculture-agroforestry realm find a particular expression on the rugged lands of the Marovo Lagoon, among its ten to eleven thousand people and some fifty villages (Figure 2.3.). Except for irrigated taro terracing which has been all but discontinued, few of the pre-colonial land use practices of the Marovo people have disappeared. All traditional cultivars remain in cultivation, despite serious crop diseases (notably the taro blight of the 1950s), a range of localised soil problems, and changes in the cultural beliefs and sociopolitical institutions that used to encourage the surplus production of, for example, yams and taro. Nevertheless the Marovo diet has become more and more dependent on the relatively recent staples of sweet potato and cassava, which have been incorporated into pre-existing swidden systems. Present-day necessities for a monetary income are partly met through cash crops (coconuts, cocoa, vegetables), handicraft production (especially woodcarving) mainly for sale to tourists, and the exploitation of marine resources such as fish, bêche-de-mer and commercial shells. There is also an expanding repertoire of often ephemeral resource "royalties" paid by non-local logging and fishing companies to the customary owners of the resources in question. But the day-to-day diet is still based to a large degree on subsistence self-sufficiency; a preference and a fact often noted rhetorically especially by village women as a foundation of a continued good 'localised existence' (**kino**).

The swidden systems of present-day Marovo interact closely with the surrounding forest. Older secondary growth contains a great variety of medicinal plants and other useful trees and shrubs, some of which are planted and others simply forming part of the regrowth succession. The tall, mature and less disturbed forest is also part of the agroforestry complex, particularly by containing old planted groves of tall *Canarium* nut trees. It is significant that nuts of two species of *Canarium* trees remain fundamentally important in Marovo people's lives and are just as integral to the agroforestry system today as in former times. This is evidenced also by the universal use in Marovo of the word **buruburu** '*Canarium* nut tree' for 'year' – in the sense of the time interval between each *Canarium* harvest. In addition, *Canarium* nuts have now attained a role as prized commodities for urban markets. This is an added importance that in many ways balances the decline of the old interisland networks of ceremonial exchange in which large leaf parcels (**boboro**) of smoked *Canarium* nuts featured prominently as an export from Marovo Lagoon, which Solomon Islanders regard as one of the main sources for *Canarium* nuts in the archipelago. These days Marovo women send seal-

Figure 2.3   Map of the Marovo area

ed plastic flour buckets (or large biscuit tins) of traditionally processed nuts on a regular basis to urban markets, and in season this provides significant household income.

This overall pattern is complicated by some intricate local variations relating to ecological factors (soils and topography) and to land distribution patterns deriving from a still-influential pre-colonial division between local-ised corporate groups of 'coastal [or 'saltwater'] people' and 'bush people'. Much intra-Marovo variation is also tied to variation in a range of later influences, such as the diverging economic orientations of three major Christian church denominations, the extent to which cash crops are integrated into swidden systems, and in recent years, direct and indirect impacts of rapidly expanding large-scale logging. Although the Marovo area has a very high population growth (slightly above the Solomon Islands national average of 3.5%), population pressures have not yet reached the extent at which local agroforestry practices are no longer viable because of ecological stress caused by the shortening of bush fallows. The Marovo Lagoon is also an area where indigenous technical knowledge generally survives and evolves, although necessarily in modified form after nearly a hundred years of colonial, Christian and capitalist influences.

The Marovo example is in many ways a remarkably rich representative of the typical Pacific Islands pattern whereby the "indigenous" agricultural systems and their knowledge bases have expanded continuously through increased contact with new species, tools and aspirations. At the end of the 20th century the Marovo Lagoon is also a particularly complex example of the rapid social, ecological and economic transformations in today's Melanesia, whereby alternative uses of the rainforest are the focal points of much heated discourse involving young and old village men and women, customary landholding groups, logging companies, conservationist organisations and other international and national NGOs, churches, and government at the three levels of local area, province, and nation.

3   Life on the Lands of Marovo

Locating Marovo

This chapter relies mainly on the "ethnographic present" as a means of introducing some basic features of everyday life in Marovo Lagoon villages, but also sketches certain aspects of the long-term history of relationships between people and land. The chapter then introduces the land and sea environments of Marovo and provides an overview of the local uses made of the forest. In line with the New Georgian perspective of extending the "social" well into what in many Western eyes would be the "natural" (cf. Hviding, 1996b), the 'life on the lands' examined here integrates the lives of people and the lives of the forest and its non-human inhabitants. The emphasis given here to the rainforest environment and its many important contributions to the Marovo way of living thus sets the stage for the next chapter's detailed examination of present-day agricultural practices. However, as will become evident, the interplay between present, past and future underlies our analysis as a whole and reflects certain deep continuities that pervade the everyday practical lives of Marovo people.

Some of these continuities are codified by the Marovo people as **kastom**: a conceptual tool of Melanesian Pidgin applied throughout the region by Melanesians themselves by invoking "selective representations of the past ... constructed in and for the present" (Keesing, 1993; for conceptual overviews and cases studies, see Keesing and Tonkinson, 1982; White and Lindstrom, 1993). In the view of Marovo people, as among other peoples of Papua New Guinea, Solomon Islands and Vanuatu, **kastom** (rendered as '**kasitomu**' in the Marovo language) is useful as an explicit reference to ostensibly historically-derived cultural conditions for localised human existence and social difference, and is thereby also a source for the legitimacy of a certain local way of life (including such prominent material dimensions as land rights). In that local sense Marovo **kastom** is also a transcultural field of discourse by virtue of defining what makes Marovo people different from others. Other continuities in the lives of Marovo people are more implicit and intangible. There are also some significant discontinuities. We recognise this and do not claim to write a definitive "agricultural history" or "forest history" of the Marovo area. Rather,

31

through moving back and forth between present(s), past(s) and future(s), our aim is to make some continuities, as well as discontinuities, explicit. Let us first give a brief sketch of the *longue durée* in some of those dimensions that combine to make a distinct "Marovo".

The Marovo Lagoon, some 700 square kilometres of extraordinarily diverse coral reefs and wide expanses of often wind-blown waters dotted with small forested islands, is delimited on the seawards side by narrow raised barrier reef islands with tall forest and jagged ocean-facing cliff formations, intersected by deep passages between lagoon and ocean. On the landwards side the wide lagoon is fringed by the rugged, rainforested and mangrove-fringed landscapes of the mountainous volcanic islands of New Georgia, Vangunu and Gatokae. Embracing the northern coasts of these three large islands, the lagoon of Marovo stretches in a southwest-to-northeasterly direction for more than 120 kilometres, from Gatokae in the south to the village of Kolobaghea near the northern tip of New Georgia Island. In the lagoon area and on the weather coasts of the main islands (Figure 2.3) lives a Melanesian population of around 11,000 (a 1997 estimate based on the 1986 national census and on a continued high population growth of 4.1%, rather more than the Solomon Islands national average of 3.5%).

These people of the eastern and southern parts of the New Georgia Group (named after its main island) form a culture complex that is generally termed 'Marovo' both by themselves and by other groups throughout the Solomons, and that is contrasted with the quite closely related Roviana area and culture complex of western and southwestern New Georgia. The name "Marovo" derives from the small Marovo Island located prominently in the central lagoon. This island was an early focus of 19th-century trade with Europeans, and its name was subsequently appropriated by cartography as a designation for the entire eastern lagoon area of New Georgia, as distinct from the Roviana Lagoon on the other side.

As applied today to a geographical area, Marovo designates the entire southeastern parts of the New Georgia Group in the Western Province of Solomon Islands. In the legal-administrative terms of the nation-state, Marovo is a provincial sub-area that comprises five "Wards". It extends from the large village of Jela at the northern tip of New Georgia, southeast to the island of Gatokae (including some uninhabited offshore islands) and westwards again to the sheer cliff coasts around Viru at New Georgia's southern end. The extent of this area roughly corresponds with present-day local perceptions of the extent of Marovo. In English parlance by locals and non-locals "Marovo Lagoon" is commonly invoked for the entire area, including the lagoon itself as well as the adjacent lands of New Georgia, Vangunu and Gatokae. The old local name for the eastern lagoon and the surrounding lands of New Georgia, Vangunu and Gatokae is Ulusaghe; an expression in the Roviana language that translates as 'above-and-ascending' and refers to the lagoon's location in the 'sunrise', 'up-wards' direction relative to Roviana. 'Ulusaghe' remains in use throughout the island of New Georgia to differentiate this eastern lagoon area from the western lagoons of Roviana and Vonavona and the northern area of Kusaghe.

Present-day 'Marovo' also includes traditional districts not within Ulu-saghe. The northernmost ward of the sub-area extends into Kusaghe, where an eponymous language is spoken. Linking old Kusaghe and Ulusaghe is the Kalikolo area which consists of most of the northwards-facing ridges, slopes and river valleys of New Georgia Island to (and including) the large Kolo river to the southeast. Finally, also within today's 'Marovo' is the Kalivarana area, today usually referred to as Viru after its major settlements around the nearly land-locked, large cove of Viru Harbour. In the cultural history of the New Georgia region, Kalikolo and Kalivarana have been important areas of conflu-ence between the three major sub-areas of Roviana, Marovo/Ulusaghe and Kusaghe.

Cultural diversity and increasing complexity

Five languages – Marovo, Vangunu, Bareke, Hoava and Kusaghe – are spoken in today's Marovo. The first of these is dominant and understood throughout all villages. It has its historical basis among the coastal-dwelling groups of Kalivarana and the central lagoon area, but in the times of missionisation is became the lingua franca of Seventh-day Adventists throughout Marovo and beyond. It is readily understood by all other linguistic groups of Marovo. Vangunu and Bareke are closely related languages spoken among the formerly bush-dwelling groups of Vangunu Island – Vangunu in villages on the south weather coast (also called Vangunu), and Bareke on the Bareke peninsula of the northern and eastern lagoon coasts. Hoava and Kusaghe, which are likewise closely related, are akin to Roviana more than to Marovo and are spoken by small groups in the northern lagoon. All five languages belong to the North-western and Central Solomons Austronesian Family (Ross, 1986) and have a considerable degree of mutual intelligibility. Yet despite a long influence by the major languages of Marovo (among Seventh-day Adventists) and Roviana (among Methodists) the minor ones remain in use on the village level, although the Bareke language is definitely on the wane among younger persons in Adventist communities. The continued presence of spoken Vangunu, Bareke, Hoava and Kusaghe reflect another domain of contrasting cultures and ways of life within the Marovo area itself: they are all known as 'languages of the bush'.

An important old dichotomy between 'people of the coast' (**tinoni pa sera**, also referred to as **tinoni pa idere** ['saltwater people']) and 'people of the bush' (**tinoni pa goana**) continues to pervade the Marovo area, even though all present-day villages are situated on the mainland shores or on small islands in the lagoon. Up to around the end of the 19th century the Marovo-speaking 'coastal people' used to operate large-scale inter-island systems of warfare and trade based on headhunting and prestige-goods exchange, whereas the lives of the 'bush people' – a more diverse number of groups speaking among them the other four languages – were focused on intensive irrigated taro cultivation in the river valleys and mountain craters of Vangunu and New Georgia. As has been argued elsewhere (Hviding, 1996a, ch. 3), the history of Marovo inter-group relations from before European contact through times of colonisation, pacification and missionisation may be seen as a sequential development of exchanges between a sea-related domain and a land-related one: between groups of coastal people and bush people. In summary, inter-group exchange in old Marovo was dominated by institutions whereby the fruits of sea and land – material objects most significantly represented by fish and taro – were bartered between coastal and bush groups. Considering the military superiority of the coastal people and their intermittent need for large quantities of taro in regional feasts based on food prestation, this exchange probably also contained some element of tribute exacted by them.

In the late 19th century there occurred a complex process of indigenous and externally-imposed "pacification" and of breakdown of the strong coastal polities. The population movement to the coast that followed gave increased access for all groups to the sea and its resources and so undermined taro/fish barter. Coastal groups exchanged use rights with bush groups, by means of an exchange of social relationships and of claims and privileges belonging to the respective domains of sea and land and their resources. Today, coastal groups and bush groups lead virtually identical lifestyles, but still people strongly emphasise group identities as being either of the coast or of the bush; demonstrable partly through the linguistic heritage sketched above. Although everyone today is both a fisher and a gardener, political control exercised on group levels remains firmly tied to the 'side of the sea' or the 'side of the bush'. More explicitly, each **butubutu** – 'corporate kin-based group modelled on cognatic descent' – control a **puava** – 'territorial estate' – that is either all-terrestrial or predominantly marine, depending on the history of the **butubutu** as 'coastal' or 'of the bush'. This amounts to the co-existence of two distinct sides of historical identity and territorial control that are somehow opposite, yet complementary (cf. Hviding, 1996a:128-130). In the course of daily activities, any person in need of something beyond his or her own world of political influence and symbolic identification must enter into negotiation with representatives of the opposite side. A taro-for-fish idiom thus remains a fundamentally important relational image – and organisational framework – in present-day Marovo.

Beyond this important distinction, contemporary social and cultural variation throughout the area mainly relates to the important role played by the doctrines of three different church denominations: the Seventh-day Adventist Church (SDA), present in Marovo since 1915; the United Church (UC, Methodist), present since 1912; and the Christian Fellowship Church (CFC), an indigenous church formed in the 1960s that fuses Methodism with strong communalism and significant elements of ancestor worship adapted from old New Georgian religion. Church membership is virtually universal in present-day Marovo. Each village adheres to one denomination only, and the material needs and organisational structures of the churches have a profound influence on everyday village life. Denominational differences also create significant contrasts in food preferences and productive orientations. In particular, SDA people (who constitute about 60% of the population in Marovo) do not eat shellfish and pork and do not chew the *Areca* or betel nuts that are all-important stimulants for any social occasion among UC and CFC people.

In social and cultural terms Marovo can therefore be seen as a small world of striking complexity. The same is true in ecological terms (Stoddart, 1969; Lees et.al., 1991; Hviding, 1995b). Dubbed the "eighth wonder of the world" by the novelist James Michener (in *Tales of the South Pacific*, 1947), and often referred to (incorrectly) as "the largest lagoon in the world" by tourism planners and, enthusiastically, by Marovo people themselves, the Marovo Lagoon is probably unique in terms of marine biodiversity. The lagoon and its adjacent lands are also remarkable for the diverse range of tropical coastal and rainforest environments contained within rather compact spatial parameters. For observers oriented towards natural scenery, the lagoon and its backdrop of mountains and crater rims reaching to over 1,100 metres is strikingly beautiful by any standard, and the area has since 1989 been under consideration for enlisting as a UNESCO World Heritage Site on the basis of what are deemed "outstanding natural and cultural qualities". Despite recent large-scale resource extraction, mainly logging, the Marovo Lagoon area as a whole retains extraordinary environmental qualities, and still contains many rather pristine areas of reef and rainforest.

The Marovo people give much emphasis to what they perceive as their unique 'way of life' (**kino**), underpinned above all by the abundant offerings of the environment and by the complex and enduring land-and-sea interactions that pervade virtually every past and present aspect of human life and ecological process in Marovo. The Marovo **kino** is, moreover, also based on a fundamental privilege that has been contested with a long series of colonial and neo-colonial agents – namely, the autonomous right of Marovo's **butubutu** to deliberate and decide, without interference, over any matter regarding the usage of the lands and seas that are theirs by ancestral title. This privilege, enshrined in customary law and therefore protected by the Solomon Islands constitution, entails a recognition of each **butubutu** to manage the use of its own **puava**, to close its **puava** to any resource exploitation by outside parties, and – when an outside agent succeeds in convincing **butubutu** leaders that it is in their best interest to do so – to open up the **puava** for such extraction (of trees, fish, minerals...) to take place.

In recent years foreign capitalist enterprises, often in liaison with the cash strapped national government, have shown fervent interest in the untapped resources of Marovo, not least those of the forest. The 1990s have seen large-scale logging by Asian companies of a large block of government-owned land (not subject to the constitutionally recognised claim to customary privilege described above) on southeast and central Vangunu, of large tracts of custo-mary land in northern New Georgia, and of an increasing number of smaller areas around the lagoon's borderlands, including some barrier islands with their significant stands of valuable hardwood trees. As elsewhere in Melanesia (cf. Barlow and Winduo, 1996) it is passionately argued by many observers, out-siders as well as Marovo ones, that these accelerating logging operations constitute the greatest threat ever to environmental sustainability in the Marovo Lagoon. The social consequences are equally potent and unpredictable. The past few years have seen alternating resistance and accommodation by land-holding groups, conflicts between their members, clashes between local and national government, hit-and-run activism by environmental NGOs, and diverse "rumours of Utopia" (see Chapters 11-12). While village women argue that large-scale logging destroys reserve garden lands outright and threatens the mangrove shellfish stocks because of increased sediment load of rivers, many men are likewise concerned over future possibilities for agricultural expansion and predict damage to the coral reefs and lagoon caused by siltation. Commu-nities that have rejected logging may still experience destruction of their gardens by migratory feral pigs fleeing logged-over forest – a side-effect that is seen by some to be the curse of logging concessions. Other village men have assumed a mantle of omnipotent "land owner" and have acted as go-betweens in negotiations and contracts with logging companies (**kabani dekuru**, the latter word a Marovo concept translatable as 'round log'). Some of these self-appointed landowners, referred to sarcastically back home as "L.O.s", have obtained what is reported to be unprecedented amounts of cash from their new Asian friends, and then have embarked on fast-spending sprees in the capital Honiara.

Such schismatic and polarising developments were in 1996-97 charact-eristic mainly of central and south Marovo where the Malaysian company Silvania Products Ltd had a reputation for particularly offensive approaches involving ecological destruction, territorial trespass and bribery. Another ver-sion is seen in northern New Georgia where more selective and apparently better controlled logging operations are run by an Indonesian company (Golden

Springs International) under stricter supervision by a landowner corporation (the North New Georgia Timber Corporation, NNGTC). The NNGTC is managed locally under the guidance of the Hon. Job Dudley Tausinga, a powerful New Georgian politician of national standing who is also a spiritual head of the area's dominant church, and who expresses faith in controlled logging as a means of furthering the lives of his people. To complicate the picture even further, the years from 1996 have also seen rumours about an extraordinarily large gold-find in the Bareke hills on Vangunu Island and plans for an enormous oil-palm plantation conditional on the clearfelling of most of that island – as well as intensifying efforts by agencies such as the WWF (World Wide Fund for Nature) and the New Zealand government (on behalf of the still-pending UNESCO World Heritage proposal) to promote eco-tourism in the lagoon area and on Gatokae, seemingly in a losing race with the loggers.

Hviding (1996a, especially ch. 8) elsewhere provides more extensive background for the diversifying resource exploitation by foreign companies and for the complicated ups and downs of Western-style conservation efforts in Marovo up to these most recent developments, which form the focus of the present book's final chapters. At this stage, a closer look at the customary relationships between groups and territories, and among land-holding groups, is needed.

Groups and territories

With its abundant and diverse marine and terrestrial resource base and rather low population densities (about half the national average), Marovo Lagoon is known as one of the richer areas of Solomon Islands. Through the 1980s, the first full decade of Solomon Islands nationhood, Marovo people themselves frequently voiced the opinion that the Marovo Lagoon and its adjacent lands contained some of the richest untapped resources of the nation, and that they definitely intended to reserve these resources for their own present and future benefit. As usual in present-day Solomon Islands, all reefs and shallow waters and most land in Marovo are held under customary law through communal "ownership". Land and sea and the resources there are controlled through customary principles by named **butubutu** which are based above all on the reckoning of shared descent, through men or women, among its members. According to this principle of cognatic descent each person inherits membership and various entitlements in the **butubutu** of both parents, and particularly strong emphasis is given to attachments to important chiefly genealogies through filiation (parent-child links). It follows that the most important members of a **puava**-holding **butubutu** – its core, basis or 'tree trunk' **(chubina butubutu)** associated with long precedence – are empowered to allocate resources among a rather large potential number of fellow members with more or less well-defined inherited entitlements (see below, and Hviding, 1996a, ch. 4).

On this background most of the **butubutu** of Marovo (and of the wider New Georgia area, where the concept is largely similar) act as localised corporate units in their management of spatially-defined estates (**puava**) of land and/or sea. The Marovo **puava** is a variant of a territorial concept widespread in Oceania; namely, the integrated land-and-sea "estate" exemplified also by the Hawai'ian **ahupua'a** (Meller and Horwitz, 1987; Kirch, 1985), the Yap **tabinau** (Lingenfelter, 1975), the very well-known Fijian **vanua** (Ravuvu, 1983) and, beyond the island Pacific, the estate concept of the Yolngu aborigines of North Australia (Williams, 1986). Depending on the ways in which socio-political and territorial subdivisions are defined, the area defined in local terms as 'Marovo' has between twenty and thirty corporate **butubutu** and homonymous **puava**: any **butubutu** that controls a territory is named after it. Assuming a basic figure for the entire Marovo area of around twenty-five corporate **butubutu** (Hviding, 1996a:377-382), ten would be regarded as bush groups, whereas the remaining fifteen would have to be divided equally between pure coastal (or 'salt-water') groups and groups of mixed coastal/bush type – the latter hold **puava** that contain significant areas of sea and reef as well as large land tracts. Then, in addition, the Marovo area has a number of other recognised social formations that are also referred to as **butubutu**, though without being associated with a **puava** in the usual sense. Representative examples are totemic non-localised matriclans, non-localised but in some respects corporate descent groups with common interest in remote inland areas no longer settled or used, and small extended patri- or matrilineages with or without territorial basis.

The rights of individual Marovo villagers to harvest land and sea resources depend on their consanguineal and affinal ties with different **butubutu**. These links are of varying strength, making the **butubutu** a less well-defined entity than the **puava** it controls. Whereas **puava** are mostly defined through a variety of landscape features that provide relatively clear terrestrial and marine boundaries (the latter less visible for outsiders but no less important), the New Georgian reliance on cognatic descent and bilateral inheritance produces more ambiguous boundaries in the social landscape.[1] Nevertheless firmly corporate **butubutu** do exist and do exercise their powers as such, making strong reference to the shared genealogical connections (through six generations or more) of their members to one or more apical ancestral persons (cf. Hviding, 1996a, 1993b). Any Marovo person relates to and has rights in the **puava** of the **butubutu** of both parents, but his or her decision-making 'strength' concerning the overall use of the **puava** entailed in such rights depend on – and are modified by – a multitude of factors concerning place of residence, adoption (which often equals demonstrable consanguinity) and consanguineal proximity to chiefly lineages. Some **butubutu** control both land and sea. Others being of inland origin – the 'bush people' – control land exclusively. Still other **butubutu** of sea-oriented origin – the 'coastal people' – control mainly reefs and sea and often just narrow strips of coastal land in addition to the offshore islands on which many of them have their villages. It is apparent, then, that there are large disparities among different **butubutu** as to the type, and extent, of their respective **puava** – resulting in significant contrasts in the availability of good agricultural land and of forest sources of raw materials and foodstuffs.

Each **butubutu**'s affairs are managed by a senior male leader, the 'chief' or **bangara**. He is assisted by a number of associate leaders, all recruited from a core of people who have 'strong' descent – i.e. with many demonstrable filiative links (through women or men) to the chiefly genealogy of the group – and are permanently resident in the **butubutu**'s area. The **bangara** supervises land allocation and manages relationships to the outside world. He is acknowledged to have overall command of the **butubutu**'s oral traditions and also safeguards a collection of heirlooms (consecrated clamshell objects, whale teeth, etc.) passed on through the generations. His associates are usually a limited range of specialists in such matters as fishing, work organisation or genealogical knowledge. At the very minimum two trusted elders (in most cases men) are appointed to perform the traditional functions of a **bangara**'s **hedematao** (lit. the chief's 'left-and-right'; in other words, his trusted associates with whom most matters of **butubutu** and **puava** are discussed deeply before decisions are made). To supplement the capacity for relating to the wider world, a number of **bangara** today have an appointed secretary to the chief – invariably a well-educated younger man of chiefly descent and not infrequently pursuing an urban career. Interestingly, communication between chiefs and such urban secretaries is not difficult these days, being facilitated by the recent establishment of radiotelephones in several villages throughout the Marovo area; moreover **butubutu** with pressing concerns on the national scene (mainly with reference to logging) have great use for such dyadic chief-secretary/village-town relationships.

Leadership succession, especially for the most senior positions and certainly for that of **bangara**, has a strongly prescriptive element of inheritance, usually from father to eldest son – provided that the old chief has named his successor (**sinoana bangara**, 'chief's replacement') before his death. Failure to do so, from reasons of conflict avoidance or untimely death, is not uncommon and tends to result in disorganised **butubutu** leadership. In any event, for **bangara** succession the general rule of male primogeniture may not be followed. Sometimes the candidate is deemed unsuitable for lack of character, and a younger brother, parallel cousin or even younger brother of the deceased chief takes over instead. More commonly these days, doubt may be cast on an otherwise respected candidate's suitability for the reason of non-Marovo residence because of urban employment (often a matter of some irony in that his position as a chiefly son has facilitated education and an urban career). In such cases, however, the town-dwelling son may often take over as **bangara** anyway as long as a well-qualified stand-in caretaker is appointed to act locally on his behalf – on the understanding that caretaker and **bangara** will keep in regular contact by letter (and today sometimes by radiotelephone). In a few recent cases women too, have been appointed to such senior caretaker posts, thereby echoing an old custom whereby a chiefly daughter could be appointed **bangara** for lack of (suitable) male offspring.

This group of 'guardians' (**ria pu chakei nia ia butubutu oro ia puava**, lit. 'those who look after the people and the[ir] territory') have many complex tasks at hand. We have already noted how the customary Marovo system of tenure over lands and seas and their resources, which has operated for generations in a context dominated by subsistence resource use and low population densities, has increasingly been challenged to cope with a variety of potentially disrupting changes. Large-scale logging, mining and fishing activities by transnational companies, increased local commercialisation of resources and rapid population growth – all these factors combine to put pressure on marine and terrestrial resources, on the tenure institutions, and on the social relationships within and beyond Marovo. In recent years, then, most of Marovo's **butubutu** have entered into a range of discussions, negotiations and conflicts with extralocal parties concerning the large-scale extraction of the area's natural resources (see Hviding, 1993b, for a concentrated example).

Marovo people tend to perceive themselves as having been rather successful in many of these meetings. In contrast to widespread and politically correct rhetoric about the vulnerability of people in out-of-the-way places to modern capitalist overtures, and about the fragility of "traditional" institutions in the face of capitalism and modernity, Marovo people see themselves as largely able to handle such encounters to their own benefit. "We have been able to influence all kinds of things for so long", they say, thereby also referring to their reputation among 19th-century traders for "sharp" business practices, and their ability to harness the energy of missionaries and missions for the benefit of the local economy and in support of customary institutions (see Hviding, 1996a; Bennett, 1987; Jackson, 1978). The strong emphasis on local autonomy also in matters of territorial control and resource management has through the 1970s and 1980s repeatedly prevented outsiders from exploiting Marovo's land and sea resources. Through to the 1990s, certain important cultural models of accountability and responsibility in Marovo terms – notably that of **varikale**, 'constituting socially reciprocal sides' (in which sense each part is supposed to act with complete accountability for its dealings, as chief to chief) – appear to have fostered a climate where representatives of Marovo's **butubutu** have managed to insist successfully that their own procedures for negotiation and contract be accorded overall dominance (Hviding, 1993b, 1996a).

The Marovo people's concern for the maintenance of autonomy in local resource control has been carried beyond the local level through to provincial and national governments. Local opposition to large-scale resource extraction has had consequences for several large ventures in which transnational companies have been seeking access to Marovo resources through legal-political channels facilitated by the national government. In 1986 the transnational logging company Levers Pacific Timbers Ltd had to cease its operations in Solomon Islands after prolonged conflict with local landholding groups of northern Marovo and Kusaghe who refused to renew logging agreements originally mediated partly by the government. Concerns over land degradation did play some part in this process, and were enhanced by the presence of pioneering Australian environmentalist groups in the early 1980s. However, local resistance was provoked just as much, and possibly even more, by landholders' dissatisfaction with what they saw as Levers' arrogant unwillingness to engage in a continuous and close relationship of joint discussions over logging practices and forest management (Chapter 9, and see Hviding, 1996a: 316-320). This is an important point of wider theoretical relevance; it indicates how resistance to such activities as large-scale logging may be based on complex concerns about political autonomy and locally correct procedure (such as **varikale**, mentioned above), rather than (as Western conservationists would like to see it) any "traditional conservation ethic".

On the 'side' of the sea, some of Marovo's 'coastal' **butubutu** have for years kept substantial parts of the lagoon off-limits for pole-and-line tuna fishing boats seeking to obtain baitfish from inshore reefs. These boats, whose operations are totally dependent on a nightly supply of live baitfish, belong to fishing companies that are joint ventures between the Solomon Islands government and foreign, mainly Japanese, capital, and access to "bait grounds" throughout the archipelago has been managed since the early 1980s through negotiated agreements with local reef- and sea-holding groups whose leaders receive stipulated "bait royalties" in return. Characteristically, Marovo opposition to baitfishing takes into account concerns over social disturbances, the divisiveness of royalty payments and the arrogance of fishing companies, as well as the more "ecological" ones about oil pollution and the fact that small fish are eaten by bigger fish which in turn are eaten by people (Hviding, 1996a:321-325; Hviding and Baines, 1994).

In a number of other confrontations during the 1980s and 1990s outside commercial interests have actually been expelled by Marovo **butubutu** leaders; relevant examples are a Taiwanese clam-fishing vessel, a Honiara-based buyer of commercial shells, Australian gold prospectors, and luxurious "live-aboard" SCUBA-dive ships operating out of Honiara. Even the long-established tourist resort at Uipi on the barrier islands in the central lagoon has not escaped confrontation, despite strong local involvement also on the management side. In one notable instance in 1987 a **butubutu** with extensive barrier reef holdings near the resort sent a letter (with copies to a large number of national and provincial authorities) demanding US$ 150,000 in compensation from the Australian proprietors for what was deemed as years of highly profitable, organised diving on the reefs in question with no fees paid to the **butubutu**. (After a long period without diving on the disputed reefs the issue was eventually resolved not by compensation, but by the signing of agreements on stipulated fees payable to the **butubutu** per tourist dive). Even representatives of overseas conservationist organisations have on occasion been told to leave Marovo, in cases where the consultants' apparent concern for the well-being of the place was perceived to be financially motivated, representing 'desire' (**hiniva**) of the profit-seeking **kabani** ('company') kind quite similar to that of logging companies (**kabani dekuru**) – and incompatible with village-level aspirations anyway. Several such instances of chasing away ships, company representatives and others have in the next run produced new approaches by those chased, resulting in arrangements with **butubutu** that allow for the return of the previously unwanted activities, but this time under terms that allow the concerned **butubutu** to define and control the situation (see Hviding, 1996a, ch. 7, for more detailed discussion). In this way "terms of trade" are agreed – for example restrictions on where foreigners can go, what compensation should be paid for any damage to trees, reefs or sacred sites, what fees SCUBA-divers should pay, and whether or not to allow the temporary establishment of non-local business in a village. In a number of these cases **butubutu** have enlisted the assistance of lawyers and of representatives of national and provincial government.

The land-and-sea-holding **butubutu** of Marovo thus frequently act to curtail large-scale commercial interests, through strong and often innovative uses of the customary politics of resource control, supplemented by rather active contacts with the nation-state's legal-administrative institutions. Indeed, autonomous control over areas and resources seems to be the focus and very essence of Marovo people's on-going involvements with outside parties, in an oscillating mix of concerns about lands and seas and political autonomy, informed by the material and symbolic interdependencies between sea and land, between reef and rainforest, outlined earlier. While much political action in recent decades has had the lagoon and its resources as focus (Hviding, 1996a), attention has from the mid-1990s been geared more strongly towards the forest and its alternative short- and long-term uses. Land disputes have escalated. The long-standing pattern of bitter intra- and inter-**butubutu** strife over smaller tracts of garden lands, a pattern for which Marovo people have attained some notoriety in the Solomons – though not as notorious a reputation for land disputes as that of the neighbouring Roviana people (cf. Schneider, 1996, 1998) – has evolved to focus on larger areas of inland or remote coastal forest, rarely visited for most of the 20th century, but currently objects of desire for logging companies.

Forested lands

We now move to an overview of the everyday contexts for these diverse courses of action: the lagoon and the land, and the daily work and community life of the seashore villages. Before dealing with present-day patterns of local resource use in Marovo, we need first to provide a brief outline of the main environmental features of the lagoon and its surrounding lands, here with an emphasis on the rainforest (further detailed material is found in Hviding, 1995b and 1996a). We refer to Figure 3.1 for an overview of the various environmental zones subsumed under the **puava** concept of 'territorial estate'.

The Marovo climate is hot and humid throughout the year, with major changes only in wind directions and tidal cycles. Annual rainfall is high, up to 4,000 mm, with some micro-climatic variations throughout the lagoon. For example, the northern parts of Marovo, with a narrow lagoon and a short distance from coast to mountains, are reckoned to receive more rain than the central lagoon area, where dense cloud columns often tower inland over the mountains of Vangunu while the coastal villages are scorched by the sun. The word corresponding most closely to "weather" in Marovo is **are**, 'wind'. From April to September southeasterly trade winds with much clear sky (and rain mostly in morning and evening) prevail, while more irregular, consistently wet northwest monsoons dominate from December to March. During the transitional period of October to November spells of calm seas and clear weather may occur for weeks on end. The time of southeast trades (**kolokolo hecha**) largely coincides with the occurrence of low tides at daytime (**mati rane**) and high tides at night (**singi ipu**), whereas the time of northwest monsoons (**kolokolo mohu**) coincides with low tides at night (**mati ipu**) and high tides during daytime (**singi rane**). While the tradewind season is regarded as dry and cool and in agricultural terms as a time mainly of harvest and decreasing yields, the shorter, wetter monsoon season is associated with heat and fecundity and is seen as the proper time for planting crops.

Recurring seasonal rhythms of winds and tides are associated with much knowledge about other cyclical events in the reef and rainforest environments – marked throughout the year by lunar and solar phenomena and by the growth and behaviour patterns or appearance of certain animals and plants. A finely subdivided calendar thus guides day-to-day practice on the basis of predictable

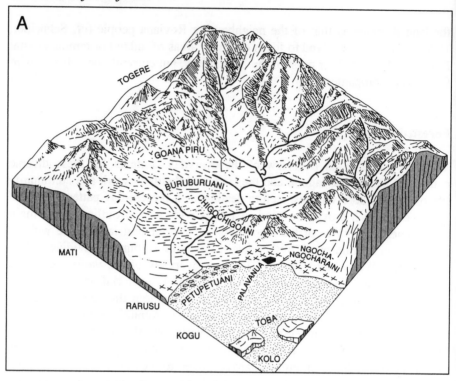

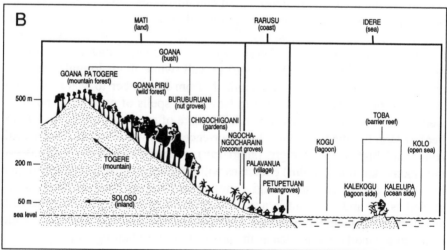

**Figure 3.1 Cross-section of land and sea environments of Marovo,
subsumed in the** puava **concept**

    A. Landscape view, based on a river catchment in Bareke, extending
inland to the summit of Mt Reku (after Wall and Hansell, 1975:97)

    B. Classification of the same environments viewed in cross-section environmental events, which include the seasonal migrations of fish, crabs and birds, the flowering of certain trees, the shifting passages of sun and moon across the sky, and the changing patterns of lagoon currents. This multi-layered calendar, where the counting of lunar months is superimposed on two main wind/tide seasons and on many other annual cycles, has profound influence on strategies in planting, harvesting and fishing throughout the year. The year itself is called **buruburu**, which is also the name for *Canarium* nut trees and thus signifies the role of *Canarium* harvests in time reckoning. In comparative Melanesian terms, this use of '*Canarium* nut tree' for 'year' signifies that New Georgians belong to a different tradition in cultural history from those whose annual cycle centres on the planting and harvesting of yams.

To a large degree the three high volcanic islands of New Georgia, Vangunu and Gatokae remain covered by tropical rainforest, in a topographical continuum of forest types: the tangled moss forests on foggy mountain tops; the more open but dry (in the sense of being located above running water) forest of high ridgetops; the tall, dense 'proper' forest of valleys and lower hills; wet coastal areas of freshwater swamps and extensive estuarine mangrove forests; and in places the sun-scorched beach or "strand" forest of the dry raised coral terraces along the coasts. Mangroves and dry coastal forests are replicated, though with some unique additional attributes, on and around the long, raised islands of the barrier reef and the innumerable small coral islands of the lagoons.

The presence of a dense forest cover also appears to characterise numerous areas scarred by bulldozer tracks and now considered to be "logged out". Unlike the logging carried out in the 1970s and into the 1980s by the British company Levers Pacific Timbers Ltd in North New Georgia (and elsewhere in the Western Solomons, especially on Kolobangara), the Asian operations underway in Marovo in 1990s have not normally included the large-scale removal of smaller trees. From the sea or air, many recently logged areas therefore still appear to have a partially intact forest cover, though with a much lower and more irregular canopy than before, and broken by the long and winding red lines of bulldozed roads and skid tracks on ridges and along foothills. Permanently degraded grasslands of *Imperata* (**rekiti**) and various ferns occur only to a very limited extent, on some upper northern slopes of Gatokae and, more recently, in patches on northern New Georgia that were more or less clearfelled by Levers in the 1970s. The latter areas are also dominated by smothering layers of *Merremia* creepers (**kualeve**), which are now, however, beginning to be replaced by an increasingly vigorous regrowth of typical forest trees; a sign of possible natural regeneration. By the late 1990s large-scale commercial logging had taken place mainly around Viru Harbour, in North New Georgia southeast towards the Tita river, and on southeast and central Vangunu.

While large tracts of the Viru land had been reforested under a long-term plan involving the national government and British development agencies (but recently taken over by a Korean company and being logged again), the other areas are by now, after incessant logging mainly from 1990 onwards, to be seen as "logged out". This means that the (mainly) Asian companies concerned no longer see it as viable to extract trees from the remaining forest. From a Marovo perspective most logged-out forest is indeed to be classified as **goana ta regocho** – 'destroyed forest' of little immediate use, though not without potential for improvement. Although not involving clearfelling, the rumoured expansion of rough-and-ready activities by the Malaysian company Silvania Products Ltd from the logged-out government-held "forest estate" on Vangunu to other areas of customary land, such as on Gatokae, may foretell modification of the lands and forests of Marovo to a degree and on a scale never before seen. Certain large "development" proposals by the same company, to be discussed and analysed in the final chapters of this book, go so far as to aim at total clear-felling – of all trees and shrubs, large and small – for the establishment of huge oil palm plantations with associated towns and ports. The future of Marovo forests indeed remains indeterminate.

In its non-logged state, the inner rainforest (**goana piru**, 'wild forest') provides medicinal bark and leaves; house construction materials (poles, vines and, today, sawn planks); woods, rope material and foliage for a staggering range of practical purposes (tool-making, food preparation, and more); trees for dugout canoes; animal protein in the form of feral pig, cuscus (a tree marsupial), fruit bats and birds; wild honey; and a further plethora of wild leafy greens and fruits.[2] Men who know the deep forest well sometimes say that in the midst of this 'wild' forest one can actually stand still in most places and just reach out one's hands all around to obtain rather effortlessly a great repertoire of what a family needs to make a living. Logging disturbance is constructed by some environmentalists as the rape of a virgin wilderness, but in fact most of the rainforest of Marovo, including areas far inland, has been heavily modified by past human activity. Though reckoned as rather 'wild' today, the upper forest of all three major islands is rich in signs of former human habitation and extensive cultivation, containing scattered groves of very old *Canarium* nut trees (associated with former settlements and irrigation sites), large numbers of stone structures such as house platforms, ancestral skull shrines and other sacred places, and the lightly covered remains of large elaborate terraces for taro irrigation. While some of these 'signs' of human presence have faded from the memory of present generations and may resurface only for present-day bulldozer operators (see Chapters 9-10), most remain in firm association with certain **butubutu**, and localised knowledge of such types of **hope** – 'sacred [or tabu] site' – are invoked to perpetuate land claims and to demand compensation from trespassing logging companies. In line with this, an increasing number of

butubutu now invite provincial archaeological field staff to record and register their repertoire of "custom sites" inland. Such surveys take place under an arrangement whereby a logging company seeking a concession to operate on customary land must pay the provincial cultural office for the archaeological work.

Moving further up above the headwaters of rivers to ridgetops, limestone pinnacles and mountain peaks, one enters zones of, as is said, "many small but very few big trees" – a forest dominated by *Casuarina papuana* and *Pandanus* trees, certain palm trees, vines and tall gingers, and with the ground covered by soft layers of dead leaves often several metres thick. With its abundance of *Casuarina* and *Pandanus* the dry ridgetop forest, it is often pointed out, is strangely similar to the similarly waterless forest of the barrier islands. These high-altitude zones are collectively referred to as **goana pa togere** 'hilltop [or mountain] forest', with the specific term **ugulu** (and, in the Hoava bush language, **saghabu** from **ghabu** 'fog') applying to the uppermost zones of stunted cloud forest. However, neither the ridgetops nor the contiguous, often cloud-obscured tangled forest of mountain tops and limestone pinnacles are visited regularly. A hunter may in rare cases pursue a feral pig all the way up there, but apart from hilltops which support certain straight-growing hardwood trees useful for axe handles, spear shafts, and the like, the high-altitude areas contain little in the way of useful items. They are widely regarded as somewhat eerie places which might best be avoided. Apart from the large and historically important, once densely populated mountain crater of Vangunu, and a scattering of high-altitude peaks that had fortified settlements in the old days, there are not many signs of past human presence in this zone. However, the historical significance of remote ridgetops is demonstrated more widely by the habit of referring to many of them as **bokuboku** (lit. 'boundary-markers'). They continue to constitute rather general yet conspicuous border zones between the different inland **puava** of Marovo, and – on New Georgia proper – also between some major bush **butubutu** of Marovo and their (historically close) counterparts in the Roviana area. They also signify the old principle whereby the extensive territories of historically inland-dwelling groups contained the headwaters of major watercourses within them; a means to ensure at least symbolic control over the means of taro irrigation.

We cannot invoke absolute remoteness to account for the lack of human uses of the uppermost forests. In fact, as for other islands of the Solomons archipelago, the forests of New Georgia, Vangunu and Gatokae are "compressed" in terms of ecological zones (Whitmore, 1969, 1990); so that a remarkable and complete range of distinct forest zones grow in Marovo on islands with a maximum elevation above sea level not more than 1,100 metres, and usually far less. Thus in the Vahole area of north Marovo, for example, a walk from coastal mangroves all the way up into the uppermost **ugulu** (or

saghabu) forest on inland peaks may be undertaken in a few hours. A comparable excursion in, say, mainland New Guinea or Borneo might take many days. This compressed nature of Marovo's forest zones has, of course, bearings on the range of forest products rather immediately accessible to coastal villagers. There are very few 'things of the forest' that may not be obtained in the course of a half-day expedition through every zone of forest.

Descending through the 'wild' forest by way of river valleys and sloping hills one passes valley bottoms where there is said to be "few, but very big trees" (in contrast to the high-altitude forest described above). Both 'slope forest' (**goana pa taba**) and 'valley bottom forest' (**goana pa nura**) are special categories in the Marovo zonation of land. Slopes are dominated by large strangler figs or "banyan" trees (**kalala**, *Ficus* spp.) as well as many palms and the large timber tree **meda** (*Pometia pinnata*). Valley bottoms in addition have useful bamboos, the large timber tree **vasara** (*Vitex cofassus*) and, down in the shade under big trees, the all-important banana-like **vaho** (*Heliconia solomonensis*) and ginger-like **sinu** (*Guillainia purpurata*) whose large leaves are indispensable for wrapping food in the stone-oven. The latter sometimes forms dense stands (**sinusinuani**) in muddy, waterlogged areas and as such are also cultivated in less favourable tracts of gardens. **Vaho** are also important in another sense in that wherever they occur in the deep forest they are held to signify that gardens were worked there sometime in the past.

Most lower reaches of hills and valleys are more heavily modified and referred to as simply **goana** ('forest' or, as in Pijin parlance, 'bush'). They are the focus of present-day agroforestry activities and indeed, with the fishing grounds, contain the major loci of everyday practice. The lower hills over most of Marovo support rotational shifting cultivation complexes where sweet potato and cassava are grown intensively in swiddens in association with a great range of other useful plants. This is described in detail in the following chapters. This agroforestry zone, generally referred to as **chigochigoani** ('area of gardens', from **chigo** 'swidden garden'),[3] also contains planted *Canarium* nut groves (**buruburuani**) of some antiquity, and in a few places there are small, recent cocoa plantings. Interspersed with swiddens under cultivation and permanent nut tree groves are fallows and secondary forest (subsumed under the term **kotukotuani**) in different stages of regrowth. Short-term fallows are dominated by dense stands of the tall, fragrant and ubiquitous **piropiro** ginger shrub (*Alpinia* sp.). Indeed, such places, called **piropiroani**, are the prototypical fallows of Marovo, being in a state of short-term transition from one cycle of intensive cultivation to another. More mature secondary forest (**kotukotuani porana**) with three to four years of regrowth contains fewer gingers but has an exceptionally large variety of spontaneously occurring trees and shrubs with medicinal and other uses, as well as certain important trees often cultivated more consciously by tending, if not planting. Examples are **lakori** (*Ficus* *variegata*), whose bark is traditionally preferred for cloth-making although specimens in recent secondary forest are usually too small); the multi-purpose **leru** (*Hibiscus tiliaceus*), otherwise most common along beaches and to some degree along cleared riverbanks); **mudu** (*Cananga odorata*), the "perfume tree" known under its Malaysian name Ylang-Ylang, whose flowers are used to scent coconut oil); the "putty-nut" tree **tita** (*Parinari glaberrima*) indispensable for caulking canoes and for handicraft work; and **pinopoto** (*Ficus copiosa*), the edible shoots of which are regularly collected. These trees can also be fully domesticated by being planted in swiddens actively under cultivation.

To sum up, this agroforestry zone of intense human activity is a dynamic continuum of interrelated stages in cultivation and fallowing. Any **chigo-chigoani** is bound to be transformed, sooner or later, into **kotukotuani**, the latter then maturing to a greater or lesser degree before being cleared for cultivation again and reverting to **chigo** (see also Figure 4.5). It should be noted that the pattern described here does not generally apply to those large tracts of land that have no major village in the vicinity. Though some more remote areas have recently been cleared in connection with the establishment of new hamlets, many remain densely forested and are only visited intermittently for hunting and gathering purposes. Although in some respects recognised explicitly as secondary forest, these areas are not usually called **kotukotuani** but referred to as **chichiogo** – which may be glossed as 'old secondary forest [with tall trees]'. In an important sense this category is intermediate between **kotukotuani** and **goana piru** – it is recognised as having evolved from cultivated lands through the former state, but it also verges on the state of 'wild'-ness represented by the latter. It is generally thought that **chichiogo** tracts have been left undisturbed for 50 years or more. The most telltale signs that an area of tall inner forest is "domesticated" **chichiogo** and not **goana piru** ('wild forest [no longer under explicit human control]') are that old settlement sites, stone terraces for taro irrigation and *Canarium* groves found there are associated with named persons and groups of quite recent generations. Furthermore, **chichiogo** areas usually contain old *Areca* palms and other trees known to have been planted by certain named persons who cultivated their gardens (including swiddens) there. In this sense ancestrally-conferred rights over **chichiogo** should, it is said, be less disputed than **goana piru**, where the history of territorial boundaries may be diffuse at best.

These interior areas effectively constitute immediately accessible reserve agricultural lands for those **butubutu** that are fortunate enough to have substantial land holdings and a low population-to-land ratio. Their status as **chichiogo** also means that they are liable for recultivation by the **butubutu** that holds recognised ancestral title over them. **Chichiogo** areas are also notable for containing large specimens of quite a few important secondary forest species, such as **lakori** (*Ficus variegata*) which in its **chichiogo** state provides exceptionally wide strips of bark for traditional cloth-making. The overlapping **piro-piroani-kotukotuani-chichiogo** continuum, with its transitional zones towards **goana piru** proper, is in essence an indigenous codification of agricultural and settlement history, and of associated entitlements in and continuous use of land. Indeed, the question of whether or not claimants are able to provide historical accounts of, and identify, inland **chichiogo** areas is often a primary issue in land dispute cases dealt with by the local, custom-oriented court. Faced by this court with the question, "Where is your **chichiogo**?", claimants are frequently challenged to identify **chichiogo** and to demonstrate their knowledge of and ancestral connections to the area(s) – for example, by locating an old *Areca* tree and adjacent garden site, or a *Canarium* grove, and relate it convincingly to known ancestral persons.

On the narrow flat coral terraces of the coast, and on slopes immediately behind villages, are extensive coconut groves (**ngochangocharaini**), bearing evidence of a recent time when copra was still the major commodity. Old coconut groves contain a large variety of other plants and are a source of several highly useful leaves, most notably those of the **hirata** climber (*Piper betle*, indispensable for betelnut-chewing) and of several small medicinal creepers. Stands of sago palm (**edeve**, *Metroxylon salomonense*), whose leaves are a main house-building material, are planted (and grow spontaneously) in muddy areas right behind the coast. The giant swamp taro (**ghohere**, *Cyrtosperma chamissonis*) is also planted here. The mainland beach zone itself (where it is not subsumed in estuarine mangroves) has its own repertoire of important trees and shrubs, mainly representatives of the farflung, typical "Indo-Pacific strand flora" (also referred to botanically as the "Barringtonia formation" [Paijmans, 1976:29-30]). Few of these plants are cultivated but several of may be tended if they happen to grow near house sites. Examples are the aforementioned **leru** (*Hibiscus tiliaceus*), the **talise** tree (*Terminalia catappa*) with its seasonal reddening and shedding of leaves (an important calendrical marker) and abundance of almond-like nuts, the large **pogala** (*Barringtonia asiatica*) whose box-like fruits are poisonous but also of medical use, and, overhanging the sea, the large **buni rarusu** (*Calophyllum inophyllum*), a main source of locally sawn timber. All these also provide shade and shelter from wind and sea. A striking feature of rocky seashores of Marovo Lagoon and the adjacent weather coasts is that dense rainforest usually grows straight down to the water's edge. The few metres of coral rubble and jagged rocks that constitute the beach zone in these areas are often left in the dark by large overhanging trees and tangled creepers and climbers, or hidden from view altogether by a lower barrier of seemingly impenetrable mangrove trees in the tidal zone.

A large number of large and small rivers cut through the steep forested valleys of the main islands and enter the lagoon in wide, shallow estuarine bays separated by low densely forested headlands of old coral rock, described above.

The lower reaches of rivers have dense galleries of vegetation including many climbers with aerial roots (particularly *Epipremnum pinnatum,* a Solomon Islands endemic that is now a ubiquitous Euro-American house plant). Sometimes growing along the riverbanks are stands of the important **hinage** or "nipa" palm, *Nypa fruticans,* which is used in house construction, especially for inner walls. In recent years an increasing number of additional gardens have been established on the banks of major rivers, behind the saltwater zone of the mangroves and the freshwater swamps dominated by the very tall **hoba** tree (*Terminalia brassii*) but also containing useful trees such as the carving wood **rigi** (*Pterocarpus indicus*). Such 'bush gardens' (**chigo pa goana**) represent an interesting expansion of the present-day agroforestry system and are examined in Chapter 8.

Where land and sea meet

In general the river estuaries of Marovo Lagoon have wide expanses of tall mangrove forest associated with them. The only major exception is the weather coast of southern Vangunu where large rivers enter the sea directly without any intermediary mangrove zone. The mangrove-dominated estuarine areas contain rich resources of shells – mainly **riki** (*Anadara* spp.) and **deo** (*Polymesoda* spp.) – and mud crabs (**kakarita**, *Scylla serrata*). In the lower, saline reaches of some rivers, large and predictable aggregations of mullet (*Mugil* spp.), a highly prized food fish, occur seasonally and are harvested by locally unique, singular netting techniques. Certain rivers, particularly in the Choe area of the southern Nono Lagoon, have large stocks of the freshwater bivalve *Batissa fortis* (highly important in Fiji, and known in Marovo as **deo Choe** after its primary habitat). The mangrove forests themselves are very important sources of wood for fuel and construction, and the large germinating seeds of the tall tree *Bruguiera gymnorhiza* (**petu ta ngo** 'edible mangrove') are an important supplementary food for some Marovo groups, who claim to have learned this way of using mangrove 'fruits' from the people of Langalanga in Malaita.

The lagoon proper, termed **kogu**, varies considerably in width, i.e. distance from mainland to barrier reefs. The northern and southeastern parts of the lagoon are fairly shallow whereas depths of 25 metres and more are common in the central parts and near the deep passages (**sangava**) to the open sea (see Stoddart, 1969 for details on the geomorphology of the Marovo reefs). The lagoon is studded with a myriad of small islands (**tusu**) many of which are covered with "strand" forest and mangrove, others planted with coconuts. Many of these islands contain ample and easily accessible supplies of good firewood, partly in the form of dead trees. Coral reef patches at various depths abound throughout the lagoon. Shallower reefs, sand bars and seagrass beds occur along some mainland coasts but are most common near the barrier reef – the extraordinary **toba**. The complex reef and island formations of the Marovo elevated barrier reef contain the most important fishing grounds of Marovo people, and consist of long, narrow raised reef islands, intersected by passages of various depths. A few sections of the **toba** are submerged at high tide, but in general the jagged limestone plateaus of the barrier islands support a dense and tall vegetation with notable trees such as the tall, valuable timber species *Intsia bijuga* (**kivili**, known under the timber trade names Merbau and Kwila), ebony (**rihe**, *Diospyros* sp.) and "kerosene wood" (**naginagi**, *Cordia subcordata*), the latter two of great value to Marovo wood-carvers but now getting increasingly scarce. The valuable coconut crab (**tupe**, *Birgus latro*), a much-prized local delicacy among Methodist and CFC groups and a market item of increasing scarcity, also inhabits this forest.

The sheltered lagoon side (**kalekogu**) of the barrier islands has thick mangrove growth and, in some areas, sandy beaches shaded by overhanging littoral trees such as the large **buni rarusu** (*Calophyllum inophyllum*), much used for local chainsaw milling. The ocean-facing side (**kalelupa**), however, most often has complex formations of reef flats, tidal pools and larger basins, coral cliffs and rocks with stunted saltwater-resistant trees, and jagged reef rims with steep drop-offs into the open sea. Among the large number of trees and other plants characteristic of the barrier island forest are some that in Marovo usage constitute "mirrors" of trees and plants of the mainland forest. For example, the hardy **chakope** tree (*Premna corymbosa*) which is often found on ocean-facing cliffs and rocks has a dry wood perfect for virtually rain-proof fire-making implements, as does the totally different lowland forest tree **hutu kaka** (*Kleinhovia hospita*). Such pairing of unrelated trees found only in mainland or barrier island forest is quite common in the Marovo-wide repertoires of forest usages, including herbal medicine. It implies that given sufficient knowledge, no one will be in want of anything useful from the forest whether hunting in the mainland bush or fishing out on the reefs.

On the weather coasts of the Vangunu and Gatokae islands the environment differs considerably from that of the lagoon. The rocky shores are exposed to the open sea, and more sheltered areas with sandy beaches are found only in some estuarine bays. The weather coasts have abundant land resources with good soils and great forests sloping up towards the inland mountains and ancient volcanic craters, but marine resources, at least within acceptable distance from the villages, are less plentiful. The remote islands and sand cays of the Hele Bar are the most important marine resource areas of the Vangunu weather coast people. The Hele islands have locally important nesting beaches for hawksbill and green turtles, both of which are much-prized seasonal feast food. Selling the hard shell of the former to Honiara dealers used to be important for supplementing weather coast villagers' modest cash income, but it has in recent years been prohibited by law, the Solomon Islands government now being a signatory of the international CITES convention.[4]

In the lagoon, along the mangrove coasts and on the barrier reef, a vast variety of fish, molluscs and crustaceans is available (cf. Hviding, 1995b, listing more than 400 Marovo taxa for fish and more than 100 for molluscs, most of which are eaten). For specifically commercial purposes there are stocks of pearlshell, trochus and other shells, bêche-de-mer and precious coral. It is often noted philosophically in Marovo that it is indeed the sea that makes Marovo so different from most other places in the Solomons (Hviding, 1996a: 167). On a direct level, the multiple opportunities for cash income offered by abundant and diverse marine resources have encouraged the development of a diversity of income sources and thereby limited the conversion of coastal forest and good agricultural land to coconut plantations. The "coconut overlay" is thus considerably less dominating on the coasts of Marovo than on many other islands of the Solomons where alternative economic opportunities have been few, whether for lack of extensive reefs or for other reasons. On a less tangible level, the maritime domain has been, and continues to be, a powerful influence in Marovo cultural identity – expressed in the history of maritime travel and overseas warfare, in the continuing importance of day-to-day fishing practice, and in the axiomatic sea-and-land/fish-and-taro equation embodied in the intra-Marovo relationships between coastal people and bush people.

Forest, lagoon and barrier reef together provide Marovo with a cultural landscape (and seascape) as well as the material resources that have been the main focus of this brief survey. A huge number of sites rich in cultural and historical meaning are found throughout the mountains, forests, seashores, reefs and islands of the Marovo area. A few examples would include: sacred sub-merged reefs over which canoe passage is prohibited even today; secret sacri-ficial limestone caves in the barrier reef with access only through underwater channels (through which it is reported that men would swim while carrying lighted embers in their mouths); rocks on ocean-facing reefs where sacrifices were made to spirit sharks; tiny coral islets upon which ancestral skulls are placed to signify tenure of the marine area in question; stone cairns along sea-shores and in the forest where burnt sacrifices were offered to spirits of fishing, hunting and *Canarium*-nut harvesting; focal ancestral shrines in the coastal or inland forest in which the skulls of many generations of chiefs are kept; remains of old settlement sites, some fortified; megalithic structures deep in the forest of only obscure origin with little if any local exegesis; abandoned stone terraces for irrigated taro cultivation; old sacred tree groves dedicated to named ancestral persons; and places that are significant by the connotations invoked by their names (cf. Hviding, 1996a, ch. 6). Such sites of significance also constitute much of the 'good things' (**tingitonga leadi**) within the **puava** of a

butubutu, and encounters with these form part of all day-to-day experience for those who work on the lands, reefs and seas of Marovo.

A continuum of forests: the Marovo perspective

In Marovo, trees and other plants are said to lead distinct lives with preferences and dislikes, associates and foes, though lacking the conscious-ness (**binalabala**) of people, animals and even fish. For example, certain plants are said to prepare the soil for others, in line with perspectives from agricultural science. Tree metaphors abound in Marovo language and refer to domains of definite knowledge, longevity, ancestry, totality and fundamental causes and purposes. **Chubi-** ('tree trunk of ...') is the ultimate expression for the very foundation of any existing object, condition, opinion and social form and speaks of existential precedence in time and space. In line with this "sociality-oriented" view different zones of forest are spoken of as hosting certain communities of typical trees and other plants which often are quite exclusive to their specific zone. This observation is commonly ration-alised by the view that these trees and other plants prefer to lead their lives together. The Marovo view is rather closely parallel to the concept of "plant community" developed in the early 20th century by ecologists like Frederick Clement and Arthur Tansley, but now criticised by Western science for beaming anthropomorphic.

The Marovo perspective is presented in Figure 3.2, which gives the local classification of forest zones and a list of what local forest experts deemed to be the typical "communities" of plants representative of each zone. The Marovo uses of each plant are also given. Of course this list is not an exhaustive account of biodiversity in Marovo's forests; but it does summarise in a systematic way information given by men and women who are recognised beyond their home villages as being among the truly knowledgeable 'people of the forest'.

Figure 3.2 builds partly on walks through continuous transects of forest – from mangroves to mountain peaks – conducted by one of the authors together with senior hunters of the Vahole 'bush' **butubutu** for the purpose of naming the important plants and examining the relationships between them. The listing follows an emically logical continuum starting with the uppermost ridgetop forest, descending through mountain sides and 'wild' forest to the general lowland forest type with slopes and valleys, through rivers, freshwater swamps and mangrove forest to the 'domesticated' agro-forestry areas of secondary forest, bush fallow, gardens, villages and coconut groves, on to seaside forest and across the lagoon with its densely overgrown islands to the complex forest of the raised barrier reef islands.

Figure 3.2 Forest zones, plant communities and their uses: the Marovo perspective

Names given are Marovo taxa with botanical identifications where available. The lists are based on information contained in Hviding (1995b). Identifications are based on a number of sources for Solomon Islands forests, notably Whitmore (1966, pers. comm.), Hancock and Henderson (1988), Henderson (1988), Henderson and Hancock (1988b) and Dowe (1989); "not identified" indicates present lack of botanical identification for the Marovo taxa concerned. It should be noted that a number of scientific identifications are tentative.

Under TYPE, plants follow Marovo categorisation, thus:
- 'tree' (**hae**); some being 'large' (with tall and thick trunks), others 'tall' only;
- '[leafy] shrub' (**rikiroko**), also including tall herbs;
- 'vine' [climbers/creepers] (**adoso**);
- 'grass' [low herbs] (**checheu**).

Certain significant plant categories depart from the main scheme:
- 'ginger' (corresponding to the Marovo term **hae piropiro**, '**piropiro**-like woody shrub');
- 'bamboo' (nominally **hae** but classified separately as **huhua hae ivu**, 'bearing resemblance to the **ivu** bamboo');
- 'palm' (nominally hae but classified separately as **huhua hae pijaka**, 'bearing resemblance to the **pijaka** [*Areca*] palm').

Under USES, the following categories define the local uses of each plant:
- fw = food, wild (f = fruits and nuts; l = leaves/shoots; t = tuber/roots/corms)

- fc = food, cultivated (f = fruits and nuts; l = leaves/shoots; t = tuber/roots/corms); includes stimulants
- fp = food preparation (wrapping, cooking implements, condiments and spices, etc.)
- me = medicinal uses (mainly curative; but p = poisonous, causative of illness)
- cu = custom significance (ritual, magic, ceremonial, decoration, objects, important folklore associations)
- sf = maritime: seafaring and fishing (canoes, fishing gear, etc.)
- ag = agricultural usages (fencing, implements, environmental indicators, fallow plants, crop management)
- hu = hunting (weapons, wildlife indicators, incidental usages)
- fd = firewood of special suitability
- cn = construction material (mainly for houses, but also fences and temporary shelters)
- ct = crafts and tools (includes carvings, weaving and other handicrafts, weapons, and toys)
- tl = timber for local use, felled and milled in villages
- te = timber for export, taken by logging companies

UGULU
'CLOUD FOREST'

		TYPE	USES									
aru pa soloso	*Casuarina papuana*	tree (large)		me	cu			fd				te?
geli	*Parinari salomonensis*	tree			cu				cn			
kokoga	*Calophyllum* sp.	tree			cu				cn	ct		
luga	not identified	climber	fp		cu							
ocha	*Pandanus* sp.	tree			cu			fd		ct		
pidiki	not identified	tree (large)		me	cu							
ramoso	*Pandanus* spp.	trees			cu	sf						
tobo	not identified	tree				sf						
vulu	Pandanaceae	shrub										

GOANA PA TOGERE
'MOUNTAIN FOREST'

		TYPE	USES									
chuvuchuvu kachere	not identified	shrub										
ijoko	*Alpinia* sp.	ginger	fp	me	cu							
keji	*Heterospathe* sp.	palm			cu							
kepukepu	*Epipremnum pinnatum* (etc.)	climbers	fp	me	cu							
kola	not identified	fungus			cu							
lomalomata	*Hernandia* sp.	tree					hu		cn			
mare	*Licuala lauterbachii*	palm	fp		cu							
micho	Zingiberaceae	ginger	fp		cu			fd		ct		
mou	not identified	tree							cn			
ngirasa goana	not identified	tree							cn	ct	tl	
pelo	not identified	palm							cn	ct		
tiva nono	not identified	tree			cu							
tobo	not identified	tree			cu	sf						te?

+ Many trees of **goana**

GOANA PIRU
'WILD [PRIMARY] FOREST'

		TYPE	USES
bebeu	not identified	tree	fwf · cu · ct
boe	*Parartocarpus venenosa*	tree	fwf · cu · ct · tl · te
buni kovo	*Calophyllum neo-ebudicum*	tree (tall)	tl · te
buni vijolo	*Calophyllum peekelii*	tree (tall)	tl · te
chagavu	not identified	tree (tall)	fwf
chuvuchuvu kachere*	not identified	shrub	sf · ag · hu
domu	aroid, not identified	climber	cu · ag
jalari	not identified	tree	cu · sf
kapuchu	*Dillenia salomonensis*	tree (large)	tl · te
keji	*Heterospathe* sp.	palm	cn
kokoga	*Calophyllum* sp.	tree	cn
lomalomata	*Hernandia* sp.?	tree	fd · te?
mala hire	not identified	tree	
rogi	not identified	tree	
vaha	not identified	tree (large)	
valo	not identified	tree	ag · ct
vosevose	*Nauclea orientalis*	tree	sf · ct

+ Most trees of lowland **goana**; those listed are typical of 'wild' forest
* The shrub **chuvuchuvu kachere** is considered to be a primary indicator of truly 'wild' forest

GOANA
'FOREST'

		TYPE	USES
adoso hokara	*Calamus* sp. (rattan palm)	climber	sf · ag · cn · ct
ara pao	*Flagellaria gigantea*	climber	sf · hu
bao	*Gulubia* spp.	palms (tall)	fwf · sf · hu · cn
beri	*Fagraea racemosa?*	tree	sf · ag · hu

GOANA 'FOREST' (continued)

Name	Identification	Form	fwf	fp	me	cu	sf	ag	hu	fd	cn	ct	tl	te
bochaka	*Actinorhytis* sp.?	palm												
bolava	not identified	tree (large)							hu		cn	ct		
bosi	*Euodia elleryana* (etc.)	trees			me	cu	sf		hu	fd	cn	ct	tl	
bue	Not identified	tree (large)							hu		cn	ct		te
chabo	Pandanaceae	tree												
chake chiri	not identified	tree (large)												
chebere chigo	*Rubus moluccanus?*	climber	fwf											
chodeke	not identified	tree												
choku	not identified	tree			me	cu	sf	ag			cn	ct		
chovuku piru	*Burckella* sp.	tree (large)				cu	sf				cn	ct		
dekedeke	*Nastus obtusus*	bamboo					sf				cn			
goliti	*Gmelina moluccana*	tree (large)					sf							
goliti patu	not identified	tree (large)												
heji	Arecaceae	palm												
hihiri	*Ficus* sp.	tree		fp					hu			ct		
hime	*Haplolobus* spp.?	tree				cu	sf					ct		
hutukaka	*Kleinhovia hospita*	tree				cu				fd		ct		
ibibu	*Cleidion spiciflorum*	tree					sf	ag				ct		
iloro	not identified	vine												
ivu	*Bambusa vulgaris*	bamboo		fp		cu	sf				cn	ct		
jakulu	not identified	tree			me	cu		ag						
jilatongo	*Laportea* spp.	shrub		fp	me	cu								
jiu	*Heterospathe* sp.	palm (tall)		fp	mep	cu					cn			
juapa	not identified	tree									cn			
katoa	Arecaceae	palms												
kerikeri	*Pangium edule*	tree	fwf		me	cu			hu		cn	ct		
kichuru	not identified	tree	fwf			cu						ct		
kikikopo	not identified	nut tree?	fwf?											
kodere	not identified	tree (large)		fp		cu					cn	ct		
kola mejara	not identified	tree										ct		

Name	Scientific name	Growth form									
kualeve	*Merremia* sp.	climber		me			ag				
kubutu	*Asplenium nidus*	fern		me							
mahi	*Physokentia* sp.?	palm							cn		
mala ghighiri	not identified	tree									
malemale	not identified	tree									
maria	*Canarium salomonense*	tree	fcf	me	cu		ag			ct	
mavuana	*Securinega flexuosa*	tree		me	cu			fd	cn	ct	te
meda	*Pometia pinnata*	tree (large)		me	cu				cn	ct	
mudu	*Cananga odorata*	tree		me	cu					ct	
muduku	not identified	tree (large)	fwf	mep	cu			fd			
mutamuta	*Amoora cucullata*	tree		mep	cu			fd			
ngirasa goana	not identified	tree		me	cu					ct	
ngoete	*Canarium indicum*	nut tree	fwf fcf	me	cu		ag				
nobonobolo	not identified	climber									
okoko	*Calamus* sp., rattan palm	climber				sf			cn	ct	
olanga	*Campnosperma brevipetiolatum*	tree (tall)			cu	sf			cn		te
pelepele	not identified	tree									
pijaka piru	*Areca macrocalyx*	palm		mep	cu				cn	ct	
poke	*Gnetum gnemon*	tree	fwf	me							
ponoro	not identified	tree									
popoli goana	*Terminalia calamansanai*	tree (tall)			cu	sf	ag				te
popoli piru	*Terminalia complanata*	tree (large)					ag				te
pucha	*Diplazium esculentum*	fern	fwl		cu	sf	ag				
pusi	not identified	climber			cu	sf		fd	cn	ct	
rapa	not identified	tree		me	cu		ag				
rekiti	*Imperata cylindrica*	grass		me	cu		ag				
reve	*Cyathea* spp.	tree ferns	fwl	me	cu						
rodona	*Cycas rumphii*	cycad		me	cu		ag			ct	
rokoroko bangara	not identified	shrub			cu		ag				
suliri	not identified	tree				sf					
tangovo	*Alstonia scholaris*	tree (tall)	fcf fp	me	cu	sf					(tl) te
tige	*Barringtonia edulis*	nut tree		me							

GOANA 'FOREST' (continued)

		TYPE	fp	me	cu	sf	ag	hu	fd	cn	ct	te
tige ta malivi	*Barringtonia* spp.	tree										
tikulu	*Calamus* sp., rattan palm	climber	fp		cu	sf	ag			cn	ct	
tiro kolo	not identified	tree (tall)				sf				cn	ct	
tita	*Parinari glaberrima*	tree			cu	sf					ct	
tiva tupi	not identified	tree				sf					ct	
tobo	not identified	tree			cu	sf					ct	
ututongo	not identified	tree										
vaho	*Heliconia solomonensis*	shrub	fp		cu		ag					
vao	not identified	tree		me	cu						ct	
vinetungu ta malivi *Entada scandens?*	not identified	climber (large)				sf		hu			ct	
vuloko	not identified	tree			cu						ct	

GOANA PA TABA
'SLOPE/HILLSIDE FOREST'

		TYPE	USES	fp	me	cu	sf	hu	fd	cn	ct	te
boloho	Poaceae	bamboo (tall)		fp				hu			ct	
heji	Arecaceae	palm						hu			ct	
kachuele	*Drymophloeus* sp.	palm						hu		cn	ct	
kalala (8 taxa)	*Ficus* spp. (banyans)	trees			me	cu		hu		cn	ct	
meda	*Pometia pinnata*	tree (large)					sf		fd		ct	te
reve	*Cyathea* spp.	tree ferns	fwl									

+ Typically most trees of **nura**

GOANA PA NURA
'VALLEY BOTTOM FOREST'

Name	Species	TYPE	USES
buni kovo	*Calophyllum neo-ebudicum*	tree (tall)	cu · ct tl te
buni vijolo	*Calophyllum peekelii*	tree (tall)	tl te
buroroho	not identified	tree	fp me cu · cn
chakita	*Semecarpus sp.*	tree	mep
chaviloge	*Piper sp.*	climber	me cu
chuvuchuvu kachere	not identified	shrub	cu
keji	*Heterospathe sp.*	palm	
kepukepu	*Epipremnum sp., etc.*	climbers	fp me cu · hu · cn
kokoga	*Calophyllum sp.*	tree	cn
rogi	not identified	tree	
sinu	*Guillainia purpurata*	ginger	fp cu · ct
vasara	*Vitex cofassus*	tree (large)	fp cu sf · fd cn ct tl te
+ Many palms			

GOANA PA KAVO
'RIVER FOREST'

Name	Species	TYPE	USES
buroroho	not identified	tree (rb)*	fp me cu · fd
chebere	not identified	tree (rb)	
choku	not identified	tree	me cu · ag · cn ct
ghalu mamutu	*Epipremnum altissimum*	climber (rb)	me · cn
hinage	*Nypa fruticans*	palm (rb)	cu sf
ijoko	*Alpinia sp.*	ginger	fp me cu · hu
iloro	not identified	climber (rb)	cu · hu
jukajuka	*Myristica sp.*	tree (rb)	cn
kepukepu	*Epipremnum pinnatum (etc.)*	climbers (rb)	fp me cu · ag · cn
leru varu	*Hibiscus tiliaceus*	tree (rb)	

GOANA PA KAVO 'RIVER FOREST' (continued)

name	scientific name	TYPE	USES	me	cu	sf	ag	hu	cn	ct	tl	te
olanga	*Campnosperma brevipetiolatum*	tree (tall)			cu	sf			cn		tl	te
pike	not identified	tree							cn	ct		
rarati	not identified	tree (rb)							cn	ct		
romo	not identified	tree					ag			ct		
tangovo	*Alstonia scholaris*	tree (tall)		me	cu	sf					(tl)	te
tui	*Dolichandrone spathacea*	tree (rb)				sf				ct		

*(rb) = grows on or along riverbank

JEMLJEMIANI
'FRESHWATER SWAMP [FOREST]'

name	scientific name	TYPE	USES	me	cu	sf	ag	hu	cn	ct	tl	te
bou	*Fagraea gracilipes*	tree		me					cn			
chabo	Pandanaceae	tree (tall)								ct		
chame	*Calophyllum cerasiferum*	tree			cu	sf		hu	cn	ct		
edeve	*Metroxylon salomonense*	palm	fw fc		cu	sf		hu	cn	ct		
ghohere	taro, *Cyrtosperma chamissonis*	herb (cult.)	fct									
hoba	*Terminalia brassii*	tree (large)			cu	sf		hu				
jukajuka	*Myristica* sp.	tree							cn			
kureu	not identified	tree							cn			
mata ihana	*Thespesia populnea?*	tree			cu	sf			cn	ct		
ngochangochara	not identified	tree	fwf			sf						
rigi	*Pterocarpus indicus*	tree (tall)		me					cn	ct		
rime	taro, *Colocasia* variety(?)	herb (cult.)	fct fp			sf				ct		
tutunu	not identified	tree									tl	te
vulu	Pandanaceae	shrub				sf						

+ An abundance of **kepukepu** and similar climbers

PETUPETUANI
'MANGROVE FOREST'

		TYPE	USES
babaheva	*Heritiera littoralis*	tree (large)	sf hu cn ct tl
bobosuru	*Myrmecodia salomonensis*	epiphyte	cu
chalu pehuru	not identified	tree (sw)*	
ivi ta malivi	*Quassia indica?*	tree (sw)	cu fd ct
koe	*Xylocarpus granatum*	tree (sw)	cu sf hu ct
kubuku	*Acanthus ilicifolius*	shrub (sw)	cu
kubutu	*Asplenium nidus*	fern	cu
ototo	*Excoecaria agallocha*	tree (sw)	mep fd
petu (>7 taxa)	Rhizophoraceae, Avicenniaceae	trees (sw)	fwf me hu fd cn ct
pipili	*Lumnitzera littorea*	tree (sw)	hu fd cn ct tl
pogala	*Barringtonia asiatica*	tree (large)	me cu sf
tototu	*Avicennia* sp.	tree (tall) (sw)	sf ct
tui	*Dolichandrone spathacea*	tree (sw)	sf ct
vevereti	*Guettarda speciosa*	tree (sw)	cu sf fd ct
vorusu	*Ceriops tagal*	tree (sw)	fwf fp sf hu fd cn
vulu	Pandanaceae	shrub	

*(sw) = **hae pa idere**; trees that grow with roots in saltwater

CHICHIOGO
'OLD SECONDARY FOREST'

		TYPE	USES
chichinoko	*Commersonia bartramia?*	tree	cn
chobochiri	*Timonius timon*	tree	me
choma	not identified (like **chichinoko**)	tree	fp cu cn ct
ivu pu	not identified	tree (large)	fd
kemacha	not identified (like **hutukaka**)	tree	cu sf ct
kokovasa	not identified	tree	sf

CHICHIOGO 'OLD SECONDARY FOREST' (continued)

		TYPE	USES
lakori	*Ficus variegata*	tree	fp cu fd ct
meda	*Pometia pinnata*	tree (large)	fwf fp cu ct te
rereta	not identified	tree	fp

+ Many plants of lowland **goana**; the ones listed are definitive indicators of **chichiogo**

KOTUKOTUANI
'FALLOW, RECENT SECONDARY FOREST'

		TYPE	USES
bichebichere	not identified	tree	me
bosi	*Euodia elleryana* (etc.)	trees	me cu sf cn ct tl
buiti	Zingiberaceae	ginger	me cn ct
chichinoko	*Commersonia bartramia?*	tree	me
chobochiri	*Timonius timon*	tree	me cn ct
choma	not identified (like **chichinoko**)	tree	fp cu ct
chopiko	*Ficus septica*	tree	me
chovacha	*Hornstedtia lycostoma*	ginger	fwf me cn ct tl
chovuku manavasa	*Burckella* sp.	tree (c)*	fcf sf cn
dekedeke	*Nastus obtusus*	bamboo (c)	sf cn
ghalu mamutu	*Epipremnum altissimum*	climber	me
hirata	*Piper betle*	climber (c)	fcl me cu
hutukaka	*Kleinhovia hospita*	tree	fd ct
jilatongo	*Laportea* spp.	shrub	fp mep cu
kakabokulu	*Ficus longibracteata?*	tree	fp
katoa	Arecaceae	palms (tall)	hu
kemacha	not identified (like **hutukaka**)	tree	cu sf cn ct
kokomu	*Costus* sp.?	ginger	me cu sf ct hu
kokovasa	not identified	tree	me cu sf ct

Name	Scientific name	Type	Uses
kole	not identified	tree (c)	ct
kualeve	*Merremia* sp.	climber	me, ag
mudu	*Cananga odorata*	tree	me, cu, ct
nabo	*Curcuma domestica*	ginger (c)	fp, me, cu, ct
natongo	*Rhus taitensis*	tree	cu, sf, ct
ogara	not identified	fern	me
opiti	*Spondias dulcis*	tree (c)	fcf
pinopoto	*Ficus copiosa*	tree	fwl
piropiro	*Alpinia* sp.	ginger	fwt, fp, me, cu, ag
pusi	not identified	climber	cu, sf, ag, ct
rereta	not identified	tree	fp
tita	*Parinari glaberrima*	tree	cu, sf
tukituki	*Macaranga* sp.	tree	fcf, fd, cn, ct
uvolo hokara	not identified	tree (c)	cn, ct, tl

*(c) = cultivated

CHIGOCHIGOANI
'GARDEN ZONE, SWIDDENS'

Name	Scientific name	TYPE	USES
apuchu	*Syzygium malaccense*	tree (c)*	fcf, ct, tl
apuchu niugini	*Syzygium malaccense*	tree (i, c)**	fcf, ct, tl
batia	bananas/plantains, *Musa* spp.	herb (c)	fcf, fp, cu, sf, cn
bini	Fabaceae (beans)	vines (i,c)	fcf, cu
bira	*Saccharum edule*, "pitpit"	grass (tall) (c)	fcf
bolivi	yam, *Dioscorea pentaphylla*	vine (c)	fcf
chalu	*Wedelia biflora*	shrub	me
ghalu mamutu	*Epipremnum altissimum*	climber	me
habichi	taro, *Alocasia macrorrhiza*	herb (c)	fctl, fp
hilele	*Solanum verbascifolium*	vine	fcf
hinahina	not identified (fragrant herb)	herb (c)	cu

CHIGOCHIGOANI 'GARDEN ZONE, SWIDDENS' (continued)

hirata	*Piper betle*	climber (c)	fcl		me	cu		
ibibu	*Cleidion spiciflorum*	tree (some c)					ag	
karuvera	taro, *Xanthosoma sagitifolium*	herb (i, c)	fct					
kasipora	*Passiflora foetida*	climber		fwf				
keto	maize, *Zea mays*	grass (tall)	fcf					
kualeve	*Merremia* sp.	climber			me		ag	
kuava	*Psidium guajava*	tree (i, c)	fcf		me			
luju	yam, *Dioscorea esculenta*	vine (c)	fct					
manioko	*Carica papaya*	tree (i, c)	fcf	fp	me			
minila	*Zingiber officinale*	ginger (c)	fcf		me	cu	ag	
nabo	*Curcuma domestica*, turmeric	ginger (c)		fp	me	cu		
ngache	*Hibiscus manihot*	shrub (c)	fcl					
omo hokara	breadfruit, *Artocarpus altilis*	tree (c)	(fcf)					
omo vaka	soursop, *Annona muricata*	tree (i, c)	fcf		me			
pinopoto	*Ficus copiosa*	tree (c)	fcl					
poke	*Gnetum gnemon*	tree (c)	fcf					
ramoso	*Ananas comosus*	herb (i,c)	fcf					
rapa	not identified	tree					ag	fd
rekiti	*Imperata cylindrica*	grass (tall)			me		ag	
songe	not identified	grass			me	cu		
talo	taro, *Colocasia esculenta*	herb (c)	fct			cu		
tige	*Barringtonia edulis*	tree (c)	fcf	fp	me	cu	ag	
tinavolu	yam, *Dioscorea nummularia*	vine (c)	fct					
tovu	*Saccharum officinale*	grass (tall) (c)	fcf					
umalau	sweet potato, *Ipomoea batatas*	vine (i, c)	fct					
uvi	yam, *Dioscorea alata*	vine (c)	fct					
uvikola	cassava, *Manihot esculentum*	shrub (i, c)	fct		me			
vaho	*Heliconia solomonensis*	herb (c)		fp		cu	ag	

*(c) = cultivated; ** (i) = introduced

PALAVANUA
'VILLAGE'

'VILLAGE'		TYPE	USES							
apuchu	*Syzygium malaccense*	tree (c)*	fcf						ct	tl
apuchu niugini	*Syzygium malaccense*	tree (i, c)**	fcf						ct	tl
bala sea	Orchidaceae	herb (c)			me	cu			ct	
boi manavasa	*Crinum asiaticum*	herb (c)			me	cu	sf			
chochoho	*Hibiscus rosa-sinensis*	shrub (c)			me	cu				
dako	*Pandanus* sp.	tree (c)							ct	
eruku	*Mangifera indica*, mango	tree (i, c)	fcf							
hae kirisimasi	*Delonix regia*	tree (i, c)								
ibibu	*Cleidion speciflorum*	tree (c)						ag		
jajala	*Codiaeum variegatum*	shrub (c)			me	cu		ag		
jipolo	*Cordyline terminalis*	shrub (c)			me	cu		ag		
kuava	*Psidium guajava*, guava	tree (i, c)	fcf		me					
kuruvete	Zingiberaceae	ginger (c)			me	cu				
laeni	*Citrus aurantifolia*, lime	tree (i,c)	fcf		me		sf			
lemana	*Citrus limon*, lemon	tree (i, c)	fcf		me					
manioko	*Carica papaya*, pawpaw	tree (i,c)	fcf	fp	me					
maria	*Canarium solomonense*	tree (c)	fcf		me	cu			ct	
ngache	*Hibiscus manihot*	shrub (c)	fcl		me					
ngochara tighetighe	*Cocos nucifera* variety	palm (c)	fcf	fp	me	cu				
omo vaka	*Annona muricata*, soursop	tree (i, c)	fcf		me					
opiti	*Spondias dulcis*	tree (c)	fcf							
opiti vaka	*Averrhoea carambola*	tree (i, c)	fcf							
oriji	*Citrus* spp., oranges	trees (i, c)	fcf							
pate	*Pandanus* sp.	tree (c)							ct	
pijaka	*Areca catechu*	palm (c)	fcf		me	cu				
pomolo	*Citrus grandis*, pomelo	tree (c)	fcf							
popoli	*Terminalia solomonensis*	tree	fwf fcf							tl
puchu makasi	*Cymbopogon* sp., lemon grass	herb		fp	me	cu				
puchupuchu	*Ocimum* sp., basil	shrub	fcl		me	cu				

PALAVANUA 'VILLAGE' (continued)

		TYPE	USES
ramoso	Ananas comosus	herb (i, c)	fcf
sedi	Plumeria rubra	tree (i, c)	ct
tagala	Polyscias spp.	tree (c)	fcl cu
tige	Barringtonia edulis	tree (c)	fcf fp me cu ag

*(c) = cultivated; **(i) = introduced

NGOCHANGOCHARAINI
'COCONUT GROVE'

		TYPE	USES
buna	Derris heterophylla	climber	sf
chuchu	Moraceae	tree	me fd
hirata	Piper betle	climber	fcl me cu
kapukapu topa	not identified; fragrant 'grass'	herb	me
kualeve	Merremia sp.	climber	me
lipalipata	not identified; small creeper	fern	me
lumulumutui	Lycopodium sp.	club moss	me
natongo	Rhus taitensis	tree	cu sf ct
ngochara	Cocos nucifera	palm	fwf fcf fp me cu sf ag hg fd cn ct tl

RARUSU
'BEACH' [ALSO OF BARRIER ISLANDS]

		TYPE	USES
babaheva	Heritiera littoralis	tree (large)	sf cn ct tl
boi piru	Crinum pedunculatum	herb	me cu sf hu
borukua	Ipomoea pes-caprae	creeper	cu sf
buna	Derris heterophylla	climber	me cu
buni rarusu	Calophyllum inophyllum	tree (large)	fd cn ct tl te

Local name	Scientific name	Type	Uses
chalu	*Wedelia biflora*	shrub	me, ct
geholo	not identified	tree	ct
kapa	*Pandanus* sp.	tree	
kidokidogha	*Scaevola taccada*	shrub	fp, me, cu, sf
koe	*Xylocarpus granatum*	tree (sw)*	cu, sf, hu, fd, fd, ct
kore erebachi	*Diospyros* sp.	tree	fwf
leru hokara	*Hibiscus tiliaceus*	tree	me, cu, sf, ag, ct
moli	not identified	creeper	fwf
nugili	not identified	climber	fwf
nute	*Morinda citrifolia*	tree	me, cu, ct
ototo	*Excoecaria agallocha*	tree (sw)	mep, cu, sf, fd
palaoto	*Palaquium* sp.	tree (large)	cu, sf, te
raraso bangara	not identified	climber	sf, ag
rarati	not identified	tree	sf, cn, ct
roko hike	*Vigna marina*	creeper	cu, ct
talise	*Terminalia catappa*	tree (large)	fwf, me, cu, sf, ct
tege	*Pandanus* sp.	tree	ct
ure mola	*Spathoglottis plicata*	herb (orchid)	fd
vevereti	*Guettarda speciosa*	tree (sw)	cu

*(sw) = **hae pa idere**; trees that grow with roots in saltwater

TUSU
'LAGOON ISLANDS'

Local name	Scientific name	TYPE	USES
ivi	*Inocarpus fagifer*	tree	fwf, me, cu, ct
kokomu	*Costus* sp.?	ginger	me, hu, ct
konu	not identified	tree	tl?
mara popoli	*Terminalia* sp.?	tree	
mavuana	*Securinega flexuosa*	tree	me, cu, fd, cn
naginagi	*Cordia subcordata*	tree	cn, ct
palaoto	*Palaquium* sp.	tree (large)	cu, sf, ct, te

TUSU 'LAGOON ISLANDS' (continued)

pilasi	not identified	tree (small)	cu	
tobo	not identified	tree	cu sf	
+ Many typical beach trees – e.g., **koe, kidokidogha, pogala, talise** – and other plants of **rarusu**				

TOBA
'BARRIER ISLANDS'

		TYPE	USES	hu	fd	cn	ct	tl	te
adoso idaka	not identified (Bignoniaceae?)	creeper (f)*	cu				ct		
ara	*Flagellaria indica*	climber (f)	sf						
ara pao	*Flagellaria gigantea*	climber (f)	cu sf						
aru	*Casuarina equisetifolia*	tree (large)	me cu						
buburata	not identified	climber (f)	cu				ct		
buni rarusu	*Calophyllum inophyllum*	tree (large) (b)**	me cu		fd	cn	ct	tl	te
burongo toba	*Euodia hortensis*	tree (small)	me cu						
chabo	*Pandanus* sp.	tree (tall)					ct		
chabo popolo	*Pandanus* sp.	tree (s)***	cu						
chaila	not identified	tree				cn	ct		
chakope	*Premna corymbosa*	tree (b)	me cu				ct		
chipuru belama	not identified	tree			fd	cn	ct		
chobu	*Macaranga tanarius?*	tree (large) (f)	cu sf		fd				
chochoruku	not identified (similar to **goliti**)	tree (large) (f)	cu sf						
chovuku piru	*Burckella obovata*	tree (b)							
chubeu	*Tournefortia argentea*	tree (f)	mep	hu			ct		
elokale	*Ficus* sp.	climber (f)	cu	hu			ct		
hilibubuku	not identified	climber (f)	cu sf				ct		
iloro	not identified	tree (f)	fwf				ct		
ivi	*Inocarpus fagifer*	shrub	cu						
jajala toba	not identified (similar to **jajala**)	tree (large) (b)	cu						
kivili	*Intsia bijuga*		cu			cn	ct	tl	te

			me	fp	cu	sf	hu	ag	fd	cn	ct	tl	te?
konu	not identified	tree (f)	me										te?
lomalomata hokara	*Herrandia nymphaeifolia*	tree (f)											
loulou	*Pandanus* sp.	tree (tall) (b)	me	fp		sf			fd	cn	ct	tl	
mala ngari	not identified (similar to **ngoete**)	tree (tall) (f)										tl	
mara popoli	*Terminalia* sp.?	tree (f)											
mavuana	*Securinega flexuosa*	tree (f)	me		cu				fd	cn	ct		
naginagi	*Cordia subcordata*	tree (b-f)							fd	cn	ct		
ngirasa	*Pemphis acidula*	tree (b)		fp	cu	sf	hu				ct		
ocha	*Pandanus* sp.	tree (f)		fp	cu				fd		ct		
pidiki	not identified	tree (large) (f)							fd				
pilasi	not identified	tree (small)			cu						ct		
popodala	not identified	tree (f)									ct		
ramoso hokara	*Pandanus* sp.	tree (b-f)			cu				fd		ct		
rapa	not identified	tree (f)						ag					
rihe	*Diospyros* sp.; ebony	tree (b)									ct		
tuva	*Pongamia pinnata*	tree (b)	me										
uvolo toba	not identified	tree (large) (f)							fd				
vao	not identified	tree (f)	me								ct		

+ Most trees and other plants of **rarusu** (except for some growing on mainland coasts only)
+ A number of typical trees of **petupetuani** (in the less diverse mangrove areas of the **toba**)
* (f) = of forest; ** (b) = of beach; *** (s) = of swamps

Vegetation classifications compared

It would be an interesting (but daunting) exercise to compare the local classification of the Marovo forest which is summarised in Figure 3.2 with an ecological assessment carried out according to the methodology of vegetation science. Reconnaisance surveys of the scientific kind were carried out by Hansell et.al. (1975) and by Wall et.al. (1979), covering mostly the various timber-rich **goana** forest types listed in Figure 3.2, and focussing especially on the floristics of the "forest estate" alienated by the colonial government on Vangunu. An authoritative recent study of Pacific Islands vegetation lists 8 "principal vegetation types" for the Solomon Islands (Mueller-Dombois and Fosberg, 1998:70-79). The 17 locally recognised vegetation zones presented in Figure 3.2 thus demonstrates that Marovo people's attention to the uniqueness of different rainforest types far exceeds the level of classification pursued so far by Western science. In general, however, the vegetation classifications of the Western scientists seem to depend on very much the same common-sense criteria as those used in Marovo – e.g., primary/secondary status, ridgetop/slope/valley bottom habitat. However, their floristic assessment is based on "objective" criteria (i.e. what species are frequent and thus "dominant" in an ecological sense) rather than the "subjective" criteria of Marovo classification (i.e. what species are normally present and are edible, useful or otherwise meaningful). Western science privileges ecological importance, whereas predictably, Marovo classification focuses on cultural significance including any manner of usefulness, as well as the presence of plants deemed to be indicators of a certain habitat.

A number of interesting observations on the relative importance of different types of forest, some quite unexpected, are fostered by the graphic lay-out of Figure 3.2. One is the extreme usefulness, for virtually any practical purpose, of the plant repertoire of true secondary forest in earlier stages of maturation (**kotukotuani**). Another is the exceptional contribution made to herbal medicine by the few plants thriving in the seemingly "barren" coconut groves and by the village areas. Many other interpretations are possible, some of which will be presented in following chapters. The interested reader will hopefully be able to make her own set of observations. Let us just note one additional item here: there are extremely few trees sought by logging companies that do not also have multiple significances for village life (see also Chapter 9). So for the time being we leave further reflections to the reader, and depart for the totally domesticated world of the Marovo village, distinctive social spaces established on the narrow strip of coastal land, backed by forest and lapped by waves. The following brief examination of village life provides some further clues to the overall frameworks for, and strategies in, the use of the rainforest.

Village lives

Marovo people live in more than forty villages and innumerable small hamlets, all coastal and some located on small islands off the mainland or in the barrier islands (Figure 3.3). Except for a few of the very largest, each village is populated mainly by people who are 'strong' members of the **butubutu** in whose **puava** the settlement is situated; the so-called 'resident' or 'ancient' butubutu (**butubutu koina**).[5] But every village and hamlet of Marovo

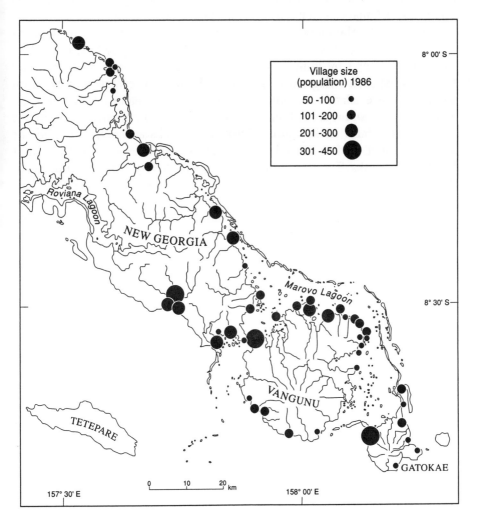

Figure 3.3   The settlement pattern in the Marovo area, as of 1986

also contains permanently settled persons who are not such primary right-holders – they may be in-laws, but also in many instances descendants of people who have at some stage in history joined the 'resident' **butubutu**, for example as slaves or as refugees from warfare. These may subsequently have been adopted into the **butubutu**. Nevertheless they tend to remain recognisable in the social landscape of the village in their capacity as **butubutu maena** ('the kin group that has arrived [from overseas]') – with little part in the absolute, ancestrally-conferred power or 'strength' (**nginira**) over the **puava** on which the village stands. Thus in every Marovo village there is a complex matrix of decision-making power in which the "descent unit" ranks supreme. It is not the village as such that constitutes a corporate, **puava**-controlling unit.

Villages (**palavanua**) of some size (from around 100 inhabitants) consist of a string of hamlets along a coastal promontory or bay, backed by more hamlets and by important community buildings such as church and school. Most such villages are located on flat land; a few, such as those on small off-shore islands are not, and tend to have a more circular lay-out. Most houses (**vanua**) are still made "traditionally". The frame is constructed from uneven 'bush sticks' (**ghinerigheri**), the walls and roofs are made of sago palm leaf, and the wooden floors are either of sawn planks or split black-palm trunks. The whole structure is supported by rather high posts. In the case of houses not built over shallow water, a sheltered work and rest space is often created below the floor. However, an increasing number of residential houses and most new community buildings are now made with roofs of corrugated iron, 'two-by-four' wooden frames and walls of sawn timber or prefabricated boards. The divisions between the hamlets of a village are often diffuse, while more spatially distinct parts of a village are closely linked by coastal paths along which are small groves of fruit and nut trees, stands of sago palm (**edeve**), small plots of largely self-tending giant swamp taro (**ghohere**), and separate toilet places for men and women among the remaining mangrove trees.

These coastal paths link together the hamlets of a village and allow access to what is, in effect, an agroforestry zone in its own right. The variety and intensity of plant cultivation within any Marovo village provide for a wide range of culinary, medicinal, ornamental and ritual needs, as well as for tool-making, construction and other purposes. Each single-household site contains a rather large minimum of such useful plants. In many ways this is reminiscent of the highly cultivated "cookhouse zone" described by Kirch (1994:58-59) for the Polynesian island of Futuna. It is difficult to overestimate the number and diversity of plants cultivated around a Marovo village, in close proximity to the domains of work to which the plants contribute (cf. the **palavanua** zone, Figure 3.2).

Generally, each nuclear family has its own residential building (**vanua mucha**, 'sleeping house') and a separate kitchen building (**vanua rejo**, 'hearth [or stone-oven] house'). Both (and particularly the latter) are often located in the tidal zone to maximise exposure to cooling sea breezes and facilitate garbage disposal. Such a nuclear family unit is usually related to several others in the same hamlet or village subdivision, as the sibling group is a common focus of co-residence in Marovo. Between the seaside houses are canoe landings where the often numerous small and large, paddled and motorised water craft of the combined hamlet are kept, whereas the costly outboard motors that are a cornerstone of present-day mobility and prestige are kept under the residential houses – or even in separate locked sheds where petrol is also stored (see Hviding, 1995a, 1996a, for details on Marovo maritime technology). Around kitchens and 'sleeping' houses, a variety of miscellaneously useful herbs, shrubs and trees are cultivated, creating a colourful, fragrant, arbour-like ambience.

The ecological diversity of the Marovo environment makes possible a varied household diet based on shifting agriculture and fishing. Agriculture and fishing are carried out at fairly constant levels throughout the year, with slight variations according to climatic cycles and to climaxes in planting and harvesting, and with additional short-term variation in fishing according to the different stages of the lunar month. Hunting (mainly of feral pigs and fruit bats), collection of shellfish from mangroves and reefs, and gathering fruits and wild greens from the forest provide important dietary supplements. Cash for school fees and for an ever-expanding range of material aspirations is obtained from various sources: by selling bêche-de-mer (sea cucumbers), pearlshell and other marine export commodities; by handicraft production (mainly wood-carving); by the marketing of agricultural surplus (particularly sweet potatoes) between villages and in the two small centres of Seghe and Batuna; as well as by remittances from urban relatives and royalties and other transient incomes from non-local resource exploitation in the **butubutu**'s area, such as tuna baitfishing or logging.

As we shall see, a pivot of the pre-colonial agroforestry system was constituted by the regular barter between inland-dwelling 'bush people' and coastal 'salt-water' people of agricultural produce for fish and other items harvested from the sea. The agricultural produce was mainly taro (**talo**, *Colocasia esculenta*, which in Marovo bears its old pan-Austronesian name) cultivated in irrigated pondfields. The material, nutritional, political and symbolic interdependencies between the produce of land and sea and between the twin identities as 'bush' and 'coastal' people have thus remained fundamental to the Marovo way of life (**kino Ulusaghe**) over the centuries.

There is a certain division of labour between the sexes whereby men carry out more maritime activities and women perform many of the day-to-day agricultural tasks. But these are not absolute divisions, and women often fish – though usually in the lagoon not far from the village shores – while many men are enthusiastic gardeners (see Bayliss-Smith, 1987, 1993, for detailed quantitative analysis of these patterns). Thus in present-day Marovo practice there are no absolute gender-related dichotomies between fishing and agricultural work. The gathering of shellfish from mangroves and reefs, however, is a heavily female-dominated activity, as the hunting in the forest for feral pigs, cuscus and fruit bats is firmly a men's activity. Further, whereas the heavy work of clearing new garden land by felling trees and cutting down and burning the lower forest layers is predominantly men's work, the gathering of wild greens and fruits from the forest (and mangroves, since the large germinating seeds of *Bruguiera* trees are an important seasonal food) is a women's domain. It is notable that whereas in the olden days the crucially important *Canarium* nuts were harvested exclusively by men who climbed the trees, today the nuts are harvested mainly by women, who pick them up after they have fallen down onto the ground. It is said that as Christianity took over during the second and third decades of the present century, climbing the tall, straight *Canarium* trees was no longer safe since the **sinare**, the old guardian spirits of nut harvesting, had lost their power – a power which was in part derived from headhunting and human sacrifice.

Women of Marovo often praise the fact that gardens are rarely far from the village. In some comparable places, such as on the steep island of Ranoga (Ranongga) further west in the New Georgia Group – an island which has a long and significant history of intermarriages with Marovo, especially among Seventh-day Adventists – one may have to walk and climb for an hour or two through rugged bush terrain to get to one's gardens. In contrast, most Marovo villages have their main agricultural areas located in the foothills and low valleys near the coast, in many cases just behind the old coconut plantations that occupy the best land behind the settlement. Furthermore, the relatively calm conditions that usually prevail in the inner parts of the lagoon make it possible for many Marovo villagers to paddle a canoe from the beach near their house along the coast to a point immediately below their garden – which gives the added bonus of not having to carry back garden produce on one's back. In the same way firewood is available from nearby lagoon islands and mangrove swamps and can be freighted home by canoe. All these factors, when added to Marovo men's reputation for being relatively helpful to their wives, combine to make Marovo Lagoon 'a good place for women', as they express it themselves. This is reflected by the observable (and quantifiable) fact that Marovo women who marry men from other islands almost without exception have their husbands come to Marovo and settle there.

4   Above the Seashore: Land Use in Marovo

Above the seashore

The sea is ever-present in the everyday lives of Marovo people. It provides them with their main and indeed often their only means of travel from village to village; it is a major source of protein food and cash income; and it has for thousands of years been the stage for encounters and relations with peoples, ideas, things and indeed worlds beyond. The histories of such 'overseas' encounters are inscribed, often quite imperceptibly to the outsider, on the lagoon, reefs, islands and beaches of Marovo in the form of 'signs in the seascape' (Hviding, 1996a, ch. 6). The reefs, rocks, beaches and cliffs next to the major passages through the barrier reef are particularly dense with place names connoting histories and events of interisland travel, warfare and headhunting, early trade with Europeans, rituals connected to fishing, and so forth.

Throughout the day, month and year every man, woman and child participates, to varying degrees, in both the work of the land and the work of the sea. Thus 'above the seashore' (**pa uluna rarusu**) is an emically logical expression that reflects the Marovo people's conceptualisations of space and place in that any movement from the seashore to the forest is perceived as being in an 'upwards' (not inwards) direction. Agroforestry – what goes on in agricultural and arboricultural terms – happens 'up' in the forest; even though that forest may well be just inland of the beach. By its reference to the proximity of the sea the notion 'above the seashore' also refers to the interdependence of sea and land in Marovo life and thought, past and present. In old Marovo the same interdependence was represented by institutionalised barter (subsumed in a fish/taro equation) on the seashore between the people of the sea and the people of the land. In practical as well as symbolic terms, a dialogical relationship between lagoon and land is always implied. The narrow forested seashore is an important zone not just of physical confluence, but also of material exchange and symbolic reciprocity.

Let us move more permanently into that 'above' realm of practice and thought introduced in the preceding chapter, where ancient and more recent histories of Marovo are to be read from a multitude of stone structures, from old groves of *Canarium* trees, and from the tell-tale presence of secondary vegetation where the forest reflects a history of swiddens and fallows, and where the sea either fades partly from view or forms a backdrop, far down below, to the sloping hillside gardens. For Marovo people – as for Western scientists and conservationists – reef and rainforest are indeed living, interrelated worlds.

Land tenure and land availability

The land-and-sea interdependence in Marovo people's life renders any simple objective correlation between population and "land availability" rather useless. It would appear that 11,000 or so Marovo people have at their disposal around 2,000 sq. km of land.[1] This gives a figure of just about 5 persons per sq. km, compared to the national Solomon Islands average of about 10. However, as we have shown this land is far from equally distributed among the **butubutu** of Marovo. There are, at one extreme, very small 'bush' **butubutu** that control vast areas of land – and at the other, there are 'coastal' **butubutu** with sizeable populations whose land holdings are limited to barrier reef islands only. Yet, the latter control vast areas – about 700 sq. km – of lagoon and reef with huge resource potentials.[2] These must also be seen as part of the total resource base available to the land-poor coastal groups. As for bush people with spacious **puava**, subjective factors (such as crop preferences or disinclinations to walk far inland) and micro-ecological circumstances (such as soil type and quality) may render part of the **puava**'s land partly useless for agricultural expansion.

In considering questions of resource availability, a simple, pan-Marovo comparison between total population size and aggregate land area thus provides few useful clues. The question about whether or not there is population pressure in Marovo today is always answerable by both yes and no, because of the crucial contribution to livelihood of the sea and its resources. That said, we shall try to account for some basic patterns in land availability and the principles and dynamics of land allocation – thereby providing a framework for this chapter's examination of present-day agroforestry and land use.

We recall once again that the basic element of land tenure is the relationship whereby each **butubutu** holds communal control of access to and use of resources in a homonymous **puava**, a territorial estate conferred through ancestral, communal title. The **puava** concept bears closer examination. On its general level of meaning as a typical Oceanic integrated land-and-sea estate, **puava** means the whole territory of a **butubutu**, embracing land, reefs and sea, in many cases stretching from the upper mountain ridges of the main island to the seashore and through the lagoon to the outer barrier reefs and beyond. On another level of meaning, **puava** is the word for 'earth' or 'soil': essentially, cultivable land. The latter use of the concept may be interpreted in terms of implying permanence and sustainability – a life-giving environmental "well-spring" dimension which is inexhaustible provided it is looked after properly. All recognised **puava** of Marovo, including some inland ones without present-day inhabitants, are defined by certain physical 'boundary zones' (**voloso**, also referring to the area thus bounded) in the form of inland mountain ridges, major rivers, river estuaries, islands and reef patches in the lagoon, and ocean passages through the raised barrier reef. These boundaries are further marked and validated by ancient shrines – stone chambers in the forest or seashore or on small islets in the lagoon or barrier reef – containing the skulls of named ancestors and heirlooms in the form of sacred clamshell artefacts.

As with the **pepeso** of neighbouring Roviana (cf. Schneider, 1996), the highly exact circumscription of any given **puava** in Marovo is not a matter of olden times but rather came into being as a response to colonial challenges, including district officers' insistence that "descent groups and their land ownership" had to be defined in a clear and precise way (Hviding, 1993b). In the earliest colonial decades, up to around 1920, several **bangara** of central Marovo Lagoon found it easy to persuade visiting district officers to construct fixed cement markers of **puava** boundaries in particularly strategic locations which were simultaneously "surveyed and registered" by the officer. This strategy, which did not involve any alienation of the land surveyed and marked, was seen by the chiefs as a way of counteracting a fuzziness of territorial holdings which had often caused strife in cases when one or a few "land owners" had sold lagoon islands or prime coastal land to white planters and traders. Simultaneously, it was the beginning of a conceptualisation of flexible **kastom** boundaries and rigid government-defined ones as parallel domains of territorial control potentially, though far from necessarily, in conflict.

Pre-colonial New Georgian society gave ample allowance to the social contradictions and overlapping claims entailed by cognatic descent and personal mobility, so that 'boundaries' were mainly seen as approximate outer perimeters of the spheres of influence radiating outwards from the core settlement(s) of a **butubutu**. This applies even today in that the apparent transgression of a boundary through fishing, hunting or gathering by members of a neighbouring group is not usually regarded as such, but rather as a recognised fact of life in terms of a strong notion of 'mutual help' (**vinari-**

tokae). In relation to agroforestry it is different, however, and until logging became the main immediate reason for land disputes, such conflicts usually erupted when somebody tried to establish a garden on the other side of the boundary towards a neighbouring **butubutu**'s **puava**, thus appropriating land for rather long-term occupation. Territorial privileges in land tenure are also recognised through the institution of asking relevant **butubutu** leaders for permission to harvest a **goliti** (canoe tree) from land which is not that of your own group. These patterns of flexibility and 'mutual help' in the handling of boundary issues are examined in detail from the vantage point of marine tenure by Hviding (1996a, chs. 4 and 7). They relate to the particular challenges posed in the New Georgia islands by open-ended systems of bilateral kinship and cognatic descent.

Because of the prevailing bilateral rules of filiation and inheritance, each Marovo person obtains rights in several **puava** – through inherited **butubutu** membership of one type or another. This creates a wide set of **butubutu** memberships for every person, so that his or her set of potentially usable rights covers a number of **puava**. But the extent to which these potentials are actually invoked and recognised depends on other factors, not least a person's place of residence. Individuals will have stronger rights in that ancestral **puava** where they live permanently or have grown up. This system produces complex, overlapping social relationships whereby each individual person has a unique set of kin relations with groups and other individuals. These relational repertoires often differ even among members the same sibling group, a fact which has consequences for the flexibility and adaptability of inter-group tenure of **puava** and resources, since every person has a number of options open to him or her regarding where, when and how to utilise resources. It has also been noted – initially by Goodenough (1955) for the Austronesian or "Malayo-Polynesian" realm, and by Scheffler (1965) for Solomon Islands – that bilateral mechanisms of allocating primary and secondary rights in communal territories and resources have some capacity to handle demographic pressure. People who have grown up with a **butubutu** that experiences population increase with consequent scarcity of land or fishing grounds may have options open to them to move to other **butubutu** with more abundant resource holdings.

Another basic element of land-and-sea tenure in Marovo is constituted by the twin concepts of **nginira** and **hinoho**, which refer to two main types of rights in a given **puava**. **Nginira** is a noun formed from the adjective **ngira** ('strong, hard, tough'), and it translates as 'strength'. In effect **nginira** entails the power to 'speak about the **puava** on behalf of the **butubutu**' – to manage the land, fishing grounds and sacred sites and to participate in joint decision-making concerning access to and the allocation and use of resources. **Nginira** is the inherited privilege of those with 'strong' membership in a

butubutu, most of whom reside in the **puava** in question. The hereditary **bangara** (chiefs) hold **nginira** on behalf of the group and make decisions jointly with elders and other influential persons. **Hinoho** is the given entitlement to use land for planting and to own and benefit from that which has been planted. **Hinoho** is a noun formed from the verb **hoho** 'to own' – which translates as 'that which is owned', 'wealth', or in contemporary Pijin or English parlance simply as 'property'. Being invariably attached to tree crops such as coconuts and sago palms in addition to garden cultivation and agroforestry in a wider sense, **hinoho** rapidly acquires a long-term, rather permanent character, and becomes part of that which in time is passed on through the title-holders' children by inheritance. The resident affinals of a **butubutu** hold (permanently granted) **hinoho** only, whereas resident **butubutu** members have **hinoho** rights as an extension of their own (or their parents') **nginira**. **Hinoho** may also be granted (particularly in the form of coastal land for planting coconuts) to persons who are from Marovo but are outside the inner circle of the **butubutu**, as a token of extended kinship or friendship, or in return for services given. Overall, **hinoho** is a very significant dimension of agroforestry, as it applies to garden blocks and tree plantings alike. The principle of largely irrevocable **hinoho** in effect transforms unmodified communal land into individually claimed land under cultivation. Although the overarching **nginira** exercised by the **butubutu** leaders and 'core' people still predominates in long-term management of the **puava**, once a tract of land has been granted – through the bestowal of **hinoho** – for transformation by way of tree planting or garden clearance, it is not likely to revert easily into the communal pool of **butubutu** land.

Everyday dynamics of land allocation

We examined in Chapter 3 how the 'dry land' (**mati**) components of the **puava** held by Marovo's **butubutu** are conceptually subdivided into a number of recognised sub-zones, which refer to topography and to typical plant communities and their uses (Figure 3.2). Superimposed on this generic system of land classification are **puava**- and **butubutu**-specific sets of place names. In addition to these important proper names of specific areas that derive from major terrain features such as rivers and mountains and also denote the valleys and forest tracts that surround them, there are names that apply to large zones of remote hinterland visited only for hunting, names for specific stretches of seashore (often extended to apply to coconut plantations and planted stands of sago palms or *Canarium* nuts immediately behind the coast), and names for small and large tracts of lower hills. In these latter tracts, which are the crucial parts of the **puava** as far as agroforestry is concerned, naming may be particularly dense and reflect an equally dense subdivision of the land.

In areas particularly well suited for intensive agricultural activity such as garden lands and secondary forest closest to villages and some more distant areas with particularly good soils, a great collection of named plots will be found. These are called **boku** ('block') or **voloso** ('bounded area', derived from the general word for boundary zone briefly examined above). Each plot is the recognised **hinoho** ('property') of one particular person, often a senior man or woman with adult children. Consequently such plots are also in effect the property of that person's descendants (**kinovuru**, 'offspring'), after the founder person named as plot-holder is dead. These named sub-divisions of attractive land, a great number of which can usually be named and identified by any adult man or woman of the associated village(s), are where the various extended families make their swidden gardens in a system of crop rotation and fallows. In practice, the adult children and resident in-laws of the person to whom a particular **puava** subdivision belongs work jointly on that land, with specific garden plots being further allocated to each member of the sibling group and cultivated by them and their nuclear families. Provided that the extended-family land is large enough, each single-family plot may permit several gardens to be under simultaneous cultivation.

When circumstances require redistribution of garden land (because the needs of a sibling group surpass the already available land) or an allocation of new land for clearing (because of the establishment of new nuclear families whose nominal extended-family land cannot accommodate them), the **butubutu**'s chief is usually approached, upon which he will consult with the elders concerned and with other advisers, subsequently to announce his decision. Alternatively, the village community may have a special committee (usually of somewhat senior men and sometimes also women), appointed in the long term by the chief for the sole task of monitoring the land distribution within the **butubutu** and organising the allocation of new blocks, or redistribution of old garden sites, as required. Sometimes there is not enough garden land in a **voloso** for all the children of the owner to inherit a share there, nor substantial areas of reserve land to be allocated by the chief. In such cases, and if their parents are both from within the Marovo area, some of the children may, when they establish their own nuclear families, move to the land of the other parent (who left his/her **puava** at marriage) to settle, live and work there on new house sites and garden plots. This mechanism of adjustment between total **voloso** size (to be divided among children) and sibling group size is an explicit recognition of the flexible workings of the bilateral system. People of the currently active working generation, usually those between 25 and 60 years of age, tend to orient themselves in agroforestry space with reference to their parents (whether dead or still living), saying: "this is the area of my father"; "my mother has her garden area here"; and so forth. But the horizons of potentially available land range beyond where parents live and work. Consider the following, rather typical example taken from 1987 field notes by Hviding:

> Raymond Lipu, a man in his early thirties of Patutiva village and primarily of the Podokana **butubutu**, is married and has two small children. His mother is of the Podokana and has her **voloso** on the New Georgia mainland not far from that **butubutu**'s secondary village on Buini Tusu, a small island immediately off the New Georgia mainland. Raymond's father is a Bareke man and is a son of one of the chiefs there. He also has a named plot inside the overall Podokana **voloso** [the **puava**], however – it was given to him by the Podokana chief when he moved to Patutiva at marriage. Raymond's father also retains land in the Bareke peninsula, which both he and his descendants [e.g. Raymond] can claim and use despite some forty years of non-residence.

What is inherited, then, is not only an indefinite share of the communally held **puava**, but also a named and delimited part of its land, with its own boundaries. From their parents, people inherit not only **butubutu** member-ship and the associated potentiality complex concerning **puava** rights, but also tangible property in the form of discrete plots. For **butubutu** with marine holdings this individualism extends into the transitional realm between land tenure and marine tenure, to the myriad of small lagoon islands inside a **puava**. These islands are also for the most parts claimed and 'owned' by specific individuals as part of their **hinoho**. Owner-ship of lagoon islands was an important issue also in pre-colonial Marovo, as observed by the British naval lieutenant Somerville in 1893-94 (Somerville 1897). However, some current claims relate to population movement during World War II when people left their large, exposed coastal villages and migrated out to temporary settlements among the small reef-studded and mangrove fringed archipelagoes of the lagoon islands so as to hide from marauding Japanese soldiers. Since those days many people have had vested interests and widely recognised rights in special lagoon islands or parts of islands. Still other lagoon island entitlements have been granted to people from other **butubutu**, including people of bush groups with little or no marine entitlements, in exchange for great favours or as a token of friendship and alliance. Except for some instances where cassava and yam gardens have been established or small single-family settlements have been founded on such islands, rights in them are mainly upheld by the planting of coconut trees. Again, it is said in such instances that lagoon islands which have had many coconuts planted on them are very unlikely to re-enter the communal land pool of the **butubutu** in question.

Generally, only certain parts of the extended family land are worked at any one time – thus, any such named subdivision will contain a mixture of recent and (possibly) mature secondary forest, ginger-dominated fallows, swidden gardens under cultivation, and garden plots under some stage of clearance. In addition, if the extended-family subdivision has a long history, there will be groves of *Canarium* nuts and fruit trees which in many ways mark the centre of the subdivision, around which shifting cultivation rotates. Other groves are located further inland or along the coast in areas not under present cultivation which were settled and cultivated by previous generations. These are also family-owned and contain old *Canarium* trees of two kinds: **maria**, *Canarium salomonense* and **ngoete**, *Canarium indicum*; the former invariably planted, the latter having larger nuts and often occurring wild too. Such old groves also contain cut nut (**tige**, *Barringtonia edulis*) and other *Barringtonia* spp., and most notably old betel nut palms (**pijaka**, *Areca catechu*). Most nut groves in upper forest are visited for nut gathering in the June-to-September period, and men on intermittent hunting or canoe-tree felling expeditions are relied upon to keep the groves relatively clear of undergrowth so as to facilitate the collection of fallen nuts in due course. The garden plots and nut groves of a family or lineage need not at all be in spatial overlap. They may be in two different areas, sometimes far apart, and people may have nut groves (**buruburuani**) in a **puava** without having any garden plot there. Such **hinoho** in *Canarium* trees may have their origin in a well-remembered filiative link (**sinoto**, 'attachment'; cf. Hviding, 1996a: 262-264 and ch. 4) with that special **butubutu** several generations ago. The fact that many people visit remote nut groves on an annual basis reaffirms the continued recognition of ancient kinship links.

Protecting the garden: boundaries, magic and mana

A named 'agricultural' **voloso** (extended-family subdivision) has its own clear boundaries within the **puava**, often marked by natural features such as streams, large prominent stones and small valleys and ridges. Many old **voloso** are also clearly marked by the existence of low stone walls along their perimeters; testimony of past generations' hard work in clearing the soil of all the larger stones, which subsequently were put to use in an attempt to fence the gardens off from feral pigs, which then were a more serious threat to crops in certain areas of Marovo. Protective fencing of gardens has largely been discontinued, not least because heavy hunting in recent decades has decimated most feral pig populations. This lack of fencing has, however, laid many gardens open to recent invasions by hungry feral pigs fleeing inner forest areas where logging operations are in progress.

The particular cultivated gardens within the **voloso** are only symbolically fenced, often with logs (from the original clearing of the site) placed rather haphazardly around the perimeters. Within each garden plot, separate divisions for different crops or rotational stages are recognised and marked, also with stones or more commonly with logs left from the clearance. These ideally rectangular, parallel divisions are termed **vilaka** 'rows' – a term that derives from the irrigated pondfields of old Marovo, wherein taro was cultivated in a perennial rotational system of distinct, parallel **vilaka** (see chapter 5). Several nuclear families may hold and cultivate different sets of **vilaka** within the same **voloso**, the latter held by one or several members of the parent generation.[3]

Less evident for the Western observer than marked **vilaka**, but immediately evident to any Solomon Islander, is a wide selection of significant shrubs, flowers and other plants whose colours, fragrances or mere presence in a garden area communicates important messages and are considered to fulfil protective functions. The two branching shrubs **jipolo** (*Cordyline terminalis*) and **jajala** ("croton", *Codiaeum variegatum*) grow in the majority of garden areas and forest nut groves and signify that the places are owned and, moreover, are imbued with certain mechanisms to deter trespass and theft of crops. **Jajala** (*Codiaeum*) shrubs have leaves with bright colour patterns; for use as garden "signifiers" yellow varieties are preferred. The **jipolo** (*Cordyline*) is also a very visible plant, with its generally dark red to copper-coloured, sometime striped, leaves. Varieties of *Cordyline* are ritually important plants throughout Oceania. **Jipolo** comes in very many types in Marovo, some named after places, districts and people, and many known to be ritual "vehicles" for certain forms of helpful magic possessed by the group that owns the specific **jipolo**; a typical technique being to slip a leaf of a 'fishing **jipolo**' into the mesh of the net before casting it. **Jipolo** plants are thus signs of attachment, fertility, and success through '**mana**-isation' (see below). Their presence in gardens and near houses is considered to dispel evil spirits and to attract benevolent ones, which traditionally were the ancestral spirits to whom the land belongs.

The presence in a garden of plants from this ritual repertoire is immediately noted by a visitor as signifying magical powers, benevolent and destructive, held by the owner(s) and cultivator(s) of the garden. In the fallows, they are considered to assist in the general protection of continued fertility of the resting garden. The colour of foliage and flowers is an issue that opens up the whole question of the symbolic meaning of colour. The Marovo people emphasise the rather universal triad of red (**orava**), white (**heva**) and black (**chinoko**) in their symbolic schemes, but they also accentuate **oha** (yellow), **buma** (green-and-blue), **bulaeri** (the dark purple-to-black colour of ripe *Canarium* nut skins) and **bupara** (brown, like soil). All these colours find a reference in the visual appearance of a garden. Yellow (**oha**) is the main colour used in Marovo to indicate boundaries and separated realms, which helps to explain the ubiquitous use of **jajala**, bright yellow croton shrubs, to mark boundaries in gardens and villages. Further in line with this, the special coconut variety called **kererao** which has bright yellow-to-orange leaves and nuts is also a frequent marker of boundaries between different extended-family sub-divisions. The presence of red, striped **jipolo** shrubs in gardens or around houses is considered to dispel evil spirits and attract benevolent ones, and this is a role they share with the small **burongo** tree (*Euodia hortensis*). **Burongo** came originally from the barrier islands and its full name is **burongo toba**, but is widely planted in 'domesticated' parts of the mainland forest. The flowers and leaves exude a strong perfume-like fragrance, of the kind that attracts good spirits and dispels evil ones (the latter are closely associated with foul smells, notably that of rotting corpses). **Jipolo**, **burongo** and yellow **jajala** varieties also invariably grow at old sacred sites of all kinds, where they are looked after and replenished should the original shrub decay. Similar properties apply, in many cases even more strongly, to the seemingly innocuous and rather small herbs **minila** (ginger, *Zingiber officinale*, whose Marovo name also means, simply, 'medicine'), **nabo** (turmeric, *Curcuma domestica*) and **kuruvete** (Zingiberaceae, a small unidentified ginger). They are often planted in swiddens along the perimeters and at corners, and have potent spiritual associations. They are also planted in fallows. Like the larger **piropiro** ginger dominating recent fallows, the lanceolate leaves of **minila**, **nabo** and **kuruvete** have distinctive appearance, some are fragrant, and the roots (rhizomes) of special varieties – notably, concerning the turmeric, of a bright orange colour – are chewed by healers and magicians (Figure 4.1).

Despite some eighty years of Christian influence and, today, a universal adherence to Protestant church denominations, old dimensions of magic, witch-craft and sorcery remain fundamentally important in Marovo people's lives and coexist rather easily with Christianity. Faith in benevolent magic and (not least) fear of malevolent magic continue to influence a great variety of small and large tasks and projects in everyday life. Should a garden not turn out the way its cultivators expected it to, fears of sorcery and malevolent spirits lurk, and counter-measures have to be taken. This may involve the immediate planting of ritual shrubs with special powers, enlisting the assistance of a magician or counter-sorcerer who will inspect and possibly 'cleanse' the garden, and pray-ers to God – all measures taken simultaneously. Prayers and church sermons in the Marovo language are, for all the three denominations, strongly pervaded by syncretist concepts rooted most importantly in pre-Christian concepts of **mana**.[4] Thus "**mana ia chigo**" ('the garden **mana**-ises' [i.e. it exhibits success and fulfills its purpose]) is habitually said of a good, fertile garden whose crops grow well.

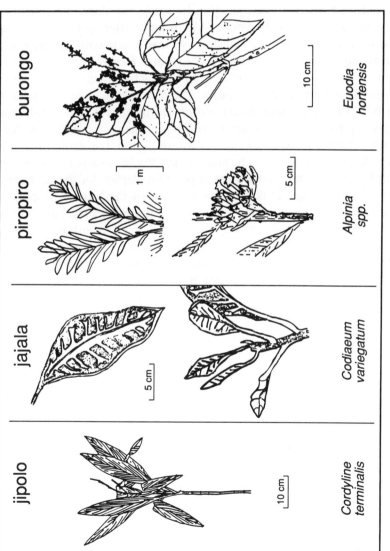

Figure 4.1   Protection from colourful and fragrant plants: jipolo, jajala, piropiro, burongo (jipolo after Sillitoe, 1983:126; burongo after Henderson and Hancock, 1988:175)

Analogous sayings apply to efficacy and success in fishing, hunting and in life more generally (including health and love). A family or **butubutu** with noticeably good gardens are said to have this as their **tinamanae** – a noun form of **tamanae**, which implies having attained the state of **mana**. In present-day Christian parlance, **tinamanae** equals, simply, 'blessing'.

But in Marovo whoever is so 'blessed' also necessarily encourages envy from others less fortunate, who may in turn enlist the help of destruct-ive garden magic in order to redress their grievance at lacking that blessing. It is reckoned that such envious people who visit your place may attempt to destroy your garden – usually from a safe distance after they have returned to their own home villages, since destructive magic is regarded mainly as an inter-**butubutu** phenomenon. Such people (**tinoni ruasai**, 'persons [of both sexes, but in most cases men] possessing destructive magic') may have a wide range of measures at their disposal. They are said to be able to send the **bichere** bird, the purple swamp-hen *Porphyrio porphyrio* that is infamous for digging up root crops, in order to attack your garden. Some, reportedly certain men from Bareke and Gatokae whose destructive garden magic is exceptionally strong, are said to be able to bury the leg of a pig in somebody else's garden soil without going there; a potent metaphor for the destruction of gardens by feral pigs. It is said that the taro of the Vahole people was spoiled by the Bareke people long ago in such a fashion, by the buried leg of a pig. Among other methods used by such people for the purpose of **ruasai chigo** ('destroying gardens') is the more direct one of going to the garden that is the object of envy and bury a small leaf parcel containing a secret mixture of substances (such as ground leaves and bark scrapings, perhaps pig faeces, and reportedly even ashes of a burnt snake) there. This may even be done in the course of a seemingly friendly visit to somebody in the nearby village. Certain Marovo persons have notorious reputations for **ruasai** work and may not generally be allowed access to gardens when they visit a village. In line with this, any notorious man or woman, or any stranger, observed in a garden area is quickly reported to those concerned. This also applies when known practitioners of witchcraft and sorcery, especially of the dreaded **pela** – a form of lethal "evil eye" malevolence considered through-out the Solomons to be particularly strong in the Marovo area – are en-countered in places they ought not to be; they may have left potentially lethal influences in gardens they have visited.

Thus the growth and well-being of a Marovo garden is fraught with many dangers, and the cultivator of a good garden appears to have reason to be paranoid. The presence of protective plants is as important in a highly successful garden (where they ward off attacks) as in a less productive garden (where the plants promote fertility). The yellow and red colours and strong fragrances of the **jipolo-jajala-burongo** plant combination promote stable conditions in a swidden. Furthermore it is significant that the arche-typal recent fallow is a dense stand of **piropiro** (*Alpinia* sp.), a tall rather woody ginger herb whose leaves have a strong, pleasant and very distinctive fragrance (for which reason they are also much used for wrapping fish in the stone oven). In this specific form of recent **kotukotuani** called **piropiroani**, the **piropiro** and its fragrance keep malevolent spiritual influences away from the vulnerable exposed soil that needs to regain its powers, and thus secures continuation in **mana**.

There are other ways of promoting growth and fertility in the Marovo garden; of '**mana**-ising' it. At the present day, apart from fragrant and colourful plants, protection against magic and the attainment of a state of **mana** is fundamentally sought by performing the prescribed Christian rituals. This involves an initial act whereby a church elder or pastor blesses (**ta manae**) a new garden, as is done with new canoes and outboard motors to ensure good catches and safe seafaring. Subsequently, regular religious acts should be carried out by the household cultivating the garden, in the form of prayers (again focusing just like the pre-Christian ones on pro-tection, safety, success, 'good fruit' and **mana**), and (especially among the Seventh-day Adventists) the weekly submission of a tithe in cash or in kind. The tithe is calculated from a thorough count of the crops harvested from the garden, and is either placed in a special tithe house for others to buy (or sometimes just to rot), or is converted into cash payable as tithe offering in church. It is axiomatic to many Marovo people that a steady flow of tithe from agriculture and fishing will provide an equally steady flow of **mana**-isation of these activities in return; and conversely, that a failure to supply tithe may well lead to disastrous failure.

Modern fertilisers find no place in Marovo gardening. In the old days, special leaves and bark pieces would be scraped and mixed and dispersed onto new land destined for taro cultivation, before clearing and planting took place. This would be associated with prayers, chanting and sacrifices at dedi-cated gardening shrines. Although modern fertilisers would seem to provide a self-evident analogy, such introduced remedies have not become popular among Marovo people. The mulching of *Canarium* trees and bananas in garden areas is regularly done by piling garden debris around the tree base, but for most crops the Marovo people insist that the ashes of burnt vege-tation are as good a fertiliser as is needed.

How to garden

The logistics of Marovo agroforestry, as opposed to the necessary social and spiritual arrangements, are basically rather straightforward:

When making a garden, you clear that place of trees and you burn the place. Then you may burn the roots of the trees also, or you wait for one year until the roots all have died. If so, you clear away the new secondary growth, then burn again, and plant. With taro, yams, **ngache** and beans you can just go ahead and plant – as long as you keep away from the remaining tree stumps. But if you want to grow sweet potato, you should start by growing pana [**luju**, lesser yams], banana or taro for six months. Then, you can plant **umalau** [sweet potato] and grow for three months which gives one harvest, and then replant twice again – altogether three harvests. After three harvests of **umalau**, you grow **uvikola** [cassava] for six months. Or, you plant the new **hikepaleke** [three-month] version of **uvikola**, which can be harvested after three months. After that you cut down and harvest the **uvikola** and let one more crop of it grow. After three or four harvests of **uvikola** when there is no longer any good fruit, you put the garden under fallow for six months to two years. This is how we do it here. But here in Bareke the hills are steep all the way from Rukutu to Manabusu, and the soil is not very good. Nono, Vangunu and Gatokae are good places for gardening. And Marovo [Island]. The soil here in Bareke is not like that on Marovo. (D. Loni of Bisuana village, 1986)

In this eloquent summary Dennie Loni, a leading man (then, in 1986, in his mid-sixties) of one of the bush **butubutu** of Bareke in central Marovo, describes the process of cultivation. He outlines a crop rotation cycle of three to five years' duration, and then the subsequent short-term fallow back to the **piropiroani** stage before a new cycle can be started. After a number of such cycles the soil will be impoverished, and a much longer fallow period with the area reverting to secondary forest will be needed. While choosing not to mention most of the daily female-dominated chores of gardening, such as turning and preparing the soil for planting, making innumerable sweet potato mounds (**botu umalau**) with a hoe, weeding, and so forth – all subsumed under the Marovo concept of **chevara** ('to cultivate [a swidden]', more narrowly translatable as 'tillage') – Mr. Loni provides us with a glimpse of the main stages in, and parameters of, present-day gardening in a typical area of Marovo. In the areas with better soil mentioned by him the cycle would be pretty much the same, except that continuous cultivation can be carried out over a longer, in some locations (such as on Marovo Island) a much longer, time-scale.

With some variations, this type of swidden garden (**chigo**), in close interaction with the surrounding fallow and secondary forest, is the mainstay of today's agroforestry. In order to gain a better appreciation of the variety of root crops, fruit and nut trees, leafy vegetables and other crops that form part of this system, we shall present maps of two representative gardens, before providing a brief listing of the wider repertoire of agro-forestry plants employed in present-day Marovo. This description is based on static morphology, in other words the form of gardens that are actually under cultivation. This account is followed by a summary presentation of the dynamic process, the different stages involved in the establishment and ongoing cultivation of a swidden. The cartographic perspective is a relatively simple one, aiming to highlight the spatial lay-out of the gardens as well as to provide a clear overview of the crops produced and relations among them. The maps also aim to present the main patterns of rotation among subsections of a garden, subsumed in the concept of **vilaka** ('block', 'row').

The first garden shown below (Figure 4.2) gives the reader an opportunity to envisage the garden that Dennie Loni and his wife Jessie were cultivating in 1986 (the ethnographic present used in the following sections) on a slope facing a stream (feeding the Kolo river) twenty minutes' walk inland from their home at Bisuana, a village of a segment of the Bareke bush people. This is a relatively compact and simple garden in terms of crop variety and extent, and it should be remembered that it is cultivated by an elderly couple with little interest in producing variety and surplus for marketing, but with a maximum concern for a good input-output ratio in terms of work. Three of the (virilocal) couple's daughters cultivate their own, more complicated gardens nearby. The other garden presented in this chapter (Figure 4.3) is cultivated in the gently sloping lowland behind the village of Michi west of Marovo Island, home of the small coastal Tobakokorapa **butubutu** who are Methodists (in contrast to Bisuana's Seventh-day Adventists). This is the garden of Jurini and her husband Tome, a very active uxorilocal couple in their forties, and shows more extended intercropping oriented partly towards marketing. Figure 4.4 gives a legend for the maps.

The two garden maps exemplify a number of basic principles in the swidden agroforestry of Marovo. In both gardens we can note the proximity of forest in the form of mature secondary growth (**kotukotuani** sometimes extending into **chichiogo**) containing a plethora of useful trees and shrubs (cf. Figure 3.2). This diverse forest dominated by the slim trunks and dense foliage of smaller trees forms a striking backdrop to the sloping garden clearings, and sooner or later becomes the subject of renewed clearing as part of a long-term cycle within the **voloso**. Both gardens are located in long-cultivated areas that form a complex of swiddens and recent fallows in short-term rotation, and older fallow bush and more mature secondary forest, some of which may not have been modified for many decades. The regenerative capacity of the agroforestry system seems to be evident for both gardens. The **vilaka** 'rows' presently under cultivation are complemented by immediately adjacent areas of recent fallow dominated by **piropiro** gingers, leafy grasses and low shrubs. The outline of recent fallow areas, standing out distinctly from the surrounding taller forest, almost mirrors that of areas currently under cultivation, both in shape and size (most clearly in the Michi example, Figure 4.3). The principle of short-term plot rotation is thus shown.

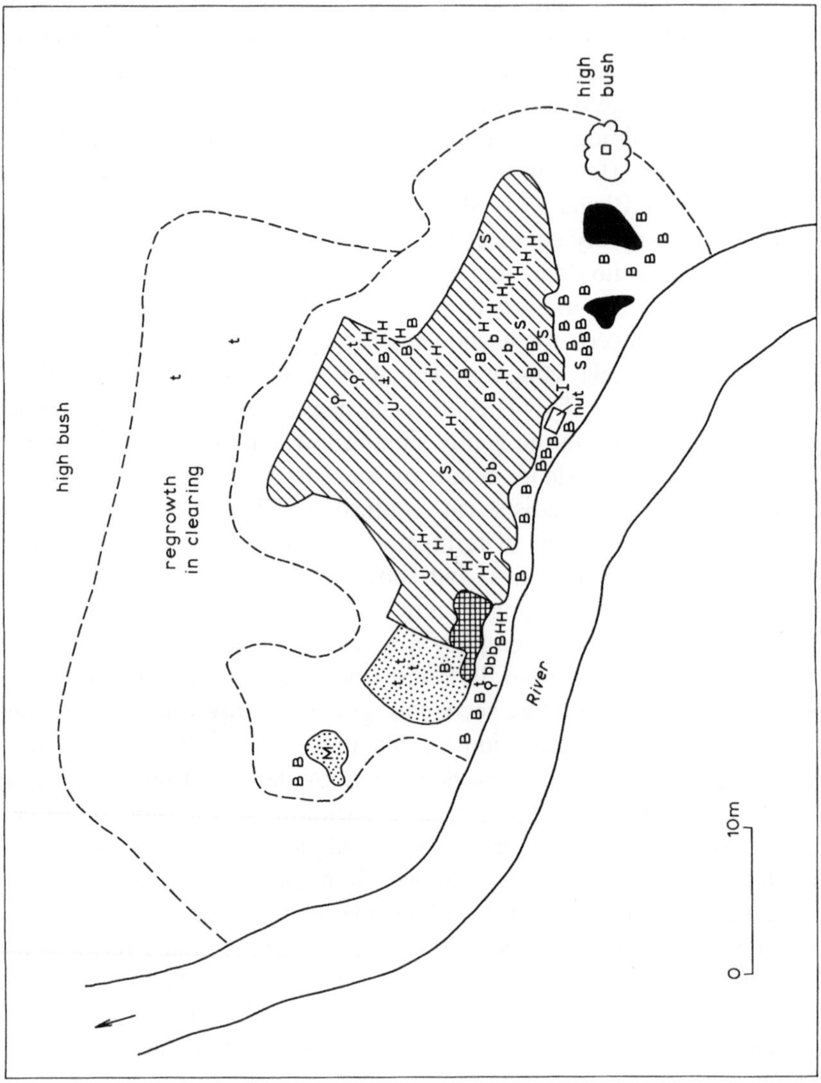

Figure 4.2   Dennie and Jessie Loni's garden, Bisuana, July 1986

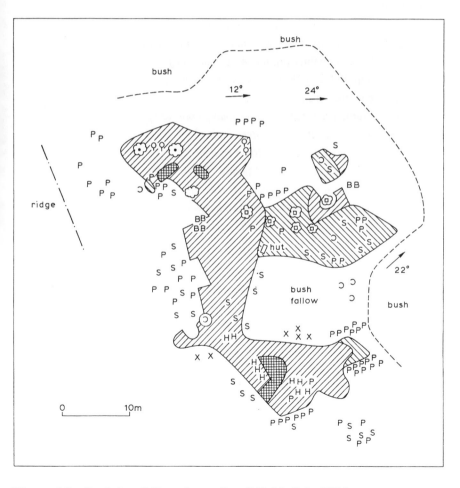

Figure 4.3   Jurini and Tome's garden, Michi, July 1986

Staple crops

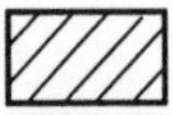

▨	sweet potato (**umalau,** *Ipomoea batatas*)
◩ ɔ	cassava (**uvikola** , *Manihot esculentum*)
▦ Y	yam (**uvi**, *Dioscorea alata*, and **luju** , *Dioscorea esculenta*)
▨ T	taro, dryland (**talo**, *Colocasia esculenta*)
■ X	Hong Kong taro (**karuvera** , *Xanthosoma sagittifolium*)

Trees and shrubs

C   coconut (**ngochara** , *Cocos nucifera*)
□   canarium nut (**maria** , *Canarium salomonense*)
t   betel-nut palm (**pijaka** , *Areca catechu*)
q   **popoli** fruit (*Terminalia calamansanai*)
X   **chovuku** fruit (*Burckella* sp.)
•   **mudu** fragrant flowers (*Cananga odorata*)
W   mango (**eruku** , *Mangifera indica*)
Ŧ   cut nut (**tige**, *Barringtonia edulis*)
ʎ   polyscias ornamentals (**tagala** , *Polyscias* spp.)
i   citrus fruits (mainly **oriji** , *Citrus* sp.)
+   papaya (**manioko** , *Carica papaya*)
U   cocoa (**kokoa** , *Theobroma cacao*)

Vegetables and fruits

A   alocasia taro (**habichi** , *Alocasia macrorrhiza*)
B   banana (**batia** , *Musa* spp.)
b   beans (**bini** , fam. Fabaceae)
H   hibiscus cabbage (**ngache** , *Hibiscus manihot*)
I   chilli (**chili**, *Capsicum frutescens*)
M   maize (**keto** , *Zea mays*)
P   pineapple (**ramoso** , *Ananas comosus*)
S   sugar cane (**tovu** , *Saccharum officinale*)
±   tomato (**tamata** , *Lycopersicon lycopersicum*)
φ   Chinese cabbage (*Brassica* sp.)
o   spring onion (**liki** , *Allium* sp.)

Figure 4.4   Legend to garden maps

The spatial layout of the Michi garden clearly shows the system of distinct **vilaka** ('rows') where, in this case, sweet potato and cassava are cultivated separately, the latter presumably succeeding previous crops of the former. Along their perimeters, Jurini and Tome's **vilaka** are rather densely planted with the market crops of pineapple and sugarcane. This strengthens the visual image of rather well-defined 'rows' or 'blocks' considered to be the hallmark of any well-cultivated garden.

From Figure 4.3 we also see the role of *Canarium* nut groves as spatial foci in the rotational dynamics of swiddens, thus signifying the importance of trees as a virtual basis for Marovo gardening. A single *Canarium salomonense* tree also has a conspicuous location in Jessie and Dennie Loni's garden (Figure 4.2). These tall, straight trees with their white bark look like nothing else in the forest and are crucial signs of **nginira**, ancestral title to land. They are indeed referred to as **chubina chigo** 'the basis [or tree trunk] of the garden'. In this sense *Canarium* trees are seen to provide the foundation for the entire life of the garden as a '**mana**-ised' plant-and-soil complex in which lives and preferences of different trees and plants interact. Individual *Canarium* trees thus placed as foci of a garden area are mulched around the base, a practice which is otherwise uncommon in Marovo tree cultivation and which indicates the unique status of these trees as markers of continued well-being. The principle of land-water interaction is evident from the Bisuana garden, which is located in a slope up from the bank of a small river. We note that taro (two types) are grown in concentrated stands in the lower parts of the garden, whereas the river bank zone is densely planted with bananas which provide shade for the taro and retain soil.

Whereas the two examples given above represent the core repertoire of plants in Marovo agroforestry of today, a great variety of other root crops, fruit trees and leafy greens are likely to be found in the swiddens, in fallows and in the surrounding, recent or mature secondary forest. In addition there are plants with important medicinal and ritual uses, particularly several leafy and woody shrubs (including many gingers), and a number of smaller trees, which are planted in the swiddens or grow in the fallows and in the secondary forest.

Work, tools, technology

Day-to-day agricultural work in Marovo is referred to as **tavete pa chigo** 'to work in the garden'. On a more general level, any activity pertaining to the long-term establishment, tending and harvesting of swiddens and taking place in the garden itself is subsumed in the all-inclusive concept of **chevara** – most suitably translated simply as 'to cultivate [a swidden]', a complex of activities in which soil tillage is central (see Figure 4.5). It should also be noted that the actual act of planting – **choku** – by metonymic extension also refers to the entire process of selecting, planting and caring for a plant and making it reproduce.[5] The actual act of domesticating a plant, not an un-common occurrence within the memory of living persons, involves bringing the plant from the state-and-domain of **piru** ('wild') to that of **manavasa** ('tame', 'domesticated', 'not running away'). As evident from its gloss, the concept of **manavasa** applies to animals as well as plants. In a longer run, certain important food plants invariably diversify into a greater number of cultivars, exemplified by the designation **talo chinokudi** for 'cultivated taros' – as opposed to **talo pirudi** for 'wild taros'.

We highlight this complicated process of transforming plants because it is a fundamental aspect of Marovo people's agricultural skills – of their ways of way of relating to their crops. Women, in particular, pursue the diversification of cultivars with great interest. Every other canoe that travels the lagoon from one village to another for the purpose of trade, exchange or visiting – or simply passing by on its way to fishing grounds – is likely to have planting material on board in the form of a few sweet potato vine cuttings or sprouting yams, sent by women of the canoe's home village to friends, relatives or affinals elsewhere. The handing-over of gifts of planting material (often elicited upon hearing that some woman somewhere possesses a particularly attractive root crop cultivar) may well form part of most courtesy visits to villages en route to a final destination. Since women rarely participate in maritime travel which is not solely for the purpose of transport to market, clinic or church gathering, they usually instruct their husbands or brothers to carry out the distribution of planting material for them.

Chevara (in daily discourse often nominalised as **chinevara** 'the work of swidden cultivation') is the work of both men and women, but on an everyday basis women spend considerably more time working in the gardens than men do. It is often remarked by Marovo women, though, that their men tend to be rather helpful where gardening is concerned. Moreover this situation is often compared favourably, and not without humour, with life in other islands in the Solomons, where the men are said to walk to and from the garden in front of their wives, carrying little else but a bushknife, while the poor women have to carry home to the village heavy loads of harvested crops, leaves for food preparation, and firewood!

In terms of the tools involved, the repertoire is simple. It invariably involves a digging stick (also called **choku**), a long machete or "bushknife" (**leboto**) and a smaller knife (**ngaloso**). Beyond this standard triad carried by every Marovo gardener, male and female, the traditional digging stick is increasingly supplemented (but not replaced) by specifically agricultural steel implements. Hoes are not uncommon tools in the preparation of a garden for planting, and they certainly ease the task of making a great number of mounds for planting sweet potato cuttings. Some spades are also to be found around Marovo villages, as are heavy picks, used by men for turning the denser soil types common in most of Marovo. The digging stick does, however, remain the primary digging and planting tool and merits some attention. It is called **choku** – in this sense a noun form of the metonymically expansive verb 'to plant', although harvesting is also part of its role. A digging stick should be made from select woods only, notably the tough **rarati** tree that grows along mainland coasts and river banks (although in practice any small tree of suitable size may provide an improvised digging stick). Its name signifies that Marovo agriculture is fundamentally about planting in prepared holes in the soil.

Harvesting of crops utilises the same tool repertoire, with the digging stick again remaining predominant. The actual act of harvesting root crops (taro, yams, sweet potato and cassava) is subsumed in the verb **heli** 'to dig'. When working with or harvesting from loose soils and sweet potato mounds the digging stick is frequently substituted by the bushknife or the small knife – or simply the hands, which remain the most fundamental tool used by any Marovo gardener in warm, loose soils, as shown by the regular occurrence of intensely painful centipede bites while working in the swiddens. The ubiquitous large centipedes (**lipata**, *Scolopendra* sp.) are regarded somewhat ambivalently, as they are also friends and helpers of the garden. They are said to keep the soil healthy by burrowing around in it, notably in sweet potato mounds under cultivation.

The tool kit of Marovo agroforestry also includes axes and string bags. Many men own axes, especially small short-shafted ones put to an endless variety of uses in the forest and gardens and at sea, often as a makeshift substitute for the bushknife. Larger axes with long shafts, often commented on as reminiscent of the headhunter's axes of the last century, are used in garden clearance and forest modification, as are an increasing number of (mostly communally owned) chainsaws. However, the most significant addition to the planting-and-digging tools is the looped string bag (**huba**), of which every woman must have at least one. Marovo string bags, that "most hard-worked accessory of everyday life" (MacKenzie, 1991:1, writing about Papua New Guinea), are invariably made from thin but tough plaited fibre ropes of bark from the **pusi** vine or the coastal **leru** tree (*Hibiscus tiliaceus*) – in a standard Melanesian fashion as "interconnected loops of bark fibres handspun into a virtually unbreakable two-ply string" (MacKenzie, 1991:1). Loosely woven in a simple fashion and rather large, they are also strong enough to hold a day's sizeable harvest of tubers, wrapped in a selection of parcelling leaves preferably from **vaho** (*Heliconia solomonensis*) or **sinu**

(*Guillainia purpurata*), two important leafy shrubs that are planted in most gardens.

In this way remarkably heavy loads are carried home by the women every day. The string bag must be properly packed, sometimes firewood is attached to the bag's outside, and a carrying strap is slung over the forehead. When men assist in this task they carry the string bag back from the garden by tying it shut and balancing it on one shoulder. Unlike in Papua New Guinea and certain other parts of the Solomons (notably Malaita), the men's string bag (in smaller versions) is not of importance in Marovo as an all-purpose carrying container for betel nut, tobacco and other personal belongings. Small baskets of woven coconut or pandanus leaf are used instead, as has been the case since 'the days of old' (cf. Somerville, 1897, who mentions the universal ownership of small bags with varied contents). The abstemious Seventh-day Adventists who are the majority of Marovo's population have few such needs anyway.

Transport to and from gardens tends to be by canoe, unless the swiddens are located immediately behind the village. The strategy followed is to paddle along the coast (and quite often into a river) to a spot immediately downhill of the **chigochigoani** – the garden area, then pulling the canoe ashore and walking to the garden through a multitude of forest (and agroforestry) zones. Mangrove swamps, sago palm stands, riverbank forest, coconut groves, bush fallows, secondary forest and valley forest are the zones that people frequently pass through on their way to and from their gardens, and this offers a great variety of gathering (and improvised hunting) opportunities on the way.

It is apparent that a full day's garden work is often done by a married couple in co-operation – a strategy which also affords a measure of privacy from the dense social life of the village. But other work groups are as common, the most frequent being several sisters and their brothers' wives going to their adjacent gardens together and taking turns at helping each other. Children also follow along on most trips to the gardens outside of school hours. In contrast the participation of teenagers, many of whom live in the villages as school dropouts, is restricted mainly to girls. While teenage boys may be taken along for heavier work such as clearing, cutting and burning, girls participate in gardening on a much more regular basis, in many cases cultivating their own gardens. This is particularly the case for unmarried mothers (of whom there are many), who are expected to grow food for themselves and their children, although they are otherwise part of larger food preparation units centred most often around their mothers' kitchens. Further information on the division of labour in gardening according to gender and age is given in the following section.

The life of the garden

Making a new garden starts with the decision that it is necessary to establish a new plot in a previously uncultivated part of the forest. The plot needs to be chosen in consultation with the **butubutu** chief. Careful planning is then required so as to mobilise the necessary labour force, with an eye to how the different stages of clearing and preparation should be timed so as to take advantage of, or perhaps mitigate, the growing conditions anticipated in the coming seasons. In Marovo, the November-to-March season generally characterised by **singi rane** (daytime high tides) and wet northwesterly winds (**mohu**) is considered to be a time of heat, humidity, fertility and intense growth, and the best period for planting any crop. Most households will strive to plant gardens well during October to December, a strategy which will invariably bring excellent crops already in January to March. After that the year is considered to take on a less agreeable cast in agricultural terms. The sunny April-to-September season of **mati rane** (daytime low tides) and southeasterly tradewinds (**hecha**) is considered to be cooler, dry and infertile. This is at best a time of final growth and harvest, but gives poor conditions for the planting and growth of most crops, and as the **mati rane** season proceeds the state of gardens is a matter of astute monitoring and much concern. The decreasing yields of garden crops in June-July and onwards, amounting to a general state of village life 'being impoverished' with people 'much in need' (**malanga**) is strikingly high-lighted by the countervailing fertility of simultaneous **pora buruburu**, ripe nuts on the *Canarium* trees. In fact the ripening of these nuts coincides with the trees shedding their leaves, this being a visual reminder – through the analogical association of denuded branches to decay – that times are indeed poor garden-wise. In a similar manner *Canarium* trees indicate the imme-diate onset of new fertility and the right time for planting when their branches turn green with new shoots and young foliage around September. Root crop cultivation is thus conceptually interdependent with arboriculture in many ways, and the environmental signs of sea, forest and weather interact to weave a dense dynamics of rather predictable agricultural seasons.

A number of crops (including the sweet potato and cassava staples) can in fact be planted and harvested at any time, and so throughout the year Marovo households are very rarely in any real danger of absolute crop failure. Throughout the months of **mati rane** there will always be some harvestable outputs from most gardens – although, as emphatically stated by many, there will never be a lot of any crop. And so the conviction remains strong that the ideal time for any planting is right before the wet northwest monsoons that usually announce their arrival with a series of squalls around mid-November. The heat and humidity is said to give planted crops a good start – certainly if by then they are already rooted in a well-prepared garden – and to give them enough strength to continue growing well during the dry weather and often scorching sun of the tradewind season. In order to have a new garden ready before the wet northwesterlies set in, it is considered sensible to commence and accomplish most of the clearance work in February to April. This will allow for cutting, felling and burning at a time when the wet season is on the wane, while giving time for short-term regrowth before final burning and tillage towards the end of the 'dry' season.

The different stages in the development of a swidden garden, all subsumed under the verb **chevara** ('to cultivate [a swidden]') are presented in schematised form in Figure 4.5 below. There are, roughly speaking, three main stages:

- **ropaini**, 'new, prospective garden site where clearing [**ropa**] is under way';
- **chigo**, 'garden under cultivation', the major focus of **chevara**;
- **kotukotuani**, 'bush fallow and secondary forest' – a stage that may lead to repeated cultivation, or to long-term fallow.

Their sequential development, and the crop rotation deemed necessary to make the most out of the soils, were sketched already in the quote from Dennie Loni that opened the preceding section. Figure 4.5 schematises key dynamics of Marovo agroforestry cycles, but some additional explanation may be useful: re-clearing and subsequent planting often takes place after only short-term fallow with predominantly ginger (**piropiro**) growth. Such short-term fallows may alternate with long-term bush fallows in which secondary forest develops, and within most larger **voloso** of extended-family garden land, fallows in all stages occur together with new and older gardens under cultivation.

There is a certain sexual division of labour associated with gardens and their development. Work in the **ropaini** is mainly the responsibility of men, who will join forces in order to clear new gardens – an activity they often say is 'work we do for the women'. While axes and long bush knives remain the major tools for heavy clearing efforts, chainsaws are becoming more common. In addition, the agricultural extension team based at the government headquarters at Seghe also offers chainsaws and chainsaw operators for hire on an hourly basis, transport to the nearest beach included. Some husbands may decide to spend money thus, in order to have the felling of the biggest trees accomplished easily. In carrying out the heavy tasks of forest clearance (**ropa**) men see themselves as transforming the male-associated 'wilderness' of the undisturbed forest into female-associated, domesticated new garden land for the women to work on (see Hviding, 1996a:155-160).

The stage of **ropaini** – forest being cleared and prepared for planting – is ideally not attained until freshly tilled soil is ready for planting. The tasks of planting, tending and harvesting crops are in actual fact usually joint efforts at least by wife and husband – although again, the nominal categorisation of gardening as 'the work of women' (**tinavete ta manemaneke**) is seen in contrast to outer-reef fishing and inner-forest hunting, 'the work of men' (**tinavete ta tinoni**). But quite a few men spend more time in gardens then they do fishing at sea or hunting in the forest. This does not appear to devalue their self-ascribed and recognised masculinity, but the continuing importance of maintaining the symbolic distinction between male and female work spheres is often illustrated by men who say about their own gardening that they do it 'to help the women'. Conversely, women often participate in work in the **ropaini** by doing many lighter tasks – 'brushing' (removing undergrowth) and collecting and burning litter – and on such occasions may say that they 'help the men'. As in that other key domain of everyday practice, namely fishing (where women often invest considerable effort in, and obtain substantial catches from, hook-and-line fishing on inner reefs), the exact definition of a domain as 'male' or 'female' does not render it a single-sex sphere of actual activity. The regular participation of men in a 'female' domain, and of women in a 'male' domain, does not necessarily diminish the genderised character of those domains (cf. Strathern, 1988 for comparative discussion of Melanesian ethnography along these lines).

The stages of garden development are more diffuse than what is implied by a step-by-step overview. The rapidly growing trees and shrubs of the secondary forest appear to be endlessly encroaching on the openness of the swiddens under cultivation. That openness is often limited anyway by the common practice of letting certain large trees remain after clearing, in addition to the "timeless" *Canarium* trees that embody the garden's fertile essence and long-term history. Some of the trees left are valuable timber species, most notably the lowland **goliti** (*Gmelina moluccana*) which is used for dugout canoes.[6] The large trees are frequently pollarded to let in the sunlight. Having them growing in the swiddens is reckoned to prevent soil erosion in the steep slopes that form the basis for most Marovo gardens. The **ibibu** tree (*Cleidion speciflorum*) has a straight trunk and dense foliage, and is another tree typically left standing when new garden sites are cleared in the forest. Since **ibibu** grows quickly it is often planted in selected locations in the garden to provide shade. Apart from such important larger trees, a variety of smaller cultivated and secondary forest trees (and the infinitely useful coconut) form part of most swiddens. Some of them are also planted in villages. Figure 4.6 exemplifies the great variety of trees in Marovo agroforestry complexes, and also includes some other plants (shrubs and herbs) not shown on the "Legend to Garden Maps" in Figure 4.4.

Figure 4.5   Establishing and cultivating a garden: the chevara **complex**

STAGE OF CULTIVATION	STATE OF GARDEN/ TYPICAL ACTIVITY	EXPLANATION
GOANA PIRU	**goana piru**	'wild', undisturbed forest
ROPAINI	**poki**	to clear away lower layer of forest
	hirama	to fell large trees
	rakoto	to cut up and collect material from trunks, branches, roots, foliage (etc.) in heaps around the biggest trees whose dead trunks may be left standing
	jupejupe	to burn collected plant litter and dead trees
CHIGO	**choku**	to plant' (**choku** also means 'digging stick'). May be done right after **jupejupe**, or one waits until new herbs and shrubs appear from ashes and then clear this regrowth away and burn it before planting
	pokipoki	regular weeding of planted fields
	heruheru	to carry away weeded matter and other garden litter and let it wither in the sun
	(or)	
	jupejupe	to burn litter, leaves, weeds, etc. in the garden

STAGE OF CULTIVATION	STATE OF GARDEN/ TYPICAL ACTIVITY	EXPLANATION
CHIGO (continued)	**habu** • **heli talo** • **(kupati talo)** • **heli umalau** • **heli uvikola** • **heli uvi** • **paju batia** • **kudu ngache**	to harvest • 'dig' taro • (replant taro tops) • 'dig' sweet potato • 'dig' cassava • 'dig yams' • 'purchase' plantains • gather *Hibiscus* shoots ('cabbage')
	choku pule	to replant a garden after harvest, with any crop
	pokipoki **heruheru/jupejupe**	to weed fields and dispose of weeds
	habu pule	to harvest again

From this stage onwards the numbers, types and succession of additional plantings and harvests depend on soil type and condition

KOTUKOTUANI	**piropiroani**	bush fallow dominated by **piropiro** gingers
	kotukotuani	secondary forest with trees
	kotukotuani porana	mature secondary forest after 10-20 years, with large trees and forest shrubs; **chichiogo** if undisturbed for several decades; eventually reverts to **goana**
	hirama pule	to clear secondary forest
	rakoto, jupejupe	to cut and burn plant debris
CHIGO	**choku**	to plant

Figure 4.6 Checklist of important supplementary plants in Marovo agroforestry

TUBER STAPLES

habichi	*Alocasia macrorrhiza*	"Elephant ear" taro; cultivated but also wild

FRUIT TREES

apuchu	*Syzygium malaccense*	Malay apple; local fruit tree, several cultivars
eruku	*Mangifera indica*	Mango; some varieties introduced, others local
laeni	*Citrus aurantifolia*	Lime; likely introduction in early 1800s
lemana	*Citrus limon*	Lemon; likely introduction in early 1800s
manioko	*Carica papaya*	Pawpaw; early 1800s introduction
opiti	*Spondias dulcis*	"Vi Apple"; a local fruit tree
opiti vaka	*Averrhoea carambola*	Starfruit; introduced fruit tree
omo	*Artocarpus altilis*	Breadfruit tree; indigenous but little used
omo vaka	*Annona muricata*	Soursop; introduced fruit tree
oriji	*Citrus spp.*	Orange; introduced fruit tree, several cultivars
tige	*Barringtonia edulis*	Cut nut; seasonal nut tree, several cultivars

LEAFY GREENS

pinopoto	*Ficus copiosa*	A bush fallow tree; shoots and young leaves eaten
tagala	*Polyscias spp.*	Woody shrubs; shoots and young leaves eaten

MEDICINAL AND CEREMONIAL

chochoho	*Hibiscus rosa-sinensis*	Ornamental shrub; flowers used medicinally
jajala	*Codiaeum variegatum*	"Croton", old cultivar; ritual uses
jipolo	*Cordyline terminalis*	Shrub of protective symbolism; many cultivars

minila	*Zingiber officinale*	Ginger; old cultivar, medicinal and ritual uses
nabo	*Curcuma longa*	Turmeric; old cultivar, medicinal/ritual uses
puchu makasi	*Cymbopogon* sp.	Lemon grass; old cultivar, medicinal uses
puchupuchu	*Ocimum* sp.	Basil; old cultivar; medicinal uses and sometimes chewed with *Areca* nuts

STIMULANTS

hirata	*Piper betle*	Climber; leaves chewed with *Areca* nuts
pijaka	*Areca catechu*	"Betel" nut palm; important stimulant
tabaika	*Nicotiana tabacum*	"Local" tobacco; 19th-century introduction

PRACTICAL USES

dako	*Pandanus sp.*	A pandanus with unserrated leaves used for mats
lakori	*Ficus* sp.	A bush fallow tree; bark used formerly for cloth
leru	*Hibiscus tiliaceus*	Multi-purpose coastal tree; growing spontaneously
pate	*Pandanus sp.*	A pandanus with unserrated leaves used for mats
tita	*Parinari glaberrima*	A secondary forest tree; nuts used for caulking and glue

Unless noted, the plants listed are cultivated and not found otherwise growing in the wild. Most are also indigenous to the Marovo area, or they are aboriginal introductions (mainly from the ancient Austronesian repertoire of useful plants). More recent introductions are identified as such. For further detail on local uses of these plants the reader is referred to the overview of forest zones in Figure 3.2.[7] Together with the major crops and trees, the supplementary plants make the agroforestry zone of well-developed present-day swiddens a rich and reliable source of most ingredients of day-to-day household life, animal protein excepted, and the wide repertoire of things usually offered by each family's "garden" indicate how **chevara** work fulfils far more than dietary and practical requirements. In a manner not unlike the emotional attachment of former generations of Marovo people to their irrigated taro pondfields (see Chapter 5), the men and women who work their swiddens today derive significant enjoyment and pride from being there and caring for this densely cultivated system.

Soil classification, soil types and their implications

In Dennie Loni's reflections earlier in this chapter on the making of gardens, the variability of soil quality throughout the Marovo area was tersely noted. Marovo people's basic inventory of distinct types of soil (**puava**; we recall the multiple dimensions of this term that also means territorial land-and-sea estate) indeed reflects the opportunities offered by those different soils for crop cultivation. Figure 4.7 gives a basic inventory of Marovo soil classification. Although not entirely exhaustive, the table lists all major categories of soils perceived in Marovo in terms of the agricultural opportunities offered by them.

Figure 4.7   Marovo soil classification

SOIL TYPE	DESCRIPTION AND LOCATION
puava	'SOIL'. Also a highly salient cultural concept referring to territories held as named ancestral estates by homonymous **butubutu**.
puava bupara	'BROWN SOIL'. Red-to-brown clay soils with greasy quality (traditionally even used for soap), but not particularly good for cultivation as sweet potato gardens have to be put under fallow after a few harvests. Common in large lowland portions of Marovo: Bareke, landwards-facing part of Marovo Island, western Vangunu, southeastern end of New Georgia, Kalikolo area.
puava chinoko	'BLACK SOIL'. Very fertile, can be cultivated continuously for a remarkably long time. Characteristic of the seawards-facing slopes of Marovo Island and certain other coastal locations where recent volcanic activity is in evidence e.g. by hot springs.
puava gegha	Etymology unknown. Infertile soil, overgrown with bush after initial gardening attempts. Various locations.

puava hokara	'PROPER SOIL'. Brown, fertile, stony soils with great capacity for intensive, long-term sweet potato cultivation. Found in parts of all barrier islands, near the sea on certain mainland weather coasts (Viru, southern Vangunu, Gatokae – especially the uplifted terraces in the Sobiro area), and in certain parts of New Georgia such as the Vahole area.
puava kolipi	Etymology unknown. Brown, rather 'dead' soil with stones, not good for sweet potatoes. Typical of many parts of Bareke and some areas of Kalikolo and northern New Georgia.
puava noti	After **noti** = 'BLACK CLAY'. Dense black clay found in a few riverine locations such as at Obo River. Formerly a trade item (cf. Somerville, 1897).
puava orava	'RED SOIL'. Alternative name for **puava bupara**.
puava ruta	'TARO PONDFIELD SOIL'. Waterlogged soils which in uncultivated state support wild **ghohere** taro (*Cyrtosperma*). Various inland, river-associated locations.
puava ruvao	Etymology unclear. A hard, rocky soil whose surface looks like stone and is hard to break and turn. Various locations.
puava toba	'BARRIER ISLAND SOIL'. A type of **puava hokara** characteristic of many areas in the barrier islands.
puava votu	'ESTUARINE SOIL'. Muddy soil mixed with leaves. Found close to river and on riverbanks.

It is clear that the major soil categories defined from the Marovo perspective may be generic and may refer to several distinct soil types as defined by Western science. The New Georgia Group's complex geology makes for great variation in soil types, as amply illustrated in the survey of "soil associations" by the Land Resources Study of the 1970s (Wall and Hansell, 1975, particularly the accompanying Map 4d). We have attempted to correlate Marovo soil classification – based on visual appearance and agricultural opportunity – with the classifications of some twenty-five different "soil associations" in the Land Resource Study – based on geological genesis and chemical properties. This turned out not to be a straightforward task. Nevertheless, some tentative observations may be made.

Marovo soil classification emphasises variations in the capacity of soils to sustain long-term sweet potato production. Following this lead we see that the reddish-brown **puava bupara** and the 'dead' stony **puava kolipi** both occur in areas that according to Wall and Hansell are dominated by soils derived from "basalt and basaltic andesites" and designated as a composite of: "Deep, freely drained, yellowish red to red clay (Haplorthox); Deep to shallow, humus-rich, freely drained, yellowish brown to red clay (Tropohumults); Deep to shallow, freely drained, brown to yellowish brown clays and loams (Dystropepts)" (Wall and Hansell, 1975:Map 4d). This soil association is claimed to be dominant in Bareke and western Vangunu as well as in southern, eastern and northern New Georgia (except coastal strips) and, notably, the Vahole area. Overall, it is considered to have low available and reserve nutrients. In Marovo, it is pointed out that the coastal hills along the Bareke peninsula are dominated by **puava kolipi** and therefore are unsuitable for long-term intensive cultivation – gardens in these hills get exhausted rather quickly. Thus in some villages of Bareke the view is expressed that land shortages are imminent, despite the vast hinterland holdings of the different **butubutu**. These villagers say that it was not like that when previous generations lived up in the bush and cultivated taro in irrigated pondfields whose water supply continuously replenished the soil. Anyhow, the soil far inland is considered to be overall better – but establishing gardens there today would mean an inordinate increase in the daily time spent on walking to and from the garden, not to mention the labour necessary for carrying home the produce without benefit of canoes. Thus the land scarcity and soil impoverishment talked about by the people of Bareke is at least partly a function of subjective preferences, and the opinion is increasingly voiced that with continuously high population increase it might be an option for some Bareke people to migrate back to the bush permanently and start intensive cultivation for intermittent marketing purposes.

The main contrast to **puava bupara/puava kolipi** in terms of sweet potato cultivation is the **puava hokara** complex of Viru, southern Vangunu, Gatokae and Vahole in northern New Georgia, also embracing the **puava toba** of barrier islands and certain uplifted coastal terraces. There is a striking correlation between this Marovo category and the Land Resource Study soil association derived from "basaltic lavas, volcanics and pyroclastics" and designated – just like the preceding association – as a composite of "Deep, freely drained, yellowish red to red clay (Haplorthox)" and "Deep to shallow, freely drained, brown to yellowish brown clays and oams (Dystropepts)" (Wall and Hansell, 1975:Map 4d). But this soil association is also considered to have "low available and reserve nutrients", a claim that differs sharply with its dominant presence in areas considered by Marovo people to be the very best for long-term sweet potato cultivation. We do not know which criteria have been used for judging the nutrient capacities of soil associations, and it is likely that the perspective is not an indigenous one of village-level root crop production in swiddens, but rather a late-colonial one of large-scale potentials for so-called "Agricultural Opportunity Areas" (Wall and Hansell, 1975).

The excellence of **puava hokara** is somewhat better substantiated by soil science when its subcategory **puava toba** is considered, however. The locations of **puava toba** – barrier islands and a few select uplifted terraces on the coasts of main islands – coincide to a large degree with "soil associations" derived from coral and associated volcanic and alluvial additions and from "limestone and volcanic detritus". Such combinations are potentially rather fertile ones, high in nutrients and minerals – and are, in the context of the ethnography of Melanesian agriculture, reminiscent of the luxurious "coral [yam] gardens" of Trobriand Islanders (Malinowski, 1935).

The extraordinary **puava chinoko**, the black soil of a few coastal spots associated with recent volcanic activity, remains a mystery as it is not mentioned in the Land Resources Study. It seems likely that this is a variety of the coral-and-volcanics complex just discusssed – in any event we note that Marovo people, particularly those inhabiting the sea-facing side of the small Marovo Island, 'blessed' by an abundance of **puava chinoko**, comment on their unique, black soil as being 'alive'. Certainly, some of the scattered locations at which this soil is found beyond Marovo Island are ones of continuing volcanic activity, most notably hot springs.

What is perceived as the very best soil of Marovo is found on the small land holdings of 'coastal' **butubutu** such as those of Bili in the south, Marovo Island, the coral peninsulas bordering the subsidiary Nono Lagoon, and Gerasi in the north. The small volcanic peak of Marovo Island, whose intensive agroforestry system is discussed in Chapter 8, is known throughout the area for the unique qualities of its **puava chinoko**. On the steep seawards-facing slopes of this rather small island, which has a present-day population density of around one hundred persons per sq. km, quite a few swidden complexes based on sweet potatoes are today in their fourth or fifth decade of continuous cultivation.

Almost as good soil conditions prevail in the inner zones of some of the wider barrier islands such as Mijanga, the southernmost barrier island in Marovo where the firmly sea-oriented Bili **butubutu** lives, and Ramata in the northern lagoon, home of the coastal Gerasi **butubutu**. The stony and brown coral-based soil soil of these barrier islands, **puava toba**, is regarded as somewhat similar to the **puava hokara** ('proper soil') predominant in the lowlands of the thinly populated weather coasts of Gatokae and southern

Vangunu as well as Vahole in the northern lagoon. It provides the people of these areas, mainly 'bush' groups, with vast areas of excellent land. Among the Methodist land-holders of southern Vangunu it is said that it is generally not necessary to clear new gardens at all, despite the abundance of reserve land. Some of their Seventh-day Adventist neighbours of Gatokae, though, are more money-oriented and have since the mid-1980s developed an impressive surplus sweet potato production destined for marketing in lagoon villages (see Chapter 8).

Some reflections on science, ethnoscience and indigenous knowledge

In this chapter and the previous one we have presented information about aspects of what may conventionally be referred to as Marovo "ethnoscience": the vegetation zones and useful plant species growing in the forests and gardens (Chapter 3), and the Marovo people's land use, cultivation practices and soils (Chapter 4). What has been presented, then, is a Marovo-centred view of agroforestry, but one that presents most of its descriptions translated into English, some of it rather technical English. Vegetation types have been related to topography and the history of past disturbance; plants have been classified by their status, whether cultivated, introduced or wild; and gardening practices have been described in terms of rotations and fallows, and the means to achieve subsistence or a marketable surplus.

Already, in the act of translation, we have moved some distance away from an account which a Marovo person would easily recognise. It is a reminder that to describe something involves decisions about the choice of words, and any word chosen will reflect the in-built structures of explanation in the culture from which a language derives. Inevitably, then, to describe is also to begin to explain. Marovo people's "ethnoscience", in the account presented above, has already been passed through the inescapable filter of translation into a language (English) that is permeated through and through with the concepts of Western science.

There is, however, a second sense in which Marovo ethnoscience has been "translated" through our account. Paul Sillitoe (1996) in his comprehensive study of the environmental knowledge of the Wola in New Guinea, points to a common error in our approach to understanding the world view of non-literate peoples. We tend to reduce their indigenous knowledge to taxonomic schemes and then expect those schemes to provide the key to an understanding of indigenous perceptions of the natural world. Ever since Linnean taxonomy has indeed been the lynchpin of our scientific perceptions, but for societies like Wola or Marovo it has some limitations:

> [K]nowledge... among the Wola, for example, is not codified but diffuse and
> communicated piecemeal in everyday life. It is to a considerable extent
> knowledge gained through experience, passed on equally by example as by
> word, transmitted as, and when, daily events require .... The knowledge is ...
> more often shown than articulated, it is as much skill as concept. (Sillitoe,
> 1996:9)

Today Marovo men and women are mostly literate, but they have little
practice in English and may not extend their reading much beyond the Bible.
To a large extent, like the Wola, "they live rather than reflect on their
environmental knowledge" (Sillitoe, 1996: 9).[8]

The epistemological problems that follow from any attempt to document
such indigenous understandings are indeed formidable. If knowledge is not
merely pragmatic – as well exemplified by the Marovo vegetation and soil
classifications – but is also more like a set of skills than a set of concepts,
something maintained and transmitted by informed experience and practical
demonstration, then such knowledge is unlikely to be explicable within an
integrated and consistent ethno-ecological theory. Indigenous explanations, if
offered, will be piecemeal, contradictory and contextualised: gardening magic
works, but then so does fire and mulch. We therefore have two epistemological
problems:

- The translation of Marovo knowledge into an English language that is
  saturated with scientific understandings;
- A form of knowledge in Marovo which is pragmatic and rooted in lived
  experience rather than articulated understanding.

Our response to these problems has been to attempt to reconcile Marovo
knowledge with scientific knowledge, and vice-versa, but with explanations
that are biased towards natural science for theory and concepts. A purely
phenomenological account of Marovo, were such a thing logically feasible,
would manage to achieve epistemological neutrality in a "symmetrical"
manner (Latour, 1987, 1993), whereas we have consciously adopted a more
partisan approach. Again the underlying reason is foreshadowed in Sillitoe's
account:

> A straightforward account of Wola environmental lore, and their practices that
> intervene in nature's arrangements, cannot address some issues which I think
> pertinent in assessing their relationship with their natural surroundings. Indi-
> genous knowledge and practices have implications which I cannot explore
> within the limited terms and idiosyncratic perspectives of Wola culture, so far
> as I have managed to apprehend these. (Sillitoe, 1996:10)

In the case of Marovo Lagoon we also follow this line of approach. Marovo ethno-science is our starting point, in a situation where our own competence is limited and in a region barely touched by systematic investigations by Western science. The geology, pedology, botany and zoology of Marovo does not extend beyond a handful of studies, few of them recent. Our scientific account of the Marovo environment, if based on the published literature, would be short and incomplete. But in presenting the small fraction of the riches of Marovo knowledge that we have been to access, we display this knowledge in Western clothing, and with embellishments derived from whatever scientific insights we have been able to acquire.

To summarise, by combining in a pluralist way the "knowledges" (cf. Worsley, 1997) of Marovo and scientific perspectives, and by presenting both in the translated form that will make most sense to a Western audience, we hope to have presented a more complete understanding of patterns and processes within the Marovo cultural landscape. In the following Chapter 5 we attempt to transpose those understandings back into the 19th century. Our purpose is to provide an ethnographically informed and scientifically valid picture of Marovo environmental relationships ca. 1840. It is against this baseline of "traditional" land use practices that we can begin to assess the multitude of 20th-century changes with which this book is mainly concerned.

5 The Wet and the Dry: Marovo Agroforestry at European Contact

Contact and networks of old Marovo

The notion of "contact" has many fallacies when applied to colonial encounters. All too often "pre-contact" is applied to instances for which "pre-European" would be the proper term, to avoid the implication that instances where "natives" encountered early European colonial agents had a momentous quality – an assumption not necessarily warranted. For Pacific Islands societies it is largely axiomatic that interisland contacts and intercultural encounters were regular occurrences and significant facts of life long before European ships emerged on the horizon. This also applies to the New Georgia Group in general (Figure 5.1) and the Marovo area in particular (cf. Hviding, nd a). In New Georgia, myths and legends about a distant past and oral histories of more recent happenings emphasise nothing so much as travel, the arrivals of new people, plants, animals, objects and knowledge, and the workings of large-scale interisland exchange and warfare. And reports by early European visitors about their encounters with New Georgians more often than not convey the impression that the latter were less than surprised at meeting the former (Hviding, 1996a, ch. 3, 1998; McKinnon, 1975; Jackson, 1978). Old Marovo prior to the first encounters with Europeans was indeed full of "contact" with other people – friends, strangers and foes.

There is no reason to suppose that the world of Marovo before European contact was in any way unchanging, and there is even less support for the notion that Marovo has ever functioned as some kind of cultural isolate. Nonetheless a certain degree of long-term political and demographic stability is suggested by the co-existence in the New Georgia Group of 14 separate languages, 11 belonging to the Austronesian group and 3 to the unrelated Papuan or non-Austronesian group (Ross, 1986; Tryon, 1981). Whereas all 5 languages – Marovo, Vangunu, Bareke, Hoava and Kusaghe – spoken today

113

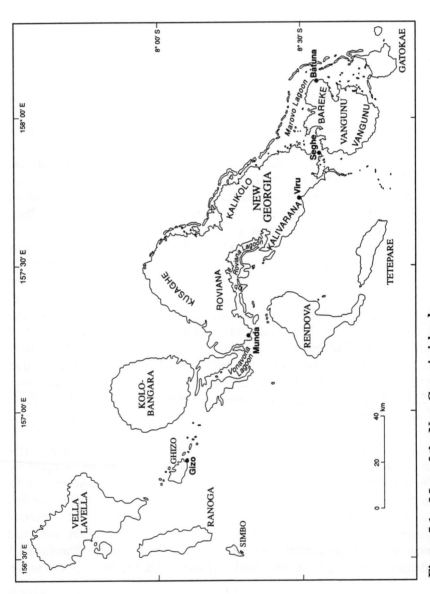

Figure 5.1   Map of the New Georgia islands

in Marovo are Austronesian and are rather closely related, the nearby people of Lokuru and Baniata in southern Rendova speak a non-Austronesian language which by virtue of its tonal characters and other attributes is deemed absolutely unintelligible by most Marovo people (who tend to comment that Lokuru speech is "like Chinese!"). Yet on the other hand these southern Rendova people are regarded as having rather similar customs to those of New Georgia, and intermarriage is frequent.

In terms of culture history, diverse origins for the various language communities of New Georgia thus seem undeniable, but the linguists do not suppose that these languages maintained themselves in isolation. On the contrary there was much contact between different areas. Wide-ranging networks of warfare, trade and marriage extended across the Solomon Islands. In pre-colonial times the coastal people (or alternatively 'salt-water people', which corresponds to the pan-Solomons category expressed in Solomon Islands Pijin as **man long solwara**) of Marovo had regular contact with the people of the entire New Georgia Group, and also with Choiseul, Santa Isabel, the Russell Islands, Savo, Guadalcanal, and probably Malaita (Hviding, 1996a; see also Findlay, 1877:773). Through these networks, objects and ideas, including those relevant to agriculture, had for generations been flowing through Marovo from the islands to the northwest – including Bougainville, thus linking up with the Bismarck archipelago – and to the southeast.

"Reconstructing" the agroforestry system

Because of these networks, the accelerating changes brought on during the 19th century were complex processes which involved not just direct Marovo/European interactions (of which there were few until after 1850), but also some indirect influences coming to Marovo via intermediaries, for example the people of Roviana and Simbo to the west, and the Russell Islands (called 'Vechala' in Marovo) to the east. Early on in the century these three groups, most notably the people of tiny outlying Simbo far to the southwest and near the routes of whaling ships, "East India men" and British convict ships en route to Australia, seized their opportunities to receive new tools, weapons, crops, commodities and ideas, and to adapt them to their needs. Introduced diseases were an uncontrolled aspect of the same process. Through their existing networks or through expanded ones, these innovators then started to influence neighbouring groups – such as Marovo, which like Roviana was a major regional power centre in command of interisland networks through strategic alliance, ritualised friendship, marriage and the sheer force of head-hunting raids (Hviding 1996a, ch. 3; for Roviana see e.g. Schneider, 1996, and Goldie, 1909). As an inevitable side effect of all these accelerating changes, the way that the environment of New Georgia was managed also began to change. Therefore, if we are to understand the way that agroforestry was transformed we must consider not only the direct, local impacts of European contact but also its ramifying, indirect and regional implications.

For Marovo and its neighbours the information sources available for this attempted reconstruction are incomplete and often ambiguous. They include Marovo's own oral histories, which are explicit about some key events and certain other things but vague about chronology; secondly, comparative inferences drawn from the vocabulary of New Georgian languages; thirdly the written accounts by early navigators and traders, which unfortunately convey little information until well after many European-induced changes were underway; and finally data from archaeological surveys, although in the Solomons these surveys have so far been of a reconnaissance nature and are not at all comprehensive.[1] We begin with oral traditions, particularly those from people with inland 'bush' origins, which provide a good outline of the way people used to live in the olden days.

Life in the bush

According to the statements given in 1986 by two of the oldest men in Bisuana (an important village of 'bush' people in east-central Marovo), unlike the present system of sweet potato and cassava production it was formerly the taro gardens that were the main source of food, together with cultivated 'pana' or lesser yam (**luju**, *Dioscorea esculenta*), yams (**uvi**, *Dioscorea alata* – many named cultivars and/or similar species, including **loko chiko** and **pokepoke** – and **tinavolu**, *D. nummularia*) and banana (**batia**, *Musa* spp. [many named cultivars]). At least five types of wild yams (**bolivi, chochore, iga, kane** and **lehu**) were also harvested in the forest. These included varieties of *Dioscorea bulbifera* (**iga**, also cultivated), *D. nummularia* (**kane**, also cultivated as **tinavolu**), and probably *D. pentaphylla* (**bolivi**, also cultivated).

Taro appears to have been the more important crop. In the Bareke bush (inland of Bisuana) it was planted in terraced pondfields or **ruta**, into which water was led from small streams. The planted taro beds were surrounded by wooden fences or stone walls, to retain the water. The channels thus created were sloping and compartmentalised so as to be able to manipulate the water flow. Although usually referred to as quite elaborate constructions with relatively large field spaces devoted to taro plants of three different growth stages, **ruta** also existed in the form of smaller fields in natural locations amenable to taro irrigation with little modification beyond simple logs for regulating water flow and inundation, such as in shallow pools in small tributary rivers and streams. Such minor **ruta** are known particularly from the formerly densely cultivated areas around the Piongo Lavata river (lit. 'the great river') in Vahole of northern Marovo, where some were still cultivated in 1996 by a few elderly couples. Small, simple pondfields may have been characteristic of New Georgia in general as family-managed supplements to the large communally-worked complexes of multiple terraced pondfields with rotational cultivation.

According to old men of Bisuana who were born while people still lived permanently inland, other important foods in the Bareke bush were *Canarium* nuts (**maria** and **ngoete**), both wild and cultivated. Many wild leafy greens and fruits were also gathered. In his description of vegetable foods in "the old days", Roviana elder George Vudere (1975:4) provides a complementary view from Saikile in Roviana Lagoon, a location where distance between barrier island and mainland is small and where seaside settlement was tied more closely to inland life than in old central Marovo. It is a similar pattern to that described by the elders of Bareke, but perhaps with more emphasis on cultivated fruit trees including mango, Malay Apple (*Syzygium malaccense*, **apuchu** in Marovo) and breadfruit.

Animal protein among the bush people came from "opossum" or cuscus (*Phalanger* sp., **binahere** in the Marovo language), fruit bats (**vahu**, fam. Pteroptidae), feral and domesticated pigs (**moa**), large eels of the river (**tulangini**, *Anguilla* spp.), mangrove molluscs (such as the abundant mud-living gastropod **ropi**, *Terebralia palustris*) and on occasion from saltwater fish such as mullets (**lipa**, *Mugil* spp.) which enter the large rivers during spawning and which were hunted with bow and arrow. Dogs were not eaten in New Georgia – they even had a sacred status among some influential Roviana groups.[2] Nor have snakes ever been eaten. The **bukulu**, a rather large tree-living lizard known to biology as the "prehensile-tailed skink" (*Corucia zebrata*, endemic to the Solomon Islands), was an important ritual food reserved for chiefs, and if anyone saw a **bukulu** in the forest but did not bring it to his chief he did so under risk of the death penalty. Some bush people are also said to have eaten, on occasion, the flesh of two larger reptiles: **erebachi** or monitor lizard (*Varanus indicus*) and, among a few groups without totemic avoidance, the dreaded **vua** or estuarine crocodile (*Crocodylus porosus*).

Despite this apparent abundance of bush food, including protein, institutionalised barter with the coastal people was of high importance. This took place at prearranged times in special locations on or near the seashore, and the open enmity that otherwise prevailed and prevented bush people from venturing out along the lagoon beaches was temporarily suspended. Nevertheless it was the women of either party who brought forth the goods, while the armed men stood watch in the background. The coastal people brought mainly fish (usually prepared in stone ovens and wrapped in leaves, but sometimes fresh), as well as coral lime, coconuts, shellfish and even seawater. This maritime and coastal produce was exchanged for taro, yams, *Areca* nuts and betel leaves, live pigs or cooked pork, and live cuscus. It should also be noted that oral traditions, as well as genealogical evidence, tells us that is was quite common for coastal men to marry bush women, especially of the Bareke area. The Bisuana elders were of the opinion that such coastal in-laws (**roroto**) could then become most frequent and trustworthy participants in the institutionalised beach barter, and so this pattern of coastal-bush marriages was a driving force in the gradual rapprochement that preceded colonial pacification. Indeed, as the Bisuana elders put it, "some coastal people were actually very good people".

Concerning the intensity of agricultural activity, the old men told one of us that in those days "before the coming of mission and government" – before about 1900 – "there was time for gardens only"; implying that the bush people's lives revolved around daily agricultural work and first and foremost around the continuous needs of the irrigated taro fields. In addition to the scattered permanent taro pondfields and the more transitory yam swiddens, the bush people of former times are also said by their descendants to have maintained a system of very large communal taro plantings – both dryland and irrigated. These **chigo lavata** ('great gardens') produced crops reserved for special occasions and were worked by the entire **butubutu**, both men and women, on whose **puava** the garden was situated. It is conceivable that these large communally worked taro crops were also destined, at least in part, for tribute exacted by the coastal people at certain points in the ceremonial cycles. It may be worth noting in this connection that the Marovo language has a specific term for 10,000 – **vuro** – distinct from "thousand" (**tina**, as in **meka tina** 'one thousand', **karua tina** 'two thousand', and so forth). According to old people **vuro** (as in **meka vuro** 'ten thousand', **karu(a) vuro** 'twenty thousand', and so forth) was reserved for counting certain important things such as massive amounts of taro for particularly large feasts. In this sense the term **vuro** indeed signifies the large-scale nature of some of the agricultural and ceremonial activities of old Marovo – in some respects not unlike today's huge church gatherings whereby one village may invite, house, entertain and feed virtually the entire population of most other same-denominational Marovo villages for two to three days on end. That the large **ruta** systems of old Marovo are likely to have produced conspicuous crop surpluses may be safely assumed on the basis of Kirch's assessment for Oceanic production systems that the expected yield (in terms of tons per hectare per year) from irrigated taro is four times greater than that of dryland taro and eight times greater than that of yams (Kirch, 1994:92-93).

The Bareke elders said that although the bush people used to live in rather large inland villages, families or other working groups would regularly stay for extended periods in small hamlets adjacent to important taro fields when that field's stage of cultivation required constant attention. Taro fields and hamlets were further associated with cultivated groves of *Canarium* nuts, and the irrigated fields also depended directly on shade from the surrounding forest and from large canopy trees left standing when fields were cleared and terracing constructed. In this sense the **ruta** were truly integral to the forest, being, as old people say, "difficult to find there in the middle of the inner forest for those who did not know where the **ruta** were" – unlike the more open yam and dryland taro swiddens more immediately associated with the larger permanent settlements inland. Some of these large settlements, such as the one at Vinuvinu in the Nono mountains of southernmost New Georgia (surveyed in 1986 by Hviding), were those of raiding groups who were by definition 'coastal' and whose war canoes were kept hidden downstream along major rivers. The sites had very extensive assemblages of buildings, ceremonial grounds, places for food preparation and agricultural areas centred on one large main hall (**erovo**) which was the residence of a chief, his warriors and their families. These were also sites to which great gatherings of warriors from other groups in Marovo and the wider New Georgia area would be invited for food prestation ceremonies (**kinolo**) during which temporary peace would (ideally) reign. The **ruta** terraces on which the Vinuvinu stronghold is likely to have depended for supplies of taro for feasts were probably located in the wide valley of the Kolo river directly to the north of the Nono mountains and facing central Marovo Lagoon. These are the customary lands of the Nono Ulu 'hill' group; a **butubutu** still recognised as such but with no present-day descendants actually living in its inland **puava**. The uninhabited Nono Ulu **puava** which has in recent years been the subject of much dispute over mineral prospecting (see Hviding, 1993b).

However, it is clearly remembered by those old enough – and further elaborated in epic tales of conquest and catastrophe including massacres (**eongo**) of whole villages – that inland settlement stability could easily be shattered by marauding coastal people in need of heads for cyclical rituals. For the coastal people of old Marovo, it is said, "a head from the bush people could be almost as good as a head from overseas", and the 'proper' inland bush people who did not maintain large numbers of warriors were particularly vulnerable to such action. Thus the bush people had to strive to obtain a thorough spacing of childbirths within each family (normally nuclear ones, though chiefs could have two or three wives): "for each woman, there must be no more than one child to carry", the old men of Bisuana reminisced.

Things began to change when warfare was on the wane and the bush people started moving towards the coast in order to plant coconuts, new kinds of work rapidly became important – and the people would neglect their taro fields and yam gardens for two to three months at a time, so that "the gardens would turn into bush [**goana**]". As another old man from the bush people of south Vangunu, on the other side of the island from Bareke, expressed it:

> Taro is big work to keep. Growing taro is like feeding a child. It is hard work to keep **ruta**, and that is why people stopped. Cassava and sweet potato are easy – you just hoe and plant, and they grow everywhere. The people of old worked hard. And they had time to work.

This explanation is a modern rationalisation of a process of taro abandonment that was probably more complex. The centrality of taro to the lives of the bush people makes it is likely that rituals of various kinds were interwoven, symbolically as well as logistically, with the cycle of **ruta** management. An analogous case may be Bolivip in New Guinea, where Crook (1998) has shown how cult leaders bear a heavy responsibility for ritual practices that promote the growth of taro, and where "The Angkaiyakmin inspect taro plants as artefacts of the social relationships producing them" (Crook, 1998:62). If in Marovo, as in Bolivip, taro health and social stability were seen as interconnected, then it seems unlikely that the reasons for abandoning the taro **ruta** were seen as entirely "economic" in character.

At the turn-of-the-century time of "great transformations", treated at some length in the next chapter, the inland village sites as well as the **ruta** were mostly abandoned as people migrated to new permanent coastal settlements, so as to gain access to new opportunities. Before that the hilltop headhunter strongholds such as the one at Vinuvinu had become disorganised and fragmented, and only relict groups of raiders maintained their activities from smaller but strategically located coastal settlements. In this process many old distinctions between 'bush' and 'coastal' (or 'saltwater') people began to disappear, although they were, and still are, maintained on other levels.

The importance of taro: linguistic evidence

Oral history and linguistic evidence provides confirmation for the special place occupied by taro in the agroforestry system of old Marovo. Myths and historical tales contain abundant references to the harvesting and eating of taro as a staple, either roasted or pounded with *Canarium* nuts in one of the many types of pudding (cf. Vudere, 1975; and Hocart, 1922, 1935 and MSS, for corresponding evidence from Roviana Lagoon and Simbo). In these 'custom stories' taro features variously, either being taken on a daily basis by women (female-headed households are a common feature in many of the stories) from **chigo** (in this case swidden gardens for dryland taro); or being harvested on a more organised scale by men and women as a **ruta**-cultivated main item in the barter between coastal and inland people; or finally as ceremonial food for the feasts managed by senior men – bartered or obtained as tribute by the coastal people, or harvested in large communal efforts by the bush people for their own feasts. The possible role of male and female 'slaves' (**pinausu**) should also be mentioned. Certainly, the coastal people used to extract forced labour (for agriculture and the manufacture of shell valuables) primarily from captives taken on overseas raids, and secondarily from Marovo bush people recruited on a more temporary basis as part of the general tribute system. There is little indication, though, that the bush people themselves kept slaves or otherwise forced labour, beyond the element of coercion implied by the hierarchical distinction between **bangara** 'chiefs' and **ngicha** 'commoners'. Thus **ruta** cultivation, which was apparently never carried out by coastal people, seems to have been characterised by relatively joint, group-wise participation of men and women – although the complex engineering work that must have gone into the construction of the large terraced pondfield systems (see Figures 5.2-5.4) is likely to have required considerable leadership efforts.

In all the languages of the Marovo area (and in the Roviana language of western New Georgia) there are separate sets of terms and concepts relating to taro, distinct from those referring to other food crops. This finds its parallel in other domains of food production: fishing for tuna and hunting for pigs (the highly-valued ceremonial protein foods of coastal people and bush people, respectively) also have distinct sets of terms that are not applied to more mundane fishing or hunting for non-prestige species. For example, in the bush language of Hoava, related to Roviana but spoken by the historically important Vahole group of northern Marovo, the harvesting of yams, sweet potato and cassava is subsumed under the concept **keru** ('to dig') – e.g. **keru kane** (*Dioscorea alata* yam) subsequently extended to the other more recent crops. However the harvesting of taro is referred to differently as **qire pole**. The latter word is a noun specific to Hoava and refers to the harvestable taro corm. The etymology of the verb **qire** (referring in Roviana to "[bringing] in taro and other foods for a feast, etc." [Waterhouse, 1949: 100]) is undetermined – but as will be seen shortly, **qire** invokes an entire complex of activities concerning taro cultivation specifically. **Qire pole** is followed by the act of **qire masedo** ('to replant the taro top') and this related set of activities is collectively referred to as **qire minaka**; **minaka** also being the general Hoava term for *Colocasia* taro, semantically overlapping with Marovo (and Roviana) **talo**. **Ruqu minaka** is an additional Hoava (and Roviana) term for the small sucker corms that are attached to, but separate from, the main corm, and that are either replanted immediately in a separate **vilaka** – a 'block', 'row' or subsection with a defined perimeter – or left to sprout before replanting, in which case they are referred to as **kiko**, which is also an affectionate personal name sometimes given to small boys.

The Hoava repertoire of words specific to taro cultivation is thus quite similar to that of the major Roviana language of western New Georgia (Waterhouse, 1928, 1949), although in Roviana *Colocasia* taro is **talo** as in Marovo. Such similarity between Hoava and Roviana languages is not un-expected, considering the significant links of Hoava (and the Vahole people) to both Roviana and Marovo and the historical importance of taro in the historically complex Roviana region where inland-dwelling and coastal groups appear to have been less dichotomised than in the Marovo Lagoon (cf. Schneider, 1996). The Marovo language is tied to coastal people and as such may be likely to reflect less preoccupation with the fine technicalities of taro cultivation. In Marovo the harvesting of yams, sweet potato, cassava and taro is more simply subsumed under **heli** 'to dig' (cf. Figure 4.5); **heli** being a cognate of Hoava **keru**. But the replanting of the taro top is referred to by a specific verb, **kupati [talo]**. There is thus no specific term for the taro top, but the act of planting it has its own term – with undetermined etymology, although postulating a link with the Roviana concept of **kupa**, 'to behead' (Waterhouse, 1949:60), may not be far-fetched.

On a general level taro cultivation in its various stages, not just that of irrigated terraces or **ruta** but also the swidden version, has a vocabulary (both in the coastal Marovo language and the bush language of Hoava) that is entirely different from that of other types of food crop cultivation – even when the same actual activities are referred to. For example, in both langua-ges there are three distinct stages of weeding when taro is concerned; the first of which is significantly termed **kiputu koburu** (Hoava) and **pokipoki koburu** (Marovo) – **koburu** being 'child'. Hoava speakers also categorise three distinct sub-sections of 'rows' (**vilaka**) of any taro field under cultiva-tion, wet or dry: **vilaka masedo** (plot of replanted tops); **vilaka ruqu** (plot of replanted sucker corms); and **vilaka kiko** (plot of sprouting sucker corms). These would form a rotational system of three-stage nursery fields and continuous cultivation.

As emphatically stated by young and old, "taro gardens are different from all other gardens". From the linguistic evidence alone it seems clear that the cultivation of sweet potato and, later, of cassava, was absorbed into the existing vocabulary for yam cultivation, whereas the distinct vocabulary for taro-growing, conferring a special status on this crop, was retained and still remains active not least in relation to recent revivals of taro cultivation.

Taro, yams and sweet potato:
evidence from early trade with Europeans

To gain an increased understanding of the Marovo agroforestry system around 1840, evidence from oral history and languages can be matched with some of the early accounts written by European visitors to the New Georgia islands. Let it be said, though, that these accounts are not always reliable and tend to refer to places and contexts that were already heavily influenced by contact with European ships. Such contacts were quite extensive in certain parts of New Georgia, as whalers and traders looked for food, wood, water and women, and bartered for trade goods such as bêche-de-mer and turtle shell. In the western Solomons these contacts seem to have begun very early in the nineteenth century. Bennett (1987:25) shows that between 1790 and 1820 there are records of 25 different ships sighting land along the southern fringes of the New Georgia group. In six cases this led to contact: four ships communicated with canoes and two carried out landings, both in Ranongga. Later contacts were also concentrated in the western part of the group, particularly with the people of Simbo who by the 1840s seem to have achieved a pivotal role in dealings with the Europeans. Probably to maintain their monopoly as trade intermediaries, they discouraged the Europeans from visiting their rivals on New Georgia island to the east, claiming the New Georgia people were "not to be trusted" (Cheyne, 1971:305). Nevertheless, it was reported already in 1839 that "European and American seasmen are domiciled on New Georgia" (Grünnadier Blahe to Admiral Maitland, 1839).

It is not known what became of this unspecified number of "seasmen", however, and for whatever reason, by 1844 the main island of New Georgia (for which read, in this context, the Roviana Lagoon area due east of Simbo) had gained a bad reputation amongst mariners. This was firmly stated by the Scottish captain Andrew Cheyne who was trading for turtle shell in the western Solomons and who provides us with the first full account of trading relationships and the kind of goods that were available in exchange. At Roviana in February 1844 he obtained "cocoanuts, bananas and breadfruit in abundance; also a few yams and sweet potatoes" (Cheyne, 1971:306). In return the people were anxious to obtain "tomahawks" (steel axes), an important new weapon in warfare but also a way to save much labour in the clearing of forest and the making of canoes.

Cheyne's reference to sweet potatoes is intriguing – and seems to be good and solid evidence for a very early date for the introduction of this crop to New Georgia. Conventionally, the sweet potato is not thought to have been present in the Solomon Islands before 19th-century European contact (Yen, 1974a). In the case mentioned by Cheyne it may have been obtained by the Roviana people from their regular exchange partners in Simbo, a safe haven for European ships since the whaling ships began to call there in the 1820s. There are also grounds for hypothesising that the sweet potato had, like so many other objects and ideas, arrived in the New Georgia Group from the Bismarck archipelago to the northwest, via the Austronesian 'salt-water' communities along the Bougainville coasts; in other words, a pre-European introduction. This is not a far-fetched alternative, considering the well-documented importance of the sweet potato in the New Guinea Highlands already by ca. 1600, amounting to an "Ipomoean revolution" (e.g. Golson, 1981).

Still another alternative explanation is that Cheyne's reference to the sweet potato is unreliable or a misidentification, but neither possibility seems likely. By 1844 Cheyne had become very familiar with all the important Melanesian food plants. In 1841, for example, he had written quite an insightful account of the agricultural system of the Isle of Pines near New Caledonia, which included the cultivation of sweet potatoes (Cheyne, 1971: 49). Adding to the evidence for early sweet potato presence in the New Georgia area, a detailed local history recently published by the chief's secretary of one of the major coastal **butubutu** of Marovo (building on oral and written recollections of two generations of elders) indeed states that "the main foods grown [in the olden days, i.e. within a time horizon of some 150 years] were taro, **habichi** (swamp taro), slippery cabbage (**ngache**), yam (**uvi**), **tinavulu** and local potato (**umalau**)" (Liligeto, 1997:97). While 'local' may seem a somewhat contrived designation for the sweet potato (conventionally used, however, to differentiate it from the tinned "English potatoes" once consumed by European missionaries), it is a widespread view in Marovo that the sweet potato has been there for a very long time. Yet it did not rise to full staple prominence until 1910 onwards (see Chapter 6).

Taro is not mentioned in the list of foods offered to Cheyne by the Roviana people, but there is no reason to conclude from its absence that taro was not a primary staple in New Georgia. The reason taro was not traded to Cheyne was probably because his landfall in Roviana brought him into contact with a coastal 'saltwater' community who were themselves dependent on barter relationships with bush communities for their regular supply of taro. They may well have had none available when Cheyne's ship arrived unexpectedly – or they may have chosen to reserve what they had for certain events deemed to be of higher importance than Cheyne's visit. Or alternatively, in line with present-day New Georgian approaches to the food habits of Europeans, Cheyne's exchange partners might simply have believed (perhaps informed by previous encounters) that Europeans did not like taro.

In 1851, a few years after Cheyne's visit, Joseph Bradley on the ship *Ariel* was trading in New Georgia. The log of the *Ariel* provides a further indication of the various items available from coastal communities. Bradley, like Cheyne, was well acquainted with trading conditions in the Melanesian islands and by 1851 had already been on shore at Simbo and parts of New Georgia Island, "up in the bush to see their houses" (Bradley, 1860:22). He records six occasions when trade took place with people in canoes during his trip around the New Georgia Group in September 1851, various items being bartered in exchange for "pieces of hoop iron about six inches long, or old files, anything in the shape of iron" (Bradley, 1860:23). Foods obtained include taro (5 mentions), yams (4 mentions), coconut (2 mentions), fish (2 mentions), bananas, mangoes, "other fruit", and eggs (each one mention). From this list, and from the absence of any mention of the sweet potato, there seems to be little doubt that when Bradley (1860:26) refers to "their usual supply of yams and tarrow" he is indeed describing the principal products of the New Georgia agroforestry system.

Seasonal as well as local factors must also be borne in mind when interpreting early European accounts. Yams are mainly a seasonal crop harvested in mid-year, and one would expect them to have been more available to Bradley (in September) than to Cheyne (in February). For bananas, breadfruit and mango, which to some degree (and certainly for mangoes) have their main season in November-January, the opposite pattern of availability is to be expected. The "abundance" of breadfruit (*Artocarpus altilis*) traded to Cheyne seems an anomaly considering the negligible role played by this tree crop in New Georgia, now as before. The fact that some people in Marovo refer to breadfruit as **omo vaka** – implying association with non-local vessels and some sort of precedence for the 20th-century introduction soursop (*Annona muricata*, in this context called **omo**) – may reflect a history of breadfruit being traded *to* European ships (cf. Leivestad, 1995).

More than 100 years after Cheyne's visit taro was still "the most important food crop" in Vonavona Lagoon, West Roviana, according to a report by the agricultural officer McNabb (1949), who listed and described 78 different varieties of taro maintained in cultivation. McNabb also reported some surprise at finding "the men quite conversant with many of the numerous varieties and quite interested in their gardens", thus implying the predominance of women in the agricultural sphere, including taro cultivation. McNabb's list shows an abundance of taro variety names connoting overseas origin – e.g. **sabasabana**, referring to the Zabana area of western Santa Isabel; **Qela**, a Roviana rendering of the Nggela islands of the central Solomons; **Buin**, referring to Buin on southern Bougainville; **Rabaul** (the district capital of East New Britain, New Guinea); **Malaita**; **Ranoqa**; and others. It reads like any list of sweet potato or cassava cultivars of present-day Marovo and illustrates the continuous interisland flow of root crop cultivars. This active, reciprocal exchange among today's New Georgia women clearly reflects, and is a continuation of, a long history of agricultural innovation.

We can summarise the above by saying that, using the available evidence from oral traditions, written accounts, and contemporary observations, a "baseline" agroforestry system for Marovo can be established. At the time when European contacts were being made it consisted of (1) irrigated taro pondfields (**ruta**) in the mature secondary forest, closely connected with (2) *Canarium* nut groves (**buruburuani**) of two species (**ngoete**, *C. indicum* and the endemic **maria**, *C. salomonense*); (3) bush swiddens with dryland taro, yams and various leafy greens and fruit trees; and (4) coastal yam swiddens (also with a diversity of additional crops) mainly worked by the coastal people. These four components stood in various relationships with each other, and the latter two in particular may be seen as two not necessarily distinct categories of "bush fallow garden".

Fat:rich::dry:poor – the role of *Canarium*

The taro/*Canarium* equation would seem the most crucial of these relationships, as summarised most clearly in the all-important feast puddings, which must consist of both of these ingredients. Without the 'fat substance' (**deana**) of smoked and crushed *Canarium* nuts, the taro will be 'dry' (**popa**) and a pudding made from pounded root crops only is regarded as a poor product. As such, it is enriched and 'wettened' by having the 'fat' nuts added. This scheme of FAT:RICH::DRY:POOR and its various complex metaphorical extensions underlie the most fundamental Marovo ideas about food, sexuality, blood, bodily strength and material sustenance (Leivestad, 1995) – and are also closely tied to the entire semantic field of headhunting, sacrifice and **mana**.

This New Georgian "wet-and-dry" complex, although representative of widespread patterns in Oceanic agriculture (cf. Barrau, 1958, 1965) has profound cultural meaning far beyond its immediate associations with crops and cultivation. The taro/ *Canarium* equation is also analogous to the taro/ fish equation forming the key principle in the institutionalised barter between bush people and coastal people in old Marovo, and being embodied in the continued symbolic distinctions between these two categories of people in present-day Marovo (Hviding, 1996a:128-130). It is notable that whereas the coastal people relied almost entirely on the bush people for their taro, they were rather more self-sufficient as far as *Canarium* nuts were concerned, as evidenced still today by the number of old nut groves (**buruburuani**) near old coastal village sites. In the Gerasi area of the northern lagoon, even the barrier islands contain a substantial number of family-owned *Canarium* groves. This reflects a long and unbroken residential history of the Marovo-speaking, sea-oriented Gerasi **butubutu** whose headhunter strongholds used to be strategically placed on tall cliffs overlooking ocean and lagoon.

The significance of *Canarium* nuts as an important mediating link between the 'wet' and the 'dry' was indicated briefly in Chapter 4 and is worthy of additional attention at this stage. It was observed in Chapter 3 that the word **buruburu** applies both to nut-bearing *Canarium* trees and to the year, thus signifying the enormous importance placed on this tree in old Marovo. Elsewhere, Hviding (1996a:262-264) has analysed today's ritual importance of the annual harvesting of *Canarium* nuts whereby dispersed relatives return to their groups' places of origin in which family members own one or more *Canarium* trees inherited through generations of cognatic links. Historically, these nuts were not collected when fallen, as they are today, but were gathered by men climbing the tall trees with special ropes and breaking off nut clusters. This was regarded as a dangerous activity – still today, a number of herbal cures specifically designed for 'people who have fallen down from trees' are remembered. Tree climbing was conducted only under the protection of the guardian spirits of climbers, the **sinare** – of which most **butubutu** had one. These spirits would cushion any fall from *Canarium* trees, sago palms, and whatever else, and protect falling people from injury when hitting the ground. **Sinare** were often the spirits of ancestors who had miraculously survived some form of ordeal in the 'wild' (see Hviding, 1995c:69-71 for an example from southern Vangunu), and were closely tied to other aspects of old New Georgian religion. Thus it is said by most elders that the demise of the power of the **sinare** resulting from the general collapse of religious-political regimes around the turn of the century made it unsafe to climb *Canarium* trees any longer.

Yet the importance of the nuts, whether collected from the ground or from above, has remained constant through centuries into the present, as has the axiom that after a season of particularly good fruit, the *Canarium* trees will have one year of poor fruit. In former times, the cracking of the nuts (with small stone hammers) and extraction of the kernels were activities for communal rituals dominated by adult men. Large leaf parcels (**boboro**) of smoke-dried nuts, preserved after long processing over smouldering fires, formed part of the currency repertoire in interisland exchange and were a major export item of *Canarium*-rich Marovo. Today, the gathering of fallen nuts is mainly a women's task, and in terms of export, biscuit tins or plastic flour buckets filled with such nuts (sometimes crushed, sometimes whole) are a major income source for the women of a number of Marovo villages.

Canarium trees, whose tall white trunks are easily distinguishable in any type of forest, are indicative of past human occupation. Since these trees cannot be propagated through cut branches but must grow from the seed, it is generally reckoned that most groves and single trees have been planted and carefully tended by past generations, or that they are the result of conscious cultivation of spontaneous seedlings in the forest whereby these seedlings were watched over and nourished (through mulching) while their surroundings were kept cleared. It is widely believed that 'the people of old' also moved seedlings found in the inner forest to groves closer to their settlements, where the small trees would be mulched around the base and pollarded as they grew. But by any standard it is the fruit bat (**vahu**) that is regarded in Marovo as the most efficient propagator of *Canarium* trees. These large bats, important in Marovo folklore as well as being a culinary delicacy, are known to be eager consumers of the soft flesh of *Canarium* nuts which they carry along and drop once the flesh is eaten. In fact the small Marovo Island which is reckoned to contain the largest density of *Canarium* trees anywhere in the area is said, according to a principal story from the oral traditions of central Marovo (Hviding, 1995c:2-24), to have received this 'blessing' (**tinamanae**) from a particular fruit bat that brought clusters of nuts all the way from Simbo far to the west.

Coastal land use: the evidence from Marovo Island

Let us now move back to the general relationship in Marovo between 'dry' and 'wet' crops. The relationship between dryland taro from swiddens and wetland taro from irrigated pondfields, amounting almost to a profane:sacred (alternatively mundane:prestige) distinction with undertones of genderisation, has already been touched upon. However, a further hypothesis appears feasible. Since there is no reason to assume that the coastal people obtained all their root crops through barter with bush people, they may well have cultivated some dryland taro in their coastal yam swiddens. The only qualification to this would be the possibility that growing taro for these groups would be a symbolic transgression of the hierarchical distinction between bush (taro) people and coastal (fish) people upon which much of their claim to power hinged, and on which the institutionalised barter of 'wet' and 'dry' things was built. No such qualification is apparent from the available information, including present-day statements.

It is worthwhile to expand the view a bit, in order to consider the agroforestry system of the fishing-and-warfare-oriented coastal people specifically. The major role of a multitude of trees also in the nearshore, lowland swidden and secondary growth complexes of the coastal people of Marovo is evident from observations of their old strongholds, such as that of the small Marovo Island which hugs the coast of mainland Vangunu in the middle of the lagoon. This steep volcanic peak, fringed by narrow coral beach terraces and with rich soil as noted in Chapter 4, had a mid-to-late 19th century population that included "four hundred warriors with axes and shields", as the saying goes. Dense settlement is evidenced by a multitude of old coastal and uphill hamlet and village sites, some terraced and fortified and some conspicuously laid out in the open along the outer seashore, and a similar multitude of dedicated stone structures including old sacrificial shrines, warriors' training grounds and canoe house foundations. As one would expect, there are no remains of taro pondfields here – the coastal people of the old days are likely to have carried out only modest agricultural activity themselves.[3] In addition, Marovo Island is virtually waterless, with only a few tiny streams.[4]

Today, Marovo Island supports a population of about 800 (in three large villages) on a total land area of some seven square kilometres, less than a third of which is under cultivation or recent fallow. The coastal people of Marovo Island are no longer able to invoke tribute or institutionalised barter to obtain their root crop staples, and with high population growth the areas of good soil are becoming scarce. As in former centuries, however, Marovo Island continues to maintain a widespread network of transactions, whereby its villagers today sell root crops and fruits even to the bush people along the Bareke coast – a reversal of sorts of the barter of olden times.

To the uninitiated observer, those parts of the island that are not under cultivation seem to be covered in rather lush rainforest. On closer examination, however, Marovo Island is revealed as an almost completely modified and still intact system of arboriculture, interspersed with open swiddens, the conspicuous tall gingers of recent fallows, and a few small spots of degraded grasslands. Marovo Island is known throughout the area to have the greatest abundance of *Canarium* trees anywhere in the Marovo Lagoon, and their conspicuous white trunks stand out all around the forest, fallows, gardens and village areas and form backdrops to modest sloping stands of coconut palms along the coast. Furthermore, a walk through the steep hillside forest reveals that a striking proportion of the other trees are species of particular importance for their fruits, their medicinal properties, their suitability for construction wood, and more. This staggering variety of useful trees, the people of the little island proudly point out, is (to quote one of them)

... something that the people of the old days created. Since they had this blessing here of having so many **maria** and **ngoete** [*Canarium salomonense* and *C. indicum*] trees growing, they planted more, and more, all around, and they saw to it that those nut trees and other useful trees that came up grew big. And they planted fruit trees, and trees for medicine. And many trees growing around the old house sites show that the people then were wise and planted good trees nearby. So the forest on this island here is not just any forest, it is really important and useful, nearly every place has good trees which you can benefit from.

To further augment their good fortune, these descendants of old headhunting groups have, according to their own claims, the best soil in all of Marovo. This is borne out by sweet potato swiddens in their fifth decade of virtually continuous cultivation in which adjacent sub-sections alternate in a way that involves fallow periods of no more than three years. Much of the island is endowed with a rich black volcanic soil that does not seem to require the longer fallow periods usual for the poorer, often brown-to-red soils of the mainland (Figure 4.7). The remarkable agroforestry-and-arbori-culture system briefly described here is explained by its present-day owners and operators as being of rather ancient origin. They themselves would not doubt that it was already in place when the first European visitors arrived.

Taro cultivation: interpreting the historical evidence

For a fuller description of the cultivation of taro we must depend on some later accounts than those of the early traders. The British naval lieutenant B.T. Somerville spent eight months in Marovo Lagoon in 1893-94 on board the surveying ship HMS *Penguin*. The Solomon Islands were then a newly established British Protectorate, and the notorious "trouble spots" of the New Georgia Group had to be investigated for purposes of colonial intervention, trade and navigation generally. However, Somerville does not describe any of the **ruta** pondfields, perhaps because he never saw them. It is clear from his reports that his local company and "great friends" were mainly men from the influential coastal groups of Repi, Marovo Island and Mugiri in the central lagoon. Indeed Somerville appears to have internalised some of the coastal people's contempt for the bush people, as shown by his reference to them as leading a "wretched life" in small, largely hidden (though nume-rous) settlements deep in the bush constantly in fear of marauding "saltwater men". The latter were, it seems, his only guides on the relatively few walks he made into the interior. And yet Somerville (1897:358) did allude to the existence of substantial inland populations. There must have been large well-organised groups operating complex irrigated taro systems, though probably already on the wane since traders and coconut cash cropping was becoming well established under self-imposed partial "pacification". For whatever reason, they escaped his otherwise eager attention.

Somerville does, however, describe in some detail the dryland cultiva-tion cycle for taro:

> Patches are cleared in the bush by axe and fire, and after a very short period of use (one or two crops) are allowed to lie fallow; when, in a remarkably brief time, they become more densely bushed than the surrounding untouched forest,

and are thus easily recognised when passing through it. The plants are neatly spaced in drill lines, and the small pits, necessary for the good growth of taro, are dug around each plant when it has got to a certain size. I have seen patches as much as two or three acres thus under cultivation. There are no native implements except a pointed stick. (Somerville, 1897:402)

How far do these "classic" Melanesian taro swiddens – very similar, for example, to those described more recently by Oliver (1955:10) for Bougainville – represent the agroforestry system of the New Georgia area before European contact? The reference to bush clearance by axes is significant, and indicates that important changes had already occurred by this time. Marovo in the 1890s was probably at least one generation removed from the end of the stone age. From visits ten years before Somerville's stay, Woodford (1890) reported that stone axes were difficult to find in New Georgia. Somerville (1897:398) confirms that in 1893 none could be purchased, having long since been sold to the traders or thrown away as useless.

One must suspect, therefore, that the swidden system that Somerville described had been expanded in importance by the coming of steel. We know from studies elsewhere in Melanesia that steel axes are 1.4-2.2 times more efficient than the stone tools for clearing trees and undergrowth (Salisbury, 1968; Clarke, 1971; Sillitoe, 1979). Because of enhanced efficiency the technological change from stone to steel must have contributed to the decline in irrigated terrace cultivation, which persisted in a few places but had disappeared altogether by the 1930s. Using steel axes for forest clearance, swiddens in New Guinea require only 800-1,200 hours of work per hectare (Bayliss-Smith and Golson, 1992), which is significantly less work than alternative systems such as **ruta**. For example, irrigated systems for taro production on Maewo in Vanuatu required (averaged over a three-year period) around 1,700 hours of work post-steel and almost 2,250 hours of work pre-steel (Spriggs, 1981:159). The need to do twice as much work per hectare to maintain the wetland system might have made sense in the political economy of old Marovo, but by the late 19th century the social underpinnings of the **ruta** were rapidly disintegrating. Before it had even come to the notice of Western scholarship, this remarkable elaboration of Melanesian agroforestry techniques was therefore being abandoned.

Archaeological and ethnographic evidence

Because they fell into disuse quite soon after regular European contact, pondfield systems have generally been neglected by those studying indigenous agriculture in Melanesia, despite the fact that the presence of irrigated terraces in north Guadalcanal was clearly stated in Mendaña's "discovery" account of 1568 (Amherst and Thomson, 1901, II:306). One exception is the study carried out in 1973 by Margaret Tedder and Susan Barrus. They uncovered traces of several irrigated pondfields deep in the interior of Kusaghe in northern New Georgia, and mapped two complete systems that had been long abandoned and overgrown by forest (Tedder, 1976). Redrawn from sketch maps by Tedder and Barrus, these two systems are reproduced in Figure 5.2, with a third system, mapped by Graham Baines in 1982 in the Vao area of southern Gatokae, also included. Tedder calculated that in the area surveyed, in the upper Mase river valley in Kusaghe district, at least one thousand people could have been supported by growing taro on 200 hectares of arable land, of which at least 100 hectares were under irrigated terraces. By contrast, in 1923 only 40-50 people, the last remaining inland "bushmen" in all of Marovo, were still living in this area. Tedder's field evidence suggested that stone-lined irrigation channels led water from side streams into the systems of stone-banked terraces. In one area of pondfields that was mapped, at Kapoara, each "step" in the flight of terraces is 8-13 metres wide, while a distance of 3-20 metres separates the stone wall of one terrace from the adjacent one in the sequence. The height of the bank or wall, i.e. the difference in elevation between adjacent terraces, is 2.5 metres. As well as inlets there are outlet channels to remove surplus water. To show such patterns in greater detail, the **ruta** system at Vao on Gatokae, mapped in a more elaborate manner by Graham Baines, is shown at larger scale in Figure 5.3, while a cross section of the Vao system, with an exaggerated vertical scale, is shown in Figure 5.4.

Oral histories were also supplied to Tedder by some of the older Kusaghe men who were young boys when this **ruta** system was finally abandoned:

> According to informants, the terraces were planted at the beginning of the rainy season, commencing with the top terrace. It appeared that the water was shut off when planting was completed but let in again later. The rain was carefully watched and if too much fell, water was let out ... [Taro varieties] used in the **ruta** were twice as big as these varieties are today. They said taro grown in the **ruta** was never diseased and never attacked by the Papuana beetle ... Our informants said that their grandfathers' whole life revolved around the growing of taro and the maintenance that the irrigated terraces required. When the people became involved in the cash economy on the coast, they no longer found time to constantly replant within every three to five days the taro shoots after removing the tubers, which is necessary in taro cultivation. (Tedder, 1976:46-47)

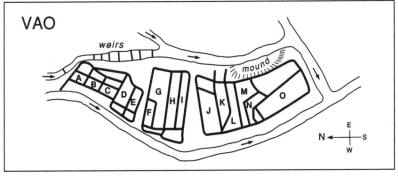

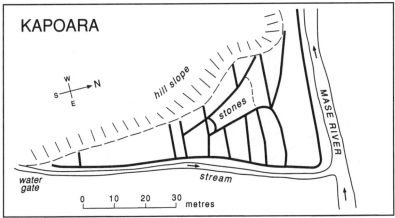

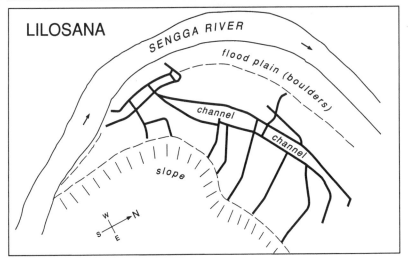

Figure 5.2 Three ruta **systems:**
the irrigated taro terraces at Vao (Gatokae Island) and at Kapoara and Lilosana
(Kusaghe, northern New Georgia). Redrawn after the sketch maps of G.B.K. Baines
(personal communication, see also Figures 5.3 and 5.4) and Tedder (1976:43).

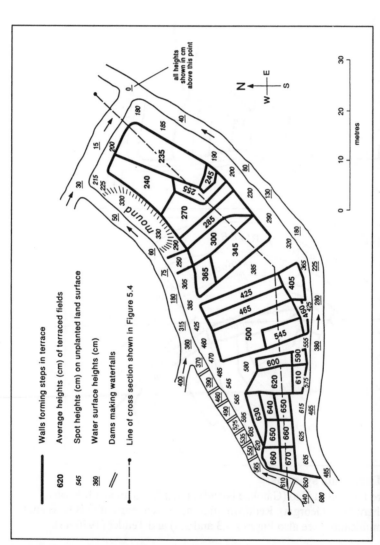

Figure 5.3   A reconstruction of the irrigated taro terraces at Vao, Gatokae Island
Based on a sketch map drawn by Graham Baines following his tape and compass survey of January-March 1982. The heights of the terraced fields are estimates based on Baines' measurements of the heights of the rock walls retaining the terraces, while the other spot heights shown are estimates interpolated from his measurements of the height of the stream water surface in relation to the adjacent land surface. The land slopes down from north to south; arrows indicate direction of stream flow.

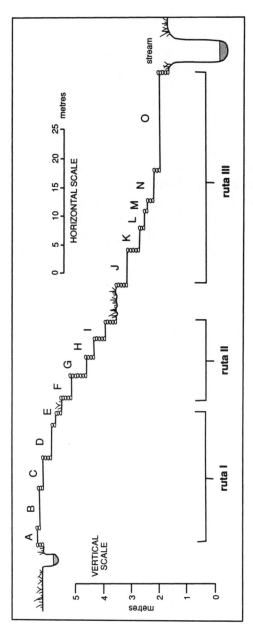

Figure 5.4 Cross-section of the Vao ruta system (vertical scale exaggerated five times)

Existing knowledge of **ruta** in the Marovo Lagoon area, especially among elders of the old bush groups of Vahole, Bareke, southern Vangunu and Gatokae, indicates that the pondfield systems there were quite similar to those documented from Kusaghe and Kolobangara. Among Marovo groups with a relatively recent past as **ruta** cultivators it is held that **ruta** were never established close to the lagoon coast. Instead, they were situated inland in the upper reaches of sloping river valleys – by the headwaters of major rivers and by smaller tributaries that fed the pondfields directly. Traces of taro terraces similar to those documented from Kusaghe can be seen today in many parts of the Marovo area, for example at Vao in southern Gatokae (Figure 5.2) and in the Vahole area of north-central New Georgia, and in several other locations inland. It is interesting, however, to note that some of the Gatokae systems, such as those of Vao near the island's southernmost weather coast, were in fact established much closer to the sea than the **ruta** of New Georgia Island. Perhaps this is a function of Gatokae's small size relative to the islands of Vangunu and New Georgia.[5]

The Vahole people of north-central Marovo were the last to abandon **ruta** cultivation. However, today there are only few remains of large pondfield terraces on Vahole land proper. The Vahole land faces the lagoon coast and today is centred on the lower reaches of the major Piongo Lavata river, where a number of smaller **ruta** were cultivated along tributaries. The remnants of the many large inland terrace systems on which the Vahole people base much of their history are to be found near the upper reaches of this river and its major tributaries, in the more mountainous Hoava and Hoeze districts located at the very centre of New Georgia Island and bridging old Marovo and Roviana. It was here that the 'true' bush-dwelling ancestral groups of today's Vahole people lived.[6] With reference to a corpus of stories and epic tales these inner lands with gently sloping river valleys are said to have been a very important area "a long time [at least 150 years] ago", with dense settlement and great **ruta** systems.

The inland basin of the Piongo Lavata is strategically located relative to both the Roviana and Marovo lagoons and is likely to have been an area of major importance to, and confluence of, the regional political systems of old New Georgia. The oral traditions of Ulusaghe proper, i.e. the lands and lagoons around southern New Georgia, Vangunu and Gatokae – attribute a similar role to the large crater basin sloping south-wards from the tall rims (> 1,000 metres) of Vangunu. At elevations from 200 to more than 500 metres, the river valleys on the southern slopes of this old volcanic core reportedly contain large **ruta** remnants in good condition, associated with several great settlement sites such as that of Rihe, a high crater location from which much of Vangunu's social basis is reckoned to have emerged in the form of six founding ancestresses (Hviding, 1996a:148-149).

None of these major areas have been surveyed by the authors beyond brief inland excursions to the lower perimeters of the inland Piongo Lavata basin and the Vangunu crater. We have therefore largely relied on oral traditions which, as indicated above, abound with tales about the size, importance and precise locations of major inland settlements of olden times. Well-known legends, tales about mythical beings and epic accounts of warfare and conquest highlight certain key settlements, some of which are referred to as 'abodes of seven thousand people', with populations that led lives structured by the requirements of cultivation and feasting cycles and tribute requirements. Activities in these great settlements centred on the cultivation of huge crops particularly of taro, the annual harvesting of *Canarium* nuts, regular feasting involving the participation of friends and allies from near and far, and – for some with a more coastal orientation – overseas trading journeys, as well as warfare and raiding sometimes in regional alliances involving virtual navies of war canoes (see Hviding, 1995c and 1996a for examples). Some of these great settlements may in their own right have been hierarchically integrated communities of taro-producing 'bush' people and headhunting (as well as fishing-oriented) 'coastal' people.

The botanical evidence

Lack of actual surveys notwithstanding, it is of great interest to note that the mapping of New Georgian forest types carried out by the late-colonial Land Resources Study (Wall and Hansell, 1975) appears to provide reliable indicators of the whereabouts of the large pondfield systems of former centuries. Most locations that according to oral traditions supported large **ruta** and associated swiddens are dominated today by conspicuous stands of the large **olanga** tree (*Campnosperma brevipetiolatum*). Tim Whitmore (1969, 1990; Burslem and Whitmore, 1996) has shown that this light-demanding tree is typical of locations where the canopy has been severely disturbed in the past. He describes vast tracts of land in northwest Santa Isabel that in the 1960s were covered with a high forest where 45% of the large trees (>180cm dbh [diameter at breast height]) were of this one species. He comments that "this particular area may well date from the abandonment of cultivations following the decimation of the local people by raiding parties from New Georgia across the Sound, which is known to have occurred within living memory late last century" (Whitmore, 1969:265). In New Georgia itself there are dense *Campnosperma* stands in upland river valleys precisely in places where oral traditions locate the old centres of bush settlement and **ruta** systems (e.g. Hoeze-Hoava, Vangunu-Rihe and southern Gatokae). The botanical evidence is a clear confirmation of what Marovo's own historians have told us. The area under **olanga** could also be a useful way to estimate the former extent of pondfield systems, and inland settlement more generally, throughout the New Georgia Group.

To follow this interesting lead, we measured the areas in the main inland zones of Marovo (Gatokae, Vangunu and New Georgia excluding Roviana) that have disturbed forest and with a dominant presence of **olanga** at canopy level, using the map of "Forest Types" from the late-colonial Land Resources Study by Wall and Hansell (1975:Map 4h). The forest types that interest us, all indicative of vegetation disturbance al least 50 years previously, are defined by Wall and Hansell (1975:Map 4h) as:

- **Flm**: Lowland closed-canopy forest with "*Campnosperma* commonly occurring";
- **Fld**: Lowland disturbed forest having a broken irregular canopy with "*Campnosperma* commonly occurring" as "scattered individuals amidst smaller often secondary trees";
- **Flk**: Lowland forest with a dense canopy of large-crowned trees, mainly *Campnosperma*;
- **Fhd**: Medium-height to tall hill forest having a broken, irregular canopy resulting from recent disturbance giving rise to gaps in the canopy and many small crowned probably secondary trees; "*Campnosperma* commonly occurring";
- **Fhk**: Hill forest "with a dense canopy dominated by large-crowned trees mainly *Campnosperma brevipetiolata*."

This map produced by the Land Resources Study is based on air photographs taken in August 1962. At that time the forest types in question covered 614 hectares on Gatokae, 3,948 hectares on Vangunu, and 2,520 hectares on the "Marovo" portion of inland New Georgia. These figures become more informative when we realise that the **Fhk** and **Fhd** types of forest are closely concentrated in hill locations where once existed the most important settlement-and-**ruta** complexes of the bush people.

For example, a tract of disturbed but *Campnosperma*-rich **Fhd** forest covers 419 hectares on the easternmost peninsula of Gatokae, where the legendary twin settlements of Tige Ulu and Tige Peka, the combined abode of 7,000 people leading lives in abundance and splendour with great feast of regional importance (Hviding, 1995c:26-47). And similarly, the western and southwestern slopes of the mighty crater of central Vangunu have more than 1,600 hectares of **Fhk** forest along river valleys, while the upper valleys of the Sagivi [Sanggivi] river which flows south right from the crater core and the foundational settlement site at Rihe are rimmed by **Fhd** forest. On the lagoon side of Vangunu there is a conspicuous 81 hectare patch of **Fhd** forest uphill at a location overlooking the present-day Bareke village of Rukutu not far from Repi, a central place for the regularised barter between bush people and coastal people. This, too, corresponds with local traditions as to where people lived and worked their taro. In New Georgia the upper reaches of the Piongo Lavata river and nearby Vahole hills are areas known for the dense presence of **ruta** partly persisting into the 20th century. In 1962 these areas were totally dominated by **Flm** forest (797 hectares) typically following the river valleys where the settlement-and-**ruta** complexes of the Kalikolo groups were located.

What do these observations imply? If we follow Tedder's approach to old Kusaghe, we might assume that a quarter of this "arable" area of 3,948 hectares was under taro (pondfield and swidden) at any one time (the rest being under fallow), and that land under taro supports 0.2 persons per hectare (Tedder 1976). This would give us $(3,948 \times 0.25):0.2 = 4,935$ people sustained by the areas of pondfield and swidden cultivation on Vangunu implied by the total disturbed area on the forest map. Some of these people must have lived in the bush, while others – supported partly by fish-for-taro barter – were basically non-agricultural 'salt-water' people on the coast.

While these figures raise little suspicion, problems arise when a more sophisticated analysis is attempted, using data on yields and frequency of cultivation. For example, if just 10% of the mapped 3,948 hectares were pondfields, being cultivated 8 years out of 10 and yielding (conservatively estimated) 20 tons of taro per hectare, and the remaining 90% were taro (and some yam) swiddens with a long bush fallow (cultivated 1 year out of 20), we come up with an annual production of 6,892 tonnes of taro for Vangunu alone. If this supplied merely half the dietary needs of the inland and coastal population, we would be looking at a "carrying capacity" of 23,767 people – probably an unrealistic figure for old central Marovo, even exceeding that implied by the number of legendary abodes of 7,000. Yet it is based on a conservative estimate of yield and fallow. Based on data from Western Polynesia Kirch (1994) argues that the Futuna equivalent of the New Georgian **ruta** is twice as productive as the modest 20t/hectare figure used by us, and for a swidden one could easily imagine land being used more frequently than one year in 20.

Less sensational estimates of the relationships between taro yields and the population of old Marovo could be attempted. Let us use Tedder's starting point again, assuming 0.2 hectare of cultivation per "head" of population, and adding our suggestion that 10 per cent of the mapped disturbed forest were pondfields and the rest swiddens. Following Tedder's estimates and the maps by Margaret Tedder and Graham Baines shown in Figures 5.2-5.4, 50% of the total **ruta** area would be in taro cultivation, the rest taken up by walls and channels. And of the swidden land, 5% would be producing taro and yams (on our basis of a 20 year cycle with one year of cropping). Each hectare of disturbed/secondary *Campnosperma*-dominated forest would then represent, on average:

> **ruta**: 50% of 0.1 hectare = 0.050 hectare under taro;
> swidden: 5% of 0.9 hectare = 0.045 hectare under taro and yams.

The total area under root crops per hectare would be 0.095 hectares. Based on a requirement of about 0.2 hectare in cultivation per person, 1 hectare would support 5 persons and 0.095 hectare consequently 0.475 persons. The population that could be supported by root crop production from the inland agroforestry regimes of old Marovo could then be estimated as follows:

> Gatokae: 614 hectares; 291 persons
> Vangunu: 3,948 hectares; 1,875 persons
> New Georgia (excluding Roviana and most of Kusaghe): 2,520 hectares; 1,197 persons.

This total of 3,363 persons does not seem to be an overly large estimate. It may indeed be too conservative. Slight variation in our assumptions would lead to higher figures, but still realistic ones. If we assume that pondfields constituted not 10 but 25% of cultivated inland areas, we reach a total population estimate for "old Marovo" of 5,665 persons. Considering the 1970 census population of 4,538 and the 1999 estimate of around 11,000, bearing in mind the density of inland settlement sites still evident, and all the uncertainties in our estimating procedures, relating **ruta** production to a population of around 6,000 is entirely justified but still a rather cautious estimate.

   Finally, in this context it needs to be pointed out that "carrying capacity" for old Marovo cannot be measured on the assumption that all taro harvested went towards feeding the population of the area. Even in today's Marovo, 'good times' are measured with reference to whether one's household is able both to feed any number of unexpected visitors while still being able to throw away substantial quantities of leftover food surplus to the needs of the household (including visitors). "These are poor times", 80-year old **butubutu** leader Dyson Kiko Jimuru of Chea village said to one of us one day in the 'dry' tradewind season of 1986, and continued, "for so many mornings now, we haven't been able to throw much food away into the sea, and nothing is left to rot!". Far from being anecdotal, this glimpse of everyday rhetoric about good times and bad points to the need in Marovo to afford waste and defines a deeper pattern of conspicuous consumption. The grand feasts of before, it is often pointed out, involved the literal throwing-away of food – hence the quantities of taro necessitating a separate number (**vuro**) for tens of thousand. Adding to this in old Marovo would be the substantial, and perennial, needs for taro as an ingredient in all the puddings being burned in shrines as offerings to ancestors and other spirits. And today's common sight of small piles of rotting crops in the village "tithe-house" – the important thing is to offer the tithe, and whether or not it is bought back again from the tithe-house for consumption by others is regarded as a moot point – is a smaller-scale echo of the "waste" that is likely to have character-ised the handling of huge taro harvests in olden times. The **ruta** of old Marovo could, and had to, produce far more taro than what was needed to sustain the people of the lagoon and surrounding lands. Attempts at quantifying "carrying capacity" must take such considerations into account.

A closer look at ruta technology

In other parts of Melanesia irrigated pondfield systems are noted for their high productivity (Spriggs, 1981, 1984, 1990). The relative importance of irrigated terraces compared to forest swiddens must have varied in different parts of New Georgia, but we believe that in general the **ruta** systems of the area were far more important that has hitherto been recognised. **Ruta** were invisible to visitors like Somerville, being hidden from the coast. With an increasing frequency of European trader contact from ca. 1850 onwards the system was soon destabilised, as **ruta** cultivation was vulnerable to dis-ruption through warfare (intensified from the first arrivals of steel axes) and population migration (intensified during a latter stage of indigenous "pacifi-cation", cf. Hviding, 1996a, ch. 3). In post-steel times its relatively labour-intensive character made it a less attractive option than forest swiddening, while subsequently (as noted by Tedder, 1976) the new demands imposed by coastal residence and cash cropping further destroyed the viability of the **ruta** system.

In some relatively isolated parts of northern Marovo, such as the Vahole area, a few **ruta** systems were under cultivation into the 1930s. There is even the possibility of continuity until the 1940s, as Japanese wartime incursions forced people to lead a migratory, secret existence for almost two years. Even today some elements of **ruta** cultivation survive here, as a few elderly couples maintain **ruta kisi** (Marovo: **ruta kiki**, 'small pondfield') along tributaries to the Piongo Lavata river where most Vahole people have 'bush gardens' and small cocoa plantations (see Chapter 8). As already mentioned, these relict **ruta** are simply small shallow pools into which water flow is regulated by means of a few logs. The Vahole people offer the following **ruta** typology:

1. The proper, large **ruta**; elaborately constructed terraced pondfield systems with rock walls supplemented by the use of water-and-rot-resistant logs (see below), cultivated by larger groups on a communal basis under chiefly supervision. They supported the full perennial, rotational three-stage system of nursery fields and continuous cultivation (plots of replanted tops, of replanted sucker corms and of sprouting sucker corms, respectively) outlined previously in this chapter. When **ruta** are talked about today it is usually with reference to this ultimate form of large-scale surplus-producing irrigation. Examples are shown in Figures 5.2-5.4.

2. Smaller **ruta** established by slight modification of a natural water pool formed in or along a stream, whereby rock walls or wooden fences are built to regulate water flow. Generally cultivated by families for subsistence purposes.

3. Small **ruta** in natural, non-modified trenches or small 'valleys' (**lolomo**) where pools are formed by a slow-flowing stream and drainage is natural through that stream or through underground channels. This type of cultivation is also for family-level subsistence, often on an *ad hoc* basis though long-lasting in particularly suitable places where they may, however, be gradually modified into the intermediate type 2.

While terrace and channel walls were mainly made of stone, wood – taken from a few special trees only – was also necessary for the construction of **ruta**. Woods used for **ruta** construction had to be resistant to waterlogging and decay. Indeed the two trees favoured most strongly for **ruta** construction are regarded as having wood that will neither die nor rot once cut. One of these is **tige piru**, the 'wild cut-nut' (*Barringtonia* sp.), a tree that occurs in wet places in the forest and that has a capacity for growing back quickly if felled. The other tree important in **ruta** construction bears further examination. This is the rather small lowland **choku** tree (probably *Fagraea racemosa*), often also called **beri** or **beriberi** in Marovo. In the Hoava language of Vahole it is called **heuku**, and in the Bareke language of northern Vangunu it is called **soku**. The observant reader will notice that its names in Marovo and Hoava (and, by extension, that in Bareke) corresponds to the verb 'to plant/cultivate' and to the noun 'digging stick'. Apparently we are here dealing with a tree traditionally regarded as being of paramount agricultural importance, most likely in its capacity as "the stuff that **ruta** were made of" and as a preferred wood also for fences that keep feral pigs out of swiddens. The **choku** tree grows near rivers. If dead, rotten bark of this tree touches your skin, you will itch and scratch.

Honey bees tend to be abundant in **choku** trees, and finally, it is said that **mago** (malevolent spirit-like creatures of the forest) are afraid of this tree and will not go underneath it. The **choku** tree, then, embodies the sweetness of honey whose producers it entices, and simultaneously it repels evil spirits. Thus it attracts the good and repels the bad and may well be viewed as a tree with a capacity for guarding over a **ruta** or swidden, as well as having wood with the right properties.

Despite the general abandoning of **ruta** from the turn of the century onwards, **ruta** remain important in Marovo people's lives. In 1996, some of the special *Colocasia* wetland varieties termed **talo ruta** were still being cultivated in Vahole in the small pondfields mentioned. And beyond such modest survivals, the 'proper', large pondfields are still in an important sense significant in today's Marovo. At the beginning of the book we quoted the concerned modern-day leader who suggested a need for reviving **ruta** cultivation. On another level, old people may comment today, sometimes quite emotionally, on the perceived beauty of a full stand of **ruta** taro in the cool shade of the partly retained surrounding forest canopy. As documented from other parts of Melanesia – e.g. the Baktaman and Bolivip of inner New Guinea (Barth, 1975:33; Crook, 1998:50) – there is an emotional dimension to taro cultivation which should not be unerrrated. The well-growing pond-field and its environs represent the interrelation of land, water, trees and cherished plant life under careful human cultivation in order to provide the most prized food, and embodying the practical, the magical and the aesthetic – thus constituting the essence of what **mana** (and a 'good life', at that) was, and is, supposed to be all about. In the words of Tony Crook, "the experience of entering one's garden to find the taros dancing, their leaf faces nodding happily in the breeze, rejoicing at the visit of their father and mother, gives evident satisfaction".

Agroforestry components and their interaction

In summary, we are proposing that the Marovo agroforestry system around the time of regular European contact (around 1840) had three major components, reflected in indigenous categorisations: irrigated, terraced taro pond-fields (**ruta**), mixed bush fallow swiddens of various types (**chigo**), and the enriched fallow of well-developed secondary forest, in particular *Canarium* nut groves (**buruburuani**). In addition, the significant gathering component of people's activities in the forest should not be overlooked, yielding then as now a great variety of edible wild leafy greens, ferns, and wild yams, as well as many important medicinal plants which are overall reckoned to be more abundant in secondary forest. Some of the range of this gathering was

described early on in this chapter for the bush people of Bareke in old
Marovo. Some hunting also depended (as it still does) directly on the agroforestry system, in that birds (such as parrots and cockatoos) and, not least,
fruit bats seek their food from cultivated trees and from surrounding
secondary forest.[7]

The **ruta** pondfields provided perennial wetland cultivation of taro on
cleared sites adjacent to streams with alluvial or colluvial soils. The **chigo**
bush fallow gardens had a complex intercropping of further taro, yams,
bananas, sugar cane, and various vegetables such as the important shrub
ngache (*Hibiscus manihot*). Yams of many types seem to have been particularly important in the coastal people's swiddens as a staple crop, though
with a marked seasonality (as indicated for Roviana Lagoon by Vudere
[1975:4]). A scattered canopy layer of useful trees was maintained in these
gardens, particularly coconuts, further *Canarium* nut trees and maybe a few
breadfruit trees (**omo**, *Artocarpus altilis*). This canopy layer also included
Tahitian chestnut (**ivi**, *Inocarpus fagiferus*), cut nut (**tige**, *Barringtonia* spp.),
the **popoli** fruit tree (*Terminalia solomonensis*) and Malay apple (**apuchu**,
Syzygium [Eugenia] malaccensis). Over time these trees would have become
an increasingly prominent part of the secondary forest in those areas that had
previously been cultivated. We do not have information on the period of
bush fallow in old Marovo, but 5-15 years is the kind of period that would
have been necessary for soils to recover their nutrient status and for the
useful shrubs and trees not to be eliminated by full competition with the
secondary forest species. This aspect of inter-species competition underpins
the view held by Marovo Island people that the rich arboriculture system of
their island's forest has long been consciously manipulated and developed.

We can only speculate at this point in time about this agroforestry
system's ecological character. However, if our reconstruction is correct, then
it has all the hallmarks of a stable and ecologically sound land use system.
Wetland cultivation of taro is inherently productive and sustainable. Yam
and taro under dryland conditions both require a high level of soil fertility,
and these crops are not normally grown more than once or twice before a site
is abandoned to bush fallow. The regeneration of secondary forest is thus
assured, since plots are recycled quickly to bush, through a stage of luxurious ginger growth that shuts out light, before the grass and weedy annual
species of degraded soils have a chance to get established. The ecological
stability of the system and its economic value are further increased by the
fruit, nut and timber trees that form an integral part of the bush fallow and
subsequent intercropping. This indigenous agroforestry system started to be
modified at a rapidly increasing rate by the direct and indirect effects of
European contact from the mid-19th century.

6 The Great Transformations, 1880-1910

Marovo agroforestry one hundred years ago

As we have already shown, by the time the Marovo agroforestry system received its first description by Somerville (1897), long-standing patterns of land use around the lagoon, and deep in the forest, were already being modified at an accelerating pace. Large-scale irrigated pondfield cultivation was probably already on the wane since traders, coconut cash cropping and a shift to coastal settlements were becoming well established under self-imposed partial "pacification" – a significant component of the oral histories told by the coastal groups themselves (Hviding, 1996a:97-99, 116-118). Somerville's account resulted from his eight months of coastal surveying work on board the HMS *Penguin* in Marovo Lagoon and elsewhere around New Georgia. While in the Marovo Lagoon, the *Penguin* used the coastal communities at Marovo Island and at Repi (some 8 kilometres due east of Marovo Island, on the mainland coast adjacent to the Bareke hills) as a main base, and there was regular, close contact with the men of these groups. The officers and men of the *Penguin* were even invited to attend funerary feasting in honour of a recently deceased Repi chief, and Somerville who was the ship's main ethnographic observer counted a number of named Repi and Marovo chiefs and warriors as his "great friends" (Somerville, 1897, nd).

Somerville's notes refer to the beginnings of major changes, not only in the use of steel axes for taro swiddens but also in patterns of trade, settlement and overall demography. The hierarchical distinction between bush people and coastal people still prevailed in 1893. He refers to inland areas as being "fairly well inhabited in the interior slopes and valleys of the hills where, in quite a small radius, huts and buildings appeared on all sides in the midst of the bush; quite invisible, however, to a passing ship or canoe" (Somerville, 1897:358). As already explained in relation to **ruta** (see Chapter 5), most of Somerville's contacts were with the coastal people, and

145

he internalised much of their dismissive attitude towards "man-bush". Thus his observations of inland life were sketchy, to say the least.

In addition, his impressions of agricultural activity would have been based mainly on observations of the dryland agroforestry of the coastal Repi and Marovo Island people. Somerville considered the variety of cultivated staple foods in Marovo Lagoon to be rather small:

> Yams are scarcely grown, as they do badly, and are very small when produced .... Taro, sugar cane, sweet potato and ... the Cape Marsh potato ... exhausts the list of vegetables under cultivation. Bananas, pawpaws and a poor species of breadfruit are the only cultivated fruits .... The coconut is, of course, the main staple of existence. (Somerville, 1897:402, 380-381)

The last remark about the coconut must refer to its growing importance as a trade item, rather than its subsistence role – although the liquid squeezed from grated dry coconut meat soaked in water was, and is, a ubiquitous "fat-enhancing" ingredient in proper Marovo cooking (Leivestad, 1995; Bayliss-Smith, 1993). There were two traders actually based in Marovo Lagoon in the 1890s, buying copra from coastal people as well as planting their own coconuts. Somerville's remarks about yams may also reflect the "saltwater bias" of his informants, or may indicate a genuine decline in the importance in Marovo of a crop that is generally regarded as more labour intensive than taro or, especially, sweet potato.

The presence of the sweet potato in Somerville's list is in fact the first evidence beyond oral history that we have for its introduction to Marovo specifically, and the first mention for New Georgia since Cheyne's visit to Roviana in 1844, as discussed in Chapter 5. The "Cape Marsh potato" is a mysterious though intriguing reference to a plant that Somerville says was grown principally in the Russell (or Cape Marsh) Islands, and which in taste was "nearly approaching the Irish potato in flavour and flouriness" (Somerville, 1897:380). In appearance it was "something resembling the appearance of the sweet potato when growing, but far better eating" (Somerville, 1897: 402). We can only presume that this was an improved variety of the sweet potato *Ipomoea batatas*, newly introduced to Marovo Lagoon as a result of the Marovo people's regular canoe journeys, for raiding and trading, to and from the Russell Islands.

The papaya (*Carica papaya*, also called pawpaw, and **manioko** in Marovo) which Somerville also mentions may have arrived by a similar route as that of the sweet potato, or perhaps was introduced by one of the white traders who were starting shore-based operations in Marovo at this time. The papaya was almost certainly absent in pre-European times, and appears to have been among the first of the many new plants (including weeds) that were becoming integrated into the expanding dryland agro-forestry system.

The rise of the sweet potato

Around the turn of the century, the dryland system was itself starting to change. As we have already indicated, it is probable that by the 1890s the large-scale taro swiddens that Somerville saw were gradually replacing the irrigated taro terraces as the main type of garden – indeed Somerville failed to mention the **ruta** technology at all, despite his wide-ranging curiosity about all aspects of Marovo life and livelihood (see Chapter 5 for alternative explanations of this information gap). By the 1890s, some fifty years of availability of steel technology may also have resulted in the more complete clearance of bush fallows, itself much easier to accomplish with steel tools but in any case a desirable preparation if sites were to be planted for culti-vation of sweet potato rather than taro. This new plant, with its perennial and much longer cropping period (up to five years, and even longer in certain places) and tolerance of poorer soils, also provided the means for fallows to be deflected towards more impoverished kinds of regrowth. However, in many parts of Marovo this new cropping pattern did not start until after 1915, when the pattern of larger "mission" villages all in coastal locations became established.

It thus seems likely that both the sweet potato and steel tools were introduced in Marovo through the trading contacts of the coastal people, whether by Europeans or by visitors from other islands in the Solomons. It is also likely that it was the coastal people who first took up intensive culti-vation of the sweet potato, suitable as it was for small open swiddens in their pockets of coastal land. Its perennial nature was a further advantage, com-pared to the more marked seasonality of yams. We can hypothesise that taking up cultivation of this new staple-type crop was a useful addition to the more prestige-oriented taro, which was cultivated mainly by the bush people and was obtainable by coastal people through barter and forms of tribute. The adoption of the sweet potato would have decreased the coastal people's reliance on bartered taro as a staple, channelling the latter more directly to the complex system of feast-giving that underpinned the pre-colonial politics of the Marovo Lagoon. Among the bush people, however, the sweet potato is likely to have remained unimportant, as reported by old people born in the bush before the turn of the century. Thus the introduction of the sweet potato did not initially upset the taro-based prestige-goods and tribute system. And significantly, the sweet potato did not greatly influence the fundamental Marovo notion that the proper components of a balanced meal are taro (as

nginongo, 'food') and fish (the latter to some degree substitutable as a main form of **binaso** ['that which is eaten with food'] by animal protein from the bush). In oral history and tales of the past, the presence of roasted taro as the staple food is universal.

Transformations and upheavals: the links to trade

The end of the 19th century also saw some fundamental changes in exchange relationships resulting from the beginnings of large-scale production of coconut for market exchange. Somerville does not directly discuss this trend, despite working mainly among the coastal communities who were the first to embrace the new opportunities of cash cropping (on the other hand his ethnographic interests lay elsewhere). He does, however, mention that in 1893-94 coconuts and copra were the main items sold to white traders, along with pearl shell and turtle shell.

Marovo people themselves consider copra to have been their first regular source of cash income in the nineteenth century. The turning point came around 1880, when planters and traders bought land on islands in the lagoon and established plantations and stations (Bennett, 1987:Appendix 5). Before this time only intermittent trading with Europeans had taken place, with passing traders purchasing turtle shell and "curios" in exchange for tobacco, pipes and iron or steel implements. There was some regularity already in this early trading contact: Findlay (1877:773) mentions that "... Sydney traders go in and anchor [in a passage through the barrier reef of central Marovo], to trade with the natives of *Repi* and *Marovo*, villages on the main island ...", and Somerville (1897:360) refers to the island of Marovo as being "... in old times the most populous and agreeable to trade at of any of the places near by ...". This regular participation in trade with Europeans by the coastal people living in and near the Marovo Island stronghold is likely to have generated a diversifying flow in both directions, causing a transformation of agriculture through the introduction of steel tools and new crops.

Traditionally the coastal people who were benefiting from this new trade had depended for much of their food supply on barter with (and tribute from) the bush communities. The sweet potato may have been one reason for the breakdown of this interdependence. But another important cause was political instability which culminated in the numerous disastrous raids, massacres and epidemics and significant depopulation that Marovo suffered in the years 1870-1900. This is remembered as a time of intermittent but rampant dysentery epidemics. Furthermore, people from other islands such as Santa Isabel, Choiseul and the Russell Islands, who had been plagued for centuries by New Georgia's headhunters, by now had obtained their own rifles and in several instances combined forces in counterattacks on Marovo.

Accelerated and more unpredictable warfare also led to some population migration. Somerville (1897:358, 399) and Woodford (1890) perhaps exaggerated when they imply that the very existence of inland population in New Georgia is related to the security that the bush provided. As we have seen, the resource base of inland forests was substantial, and taro production at least was responsive to intensification in response to coastal demand. On the other hand there is some archaeological evidence from northwest New Georgia of coastal village abandonment in the 19th century, which supports the notion of depopulation and possibly settlement migration inland (Reeve, 1989:63; see also Hviding, 1996a:83, 393n8). Warfare had certainly escalated since the 1840s, with the introduction of tomahawks and rifles and the steel technology that freed men's labour time (McKinnon, 1975). In the twenty years prior to 1893 headhunting "had almost annihilated some villages, and driven the wretched remnant back into the bush, thus giving the appearance of absolute depopulation" (Somerville, 1897:410). Marovo Island, for example, had been reduced since 1885 from about 500 people to less than one hundred – at least according to Somerville (1897: 399). Although no disasters of such magnitude form part of the oral histories of Marovo Island people, these years are nevertheless talked about as fraught with misfortune, disease, political conflict and general disruption.

In these circumstances the institutionalised bush/coastal barter must have diminished. For the relict communities on the coast, this provided an added incentive to grow a high yielding, short fallow crop like the sweet potato. The full story of this crop's diffusion into the Marovo Lagoon cannot now be reconstructed, but by 1910 with the end of headhunting and the migration of all settlements to the coast, the pre-conditions for the sweet potato's full integration into the Marovo agricultural system were well established.

The years 1880-1910 were therefore a period when coastal people increasingly took up intensive agriculture, while bush people settled on the coast and increasingly took up fishing. Whereas formerly, bush people did not even venture out to the open coasts of the lagoon, increased inter-marriage now combined with permanent reciprocal exchanges of use rights to give both groups extended access to both land and sea resources. This was a time of settlement upheaval, group fission and reorganisation in Marovo. Splits at the former stronghold on Marovo Island already around 1870 had caused several ostracised groups from there to form strong friendly links with the bush people of Bareke in northeastern Vangunu, thereby obtaining garden land in exchange for, first, protection, and later, fishing rights. These were the Repi people who became Somerville's "great friends" in 1893. The collapse of the barter system started, and a more flexible integration of agriculture and fishing and of coastal and bush identities began to develop, as inter-group hostilities diminished, and as the energy-demanding centralised 'salt-water' polities of coastal people crumbled.

From headhunting to horticulture

It therefore came about that when missionaries arrived in 1912-1915 they found a number of former headhunting chiefs now peacefully preoccupied with cultivating large swidden gardens on coastal land obtained from bush people in-laws, rather than organising warfare and bloodfeuds, exacting tribute and giving regional feasts with invited chiefs and warriors from near and far in the New Georgia Group. The headhunters had become dedicated "horticulturists", and it is said by old people of Marovo that many a tough man who had previously rarely set foot in a garden now showed great concern for the finer technicalities of swidden cultivation.

The heightened value of good garden land and agricultural activities, and a complete collapse of the prestige-economy system of warfare and exchange is highlighted by the following statement given in 1915 by Tatagu, a former leader at the Marovo Island headhunter stronghold which after a long history of internal conflict disintegrated around 1910. By 1915 Tatagu had thus been stripped of much of his formidable power and was spending the greater part of his time as an agriculturalist and in-law on the land of his wife's 'bush people' at Bareke. When approached in his hill garden by a pioneer Seventh-day Adventist missionary who asked him, in his still recognised capacity as a man of power, for permission to establish a mission school on Marovo Island, he is reported by his brother's son as having replied: "I want my children to go to school, but today I cannot say yes, because I have no ground" (Pana, 1965). Only ten years before, having very little land was a fact of life for Marovo's coastal people, and would not at all have interfered with the capacity of a chief and strongman like Tatagu to say yes or no in important political matters. The decision-making power that once was based on the economy of warfare, prestige and exchange had collapsed by 1915, to be replaced by new sources of economic power and prestige.

The abandonment of taro pondfields

In pan-Marovo terms, the incentive to produce surplus taro may have diminished rather rapidly as the structure of authority, dominated by powerful coastal groups, collapsed in the period 1905-1915 under the combined attack of colonial rule and mission influence. On a lesser scale, though, the key position in Marovo feasts occupied by puddings made of taro baked with *Canarium* nuts continued, and was noted by the traveller Paravicini (1931: 176) in the 1920s and by the colonial officer Tom Russell (1948a:319) right after World War II. This pattern continues until today (cf. Leivestad, nd), and as will be shown in Chapter 8, taro cultivation has experienced something of a revival since the late 1980s. But with the demise of chiefly strongmen and the complete collapse of the headhunting-based ceremonial cycles, feasting and the associated puddings were quickly integrated into the domain of the Seventh-day Adventist and Methodist churches.

Historical material from Marovo, combined with documentation from elsewhere in the Pacific of the role of "big men" and chiefs in mobilising surplus production, for example in irrigated taro cultivation on Aneityum in Vanuatu (Spriggs, 1990), suggests that the Marovo **ruta** systems were to a large degree organised by and for the chiefs. The tribute system itself may well have been based on rather long-term hierarchical relationships between bush chiefs and coastal chiefs, whereby the former would have mobilised the 'common people' of their own **butubutu** for heavily intensified taro production according to the cyclical ceremonial needs of the latter. Certainly the category of **ngicha** (male and female 'commoners' or 'people who serve'), distinct from but bound to the superior "troikas" (Keesing, 1985) of **bangara** ('chiefs'), **varane** ('leading warriors') and **chiama** ('priests'), is said to have formed the major working segment of any **butubutu** of old Marovo (though probably most markedly among the coastal groups). This hierarchy would enable the leaders of most **butubutu** to rely on a large and stable workforce of their own for meeting the perennial, seasonal and sporadic requirements of **ruta** cultivation and engineering. Furthermore, traditions from the bush groups of Vangunu and New Georgia indicate stable cooperative arrangements among sets of neighbouring, closely related **butubutu**, whereby work organisation for **ruta** purposes could reach conspicuous levels ranging across the subdistricts of old Marovo.

While the war leaders and priests were to disappear altogether, the role of the pre-colonial chiefs was only partially replaced by the church, as Christian festivals became alternative occasions for the production of taro puddings. But taro no longer needed to be counted in the ten thousands – and family-based swidden cultivation, pooled on a rather egalitarian basis for ceremonial occasions (though still along the principle whereby common people are "managed" by chiefly people), provided what was needed. However, a variety of inter-**butubutu** arrangements in agroforestry have continued to flourish through the entire 20th century for a range of church purposes, often arising from the churches' need for large annual offerings. One notable example was the large-scale cooperative scheme of copra production, transport and marketing organised by district headman (and customary chief) Ishmael Ngatu in 1933, building on a long history of "gift copra" production for the Methodist and Seventh-day Adventist missions (Bennett, 1987:244). The most striking example of institutional arrangements on inter-**butubutu** levels is more recent and is indeed heavily based on customary precedents: the syncretist Christian Fellowship Church has, since its inception in the late 1950s as a breakaway movement from the Methodist church, expanded to become a political and economic framework for most **butubutu** of northern New Georgia (see Hviding, 1996a:122; Bennett, 1987:299-301; and this book's Chapter 9).

It is usually the case that the disintensification of agriculture, in this case the progressive abandonment of the Marovo **ruta** pondfields, has multiple causes (cf. Brookfield, 1972, 1973, 1984, 1986; Leach, 1999). Population decline, political change, settlement migration, and changing values and technologies all play some part in what was, in the Pacific, a widespread process in the 19th century. More archaeological survey and oral history research is needed to strengthen the case for the importance of the **ruta** pondfield systems in New Georgia, but the evidence already available suggests that agriculture in Marovo prior to European contact had strong elements of stratified organisation based on irrigation and redistribution and was not simply, and perhaps not primarily, a swidden system of shifting cultivation – even though that it was what it subsequently became.

7 Colonialism, Coconut Overlay and the "Age of Development"

On writing histories of colonialism

Up until the era of formal colonialism, writing the history of places like Marovo is a task of imaginative reconstruction. Any such history is a patchwork stitched together from various small scraps of knowledge. In Chapters 5 and 6 we offered a version of Marovo agroforestry in the 19th century and its transformation in the period 1880-1910. We are confident that the general outline provided, including that of the momentous events around the turn of the century, gets as close to the truth as is possible with the available sources. Of course we cannot be so confident about certain details.

In this early "contact" period the necessity for a historian to contextualise the sources is almost self-evident, as the information available is not merely thin, it is also so obviously slanted. Captains of trading vessels in the Solomon Islands were minding their own business, not documenting the lives of Solomon Islanders for posterity. What we might call "ethnographic" information is limited, in the few cases where traders left any records, to facts about the islanders that might help others to trade successfully and in safety.[1] Likewise the more literate visitors, the Somervilles and the Woodfords, all carried with them a heavy ideological baggage of social darwinism and other narratives of the imperial project. And the fading memories of the indigenous people, or rather such versions of these memories as have survived, are themselves tinged by hindsight, nostalgia and awe at the transformation in world view which colonised peoples (and indeed most people on earth) have experienced in the 20th century. For all of us, our 19th century past has become a foreign country that is difficult to revisit.

When we reach the period of formal colonialism, at least in rather thoroughly administered and missionised places like Solomon Islands, the task for an historian becomes rather different. For one thing the sources become more plentiful, so that eventually there is almost too much information. There are the colonial archives of administration and commerce, which for Solomon Islands have been brilliantly employed by Judith Bennett

153

in her history of commercial agriculture and forests (Bennett, 1987, 1995, in press). There is a large mass of oral history which can readily be assembled from the memories of a range of eye witnesses, people who actually participated in or observed the unfolding of events in the 20th century. And finally the landscape itself provides a kind of text which the literate can read, if they are sufficiently tutored in the languages of Western science, indigenous knowledge and local cultural meanings.

Some of the problems of bias still remain, of course, and they are particularly prominent if we use written sources to establish change in the indigenous sector and in the subsistence sphere, as opposed to their use for tracing the arrival of things "modern". Most of the literate observers of the Marovo scene whose writings have survived were Westerners, and their world view still needs to be contextualised even though their cultural background is disturbingly familiar (Somerville, for example, wrote articles for anthropological journals). Behind their mask of objectivity lies a whole series of unexamined assumptions, hidden agendas, and areas of ignorance of which knowledge of the local language is the most obvious.

The problem can be highlighted by caricature. Tourists today face acute problems of communication when visiting places like Marovo Lagoon (see Hviding, 1998a). If we can judge the accuracy of their impressions by what they write in the Visitors Book in tourist lodges, or by the accounts they post on the Internet when they return home, then their limitations as observers become all too obvious (see Chapter 12). To colonial administrators and other foreigners with long-term residence, the language barrier may have seemed more slight. After all, by about 1920 English-based Melanesian Pidgin was being spoken by an increasing proportion of the population, and it seemed (then as now) to provide an easy entry into knowledge of the Melanesian "Other". This illusion is as insidious as tourists' bland assumption of effortless "empathy", and also needs to be critically examined.

It is important also to remember that practically everything written about Marovo in the 20th century is self-consciously "authoritative" in a rather insidious way. First it is largely a male gaze.[2] By and large these observers were white men operating in a masculine, colonial world in which their every act was an embodiment of authority. When they asked questions they invariably received answers, of some kind. When these answers were written down, as a form of knowledge systematised according to the categories of Western science, then the apparent authority of the text is difficult to resist.

Fortunately in the 20th century documents and reports are not our only source. There is also the cultural landscape, which when interpreted for us by those people whose actions have shaped it, constitutes a vast storehouse of knowledge – as we have already indicated in Chapters 3 and 4. And there is the evidence from ethnography. In the history that follows, we blend these insights from landscape and ethnography with insights gained from historical sources. In this way we hope to offer a secure basis for establishing patterns of change in Marovo Lagoon in the 20th century. In so doing we hope to avoid writing an historical narrative that is itself permeated with certain other "narratives" – those insidious and empowering visions of Marovo's past, present and future that we will consider in a more explicit way in the book's Epilogue, in Chapter 13.

"King Copra": origins of the coconut overlay

As described in chapter 6, the coastal lands of Marovo first started to under-go conversion to a new cash crop (coconut) in the wake of great transfor-mations, ca. 1880-1910. This conversion was in the service of what, else-where in the Pacific, became known as King Copra, and it followed the lead of the white traders who from about 1880 onwards were acquiring land on islands in the lagoon and outer barrier reef for coconut plantations (for the most part they used labour from other parts of the Solomons). At the begin-ning coconuts were probably planted by the Marovo people in new swiddens that, initially, were interplanted with food crops until the shade from the coconut palm canopy began to prevent any further intercropping. This grew to a large-scale, pan-Marovo phenomenon in the 1920s and 1930s, at a time when it became clear to everyone that the newly established British Solomon Islands Protectorate signalled a permanent transformation in the political economy of Marovo. Coconuts as a new form of agroforestry was quickly perceived to be the best route towards new wealth and status.

The people's incorporation into the Methodist and Seventh-day Adventist churches was accompanied by rising aspirations in commerce, and by the active role of the churches in getting villagers to establish coastal coconut plantations.[3] As **butubutu** after **butubutu** was converted in the very active 1915-1925 period every new church established and built was accompanied by the planting of large numbers of coconut trees in neat "drill lines", usually on coastal plains or low slopes immediately adjacent to the village. The process was often supervised by the first "missionary" of a village, frequently a Marovo man selected from a previously converted community. The ensuing copra production would in turn underpin not only the villagers' mandatory tithe and "Thanksgiving" offerings to the churches, but in addition the "head tax" imposed by the colonial government on all adult men.

These changes were well underway by 1929, when the Swiss traveller Eugen Paravicini visited the Marovo Lagoon on an extensive tour around the

British Solomon Islands Protectorate – but he fails to mention them. In his book *Reisen in den Britischen Salomonen* (1931) he enthused about the natural beauty of Marovo, and reported that he found the people not only likeable but "richtige Herrenmenschen" (Paravicini, 1931:174-175), in stark contrast to his impression of the inhabitants of Malaita. But in common with many such travellers searching for some kind of Paradise Lost, Paravicini's main feeling was one of nostalgic regret for an exotic past that was already almost out of reach in this post-upheaval time of depression and de-population:

> Unfortunately the population is disappearing very rapidly. Before the [First] World War it was estimated to consist of 15,000 souls, now there are only about 800 natives left. In those days the interior of the islands would have been densely populated, while today all villages lie on the coast and the interior is empty of people. Only behind of Viru, along a river, are a few small inland villages still to be found. Two dysentery epidemics were responsible for this huge depopulation; yet they can hardly be the only cause, for today the population is still decreasing, even though the disease no longer claims any victims. (Paravicini, 1931:175, translation by Edvard Hviding)

Paravicini gives more emphasis to the headhunting customs and material culture of the recent past than to daily practical life. Indeed, if we can believe his account then his informants, mainly old chiefs, seem to have been preoccupied with little else than reminiscing about the exploits of former times. Yet he did sketch the agriculture of the time, however briefly:

> The daily diet is provided for by agriculture. The most important cultivated plant here is the taro, while in addition yams, pana, sweet potato and bananas are grown. The greater significance of taro than yams is demonstrated by the fact that it is only taro harvests that are celebrated with feasts. The finely grated taro corms are mixed with the pounded nuts of the *Canarium* tree, shaped into balls and simmered in hot water. The *Canarium* tree is ... not planted, however all undergrowth is cleared around wild-growing specimens in the forest. (Paravicini, 1931:176-177, translation by Edvard Hviding)

Ruta irrigation is not mentioned, and this is consistent with Paravicini's assertions about a virtually total depopulation of the interior before 1929. It is also Marovo opinion that pondfields were largely abandoned by 1930 in favour of mainly coastal swiddens. It is clear, however, that as late as 1929 taro remained the most important crop and the only proper ceremonial food.

Happily neither the dire forecasts by Somerville (1897) about the eventual extinction of the New Georgian peoples nor Paravicini's pessimistic views of the immediate future were ever borne out. The period 1910-1930 was one of low activity, stabilisation of population after epidemics and migrations, and social consolidation, in the aftermath of the "great transformations". In retrospect we would emphasise a growing focus of activities centred on the church and coconut plantations. Yet these two processes were not mentioned by Paravicini apart from his remark that many lagoon seashores were dominated by the "mighty crowns of coconut palms swaying mildly in the sea breezes" (Paravicini, 1932:4).

Despite the silence on this matter of Paravicini, who unfortunately is one of the main external sources for this "quiet" period preceding World War II, we firmly believe that the spread of Christianity and copra-making were fundamental changes in Marovo society at this time. Moreover, we believe the two processes were closely linked. While the churches rapidly built up considerable copra-related infrastructure in competition with the traders and resident planters, the 1930s also saw the development in Marovo of an indigenous scheme for making and shipping copra on a cooperative basis. This scheme, mentioned in Chapter 5 as an example of historical continuity in inter-**butubutu** organisation of agroforestry, was led by Ishmael Ngatu, a customary chief of the "mission" village Patutiva and also the district headman (a colonial appointment). Although it was to be of rather short duration it is one of the first examples of a large-scale commercial enterprise wholly organised by Solomon Islanders (Bennett, 1987:244).

What happened in Marovo at this time is very parallel to the changes occurring in other parts of Oceania. In the Lau and Lomaiviti islands in eastern Fiji, for example, Brookfield described the spread of coconuts after 1870 as a process covering more and more of the productive land of coastal lowlands, and as a means for money to penetrate large parts of the wealth economy. Eastern Fiji became much more than a coconut economy:

> It became a coconut society ... Large inland and coastal areas ceased to be cultivated, people who were moved away from their improved land often adopted less intensive cultivation methods with the new and less demanding crops [sweet potato and cassava] in their [new] settlements. A "coconut overlay" spread over land and society alike, blanketing former differences in resource use and production systems. (Brookfield et.al., 1977:155-164)

The "coconut overlay" in Marovo occurred several decades later than these changes in Fiji, and its impact was perhaps less complete. Nevertheless the spread of coconuts and copra making had equivalent effect on the agroforestry system. With the increased (and by 1930 almost total) coastal nucleation of settlements, including some "mission" villages of a size never seen before, and with an emerging coconut overlay, the more tolerant sweet potato was becoming ever more important in many parts of Marovo. Cassava was also established in Marovo from the mid-1920s, having been introduced by a "native medical practitioner" returning from training in Fiji in 1923

(Russell, 1948b:2). The introduction to most Marovo swiddens of this new crop, yielding good harvests on the poorest soils, was accompanied by many other "exotic" roots, leafy vegetables, fruits – and weeds. Some of the range of these introductions was indicated in Chapter 4 (Figures 4.2, 4.3 and 4.6), but overall this period of planned and haphazard introduction of new plants is poorly documented, as well as being a topic which Marovo people's own story-telling traditions are little concerned about.

With increased ties between Marovo and the world economy, this period also saw a number of short-lived agroforestry enterprises based on existing plants. For example, "ivory nuts" (the hard fruit kernels of the sago palm *Metroxylon salomonense*, **edeve**), were obtained from a large sago palm plantation on swampy coastal land south of the village of Pejuku on Gatokae. The nuts were exported to overseas buyers, and the plantation was operated by a company, with workers from other islands, mainly Makira. As for other foreign enterprises the ivory nut plantation was terminated by the war. The hard "ivory nut" did not regain significance until the mid-1990s, when a few wood carvers discovered its merits for the production of tourist handicrafts in the form of very small, exquisitely detailed carvings of sharks, turtles and other animals, shaped in ways offered by the circular nut.

Alongside the shift towards coconuts, sweet potato and cassava there was therefore an increase in the overall diversity of the economy. Dependence on the new crops was never as complete as in areas like Fiji, and was interrupted by substantial fluctuations caused by rivalry between European traders and the churches and by the exigencies of the world economy. These years of adjustment to the new opportunities of the first phase of colonisation came to an abrupt end with World War II, which disturbed Marovo (and the rest of the Solomons) in a totally different way.

World War II: exodus and disruption

In 1939, when the war broke out in Europe, copra prices at first rose, but only for a short while as international trade was soon thwarted by the spread of war. Marovo people, as other Solomon Islanders, came to experience the full wrath of modern warfare as their islands, forest, beaches and lagoons in 1942-43 were turned into a major stage of the Pacific War "theatre" of American and Japanese forces (USP, 1988; Bennett, 1987: 285-310; White and Lindstrom, 1989). The New Georgia Group became a scene for the major American offensive during 1943 against the Japanese who had retreated and established air bases there after being defeated at Guadalcanal. Being at the eastern end of the New Georgia islands the Marovo Lagoon saw little large-scale fighting. However, incursions by Japanese launches that involved some random killing of villagers and the plundering of coastal food gardens, as well as the warning of mighty and impending attacks on the entire New Georgia Group by Americans, resulted in a large-scale exodus from the coastal villages of Marovo. Some fled out into the lagoon to hide in the dense bush of the larger islands there, while most established provisional hamlets up in the mainland forest. This was, as some old men and women of bush **butubutu** have expressed it, almost like hiding from the marauding headhunters of the coastal people in the old days. But the **ruta** were long abandoned and overgrown, and there were many disincentives for clearing new large swiddens.

So the years 1942-43 are remembered as a time of hardship, when people subsisted on what they could harvest by visiting neglected coastal swiddens, supplemented by wild yams, leafy greens, and some hunting. Fishing and lagoon travel was deemed by many to be too dangerous, and was also discouraged by the only long-term wartime colonial presence in Marovo, the coastwatcher Donald Kennedy who had established head-quarters at Seghe and built up a guerilla "army" recruited partly from among the sons of former New Georgian headhunters (Boutilier, 1989).[4] European planters and missionaries withdrew altogether from Marovo during the war, and these years consequently saw a total collapse of the market economy, the churches and colonial administration, and a temporary return to bush subsistence.

When the Americans did come to Marovo in 1943, Marovo men were recruited in numbers as carriers, scouts, barge pilots and camp labourers, many following along as the offensive was carried further west. It represent-ed a remarkable encounter between Solomon Islands villagers and the machinery of large-scale western warfare. Bennett (1987:288-289) notes how "the scale of operations, to say nothing of the great sea battles and over-head dogfights, was bewildering" and mentions how on 15 August 1943 4,600 U.S. troops landed on the Bilua coast of Vella Lavella (further west in the New Georgia Group) with 2,300 tons of supplies. Many Marovo men who worked for the Americans also recall how they were at first baffled and then delighted by the egalitarian friendliness of U.S. soldiers and officers – so unlike the austere aloofness of British colonials and the often brusque and brutal demeanour of alcoholised traders of many nationalities. Indeed, World War II did not only disrupt the pre-war village life, agroforestry and fishing of Marovo people. As elsewhere in the Solomons, the experiences gained during the war also transformed many aspects of the relationships between local villagers and Europeans, not least British colonial officers. The war thus was a longer-term, important catalyst to social, economic and political change.

Post-war, and the late colonial era

In Malaita and parts of the Eastern Solomons the post-war period saw the development of cargo cults and similar social and political movements, but Marovo like the rest of the Western Solomons responded to the wartime experience in a different way. It is true that in North New Georgia the local "prophet" Silas Eto established his breakaway Christian Fellowship Church (CFC) in the 1950s, but there are many differences between the CFC and cargo cults. Elsewhere the post-war years saw the re-establishment of "business as usual". Perhaps the "great transformations" (ca. 1880-1910) and the coconut overlay (ca. 1910-1940) had altered values in the Western Solomons more substantially than the more tentative and partial changes that were underway on islands like Malaita. But there is a sense, too, that social systems on islands like New Georgia, with their maritime tradition and far-flung exchange networks, had always been more outward looking. Genera-tions of leaders had been eager to adjust to new opportunities, whether it was the acquisition of steel tomahawks, sweet potato cultivation, the adoption of Christianity, or money making through copra. Both the churches and the colonial government responded to this aspect of Marovo culture and society by rapidly re-establishing its administrative infrastructure, to counter any local dissatisfaction and mistrust in the post-war Western Solomons.

The world of commerce was changing in ways that promised much greater Marovo participation. Most of the European planters, some of whom had been resident in Marovo since the early years of the twentieth century, did not return after the war. Their plantations either were abandoned or were taken over by large companies (such as Burns Philp, Levers and R.C. Symes) which posted their own managers, often part-European sons of former traders. However the coconut overlay remained. For forty years after the end of World War II copra remained the mainstay of the Marovo cash economy, although not quite on a scale of some other islands (e.g. Choiseul) where a lack of alternative income opportunities from marine resources led to a total dependence on copra. Marovo people point out that much of their coastline still has rainforest growing right down to the seashore which, they say, testifies to their only partial dependence on copra. The availability of some other income sources certainly helped helped them when copra prices finally collapsed in the mid-1980s. There is so far no sign that copra can re-gain its role as the major cash crop.

What was happening in the subsistence sector, always the less visible component (for outsiders) of the Marovo agroforestry system? We are fortu-nate to have a rather full account by a district officer, Tom Russell (later a key figure in the colonial administration of the 1960s), which is worth quoting at some length:

The diet of the people is a monotonous one, consisting mainly of roots grown in the gardens, relieved by fish when available, crabs and molluscs with occasional pigs for those of Methodist faith. Domesticated pigs are kept in small enclosures made of stakes ... at a short distance from the villages. Wild pigs which ravage the gardens on the mainland are hunted by dogs and killed on occasions. Poultry is kept in small quantities.

The gardens do not differ from these in other parts of Melanesia. Shifting cultivation is employed but a simple rotation of crops is understood, and a permanent stand of fruit-trees in several places visited seems to be the pivot round which the system of cropping rotates. Gardens at *Penjuku* [northwest Gatokae] are a good argument for this contention. In the gardens *taro* is the principal crop, but alocasia, yam, potatoes, sweet potatoes, sugar-cane, maize, *kassava*, pineapples, bananas, breadfruit, soursop, limes, pumpkins and beans grow in various amounts. Malay apple ... [Marovo **apuchu**] is grown, and a fruit called *Opiti* ... which has a sweet flavour. Canarium almonds become ripe in September. *Kassava* has an interesting history in Marovo, having been introduced in the 1930's by a native medical practitioner returning from Fiji. In some of the villages where soil is bad for *taro* cultivation, this has completely supplanted *taro*, and together with sugar-cane is a common growth in the immediate vicinity of the houses, whereas the other crops are relegated to the gardens sometimes several miles distant.

A reason given for the failure of *kassava* to spread in other villages was that *taro* was the chiefly food, and that no other crop could supplant it. To a visiting chief or relative no other food was possible. My informant quoted with scorn the habit of the people of Simbo, 'Where *taro* cannot grow because of the volcano: they use bananas as we use *taro* to mix with [*Canarium*] nuts in puddings.' (Russell, 1948a:317-318, italics in original)

This description of gardens as of 1946-47 refers to the large Seventh-day Adventist community of Pejuku, a typical early "mission" village still almost entirely surrounded by extensive coconut plantations dating from the 1920s. It is clear that by the post-war years a wide range of introduced crops were well established. The date Russell gives for cassava's introduction ("1930s") is probably incorrect, and contradicts what he says elsewhere in a tour report (Russell, 1948b) where the year 1923 is specified. This latter date matches the recollections of village elders, who are usually quite exact in pinpointing momentous events and birthdates by referring them reciprocally to each other. As for Russell's puzzling reference to "potatoes", this surely applies to the "pana" or "lesser yam" *Dioscorea esculenta*, called **luju** in Marovo.

The Pejuku gardens described by Russell, as well as his general state-ments about crop rotation, also highlight the longevity and continuity of other key aspects of Marovo agroforestry. The interdependence of trees and root crops in the swidden gardens of Marovo is clearly shown. His reference to permanent stands of "fruit trees" as the pivot of crop-and-fallow rotation probably applies to *Canarium* nut groves (**buruburuani**) and the cut nuts and various fruit trees that are associated with them. In his tour report Russell (1948b:2) comments that "manure is unknown" (not unexpectedly since he also notes that cattle are absent and domestic pigs few), thus noting the sole dependence in Marovo agroforestry on ash as the only "fertiliser". Finally, Russell's example gives us ample indications of the all-important role of taro as the only proper, 'true' food on special occasions and in special relationships.

In retrospect we might see this time as something of a turning point in Marovo agroforestry this century. The coconut areas were highly productive and were to enter their most profitable period in the early 1950s. Meanwhile the food gardens maintained a coexistence of old and new. We can see from Russell's account that taro and sweet potato/cassava were dichotomised, the former being tended in small plots close to village houses (on those flat coastal areas still lacking coconuts), whereas the latter were grown in larger gardens further inland. It was soon after this time that epidemics of virus disease in taro began to attack and eventually destroy the viability of taro, leaving people with a complete dependence on sweet potato and cassava. As a result the agroforestry system began to be characterised much more as a monoculture, although the dynamics among swiddens, fruit trees, fallows and secondary forest continued. We may turn to Tom Russell's 1948 tour report for a glimpse of the impending doom over New Georgian taro. He states that

> Disease of taro which had all the characteristics of the specimens brought back from Choiseul was notified, and in some cases inspected in the following villages: - Parengete, Vura, Penjuku, Sombiro, Michi and Vakambo [a range of villages that covers most of the Marovo area and most of the range of soil types]. This was only elicited by questioning and there was no thought of reporting it, as it seems to be a normal hazard of taro cultivation in Marovo. The remedy which was explained at several different villages was simply to leave the taro in the ground. The leaves wither away and some time later new shoots appear. These are transplanted and are normally healthy. Several beds of taro grown in this way from diseased plots were seen. This would seem to confirm that it is a worm disease of some kind and not bacteriological in nature. (Russell, 1948b:2-3)

A memorandum from Russell's superior dated three weeks after the tour report and appended to it when filed reflects the concerns over taro disease, but also gives a rare example of colonial attentiveness to the potential value of the unwritten but empirically tested knowledge possessed by villagers about such topics as agriculture – in this case Marovo peoples' own remedy for taro disease:

Agriculture. The relevant portion of your report has been sent to the Senior Agricultural Officer. The alleged 'cure' for taro disease should be borne in mind when touring other sub-districts. (Russell, 1948b, appendix)

A further perusal of district officers' reports from Marovo in the period 1948-50 shows the mounting concerns about the taro disease and the uncertainties as to what form of disease this was – beetle, worm, or bacteria. The reports also, however, note that the food supply in Marovo remains "good" to "excellent", with taro remaining the staple crop though buffered by the widespread diffusion of cassava into former taro gardens. Overall, the havoc wreaked on root and tree crops by abundant feral pigs, and to a lesser extent by even more abundant flocks of cockatoos, appear as a more imminent threat to gardens at this time. District officers report having received many requests for shotgun cartridges from villagers who wanted to get rid of the cockatoo "pest".

For taro, things went from bad to worse in the following years, and it is said in Marovo that by 1965 there was virtually no taro left. Epidemics of virus disease, the "taro blight", had wiped out taro cultivars on a large scale. Elders say that this would never have happened if they had continued growing taro in irrigated pondfields, since it is reckoned that irrigated taro was never attacked by any diseases or insect (cf. also Tedder, 1976:46-47). But with the complete shift to dryland taro in swiddens, the ground was "laid open", so to speak, for the rapid spread of this disease. With the demise of taro, the agroforestry system of Marovo had attained the state which corresponds rather closely to the "present-day" picture which was presented in detail in Chapter 4. Only the giant swamp taro *Cyrtosperma chamissonis* (**ghohere**) remained, a crop grown rather extensively in some coastal swamp locations. The huge but rather coarse corms of giant swamp taro are today regarded mainly as food during shortages of sweet potato, and during the November-to-February season of northwesterly winds when persistent rains may prevent people from going to the main gardens far from the village.

Fortunately copra production went ahead strongly during these dramatic events in the subsistence garden sector. There were price fluctuations, but large numbers of new coconuts were still planted, many on newly allocated blocks on lagoon islands or for the coastal groups even in the barrier islands, since little coastal land not already subject to the coconut overlay was left. A detailed census of households made in 1987 by one of us (Hviding) in the two villages of Rukutu (central Marovo, Methodist) and Tamaneke (north Marovo, Christian Fellowship Church) shows that it was common for nuclear-family households of not too recent establishment to possess 500 or more coconut trees. Quite a few more extended households centred on late-middle-aged couples with one or two resident married children had 2,000 or more coconut trees planted in one or more locations. Yet, in the 1990s, Marovo people usually comment quite laconically that coconuts can now be used only in cooking and for feeding pigs, if not the tree itself is felled so that the wood can be used in the tourist carving trade. There is almost no new planting of coconuts today, except for some carried out by a few optimistic individuals, and by Christian Fellowship Church communities who still maintain communal copra production despite the low price.

The late colonial era also saw increased government investment in infrastructure, education, transport, and so forth. In the 1960s and 1970s this was supplemented by the emergence of the indigenous Christian Fellowship Church as a powerful agent of autonomous rural development. Echoing the short-lived enterprises of then 1930s, the CFC went ahead and bought ships and established copra buying-and-shipping schemes ranging throughout the New Georgia area. The establishment in pre-Independence years of extended local government and the beginnings of "rural development" rhetoric also focused partly on securing the infrastructure necessary for successful copra production. "The age of development" and its associated rhetoric continued after independence in 1978, but the value of copra, its main engine in the rural economy, was already in decline. The year 1986 was the last year when people (in Marovo at least) produced copra in a serious way.

The age of rural development projects

In her history of Solomon Islands colonialism and trade Bennett (1987:312) describes the period 1955-65 as the decade of "paternalistic policies for progress". The British authorities were beginning what they imagined was the long road towards ultimate independence for their Pacific Islands colonies, although in the end that road proved to be much shorter than anyone envisaged. Government was now almost synonymous with rural development, and any project was better than none at all. An increasing variety of schemes was initiated, some organised by outsiders and others by local entrepreneurs. The pace quickened in the 1970s and, particularly, the 1980s, in the search to supplement or replace copra as the mainstay of the cash economy. These schemes included commercial fishing (invariably failing for lack of reliable shipping to bring iced fish to Honiara), cocoa planting (failing partly from the serious drop in world market prices just when it was becoming established in Marovo), and cattle projects (dismal failures in this context of historically non-fenced gardens, and resulting only in the establishment of a small resident population of feral cattle in the forest).

Indeed, one could argue that projects, expert advisers and foreign entrepreneurs have been a rather constant feature of Marovo over the last decades. With or without the efforts of outsiders, the Marovo people have accessed an increasing diversity of cash income sources. These include wood-carving and other handicraft production, marine products (commercial pearlshell, turtle shell and bêche-de-mer), marketing of crop surpluses, remittances and royalties. Together they provide a strong buffer in the era of failed development projects and fluctuating and declining copra incomes. Thus despite the failure of any one source of income to replace copra entirely, the people of Marovo have tried a great variety of new ways to gain value from their resources, at the level of individual, household or community.

Of course many of the schemes tried have been shortlived, and the financial returns have been disappointing. Yet there is a sense in which in Marovo none of this really matters. For one thing surplus is shared quite widely, along bilateral kinship networks. Secondly, the meaning of wealth in Marovo as elsewhere in Melanesia is still very different from what development models generally assume. To any economist, to contemplate so many development "failures" in Marovo must be distressing. Such experts tend also to look at what people spend their money on when cash is available, and they despair at so much frivolous or unproductive expenditure. Yet in Marovo reality, for most people and for much of the time, money is desirable but not essential. The notion of "subsistence affluence" is still highly relevant to Marovo Lagoon because almost all necessities of everyday life can be produced by every household from land and sea. The agroforestry system is a highly dependable source of food energy; the forest gives an almost inexhaustible supply of firewood, timber, thatch and vines, herbal medicines and animal protein; while the lagoon and the barrier reefs are a rich source of fish, shellfish and other foods.

In consequence the realm of money can be reserved – once children's school fees are paid – for risk, speculation and conspicuous consumption. It has become the domain in which men compete for status, but the outcome is not a matter of subsistence or survival. All this helps to explain why, from the 1980s onwards, there have been more and more concessions by customary land-and-sea-holding **butubutu** (or rather by certain of their leaders and spokesmen) to transnational logging, fishing and mining companies. This can be seen as one symptom of a continuing struggle to find a satisfactory alternative to copra (Bayliss-Smith, 1993), but to assume that in Marovo (so-called) economic decision-making is just a knee-jerk response to market failure, is to adopt not merely the language of economics but also its economistic assumptions about the way the world works. We may choose to regard logging as affecting "forest reserves" and "sources of income", but in fact it needs to be explained as also a form of status-seeking behaviour by new leaders, the "headhunters" of the modern age. The scale of such strategies may be notable, as shown by a remarkable recent example. In 1996 persistent rumours had it that one prominent "land owner representative" had managed to spend more than SI$ 400,000 – cash advances received from Asian logging companies in return for felling concessions on customary land (cf. Chapter 9) – on just three months of hectic partying and gift distribution in Honiara. For him the only material results were one new house in town, one at home in Marovo, and a boat with a powerful outboard motor.[5]

Forest futures: the "objective" view

Lieutenant Somerville's (1897) sinister prediction that the development of the forest tracts of New Georgia must await the coming of a "more industrious race" was not fulfilled by the first wave of capitalist entrepreneurs in the period from around 1880 to 1920. The efforts of white settlers to establish coconut plantations barely extended the "developed" area beyond the lagoon islands. Nor was this aim ever achieved by the British colonial government, despite hints by development planners that what New Georgia really needed was immigration by "outside labour" (Wall and Hansell, 1975:166). The current capitalist wave has its origins in East and Southeast Asia, and in the aftermath of logging there is a proposed scenario of massive oil palm plantations on Vangunu, with a projected town of 10,000 people (see Chapter 9). In this chapter our focus is not on these external threats to the Marovo forests so much as on the view from the inside. But since the inside view is increasingly being informed by the "objective" assessments of outsiders, it is to these that we now turn.

Over the last twenty years the population of Marovo will have doubled from about 5,400 in 1980 to a projected 10,700 in 2000, and many people in the area are starting to believe that this population explosion threatens to put real pressure on subsistence resources. From a scientific perspective, and considering the resources of Marovo in an aggregate way, it is easy to dismiss these feelings as having no rational basis. For example, if we disregard the more than 700 sq. km of coral reefs and lagoon in Marovo and consider just the 1,500 sq. km of land, then we can estimate a population density in the year 2000 of just seven persons per sq. km. By world standards, and even by Solomon Islands standards, this is a low figure. There appears to be plenty of room for a wide range of future alternatives.

Such indeed was the "objective" view of optimal resource management expressed in Wall and Hansell's (1975) study carried out for the British Government's Ministry of Overseas Development. It was part of a large project covering the whole of the British Solomon Islands Protectorate. Land resources in New Georgia were measured on the basis of slope and soil quality, while current land use was assessed from air photographs. Wall and

Hansell reported that in 1969 the island had an average population density of only 3 persons per sq. km, making use of the total land resources as follows (with 1 sq. km = 100 hectares):

Subsistence gardens and young regrowth	2,040 hectares
Old garden regrowth	1,345 hectares
Coconuts	1,700 hectares
Towns, villages and airstrips	260 hectares
Logged areas	325 hectares
Total area used	5,670 hectares
Total area unused	214,700 hectares

These data suggested to the planners that in 1969 only 2.4% of the total area of New Georgia was being "properly" used, mostly around the coasts, and it was a similar story on Vangunu, Gatokae and nearby islands such as Kolobangara. Logging operations had begun to "open up" parts of Kolobangara and New Georgia (see Chapters 9-10), but in most areas inland areas remained "empty", with both Vangunu and Gatokae being "little used islands" (Wall and Hansell, 1975:52, 165).

The report identified a series of "Agricultural Opportunity Areas" (AOAs), where it was recommended that development efforts by the colonial government should be focused. For example, West New Georgia AOA was reported to contain extensive hill areas everywhere suitable for tree crops, and in places land that would be suited for spice and annual crops and probably also cattle grazing. However, in the area identified there was absolutely no resident population, and with other nearby areas also ripe for agricultural development the consultants foresaw a potential labour shortage: "The presence of the Roviana AOA and the West New Georgia Terrace AOA nearby signify a potential competition for labour, and unless outside labour is permitted to enter the region on a large scale the full potential of the land will not be realised" (Wall and Hansell, 1975:166).

It is not surprising that not one of these Agricultural Opportunity Areas has so far been developed in the manner envisaged. Independence for Solomon Islands in 1978 spelled the end for the grandiose development schemes of the late colonial era. The new constitution's respect for the rights of customary land owners and the new role for provincial government have both put obstacles in the way of centralised development planning. In any case, central government does not have the money to invest in such schemes. Instead, in Marovo as elsewhere, it is the alienated land which has attracted outsiders seeking to develop business enterprises: most notably, Australian entrepreneurs at Uepi Island tourist resort and the Solomon Islands Government itself offering logging concessions on Forest Estate Land (alienated in the 1960s) at Viru Harbour and on Vangunu. Except as temporary workers at these places, immigrants have not so far entered the Marovo Lagoon in significant numbers.

Timber trees through local eyes

In order to gain additional perspectives on the "insider" view of the Marovo rainforest, let us shift briefly to the urban scene. One of the most prominent buildings on Mendana Avenue, the absolute main street of Honiara, is the new, air-conditioned and rather ostentatious office of the National Bank of Solomon Islands (NBSI). In the international department on the ground floor is an eye-catching display of the commercial timbers of Solomon Islands. There are eight panels of beautiful polished woods, each of which is identified with a brass plaque bearing the Latin name of the tree and the common Solomon Islands trade names of its timber:

BUTI *Gmelina moluccana*
AKWA *Pometia pinnata*
MILKY PINE *Alstonia scholaris*
PENCIL CEDAR *Palaquium* spp.
BA'ULA *Calophyllum kajewski*
ROSEWOOD *Pterocarpus indicus*
NULI *Terminalia brassii*
VASA *Vitex cofassus*

The various visitors to the bank are likely to receive the messages conveyed by the polished wood panels and brass plaques in different ways. At the purely aesthetic level, there is a message that everyone can appreciate about the exquisite lustre, grain and colour of the various hardwoods. The average businessman (unless he is from a logging company) or the average tourist (other than a stray botanist) is unlikely to give the actual names of the eight woods much attention, unless it be a raised eyebrow at the rather contrived imitation of well-known English woods in three of them.

Solomon Islanders, on the other hand, are likely to see beyond the aesthetic level, and will ask themselves questions about the other five names, all of which are in the Kwara'ae language of Malaita, which was adopted by the Forestry Division in the 1960s in an attempt to reach some level of standardisation in this island world where some 85 languages each may have several hundred names for trees and other plants (see Whitmore, 1966, for a magnificent example of this innovative approach, and Hviding, 1995b, for a Marovo-centred perspective). The five names in question have close cognates in many other languages of the Solomons and would thus be recognisable to many people from different parts of the archipelago.

At the level of symbolic meanings, Solomon Islanders might also ask themselves some more political questions about these icons of forest wealth, these lustrous glowing panels displayed in this air-conditioned temple of money. The bank is of course a place where few of their countrymen, not to say women, will ever set foot. Solomon Islands villagers, if they do have a relationship to the NBSI, do so as holders of modest passbook accounts. They do their bank business in SI$ only, and visit the rural NBSI branches or the less pretentious head office nearer to the centre of town. Only a few venture down into the basement of the international branch, which is where domestic bank business is transacted.

Where the eight hardwoods are displayed is in fact the nerve centre of international transactions. This is where export credits are negotiated and where foreign currencies are exchanged. Upstairs even more arcane transactions take place, involving larger sums and electronic means. The eight key tropical hardwoods serve as an apt symbol of this exported Solomon Islands wealth, rather like the sheaves of wheat and the fleeces of wool that adorn rural banks in agrarian Europe.

Beyond their aesthetic, narrative and symbolic levels of semiology, any villagers gazing at these eight wood panels would in any case recognise most or all of them at an iconic level, simply by looking at their colour and grain. From this, the disturbing realisation could well ensue that the commercial timbers eagerly sought by logging companies tend to come from trees that in some way or other are of key importance to everyday life in the village. Taken together, these eight species are major or sole providers of raw materials for a wide range of indispensable items such as canoes, paddles, tools, commercial woodcarvings and locally sawn planks for today's family houses, churches and school buildings. They also meet many other needs in a spectre of distinct yet interwoven domains from religion and ritual to everyday food preparation.

To further investigate the hypothesis that the most important commercial timbers are simultaneously among the most important resources in the subsistence-based village economies of Solomon Islands, Figure 7.1 provides more detail on the relationships of commercial timbers to everyday village life, from a Marovo perspective. The twelve commercial timbers listed in the table were chosen on the basis of published and unpublished material from the Solomon Islands Forestry Division, Levers Pacific Timbers and the SWIFT (Solomon Western Islands Fair Trade) "eco-timber" project (see Chapter 11). They are listed in terms of their current importance to the logging industry.[6]

Figure 7.1   Twelve commercial timbers and their local uses in Marovo

NAMES (scientific, common trade names, Marovo)	COMMERCIAL IMPORTANCE	SIGNIFICANCE IN MAROVO
Calophyllum neo-ebudicum and *Calophyllum peekelii* Bintangor **buni soloso** (generic for **buni kovo** and **b. vijolo**)	Major	Two tall tree species of inner forest; both increasingly used for local planks, milled with chainsaw by villagers at the felling site or after being towed downriver
Campnosperma brevi-petiolatum Solomon Islands Maple **olanga**	Major	A tall tree of the forest, often near rivers; a preferred wood for local chainsaw milling, and for key accessories of dugout canoes
Pometia pinnata Pacific Maple **meda**	Major	A large tree of inner forest and **chichiogo**; plank buttresses preferred material for axe handles; wood a favourite fuel for slow-burning fires
Terminalia brassii Dafo; Terminalia **hoba**	Major	A large, very tall tree that grows in extensive stands (**hobahobaini**) in freshwater swamps behind the mangrove zone; good hardwood for local planks
Vitex cofassus Solomons Vitex **vasara**	Major	A large tree of the lowland forest; buttresses and trunk important wood for paddles, canoe parts, spearguns, planks and other building material (including saltwater-resistant posts), mortars for ceremonial puddings, and more; also a good fuel for slow-burning fires
Intsia bijuga Merbau; Kwila **kivili**	Major/secondary	A large and tall tree of coastal forest, mainly in barrier islands; very hard wood with a wide variety of construction uses (not least saltwater-resistant posts); also used for axe and adze handles

Alstonia scholaris Milky Pine **tangovo**	Secondary	A very tall tree of the lowland forest, often near rivers; traditionally a 'spirit tree' not normally to be felled; however, buttresses were required wood for war canoe prows, and less frequently the trunk was used for war canoe planks; buttress wood used for net floaters; sap and bark used medicinally; wood today sometimes milled and planks used for church buildings
Calophyllum inophyllum --- **buni rarusu**	Secondary	A large, twisted beach tree of barrier islands and mainland; important wood for local planks; dead wood excellent for slow-glowing fire sticks; sap of leaves used medicinally
Dillenia salomonensis Dillenia **kapuchu**	Secondary	A large and tall tree of the inner forest.; wood regarded as 'weak' and not much used in Marovo, though sometimes taken for chainsaw milling
Gmelina moluccana Pacific Gmelina **goliti**	Secondary	A large, fast-growing tree of the lowland forest; of utmost importance in being the only truly good tree for making dugout canoes of all types and sizes
Pterocarpus indicus New Guinea Rosewood **rigi**	Secondary/low	A tall, fast-growing tree mainly of freshwater swamps; wood is very good for planks and has been used for small dugout canoes; main importance as first-grade carving wood, significance increasing with shortage of ebony (**rihe**, *Diospyros* sp.) and kerosene wood (**naginagi**, *Cordia subcordata*)
Terminalia spp. Pacific Maple **popoli goana, popoli piru**	Secondary	Tall trees of the forest. Good for planks and sometimes used for local chainsaw milling

We can reach a number of conclusions, many of them virtually self-evident. The trees in question are among the largest of the forest, some of them are quite easily accessible, and moreover it comes as no surprise that in Marovo as elsewhere in the Solomons villagers appreciate good, hard woods in large pieces – just as the loggers do. Most notable among the trees listed is perhaps the tall, straight **goliti** (*Gmelina moluccana*) – the canoe tree, without which transport would simply be impossible for most Marovo villagers. These lowland trees are often owned by individuals, and sometimes single trees are even inherited. The are invariably left standing when new swiddens are cleared, and can be regarded as integral parts of the agroforestry system. In the cases where villagers have had a definite say (as customary landowners) in negotiations with logging companies, it has usually been stipulated that both **goliti** and **rigi** trees are not to be felled. Yet this has proven difficult to monitor, and more than a few **goliti** appear to have ended up as logs in the holds of timber ships rather than as dugout canoes on the lagoon. By some villagers of North New Georgia, though, it is noted that the most recent logging operations there by a Malaysian company have by-passed – according to an agreement with the landowners' corporation (see Chapter 9) – both **goliti** and **rigi** trees.

Another trend visualised by Figure 7.1. is the much-increased local need today for large sawn planks derived from one's own forest. Melanesian modernity on the village level, coupled also with a measurable shortage of sagopalm leaves in many locations, has promoted a new type of 'permanent' house which has walls made of vertical plank panels (rather than the imported prefabricated boards used in the 1970s) and a roof of corrugated iron. For an even longer period of time, plank walls have also been preferred for larger communal buildings such as churches and schools, and plank floors have been *de rigeur* for virtually any permanent dwelling house since the days of prefabricated boards.

In Marovo such a preference for sawn planks can partly be traced back to the operations during the 1980s of a fairly large sawmill at the SDA headquarters in Batuna. During these years the sawmill purchased logs, mainly of **buni** (though not the twisted beach species), **kivili** and **vasara**, from villagers. The arrangement was sometimes for cash but more often was an agreement whereby villagers would receive sawn planks equal to the volume of two logs for every ten logs they supplied. In what appears to have been a rather sustainable – and certainly labour-demanding – system, size-able quantities of easily accessible trees were felled, barked and dragged down to the nearest river estuary or beach by family groups or community organisations, to be towed to Batuna by the sawmill's launch. In this way new technologies have allowed Solomon Islanders to enlarge the range of hardwood species with local uses. Chainsaws and sawmills now enable them to utilise woods that would have been difficult to process in the age of steel axes (and virtually impossible to use with the stone age technology that prevailed before about 1850).

Local hardwood demand is also increasing for other reasons. The shortage of good trees along the coast and immediately inland today, as well as entrenched construction preferences, increases the importance of large **buni** (*Calophyllum peekelii, C. neo-ebudicum*) and **olanga** (*Campnosperma brevipetiolatum*) from the more remote forest. The same is true even for the large **hoba** (*Terminalia brassii*) which is still abundant in some freshwater swamps, and what few are left in the barrier islands and along the mainland coasts of large seaside **buni** (*Calophyllum inophyllum*). For the recent (1996-97) construction of a large new church in Chea village on Marovo Island, several of the locally disregarded **kapuchu** (*Dillenia salomonensis*) were felled in a nearby sago swamp and processed by chainsaw. **Popoli** (*Terminalia* spp.) and the very tall **tangovo** (*Alstonia scholaris*) are also being targeted today, although the latter as a 'spirit tree' is regarded as off-limits for profane purposes by a number of Marovo's **butubutu** (notably, it has been used in a few cases of church construction – thus retaining its place in the spiritual sphere). Likewise **vasara** (*Vitex cofassus*) has a long-standing importance as a significant all-purpose tree, and **kivili** (the valuable Merbau, *Intsia bijuga*) has traditionally been, and remains, the most widely-used timber for thousands of house posts in Marovo's coastal zone, where most kitchen buildings and traditional residential houses are still built from bush materials. **Rigi** (*Pterocarpus indicus*), now emerging as a local carving wood of key importance given the increasing shortage of ebony and 'kerosene wood', is also the potentially sought-after "Rosewood" of logging companies. Indeed a belief is often optimistically expressed by village carvers that **rigi** is in reality subject to a government export prohibition (a belief not supported by the fact that the SWIFT "ecotimber" project [cf. Chapter 11] reckons **rigi** as one of its five to six target species). In fact **meda** (the commercially important *Pometia pinnata*) is the only one of the twelve species listed in Figure 7.1 that does not have an actual or potential major usage in Marovo, although even **meda** is a "niche" wood for certain very specific purposes.

Thus eleven out of twelve commercial timbers that are targeted by logging companies come from trees that provide key resources for everyday village life in Marovo villages. Two of the timber trees have such fundamental significance for Marovo people's daily lives that they can hardly see themselves living without them. Competition for timber trees seems likely to increase, given the growing – and irreversible – preference for plank-built, longer-lasting village housing.

Options for the twenty-first century

The fact that most of the forests of Marovo survived to the end of the 20th century almost intact has enabled them to be discovered by a new wave of external consultants concerned with promoting conservation rather than "development" of the forests. Lees et. al. (1991), for example, carried out a study which identified a huge forested area in the catchment of Marovo Lagoon in order to recommend it for "forest protection": "The proposed protected area has been little disturbed: hurricanes are infrequent and of low intensity, and human impact has been limited to gardened land and some timber removal on Vangunu and Nggatokae. The result is a region of extensive primary rain forest including undisturbed forest community transitions from the sea to mountain tops" (Lees et.al., 1991:95).

In 1996 there was abundant evidence that this situation of undisturbed tranquillity was about to be overturned. We believe that Marovo Lagoon is soon going to about to enter a new period of radical change in the way that people use its forests, comparable to the great transformation that we have identified as characterising the period 1880-1910 (see Chapter 6). The stimulus, now as then, is external, but the pace and direction of change will be controlled by certain individuals in Marovo and by the internal dynamics of Marovo society. In the chapters that follow we review the options for change under a number of different headings, which can be summarised as follows:

Adapting the indigenous agroforestry system. A process of diversification and intensification is taking place in the indigenous system, to take account of the relentless rise in subsistence demand following half a century of population growth. Today's agroforestry is also implicated in the increasing dissatisfaction being expressed in Marovo with the people's marginal economic status, as the area is touched by rumours of something that elsewhere is called "globalisation", and by a yearning by the Marovo people for a greater participation in this process, by becoming the consumers of more than fish and meat and tubers, fruits and leaves from the reef and the forest. Within Marovo some fundamental questions are being asked, but so far what we see is mainly a series of incremental changes and adjustments in Marovo agroforestry, and therefore a continuation of what we have analysed for the historical period in earlier chapters. The changes in agroforestry that are now under way are the subject of Chapter 8.

Selling the forest to outsiders. A radical alternative to the rather conservative resource development policies that the Marovo people have adopted in the past would be the logging option. The leasing of land to logging companies has become an increasingly attractive option in the 1990s, in order to take advantage of the high prices available for tropical hardwoods and the ease with which deals can be fixed up with Asian companies in the political climate that has prevailed in Solomon Islands for most of the past decade. The past, present and potential future of logging in the Marovo area are the subject of Chapter 9.

After logging: the management of reforestation. Quite new forms of agroforestry are not merely conceivable but are actively being pursued in other parts of the Western Solomons. Reforestation using exotic species could be a sustainable use of land once under primary rainforest, producing a steady stream of either logs or pulp for export as well as sawn timber for local markets. Another alternative could be reforestation with certain local trees, maybe not as fast-growing but of high value in the international market for choice tropical hardwoods. The experience of large-scale plantation forestry on Kolobangara Island, and the rejection of this option so far by some groups in Marovo (as well as some alternatives proposed by them), are reviewed in Chapter 10.

Small-scale logging of the existing forests, to meet local demand. Instead of the quick money provided (especially to the logging company) by round-log exports, the alternative option of locally owned and sustainably managed forestry is being proposed. The technology would be inexpensive and its environmental impact would be restricted, in contrast to the capital-intensive, wasteful and destructive methods of the logging companies. These 'walkabout sawmill' methods should, it is claimed, be a means to provide a sustainable livelihood and plentiful sawn timber for local housing. However, despite NGO enthusiasm and some local support, actions by central government to pursue this option have so far been negligible. The reasons for this paradox are explored in Chapter 11.

Conserving ecosystems for the future, and for eco-tourists. Some have argued that environmental conservation is the new moral discourse of the West, providing a new Utopian vision. Environmentalists tend to see eco-tourism as almost the only acceptable face of capitalism, since it is the only way so far devised whereby insiders and outsiders can simultaneously live and enjoy the benefits of Utopia without destroying it. According to this new paradigm, an earthly paradise (not to be confused with the village named Paradise in north New Georgia) cannot be found in a world too much tainted in capitalism. Instead we should cherish those few remaining places that can serve, for the 21st century, as a new Garden of Eden. If possible the Garden should be in the state of nature that existed before Adam and Eve took up agroforestry. Any remaining examples of paradise – such as Marovo Lagoon – are also seen as storehouses of undisturbed biodiversity and places that "we" have a moral obligation to conserve. The World Heritage Site proposal for Marovo Lagoon, and the eco-tourism that might make this proposal feasible, are reviewed in Chapter 12.

In many parts of Solomon Islands not all of these options could be regarded as serious scenarios for the future management of the forests. In densely-settled parts of north Malaita, for example, most of the land is now converted to cultivation with short grass or shrub fallows, and the challenge is to find any way in which useful trees can be accommodated within a landscape that is under intense population pressure (Frazer, 1987). In such areas indigenous agroforestry has already been intensified beyond the point where woody regrowth can find a place in the cycle, so that building materials and fuelwood can no longer be provided from local sources. If trees can be introduced as some kind of crop, it is likely that the land will afterwards be re-used for food production, with the tree products that the people still need being supplied by trade with other parts of Malaita that are not yet deforested to the same degree.

Marovo Lagoon, by contrast, like most of the Western Solomons, is at the other end of the spectrum. Despite population growth, inroads from large-scale logging and other pressures, choices for the future do include all five of the options outlined above. There are even other options such as biodiversity prospecting which as yet are scarcely on the horizon. First, however, we need to consider the existing agroforestry system in Marovo. How far can it adapt to new needs, and in the future how far can it continue to fulfil successfully the wide range of needs that it has supplied in the past.

8 Towards the Twenty-first Century: Adapting the Indigenous System

Subsistence affluence at micro-scale

If the Marovo economy is growing more complex, then so also are the gardens which form its subsistence base. Since about 1980 we can trace a process of growing differentiation among households and among villages in different parts of Marovo. For some people, work in the gardens has remained the main source of livelihood within household economies primarily focused on subsistence production. For others gardens have become just another component, though invariably an important one, in a diversified "peasant"-type enterprise. Still other households may at times find they need to purchase their daily root crop requirements from those who concentrate on agroforestry. These include households whose members invest most of their time in wood-carving (by the men), handicraft production (by the women), the collection and preparation of *Canarium* nuts for sale (by the women), or commercial fishing and collection of "marine products" (by the men).

The post-war era of "rural development" in Marovo Lagoon has thus witnessed a rising tide of social and economic change (see also Hviding, 1996a; Hviding and Baines, 1994; Bayliss-Smith, 1993). To examine how far the process outlined above have had a differential impact on the Marovo agro-forestry system, four communities were selected in 1986 for detailed fieldwork by one of the authors (Bayliss-Smith) following consultation with Hviding about which communities to study. To encompass as much of the economic and, perhaps, the ideological variation that has emerged, we decided to choose four communities with contrasted characteristics in terms of church denomination, market access and involvement, land availability and quality and bush/coastal **butubutu** identity. Villages chosen for study were Bareho on the subsidiary Nono Lagoon of southwest Marovo, Michi in central Marovo, Bisuana on the Bareke peninsula of north-east Marovo, and

Vakabo in the narrow northern arm of the lagoon. Their contrasting characteristics are shown schematically in Figure 8.1 below.

Figure 8.1   Contrasting characteristics of the four sample villages

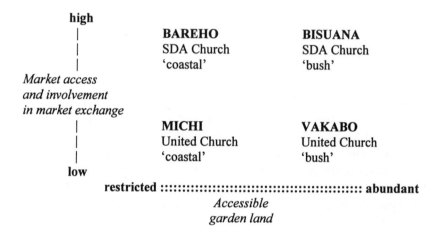

In these four communities information was collected on population structure,
and on land use, diet, work and income among fifty households for a total of
584 household-days, in a four-week period in July-August 1986 (Bayliss-
Smith, 1993). Furthermore, all the gardens of certain households were
mapped, representing a total sample for Marovo of 15 house-holds (Bareho
3, Bisuana 3, Michi 7, and Vakabo 2 households). The sample size per
community is not sufficient to justify detailed comparisons, but taken
together some meaningful generalisations emerge from the total of 15
households that were covered (Figure 8.2). This population amounted to 93
persons (41 productive adults and 52 dependents) cultivating on average 384
square metres of root crops per household, mainly sweet potatoes and
cassava, alongside a wide range of useful trees, fruits and vegetables. Sweet
potato alone occupied 71 per cent of the area under root crops. The old
staples of the 19th century, taro and yams, together occupied a mere 4% of
the area (Figure 8.2).

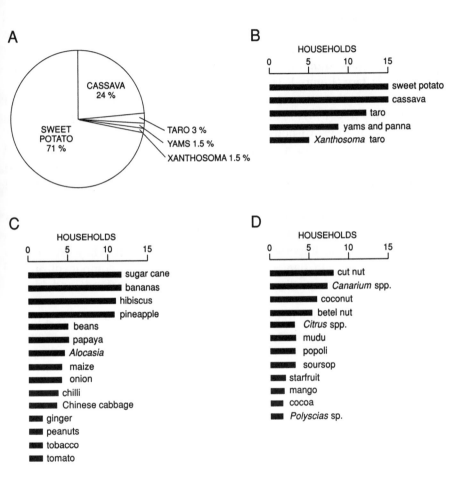

Figure 8.2 Gardens being cultivated by 15 households in Bareho, Bisuana, Michi and Vakabo (1986)

A. Per cent of the total cultivated area under various root crops
B. Number of households cultivating various root crops
C. Number of households cultivating various minor crops
D. Number of households with various useful trees growing in their gardens

NOTE: Some minor crops are also cultivated in the village, and many useful trees are growing in former gardens and village areas. Data from tape and compass maps, July-August 1986.

Less systematic observations by both authors in 1996 suggest the situation had changed very little over the intervening ten years. It is clear that sweet potato and cassava have become the predominant staples of the Marovo people and that taro has almost vanished from the scene. The 1986 diet survey quantifies the extent of this transformation (Bayliss-Smith, 1993:20). Out of a total of 590 household-days of food consumption in the four villages surveyed in 1986, 550 included sweet potato, 234 cassava, 16 yam (**uvi**, *Dioscorea alata*), 22 lesser yam or 'pana' (**luju**, *Dioscorea esculenta*) and 21 taro (Figure 8.3)

This means that sweet potato was eaten by every surveyed house-hold virtually every day (87-97% of household days in the four villages). Cassava was eaten on 29-53% of household days, partly as a cooked root crop but more importantly as the main ingredient in puddings made from grated cassava, mixed with coconut cream and (sometimes) roasted and crushed *Canarium* nuts. In this respect cassava has directly replaced taro, which used to be the staple ingredient in these puddings before. Baked in the stone oven on a regular basis, several times a week by many households, cassava-based puddings (still retaining the names that they used to have when made with taro) are in effect an important staple in their own right. They are also, as mentioned initially in Chapter 1, the essential mediating component of food symbolism in that they may be both **nginongo** 'staple food' and **binaso** 'relish'.

No other subsistence food can match the importance of the sweet potato and cassava staples, but other crops are important supplements. For example, **luju** ('pana' [lesser yams], 15% of household days), bananas (15%) and *Colocasia* taro (**talo**, 14%) were of significance in Bareho, a small-island SDA village of coastal people with very good soil (**puava hokara**, cf. Figure 4.7) on the adjacent flat coral land. In the SDA (and bush people) village of Bisuana in Bareke, the giant swamp taro (**ghohere**, *Cyrtosperma chamissonis*) was an important supplement (15% of household days), and likewise in Vakabo, a small-island Methodist village of mixed coastal-bush people in the northern lagoon (12%). Less important though still significant supplements in all four villages were greater yams (**uvi**), *Xanthosoma* taro (**karuvera**), sago (in the form of puddings baked from the extracted pith of fallen trunks, an uncommon food in Marovo) and maize. As a purchased carbohydrate, rice featured in household meals on 50-58% of days in Michi (a Methodist village of coastal people in the central lagoon), Bisuana and Bareho, but only 30% of household days in the more remote, less monetised village of Vakabo. Biscuits, flour based cooked foods, noodles and milky beverages appeared in only 5-10% of household days, and less in Vakabo. Coconut is the most common source of fat in the diet, and coconut cream was used for cooking on about half of all household days (range 42-58%).

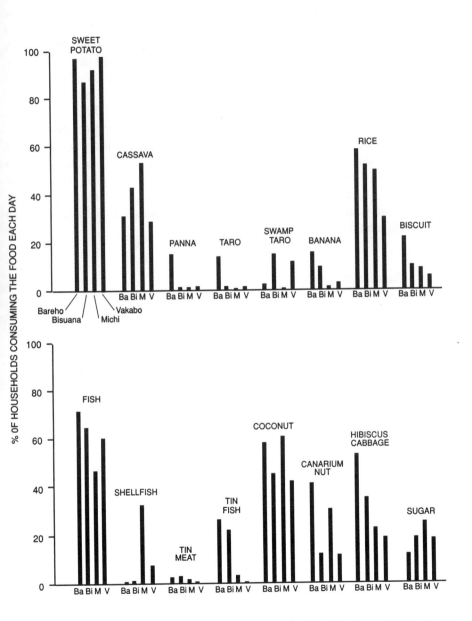

Figure 8.3 The significance of root crop staples in household food consumption
Results of a survey of 129 household days of food consumption at Bareho, 139 at Bisuana, 173 at Michi and 149 at Vakabo, July-August 1986 (source: Bayliss-Smith, 1993:18-20).

At the time of the survey *Canarium* nuts were coming into season, and fresh or smoked they were recorded often (on up to 45% of household days), particularly among the coastal people at Michi and Bareho. Other nuts (cut nut, and the recently introduced peanuts) were less important. Vegetables are dominated by **ngache**, the shoots and leaves of the cultivated shrub *Hibiscus manihot*, which were eaten on up to 53% of household days. Wild leaves and fruits such as mangrove pods and the forest fern **pucha** (*Diplazium esculentum*) were eaten less frequently, but on up to 9% of household days among the SDAs of Bisuana. Thus, root crops grown in people's own subsistence gardens, as well as a core variety of other plants in the agroforestry system, remain as the very 'basis' (**chubina**, 'tree trunk') of the Marovo **kino** 'way of life' – reflecting the all-pervasive view of root crops as the basic 'food' (**nginongo**) that relates to any manner of protein and vegetable **binaso** 'that which is eaten with food' obtained through fishing, shellfish collecting, hunting and gathering.

Four villages compared

The statistics of land use and diet discussed above and the generalised perspectives on land use given in Chapter 5 do hide some significant variations among the four sample communities in their agroforestry practices and food usages – and it is these variations, representative of pan-Marovo variation a wider scale, that we now consider in more detail. On the basis of further fieldwork periods since 1986-87, and from our general background knowledge of the history and ethnography of the area (cf. also Hviding, 1996a), the following description of the four villages in effect constitutes a micro-history of sorts of land use and socioeconomic transformation with a focus on the recent decade. We start with the northern village of Vakabo, representing the "abundant garden land/restricted market access" of the range as shown in Figure 8.1.

Vakabo

The population of the present-day village of Vakabo originated with the bush peoples of the Nono mountains and the upper Kolo river basin. Referred to as the the Nono Ulu and Luga people, these past generations were important in the inland politics and economies of southern New Georgia, having connections to 'coastal' polities both in the Kalikolo area of northern Marovo Lagoon and in Nono Lagoon to the south. A slow but gradual seawards migration through a succession of settlement sites, each associated with the focal leader of a specific generation, led to the final settlement of this **butubutu**, usually referred to as the Luga people, on the coast in the later years of the 19th century. Intermarriage with certain smaller coastal groups had by then already placed large areas of barrier islands and reefs under overall Luga control, though with considerable influence wielded by more powerful coastal groups to the northwest and southeast. Initially being concentrated in an estuarine location at the river One some five kilometres to the southeast, the people moved to the raised coral island of Vakabo around 1910, and it was there that they were contacted soon after by the Methodist Mission (later to evolve into the United Church). The village of Vakabo, well-placed with equally easy access to the forest, mangroves and large rivers of the mainland and to the fishing grounds of the barrier reef (through the wide, deep Mogo Passage), thus has a long and stable settlement history. At about 2 sq. km Vakabo Island was too small to allow for gardens, other than small 'house gardens' of cassava and sweet potato. Tree crops of many kinds abound around the island, which today has hamlets strung out along most of its shores. As on all lagoon islands, there is also a complete lack of water on Vakabo Island, necessitating daily canoe trips to the nearby mainland in order to fetch fresh water for drinking and cooking and drinking, to bathe, and (for the women) to do the household laundry.

Thus Vakabo people have from the outset had a close association with the mainland, and at the time of the village's formation the coastal lands close to the large Obo river were divided into blocks (**boku**) by the chief and distributed among the various families along the patterns described in Chapters 3 and 5. These blocks are still held by the descendants of those family heads (whether male or female) who were involved in the original allocation, and are still worked by them in a daily round of activities involving food and water. Land as such is plentiful inland, but much of it is steep and rocky, and really good garden land beyond the coastal lowlands is far away in higher valleys usually visited only intermittently for the hunting of feral pigs. As Vakabo expanded its population, sites for gardens did of course become scarce in some blocks. However, land can be borrowed from other families provided that the borrower does not plant long-term tree crops (coconut, breadfruit, *Canarium* nut, etc.) but only root crops, vegetables, bananas or betel nut.[1]

In 1986 the biggest concentration of Vakabo people's gardens was on the mainland in the lower reaches of the Obo river, on terraces that back on to colluvial slopes. The example in Figure 8.4 (cf. Legend to Garden Maps, Figure 4.4) is a garden on a river terrace 2-3 metres above the Obo, a level that was last flooded in 1979, which was also the year that this particular garden was previously in use. A mature betel nut tree dating from the late 1970s still survived, together with an older coconut palm. Otherwise the site was open. The cropping cycle in this area was stated to consist usually of three to four years of bush fallow followed by three years of cropping, in the following cycle:

Year 1: Sweet potato crops 1 and 2
Year 2: Sweet potato crop 3, cassava crop 1
Year 3: Cassava crops 2 and 3
Years 4 to 6 (or 7): Abandoned to fallow
Year 7 (or 8): Renewed clearance for sweet potato

On better soils small patches of yam, pana and taro are grown in years 1 and 2, and also scattered papayas and bananas. The cassava is interplanted with sweet potato in the third (sometimes second) sweet potato crop, and then takes over. A few pineapple plants are grown in the last cassava crop before abandonment. On these fertile alluvial soils a vigorous bush fallow creates quite a dense cover within three or four years, enabling a new cycle of cultivation to begin.

The particular example shown in Figure 8.4 is a garden that is partly in year 2 and partly year 3 of the cropping cycle. As well as the usual root crops there are some plants of *Alocasia* taro and some beans. Some cut-nut and betel nut trees represent the only long-term additions to the canopy layer, while the isolated mature coconut testifies to a previous gardening episode 20-25 years before. By general agreement these prime gardening sites are not to be planted with coconuts or other tree crops. This is to prevent ownership becoming 'frozen' and to ensure continuity of food cropping.

By 1986 there was in any case little incentive to grow more coconuts. Vakabo was too remote to be visited by many ships even during the times of good copra prices.[2] Our survey showed that in mid-1986 average incomes in Vakabo were only SI$30 per month per household, the lowest level in all four villages surveyed, and for many there was insufficient money to provide for basic needs such as sugar, tea, soap and tobacco. Whereas for the more prosperous communities of Marovo agroforestry is only part of a wider system of production, in Vakabo gardening is still the primary focus. The gardens have to be large, diverse and productive, and in view of their central importance in the Vakabo economy it is fortunate that the people here still have access to plentiful land, even if in inaccessible locations.

The river terraces used in 1986 permitted a 43-50 per cent ratio of cropping time to fallow time. The system thus appeared sustainable for the foreseeable future, but in a situation of poor market access agroforestry can only support a livelihood of subsistence affluence. In Vakabo there is therefore every incentive to integrate more cash crops into the cropping system, and there were some initiatives in the late 1980s to plant cocoa in new blocks in-

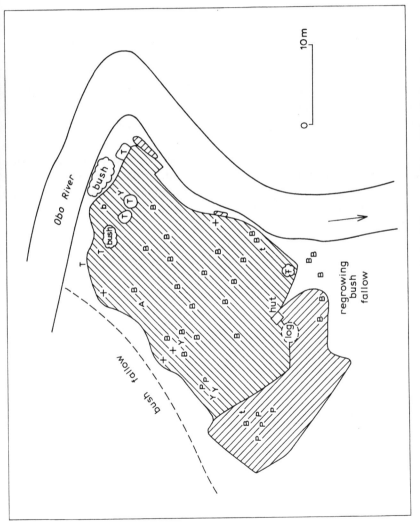

Figure 8.4 Garden at Vakabo in years 2-3 of the present cultivation cycle

land along the Obo river. This was part of a short-lived intensification of cocoa organised around a "Marovo Cocoa Farmers' Association", but failing prices and transport problems caused its downfall. With a background of perennial "project" failures it seems inevitable that in Vakabo the people will be tempted to permit access by outsiders to the inland forests and mineral prospecting rights, in return for what might be perceived as a secure source of income.

In recent years the barrier islands of Tatama and Avavasa have become the focus of a concerted effort by **butubutu** leaders at allocating more well-defined and permanent, family-specific 'blocks' (**boku**). And simultaneously, the tall primary forest of both islands was selectively but rather extensively logged in 1992-93, in an enterprise initiated by some Vakabo people and involving, in addition to substantial labour input by villagers, the mechanised contribution of an Asian company based at Viru Harbour and the direct export of round logs on Asian ships. These efforts, which stripped the islands of a variety of tall valuable trees as well as of large littoral *Calophyllum* trees, appeared to be motivated both by cash-earning aspirations (in a perspective of long-standing relative deprivation) and by the perception that the rapid mechanical clearance of new land for gardens and plantations was useful. Perhaps ironically, in 1996 the immediate availability of ready garden land in the barrier islands garden land was reported by Vakabo people to be of the utmost importance, since flocks of feral pigs displaced by the logging in the northern New Georgia areas of Gerasi and Kusaghe were migrating into the Obo River area destroying mainland gardens with alarming frequency. In an immediate short-term perspective, the fate of Vakabo people's mainland gardens thus appears most uncertain, and there are acute needs for alternative land. In the short and medium term the fertile soils and rather abundant land of the barrier islands (much of which is partly cleared after recent logging) appear to be sufficient to serve these new needs, and a significant shift in Vakabo land use orientations towards the barrier islands may be imminent.

Bisuana

Bisuana village is different from Vakabo in being a Seventh-day Adventist community with much involvement in marketing, and in being close to an abundant fresh water supply provided for by a waterfall (now piped to the village). Nonetheless there are many similarities in the bush origins of its inhabitants, in the extensive land area controlled by them as their **puava**, and in their continued strong involvement in gardening activities. The village is located on the large Bareke peninsula in north Vangunu on a headland backed by steep hills and valleys. Like Vakabo, Bisuana is a long-established village, dating from around 1900 when several smaller segments of a major bush-dwelling **butubutu** 'came down and out' (**horevura**, cf. Chapter 6) from their scattered hamlets in the lower foothills as the dangers of headhunting and warfare ceased with the collapse of the coastal polities.[3] The new community at Bisuana had abandoned irrigated taro cultivation and were set on the cash cropping opportunities offered by the presence of copra traders in this central lagoon area and facilitated by pacification. The area around Bisuana and the neighbouring villages of Gasini and Malavari was also where a number of former headhunting strongmen settled with their bush in-laws around the turn of the century and themselves took up active swidden cultivation on the coastal slopes.[4]

Today some of Bisuana's gardens are still in the long-cultivated, sloping secondary bush immediately inland from the village (see Figure 4.2 for an example). They are focused on the usual sweet potato and cassava cycles as outlined by Bisuana elder Dennie Loni in Chapter 4. It is notable that Bisuana people themselves, like the majority of Bareke people, emphasise the agricultural limitations posed throughout the peninsula by the poor quality of soils and the extraordinarily rugged terrain not far inland. Beyond these main gardens, Bisuana people also cultivate swiddens a few kilometres away on river terraces along the Kolo river (not to be confused with the much larger Kolo river of southeast New Georgia, not far from Vakabo), and here significant amounts of yam (*Dioscorea alata*) and 'pana' (*D. esculenta*) are still cultivated by some of the older men and women as part of the following cycle:

Year 1: Sweet potato crops 1 and 2
Year 2: Pana or yam
Year 3: Harvest patches of banana and **ngache**, and abandon
Years 4 to 6 (or more): Bush fallow

Less dedicated gardeners may not bother with pana or yam in year 2, and may simply plant cassava crops in year 3. The information obtained was not very explicit about fallow lengths, but as at Vakabo 3-4 years seems to be normal. Some of the hill slopes near the village have been used and reused ever since the turn of the century, and have a somewhat degraded regrowth of tall grassland dominated by *Imperata* (**rekiti**). The grassland is interspersed with small bushes and, in places, gingers of the **piropiro** and **ijoko** types (*Alpinia* spp.), the former being regarded archetypal fallow vegetation (see Chapters 3-4). Whatever its duration, the fallow is clearly too short for proper forest regeneration. An example of a garden in this somewhat degraded area is shown in Figure 8.5.

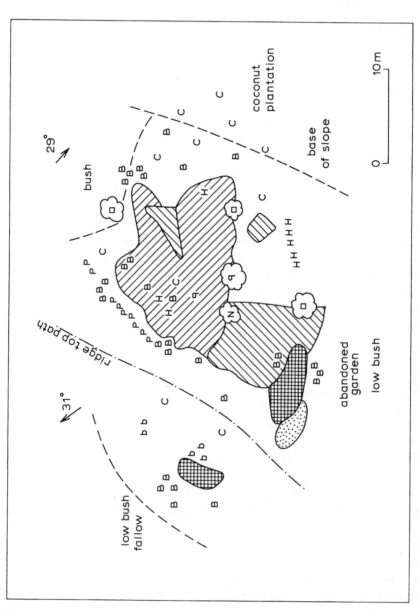

Figure 8.5   Garden at Bisuana on long-used, degraded land

Degradation of the garden land accessible to Bisuana is one of the consequences of almost a century of settlement nucleation. Another related problem is the imminent scarcity of land, a threat commented on by many; their subjective view thus in stark conflict with any objective measurement of land availability. Despite containing ample areas of unused hinterland, the **puava** over which the **butubutu** resident at Bisuana have primary control is seen as rather unfavourable for the expansion of agriculture. As elsewhere in the Bareke peninsula, the brown, stony soils are infertile even in the short runs of swidden cultivation cycles, while the steep topography with narrow valleys and limestone cliffs and pinnacles mediates against agricultural expansion beyond the more gentle terrain of the coastal hills.

In 1996 a more immediate problem, as in Vakabo, were the ravaging bands of displaced feral pigs, coming across the mountains from the logged areas of Gevala on southeast Vangunu. The pig problem at Bisuana and nearby villages is exacerbated by the fact that Seventh-day Adventists do not hunt pigs.[5] The ironic consequence for Bisuana is that its former role as a food exporting community has been reversed. The old taro-for-fish system that linked the Bareke bush people in exchanges with the coastal people of old Marovo has been replaced by the transport of sweet potato from 'coastal' people, such as the villagers of Chea on Marovo Island, for sale among the bush people along the Bareke coast. In yet another reference to the 'blessing' of the excellent soils on the small Marovo Island, a number of men and women of Chea pondered in the 'dry' tradewind season of 1996 over the curious fact that they, with their negligble garden lands, should now be able to market surplus root crops to the Bareke people who were "hungry despite their masses of land".

The economic future of Bisuana's households thus seemed rather precarious. As in all Seventh-day Adventist communities, Bisuana families are required to raise considerable sums of money for children's school fees, amounting to around SI$250 per child per year in 1996. Agricultural crops can only contribute a fraction of this, carving woods are becoming acutely scarce, and access to commercial marine resources such as fish and trochus shell depends largely on the generosity of reef-holding coastal **butubutu** – something that is actually facilitated by the large number of marriages between coastal men and Bisuana women. As a result the Bisuana people were in 1996 eagerly pursuing a range of more or less speculative future scenarios, ranging from coastal aquaculture of giant clams and pearlshell via "eco-tourism" to mining and logging by foreign companies. While logging companies have so far expressed slight interest in entering the very rugged terrain of northern Bareke, representatives of an Australian mining company has actively but discretely been prospecting for gold in mountains behind Bisuana. Throughout 1996 a sequence of rumours concerning fabulous gold finds in Bareke were variously launched, confirmed and denied by different parties, as Bisuana people continued to go about their day-to-day gardening work.

Thus perceived scarcity is stimulating an entrepreneurial response, but in a context where subsistence affluence continues to prevail. Despite stated pessimism and beliefs that things were much better 'before' (not an uncommon attitude in Marovo), and despite the obvious reliance on intermittent purchases of root crop staples, there were few signs in 1996 of abject poverty in Bisuana, nor of food scarcity. If we look at it in isolation the agroforestry system in Bisuana shows some signs of strain, but viewed in a wider context what we see – and this is typical of Marovo Lagoon – is a resilient economy that continues to benefit from socially flexible land and sea tenure and reciprocal practices of trade and barter.

Michi

Like Vakabo, Michi is another United Church community, and as usual in the Marovo Lagoon this denomination implies less involvement in the market economy, not least since the demands on each household for children's school fees are less severe (United Church villages have government-funded primary schools). In Michi, cash incomes per household in mid-1986 averaged SI$ 53 per month, a lower level than in both of the SDA villages (Bisuana SI$ 71, Bareho SI$ 83). However, in contrast to Vakabo or Bisuana, the agroforestry system at Michi village reflects the inhabitants' 'coastal' rather than 'bush' identity, and in consequence we see a relative shortage of prime sites for gardens. Although the Tobakokorapa **butubutu** resident in Michi have ancestral title over a larger area of land than other 'coastal' **butubutu** do, the limited area of land actually accessible is nevertheless of rather poor quality.

The village itself (sometimes referred to as 'New Michi') is located on a dry coral peninsula of the Vangunu mainland, having moved there in 1939 when the original village location, a small coral island just offshore, split and crumbled during an earthquake (this island is now "Vanua Rapita", an ecotourism resort; see Chapter 12). Historically, the Tobakokorapa people were part of a larger polity centred on the headhunter stronghold of nearby Marovo Island. After partly breaking with that stronghold following adultery and subsequent internal killings around 1850, these people settled more permanently at the northwestern end of Vangunu, whereupon the distinct **butubutu-puava** entity of Tobakokorapa came into being. Nevertheless, they maintained a role as the Marovo Island centre's westernmost "gatekeepers", watching over lagoon traffic from northwards and from Jae Passage to the south. The present village site is adjacent to a tract of land called Kachekache, which was once a coconut plantation belonging to a white trader. Title over the Kachekache land has, however, reverted to the Tobakokorapa **butubutu**. Following the copra slump the coconuts have been almost entirely neglected except for subsistence consumption, but meanwhile they symbolise the "coconut overlay", occupying a large area of the best and most accessible land.

For some 40 years now the Michi people have for used and reused for their gardens the volcanic soils on the lower slopes of the Subolo ridge, about 3 km or half an hour's walk east of the village. This area supplies all root crops, firewood, vegetables and fruits other than the coconut. An example of a garden in this area was examined in Chapter 4 (see Figure 4.3). The hillsides here are quite steep (up to 31 degrees), but the soils seem physically stable and so far are reasonably productive. The cropping and fallow cycle is as follows:

Year 1: Sweet potato crops 1 and 2
Year 2: Sweet potato crop 3, cassava crop 1
Year 3: Cassava crop 2, pineapples and sugar cane planted
Year 4: Abandoned after pineapple and sugar cane harvest
Years 5 to 7, 8 or 9: Grass and bush fallow

In the past, Michi people say, repeated cassava crops were possible, but today two is the maximum. The area having been used now for 40 years, some deterioration in soils can be expected. Nevertheless with 2.5 years of root crops and 3-5 years of fallow, the system still has a 33-45 per cent cropping: fallow ratio. An example of such a garden is shown in Figure 8.6

All adults in Michi are supposed to manage individual gardens, although these gardens are contiguous with those of their children or siblings. Usually, as members of families that live together, the food production of individuals contributes to a collective kitchen. As well as gardening, Michi men and women are heavily involved in fishing and shellfish collecting, and the food resulting from this activity compensates for the fact that the gardens have largely become sweet potato/cassava monocultures. Yam and pana are very little cultivated, while taro is practically non-existent. There is giant swamp taro (*Cyrtosperma*) growing semi-wild, but it is seldom eaten.

In 1986 no one was cultivating gardens outside the area of overused hill sides at Subolo, as alternative bush sites were regarded as too remote. By 1991, however, a few new bush gardens had been established near rivers further south in the Jalire Bay, an example of the pioneer settlement process that we discuss later on in this chapter. So far the more drastic alternative of clearing new gardens within the little-used coconut plantation at Kachekache

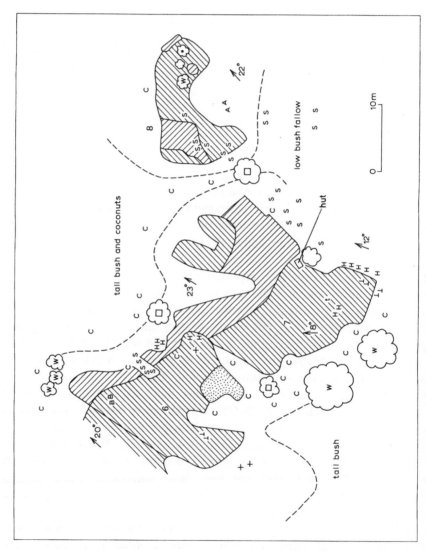

Figure 8.6 Garden at Michi showing stable long-term use

has not been adopted. Reversing the "coconut overlay" and establishing new hamlets in remote bush gardens were both immediate options that Michi people will need to pursue in future, in view of the growing pressures upon the existing agroforestry system. In 1996, a large segment of the Michi population had a new village site cleared by bulldozers (hired from a logging company), several hundred metres inland of the present beach site. There were plans to 'open up' more remote areas of the bush for gardening. Meanwhile, those households remaining in the old village placed great faith in stable incomes from the ecotourism project Vanua Rapita (analysed in Chapter 12) and envisaged a future perhaps less dominated by daily garden work.

Bareho

The island village of Bareho is a Seventh-day Adventist community, established early on in the 20th century by the 'coastal' Nono **butubutu**. This group's history of headhunting and wider political influence was closely tied to control over the small Nono Lagoon, an island-studded cul-de-sac of rather shallow water strategically located right outside Jae Passage, the southwestern entrance to the Marovo Lagoon. From the combined basis of coastal strongholds, hamlets on many of the islands of the small lagoon, and fortified hill settlements, former generations of Nono people had an important role in the continuum of coastal polities from Roviana in the west via the central Viru area to Bili and Gatokae in the east. Bareho is the village of a sea-oriented segment of the larger Nono group (whose past inland dwellers, the Nono Ulu people, have descendants in many lagoon villages, including Vakabo). The **butubutu** of present-day Bareho is therefore referred to habitually as the Nono Kogu people, thereby differentiated from Nono Ulu.

Bareho, then, is like Michi in terms of the history of its people and its shortage of good garden land within a reasonable distance of the village. However, as Bareho itself is on a small lagoon island (about the size of Vakabo, but lower and flatter with many areas susceptible to waterlogging in heavy rain) and all gardens are located on the immediately adjacent raised barrier reef, the soils and topography are quite different. Bareho's gardens are on almost flat land in the Savele area, a raised reef terrace attached to the low-lying, swampy southeastern tip of New Georgia. Savele soils are derived from limestone, and the terrain with its mixture of ragged coral ridges and more gentle expanses of cultivable soil is not dissimilar to the environment of the "coral gardens" of Trobriand fame (Malinowski, 1935). The gardens worked by Bareho people at Savele indeed fall under the special Marovo category of **chigo pa toba**, 'barrier island garden', with opportunities and constraints somewhat different from the agroforestry zone of the mainland.

For most villagers of Marovo **chigo pa toba** are a type of intermittently worked 'bush garden' (see below) often associated with family-owned coconut plantation, but for the people of Bareho (and several other island villages near the barrier reef) "coral gardens" (Figure 8.7) are the normal context for everyday food production. Blocks of Savele land have been divided among the various Bareho families, and some areas have been under repeated cycles of cropping for 60-70 years. As a result the land seems to be somewhat less productive than at Michi, and much less productive than at Vakabo or Bisuana. The fallow has degenerated to a regrowth of tall grasses and ginger plants, and scattered shrubs and thin trees produce a broken canopy.

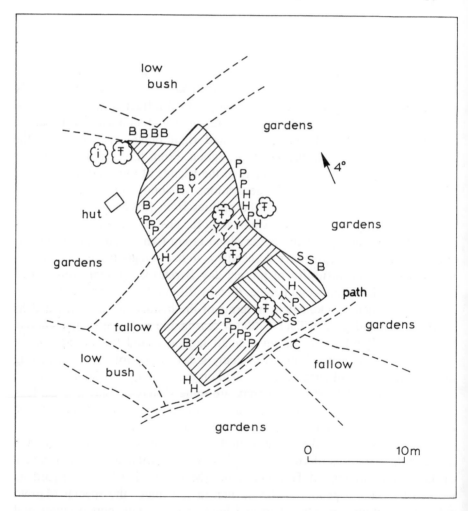

Figure 8.7 Garden at Bareho on limestone soil

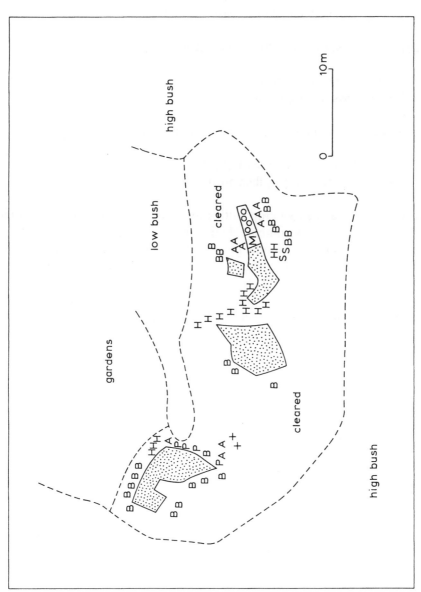

Figure 8.8 Specialised taro garden at Bareho

The precise cropping cycle in Savele depends on a family's land scarcity and on opinions regard-ing soil quality. On the best sites four main crops are possible:

Year 1: Sweet potato crops 1 and 2
Year 2: Sweet potato crop 3, cassava crop 1

Less promising sites switch to cassava after year 1:

Year 1: Sweet potato crops 1 and 2
Year 2: Cassava crops 1 and 2

The poorer sites are now being fallowed after 18 months of cropping:

Year 1: Sweet potato crops 1 and 2
Year 2: Cassava crop 1, then abandon

Everywhere in Savele root crop cultivation ceases in year 3, but a few pineapples and bananas may continue. Fallow lengths seem to be variable. Some areas are given only six months of grass fallow before more root crops are planted, but 3-4 years of grass/bush fallow is more usual. An example of one such garden is shown in Figure 8.7.

As at Vakabo a few specialised taro gardens still exist at Bareho, outside the main gardening area and usually in small swidden plots surrounded with secondary bush. An example is shown in Figure 8.8. Here the cropping pattern is quite different:

Year 1: Taro, interplanted with banana and **ngache** (*Hibiscus manihot*)
Year 2: Harvest banana and **ngache**
Years 3-6: Abandon to bush fallow
Year 7: Clearance, and replanting with taro

By cropping taro only one year in six soil fertility is maintained and, it is hoped, the taro pests and diseases can be kept in check. It is tempting to view this type of garden, which today is for household consumption only, as a survival of the dominant taro swiddens of the 19th century. The ratio of cropping time to fallow time (ignoring banana and vegetables like *Hibiscus manihot*) is 1:6 or 14%. This compares to 33-40% for the normal sweet potato/cassava system, and is a measure of the enhanced land use intensity made possible by the new crops. The example of Bareho also shows how ecological stability can be reduced as the tree fallow's role is almost eliminated after repeated sweet potato/cassava cropping cycles and a shortened fallow.

Pressure and transformation

The four villages illustrate the variability in agroforestry practices that exists in present-day Marovo, reflecting variations in physical and cultural circumstances. For particular sites the main threat to the system's sustainability comes from a lengthening of cultivation periods, which sweet potato and cassava allow, and from a shortening of fallows which proximity to the village and lack of alternative sites encourages. While the 'bush' people of Vakabo and Bisuana have a varied and plentiful supply of bush land, the 'coastal' people of Michi and Bareho face much heavier constraints. We see unmistakable signs of ecological stress after 40 years (Michi), and more critical ecosystem degradation after 70 years (in Bareho) of sweet potato/ cassava and short fallows. There is no doubt that in both cases new land will have to be found soon, as the diversity of the system deteriorates and its sustainability comes into question.

Fortunately in Marovo there are always alternative income options, for example in fishing, shells, commerce and handicrafts – as well as, for several 'coastal' groups with predominantly marine **puava**, regular "royalties" from bait-fishing by the tuna industry (Hviding, 1996a:314-325). Within agroforestry there are also some important changes. We can summarise these as selling garden produce, moving gardens inland, and establishing new hamlets. Taken together these three trends have the capacity to transform the future map of Marovo agroforestry. Each will now be briefly reviewed in turn.

Selling garden surpluses

As previous chapters have shown, exchange and trade of garden produce are nothing new in Marovo, but in the 1990s we see unmistakable signs of an increased local commercialisation alongside a further diversifying of crops and garden sites. When copra (until the mid-1980s) and commercial fishing (throughout the 1980s) were in vogue, agroforestry stagnated quietly in the background. Today these activities have faltered (although short-lived commercial fishing enterprises keep emerging), and unless and until logging takes over, agroforestry comes into its own. It is increasingly common these days to see the small-scale marketing by women of garden produce – both new and traditional crops. This takes place either within their own village or at the large weekly markets held at Batuna, and it involves most of the people of the central and southern lagoon. There is also some inter-village marketing which takes place during the twice-weekly calls by inter-island passenger ships at the village wharves in Patutiva (on Jae Passage) and at Gasini (in Bareke).

To the younger generation in Marovo this intensification of marketing seems like a new departure. Sometimes it is not so much trade as barter, with garden produce being exchanged for fish or other food items. Viewed from an historical perspective, however, these transactions are reminiscent of the coastal-bush, fish-taro exchanges in old Marovo. In the villages (around 1990) typical prices were SI$ 8.00 for a coconut leaf basket (or a 25kg rice bag) of sweet potatoes, SI$ 1.50-3.00 for a pineapple, SI$ 0.50-1.00 for five *Areca* nuts, SI$ 4.00 for a water melon, and SI$ 8.00 for a full stalk of small sweet bananas. In Batuna and at the ship markets, prices were typically 30-60% higher, but still well below the urban level.

This increase in local marketing, together with noticeable increases in the amount of produce (mainly sweet potatoes) sent on the weekly ship to relatives in Honiara and a rise in the frequency of village fund-raising activities based on the sale or exchange of food, indicates that the subsistence-based Marovo agroforestry system produces a growing surplus. The surplus must come from a larger area in cultivation per household rather than from increases in yield. Alongside this new source of pressure on accessible land is the current rapid growth in population, resulting in a concern over shortage of garden land – an opinion now being expressed by many people throughout Marovo. These concerns and people's response to them take various forms. For example, among the coastal groups who have never possessed much land, an increasing number of young men have married women from bush groups with abundant garden land, and have moved to settle in their wives' villages – thus reflecting another pattern of past generations (cf. Chapter 6). But perhaps the most notable development in recent years is the expansion of the household's gardening to several sites, constituting a significant expansion of the range of agroforestry activities.

Into the forest and up the rivers

As has been shown, the typical 20th century Marovo household has tended to concentrate its gardening activities on the intense cultivation of one site at a time, with internal crop rotation and often short-term fallow. These gardens were located as close to the village as possible, above the coconut groves or alternatively above an easily accessible seashore further along the lagoon coast from the village. Increasingly nowadays, however, each household is starting to cultivate other types of garden. The nearby, open swiddens dominated by sweet potato and cassava remain the basis of daily food production, but are now being supplemented by small but highly diverse plots immediately around village houses containing medicinal plants, a little sweet potato, cassava and taro, and some fruit trees. However, the cultivation of new gardens in more pristine areas is a more important trend. It represents a process of expansion that reflects simultaneously land shortage and land abundance; good swidden land within reasonable distance for daily visits is growing scarce, while most **butubutu** (even the coastal ones) seem to have enough reserve land for people who need to expand their agroforestry activities.

The general Marovo term **chigo** – 'garden' – is now applied to a new type called **chigo pa goana** – literally 'garden in the forest' (usually in areas of tall mature secondary growth), or sometimes **chigo pa kavo** – literally 'garden by the river', latter referring to a much-used location, chosen for reasons of access as much as of soil quality. Among groups with control over barrier islands **chigo pa toba** ('barrier island garden', mentioned above in the context of Bareho) – and even **chigo pa tusu** ('lagoon island garden') are also becoming important agricultural supplements, although there is a general preference for locating secondary gardens in the mainland forest whenever possible. These new gardens are a direct outcome of conscious policies by many **butubutu** leaders to open up the more remote parts of the **puava** for diverse gardening purposes, thus relieving some of the pressure on the centrally located parts. For many Marovo communities, the areas thus 'opened up' are relatively flat coastal or riverine land, often located in shallow bays where mangrove swamps and mosquitoes discourage permanent settlement, and commonly a couple of hours' paddling from the village. For others, the newly opened land may be located closer to the village but in areas not readily accessible because of steep topography, extensive swamps, dense mangroves or other inhibiting factors.

We shall use the term "bush garden" to distinguish these agroforestry sites from the open swiddens we here call "village gardens", denoting the latter's proximity to, and often integral part of, the extended 'domesticated' village space. Bush gardens are usually located as close as possible to a river or a lagoon seashore, on the relatively flat land behind – in Marovo terms always 'above' (**pa uluna**) – river banks, coastal mangroves or sago swamps. Access to bush gardens, then, is primarily by canoe through mangrove channels or rivers, as far upstream as possible. Nevertheless, unless its owners are so lucky as to have secured a prime riverbank site, bush gardens may be located as much as half and hour's walk through the forest from the farthest point upstream to which a canoe may be paddled. This remoteness is not such a problem as it seems, as bush gardens do not require such frequent visits as the everyday work of open swiddens. Bush gardens are characterised by relatively subdued light, humid soil and a modest growth of weeds, reflecting their secluded location within largely undisturbed old secondary forest, or even primary forest in some cases. Regular regular weeding is simply not necessary – it is reckoned that most bush gardens can tolerate at least three weeks of absence by the owners. Cultivation of bush gardens is rather characterised by a full day of work, involving at least husband and wife and often a large family in diverse tasks of planting, tending and harvesting.

A typical bush garden contains a different, and larger, variety of plants than those cultivated in village gardens. Especially notable is the revival of taro and yam cultivation. Taro, the old staple crop, ceremonial mainstay and 'proper food' of Marovo, is having something of a renaissance in today's new bush gardens by the extensive planting mainly of non-disease-prone cultivars of **talo** (*Colocasia esculenta*) but also of introduced types of *Xanthosoma*. Yams (mainly varieties of *Dioscorea alata* and *D. esculenta*) are grown in increasing quantities in bush gardens, and much recent attention has been given to finding the right types and quantities of small trees for yam poles and trellises. Among fruits and leafy vegetables commonly cultivated in bush gardens are citrus, Malay apple (**apuchu**, *Syzygium malaccense*), cut nut (**tige**, *Barringtonia edulis* and related species), the betel nut palm (**pijaka**, *Areca catechu*) and a few coconut trees, mainly for snacks and food preparation during gardening work. In addition there are other plants that are commonly found in village gardens, such as bananas and **ngache** (*Hibiscus manihot*), and many other small and large trees, shrubs, climbers and creepers. Some of these are reckoned to be only semi-domesticated and are hardly recognisable from the surrounding forest, but are valued for their yield of fruits, nuts and leafy greens as well as for providing fragrances, medicines, ornamentation, and much else. Sweet potato and cassava are not so commonly planted in bush gardens, with the exception of those gardens that are located in open, flat terrain on cleared river banks or at barrier islands.

All in all, then, this new cultivation pattern is a diversified form of agroforestry, with a large number of crops being cultivated in a complex multilayer system that gives considerable protection from the sun and rain. Soil moisture is retained and erosion by the heavy rains is inhibited. In this sense the bush gardens of today's Marovo mimic many of the resilient qualities of the unmodified forest and avoid many of the regrowth-and-weeding problems associated with open swiddens. Bush gardens thus reflect many of the characteristic attributes of sustainable shifting agriculture in rainforest environments as set out in classic studies from Southeast Asia by Conklin (1957), Geertz (1963) and others.

The bush gardens reflect more the wish to diversify subsistence agriculture than the need to generate a surplus of the regular staples. Characteristic of recent bush garden cultivation is the desire to take up again, if not old agricultural practices, then at least some traditional crops, like taro – and the desire to collect together as many of the useful plants of the forest as possible in a compact, controlled site as a continuously available resource. Most of the produce from bush gardens is directly consumed by the household. They have not only relieved the pressure on the open swiddens, but also provide a diversification of household staples which enables many households to channel more sweet potato crops into marketing or exchange.

The cocoa connection

Some bush gardens are associated with adjacent groves of cocoa, Marovo's most recent cash crop. The requirements of cocoa seem to coincide with those of the bush garden, and visits to the two are often combined. To some extent the cultivation of bush gardens is actually a direct result of new initiatives in cocoa planting. In the late 1980s the leaders of many **butubutu** established a policy where cocoa was to be established on previously uncultivated land, so as not to create further pressure on the land close to the village. When announcing these policies, **bangara** and their associate leaders invariably referred to the detrimental long-term effects of covering most of the good garden land immediately behind villages with coconuts, a wrongdoing committed through several generations. By the 1980s the universal presence close to, and along, village coasts of increasingly useless coconut trees (which are very difficult to remove altogether since the root system is so extensive) was deemed to have done more than enough damage to the availability of good land near villages. Giving heightened priority to food crops on easily accessible land was thus assured by relegating new cocoa plantings to the remote forest – combined in many instances by the beginning removal of surplus coconut trees close to villages. This 'opening up' of the more remote forest for cash crop purposes rapidly led to regular visits to and modification of these tracts, and eventually encouraged the establishment of these new and diverse gardens.

A rather extreme case of this move back to the bush is provided by the villagers of Tamaneke in northern Marovo. This important community of the Christian Fellowship Church was in 1995 and 1996 making a concerted effort to develop much new agricultural land along the Piongo Lavata river. The area is the spatial and spiritual focus of the very large **puava** of the Vahole **butubutu** whose historical role in taro irrigation was discussed earlier. Community leaders (leaders of the CFC and the chiefly core of

Vahole) have directed each of Tamaneke's thirty or so households to clear land on allocated blocks along the inland riverbanks, and to interplant 500 new cocoa trees with dryland *Colocasia* taro. It is envisaged that taro cultivation can continue among the growing cocoa trees until the latter begin to bear fruit. This initiative signalled a strong revival of taro as a staple among the Tamaneke people, and much enthusiasm has gone into the combined effort of providing taro for today while establishing cocoa as a source of cash income for the not too distant future. Enthusiasm for taro indeed led some older men of Tamaneke to question the wisdom of planting cocoa in these new riverside gardens. Referring to the unique suitability of the soils there for taro cultivation, they maintain that it would be a waste to fill this good land with cocoa – a cash crop whose price fluctuations have been notorious (cocoa prices paid to village growers in mid-1996 were SI$ 3.00 per kilogram). There is reason to believe that Tamaneke people would have been less enthusiastic about the Piongo Lavata garden enterprise if taro revival had not been so much part of it.[6]

Of course, visits to bush gardens yield more than cocoa or harvests from the gardens themselves. Getting there involves travel by canoe and on foot, often by entire family groups, through a number of fertile ecological zones such as mangrove estuaries, swamps with stands of sago palms and giant *Cyrtosperma* taro (**ghohere**, planted but rarely tended), and undisturbed forest. A number of things can be harvested en route, such as medicinal plants, mangrove shells and mud crabs, building materials, firewood and wild edible plants including ferns and mangrove fruits. It is not uncommon for families or couples to stay for a few nights in a simple hut built in the bush garden. Apart from the ostensible focus on taro cultivation and the tending of cocoa, such visits may lead to hunting trips in the forest, and they provide relaxation from what is often complained about as the demanding sociality of village life.

Hamlets, entrepreneurs and proto-peasants

An even more fundamental present change in Marovo is basically a response to the same pressures of population growth and land scarcity that has promoted bush gardens, but it involves not just the agroforestry system but also the entire settlement pattern. The 20th century map of relatively few and rather large nucleated coastal villages began to dissolve in the late 1980s. We see a growing tendency for extended families to move away from large villages and settle in single-family hamlets. Just as the recent bush gardens have parallels in remote gardens developed by coastal people on bush people's land in the early years of the 20th century, so the process of hamleti-sation shows a return to past patterns.

The new hamlets are often one-family settlements located some distance along the coast from the main village, many of which date from the arrival of missions from around 1915. Population growth and the resultant shortage of easily accessible garden land are the main reasons why a family decides to leave the main village, clear an entirely new site for settlement and gardening, and set up a small village all on their own. This trend is not altogether new, and we can find examples new hamlets established a decade or two ago are now actually growing into larger villages in their own right, as the children of the original settler family marry and set up their own households. The building of a church is a major breakthrough in the status transition from hamlet (**palavanua kiki**, 'small village') to proper village (**palavanua**, cf. Chapter 3). However, the majority of these 'small villages' throughout Marovo are of recent origin. Most of them are in new locations within customary **puava**, allocated to and cleared by the founding family, but some are established on former settlement sites dating from pre-colonial times. Among coastal butubutu, an increasing number of hamlets are being established in the barrier islands, with maximum opportunities for fishing and the collection of "marine products", and with the absence of water no longer being a problem as rain-water tanks fed from iron roofs become a norm. A number of hamlets have been established on formerly alienated land (most often abandoned European-owned coconut plantations) now purchased and registered as "perpetual estate" by its owners, who are often descendants of the people who originally sold the land to planters in the late 19th century.

What we see here is the Marovo version of the "homestead" movement noted in many other parts of the Pacific, for example in Fiji, where the new homesteads are strongly linked to peasantisation and the desire to establish more individualised land rights (Bayliss-Smith et.al., 1988; Brookfield, 1988). In Marovo Lagoon these social changes are also underway but in a more restrained form. People say that life in the old villages is simply too socially 'dense' and practically demanding. This applies especially to the numerous villages on small islands just off the coast, of which Vakabo and Bareho are examples (although these two islands are relatively large compared to the locations of some other villages of this type). Life in such "offshore" villages has the added discomforts of the need to paddle to the nearby mainland for gardening, for obtaining fresh water for drinking, and for doing one's laundry. New hamlets typically have their gardens only minutes' walk away from the house and their own freshwater source just nearby. But there are other cases where persons of entrepreneurial leanings, agricultural or otherwise, establish their own hamlets in order to pursue intensive economic activities without being constrained by the spatial limits, social obligations and communal work requirements of large villages.

In support of this "proto-peasantisation" model it is significant that it is predominantly the hamlet families who operate petrol sales (an important form of small business in this area of heavy reliance on outboard motors for fast transport), outboard motor servicing, marine products purchase, dugout canoe manufacture and other commercial activities, in addition to intensive market gardening and sometimes even copra production. Some hamlet founders simply express a desire to get away from the main village because of social conflict, or because of the environmental undesirability of that village site. In yet other instances, larger-scale village fission may occur because of population pressure or because of land disputes or other quarrels, thus instantly forming a larger-than-hamlet size "new" village settled by a portion of the population of the split village. Most recently, there have been at least one case where a major village has split following the conversion to a new evangelist church of a minority group.[7]

On the most fundamental level of **butubutu-puava** relationships, the spread of new hamlets along the coasts of the lagoon is seen as an extension of the fundamental **nginira** 'power' – or ancestral title –held by the group over its territory and all resources therein. Some **bangara** say that it is a good thing if some families move from the main village(s) to set up their own hamlets. This position is not taken by the chiefs simply out of concern for population pressure and land scarcity in the village. Rather, the profusion of hamlets since the late 1980s is considered by chiefs to be a significant expansion of the surveillance opportunities of the **butubutu** as a whole in a time when a staggering variety of resource-hungry agents of foreign capitalism descend on the Marovo Lagoon. The more eyes there are along the coastline of a **butubutu's puava**, the sooner can unwanted intruders be spotted and, if necessary, chased away – in the old but persistent Marovo exorcist tradition of **chitua**, 'driving out malevolent agents and powers and unwanted persons'.

In summary, many of the new 'small villages' of Marovo are pivots in agricultural innovation and commercial entrepreneurship. While their inhabitants follow well-established Marovo patterns of trying out new things as well as minimising economic vulnerability by maximising diversity, these small and rather dynamic communities also look to the future. In a number of ways the diverse, "modernist"-oriented adaptation of some hamlet-dwelling entrepreneurs, including activities like intensive cash cropping, modest cattle ranching, the performance of scarce services (such as well-stocked trade stores and outboard-motor repair) for payment, and buying of marine products, make them seem less dependent on the traditional backdrop of vast expanses of reserve forest.[8]

9 The Forest as Commodity: Selling Logs to Asia

Logged landscapes

In previous chapters we have traced the Marovo people's multiple uses of the rainforest over many generations. All these uses involved some degree of disturbance to the forest, but even clearance for cultivation – the most drastic of these disturbances – did not have a lasting effect. Instead the rapid regrowth of secondary forest paved the way for the development of **chichiogo** – a mature forest with tall trees, enriched with useful species but basically resembling undisturbed primary forest (cf. Chapter 3).

Today there are some more visible transformations, rather striking to those travelling by air between the New Georgia islands and Honiara in the low-flying Twin Otter or Islander aircraft used by Solomon Airlines on these routes. Large-scale logging with heavy machinery has inscribed the land with wide red roads of compacted clay running parallel to the coast and snaking their way inland along ridges. The roads are flanked by swathes of broken forest in which the red patches of eroded clay can be seen beneath the tattered fragments of canopy. Here and there totally clear-felled patches more or less bare of vegetation show the "log ponds" where logs were accumulated after being felled and dragged out of the forest, or the sites of temporary camps, or simply places where felling has somehow got out of hand.

The recent (and current) operations of certain Asian logging companies create, at worst, a chaotic blighted landscape scarred as if by modern warfare. For example, on the Gevala lands of southeastern Vangunu we see a twisted, seemingly irrational embroidery of roads, some leading nowhere into culs-de-sac on terrain too steep to be traversed even by logging machinery. The surviving vegetation is a patchwork of low, ragged shrubs and creeping vines, irregular patches of small trees, and a scattering of tall trees left as a pathetic reminder of the forest that used to be. The streams are clogged with scattered tree trunks and the rivers, particularly the mighty Gevala system, discharge red silt into the inner reaches of the lagoon.

205

In contrast, those flying further along westwards over New Georgia Island may catch glimpses of the flat land between the silted waters of Viru Harbour and the Kalena Bay of the Roviana Lagoon, where the improbable straight lines of uniform trees indicate a different history. Here less recent logging was succeeded by large-scale reforestation, carried out by government agencies. Over the mountains to the north and west the picture is again a different one. Here a single, very wide road – in places appearing white from its predominant gravel surface – runs parallel to the coast in a curve from the Kusaghe lands into the northern reaches of Marovo Lagoon, and signifies the apparently more well-regulated activities of another Asian logging company whose operations have taken over where a late-colonial European predecessor left. On the logging concessions of northern New Georgia, the lands at first glance appear to be still rather well forested with a remaining canopy. From the ground, quite a few valuable **goliti** (*Gmelina moluccana*) and **rigi** (*Pterocarpus indicum*) trees may be seen still standing.

What has happened to these lands, what *is* happening to them, and what are the areas likely to turn into? How have Marovo people handled this new intruder – the foreign logging company? This chapter addresses the long and complicated history of logging and its many ups and downs in the Marovo area.

Logging, politics and secrecy

It is extraordinary, but significant, that the logging industry in Solomon Islands should be so poorly documented at the present time. The logging boom of the 1990s has probably engaged more Solomon Islanders in discussion and disagreement than any other topic (including churches and Christianity) ever has done. In this decade national politics became reduced almost to a single issue, which played a key part in changes of governments and which almost caused a collapse of diplomatic relationships between Solomon Islands and its main aid donors such as Australia because of stark differences over logging policy and practice. In the 1990s the logging industry grew to become the mainstay of the national economy. Since 1993 round logs and timber have provided each year at least 50% of the total exports of Solomon Islands, while the export duty on logs alone provides for the government one-quarter of all its revenues (Anonymous, 1996). However, despite the industry's massive contribution to the national economy there are no official statistics on the volume of logs produced by different areas, and no published information on the benefits that accrue to local people. How much timber has been produced recently on the islands of New Georgia, Vangunu and Gatokae? How much in royalties is being paid to customary landowners in Marovo? And what is the future potential of the forests to generate a sustainable income from logging?

These seemed to us to be legitimate questions to ask, but they have proved to be difficult ones to answer. The Statistics Office of the Ministry of Finance told us in August 1996 that there was no particular reason why they should not produce regional data on timber production, but that no one in authority had ever instructed the statisticians to carry out such an analysis. The most recent data they had available was for 1988. However, the task of statistical collation has been undertaken by others. The NGOs estimate that by late 1995 Choiseul and Western provinces were supplying 76% of the country's revenue from exported round logs (Bennett, in press). In this same year it was calculated that over 90% of government expenditure took place in Honiara, the capital (John Roughan, pers. comm.). It is not surprising that provincial leaders should become increasingly critical of the huge scale of this regional "subsidy", which props up a government regarded by many people in the Western Solomons as greedy, inefficient and corrupt. Some regional data were collected together by Campbell (1994),[1] and were leaked to us by a disgruntled expatriate consultant. The data show that Western Province (mainly New Georgia) contributed 66.6% of Solomon Islands log exports by volume, and almost as much by value, in the period January-August 1994 (Figure 9.1).

A particular bone of contention was the fate of the "timber levy", a 7.5% tax of the f.o.b. value of exported logs. Although originally envisaged as a tax on logging companies that would finance reforestation by the government, the timber levy was diverted into central government coffers while the Forestry Division was funded from aid money. From 1990 to 1994 Prime Minister Solomon Mamaloni resisted all efforts by provinces to claw back the timber levy, which climbed to over SI$ 4 million in annual income during those boom years. In 1994 the new government of Francis Billy Hilly, the National Coalition Partnership, showed itself to be responsive to provincial pressure. In October Billy Hilly announced that 20% of all logging taxes, including the levy, would go back to land owners, but unfortunately for them the NCP government collapsed in the following month and Mamaloni was back.

> One of Prime Minister Mamaloni's first moves was to reduce the 20% to the old rate of 7.5% levy to be held in trust for land holders' and/or area councils' reforestation projects. Although Premiers such as Malaita's David Ueta kept reminding the national government, the finance did not materialize. (Bennett, in press, Ch. 13)

Central government could control the proceeds of logging more easily than it could stifle debate. Australia, New Zealand and EU aid donors became increasingly critical of the mismanagement of the timber industry but were powerless to intervene.

When Keith Campbell's data were discussed in Honiara at a Conference on Forest Policy and Law in October 1994, there was a meeting of provincial delegates at which a resolution was passed "that forestry be devolved to the Western Provincial assembly to pass such ordinances as may be necessary to exercise control [over logging operations]" (Ministry of Forests, 1994:108). A political response by the Mamaloni government was to propose legislation in 1996 that would, in effect, abolish most powers of the provinces, in an attempt to cut out all intermediate levels of administration between central government and Area Councils. Not surprisingly this proposed legislation was strongly opposed by several provincial premiers. By late 1997, after the change to a new government led by Prime Minister Bartholomew Ulufa'alu, it was still not in force.

Figure 9.1   Solomon Islands log exports by province, January-August 1994

Province	Volume (cu. m)	%	Value	Value (%) (mill. SI$)
Western	265,298	67	31.96	64
Choiseul	54,988	14	8.22	16
Malaita	25,601	6	3.61	7
Isabel	20,330	5	2.54	5
Makira	21,822	6	2.50	5
Guadalcanal	10,568	3	1.32	3
SOLOMON ISLANDS	398,624	100	50.15	100

Source: Campbell (1994:4)

With most government expenditure taking place within Honiara itself, the large contribution that islands like New Georgia make to national revenues is readily seen as a political embarrassment. Such information exacerbates the widespread feelings in Marovo and elsewhere of neglect by government. Logging can easily be construed as part of a process of deliberate impoverishment, whereby a revenue-hungry centre extracts wealth from the resource-rich periphery. In the rather fevered atmosphere of 1996, in which virtually all politics in the Solomons were linked to logging, it was easy to imagine there was a conspiracy not to reveal any information about the industry.

During our fieldwork in 1996 we hoped that perhaps the various studies already carried out by overseas aid consultants could help us in our search for information. The timber industry of Solomon Islands has already been examined in detail as part of the recent aid programmes of the European Union, Britain and Australia. However, enquiries to the relevant officials at the British High Commission in Honiara were answered by a secretary, who was candid about the fact that logging was a politically sensitive issue and therefore no information could be provided at the present time – perhaps the Australian High Commission might be in a better position to help? We enquired there for access to the Forest Inventory reports that were produced under an AusAid programme (but which were still "non-accepted" by the government), and met with an equally blank response. All requests, we were told, must be made in writing to the Australian High Commissioner. We asked for a sheet of paper and one of us wrote out a polite letter on the spot, which we handed in to the desk clerk. After some mutterings in the back office, the response came back that unfortunately any letter takes several days to process. However, copies of the reports were sent to us at a Cambridge address a few weeks later.

Why should so many aspects of logging in Marovo Lagoon (or any-where else in the Solomons) be shrouded in such secrecy? Why is it that much of the information in this chapter has had to be pieced together from leaked reports, newspaper articles, and the rumours spread around after village meetings, during local beer-drinking sessions in Honiara, Gizo and Munda, and among the expatriates and urban elite Solomon Islanders who gather for lunch on the cool terrace of the Mendana Hotel in Honiara? Logging has become the focus of politics, litigation, media attention and gossip at all levels of Solomon Islands society, and a dominant theme in the presentation of Solomon Islands in international media. For some, logging is almost a cargo cult for the millennium, while for others it is the work of the devil. We believe that logging has the potential to transform Marovo society and economy, achieving a series of changes as far-reaching as those accomplished by the sweet potato or copra in the 19th century (see Chapters 6-7). Yet in many ways we can document the present-day impact of logging with less confidence than when reconstructing the outcome of those earlier transformations which, because they are now history, now seem somehow logical and even inevitable. Our attempt to analyse the recent history of logging, in New Georgia and for the Solomons in general, must start with the recent demise of copra, that long-standing rural commodity of the Pacific Islands.

The decline and fall of copra

The contrast between the hidden secrets of the timber industry and the utterly transparent coconut industry is dramatic. Copra, for so long the main export of the country, has an entire marketing organisation devoted to regulating its price and monitoring its production and quality. Every three months detailed statistics are produced for quite small geographical areas, showing copra production for both "smallholders" and "plantations". In this way we can reconstruct the changes in copra production in Marovo Lagoon over the past twenty years in some detail (Figures 9.2 and 9.3).

Yet for the Solomons as a whole copra has been declining in importance since its heyday in the 1960s. Copra has not been the principal export of Solomon Islands since 1979. Since then, apart from 1984 which was an exceptional year of world shortages and boom prices, copra has been in decline. It has been overtaken in the list of exports by fish, timber (mainly round logs), palm oil, and even in some years cocoa. In 1995 its contribution to Solomon Islands exports was only SI$ 33 millions, or a mere 5.7% of the total (Central Bank of Solomon Islands, 1996a:27). Moreover there seems little prospect that this decline can be reversed (see, e.g., Bank of Hawaii, 1994). In early September 1999 (as this book went to press) Radio Australia in fact reported that the Solomon Islands Commodities Export Marketing Authority had announced plans to end all copra exports by the end of the year, and to develop processing in the Solomons of coconut oil and consumer products for both export and domestic use. To this end, it was reported, copra processing mills are being established in all provinces. Yet it remains unclear to which degree this radical move will manage to re-establish copra production as a rural mainstay.

King Copra, it would seem, has had his day. Dominant in the cash economy of Marovo for almost a hundred years, copra's precise origins in the village economy are difficult to trace, as we discussed in Chapter 7. However, because of the fantastically tight monitoring system that was set up in the days when fluctuations in copra production really mattered, the death throes of copra can be followed in minute detail. Statistics for copra shipped from Marovo Lagoon in sample years show that production was high in the early 1970s, but fell with low prices in 1975. By 1978 the price had recovered, and it reached a peak in 1984. Producers in Marovo responded to this opportunity, and tripled their output from around 300 tons in the mid-1970s to nearly 1,000 tonnes in 1984. Thereafter there was a spectacular collapse. By 1987 production had fallen to 164 tonnes, and by 1994 no copra or only token amounts were still being produced in Marovo, amounting to just 10 tonnes in total (Figure 9.2).

Figure 9.2 Copra production in Marovo Lagoon, 1975-1994

Year	Copra price per tonne		Production by grading station (tonnes)					Value of total copra production (SI$)*
	World US$	Local SI$	Gato-kae	Va-ngunu	NW Marovo	Viru	Total	
1975	239	129	63	24	173	23	283	36,507
1978	458	233	63	28	220	0	311	72,463
1980	454	318	102	227	108	0	437	138,966
1984	710	479	263	377	137	187	964	461,756
1987	309	327	141	3	5	15	164	53,628
1991	287	400	30	9	0	3	42	16,800
1994	418	689	2	4	0	4	10	6,890

*Calculated from local price

Sources:
Copra prices: Statistics Office 1995, Table 3.1
Production: Statistics Office 1985, Table 5 (i), and quarterly Statistical Bulletins of Statistics Office, Honiara, for 1997, 1991 and 1994.

This fall in production has been matched by a decline in its value, particularly when dollar values are calculated in terms of their real purchasing value. Throughout the past two decades persistent inflation has eroded the value of the Solomon Islands dollar, which was worth US$ 1.26 in 1975 but has subsided to only US$ 0.20 in 1999. Since Solomon Islanders spend a high proportion of their income on imported goods, the declining value of their dollar impacts greatly on the retail price index. Figure 9.3. shows what each year's copra production was worth in 1994 prices, adjusted to take into account the changes in the retail price index.

At the same time populations are growing rapidly. Over a period of twenty years the population of the Marovo Lagoon area has almost doubled, from an estimated 5,350 in 1975 to around 10,000 people in 1996. The statistics in Figure 9.3 show the contribution of copra to the Marovo economy on a per capita basis in the period 1974-1994. In the 1970s copra generated an income equivalent (in 1994 values) to SI$ 50-100 per person per year, rising to a peak of SI$173 per person in the boom year of 1984. Just three years later copra production had been abandoned by most villagers of Marovo, and in the 1990s it was contributing each year less than SI$ 3 per capita to total cash incomes.

Figure 9.3 Value of Marovo copra production, 1975-1994, at 1994 values

Year	Total production (SI$)	Honiara retail price index 1985 = 100	Total copra production, 1994 value (SI$)	Population of Marovo	Copra income per capita, 1994 values (SI$)
1975	36,507	(38)	276,204	5,350	51.63
1978	72,463	(49)	425,160	6,400	66.43
1980	138,966	56.3	709,640	7,250	97.88
1984	461,756	91.4	1,452,460	8,400	172.92
1987	53,628	126.1	122,268	8,950	13.66
1991	16,800	211.8	22,805	9,400	2.43
1994	6,980	287.5	6,980	9,650	1.40

Sources:
Copra production: see Figure 9.2.
Honiara RPI: Nankivell, 1991, Table A7; Central Bank of Solomon Islands, 1996a, Table 4.1. The modern RPI did not begin until 1980; the 1975 and 1978 figures are our estimates based on changes in the exchange rate.
Population: Interpolated/extrapolated from 1970 estimate of 4,538 (Statistical Office, 1971, Table 1.5), 1976 census of 5.561 and 1986 census of 8.865 (Statistics Office, 1995, Table 1.2.5), and 1992 estimate of 9,500 (Hviding and Baines, 1992).

It is in this context of a dramatic collapse in copra that the forests are being seen as the economic salvation of Marovo Lagoon. Unless and until copra returns to the central place that it once occupied, the Marovo people are obliged to look elsewhere for ways of meeting their needs for money: fish and vegetable marketing, shells, handicrafts, and tourist lodges are all being tried. However, increasingly it is the forests that are seen by outsiders as the most valuable market commodity that Marovo Lagoon has to offer. Whether or not in future it will be Asian logging companies or Marovo entrepreneurs who control the resource, it seems inevitable that logging will constitute the next phase in the evolving relationship of Marovo society to world capitalism.

Origins of logging

Outsiders did not always look upon Marovo's rainforests with such covetous eyes. Again, we turn to the British naval lieutenant B.T. Somerville who, just over one hundred years ago, spent eight months doing hydrographic surveys in Marovo Lagoon on board HMS *Penguin* (see Chapter 5). Like most Europeans of the time (and unlike earlier naval officers who were always on the lookout for ships' masts and spars) he saw nothing of value in the Marovo rainforests as such. Instead, he looked forward to the day when these seemingly "fertile" and plentiful lands might, through better management, be transformed into plantations of useful crops such as tea, rice and coffee – a process, he thought, which implied colonisation by "a more industrious and energetic people" (Somerville, 1897:411).

It was the same story elsewhere in the Solomons. In 1911 Charles Woodford wrote optimistically in the *Handbook of the British Solomon Islands Protectorate* that "a quantity of valuable timbers are known to exist, for which a market will eventually be discovered" (BSIP, 1911:31), but it was not until 1924 that the stands of kauri pine (*Agathis macrophylla*) in Temotu Province began to be logged (Lees et.al., 1991:178). Even so, prior to 1958 government revenue from timber exports rarely exceeded A$ 1,000 per annum (BSIP, 1963:33), a tiny fraction of the total. Forests covered most of New Georgia and the other islands, but neither the market nor the technology existed to make exploitation worthwhile.[2] Far from being a source of profit, felling trees was the price that had to be paid if land was to be brought into agricultural production.[3]

By the late 1950s, in addition to kauri forest logging on Vanikoro there were small sawmills at Tenaru (Levers), Buma (Roman Catholic mission), and Batuna in Marovo Lagoon (Seventh-day Adventist Mission), but the market for this timber was mainly local.[4] In 1963 timber exports still provided less than 4% of the Protectorate's exports, compared to copra's 91% (BSIP, 1965:22). The year 1963 marked a turning point, with the formation of Levers Pacific Timber Company as an offshoot of a multinational with logging experience in Africa. A market for hardwood logs was growing in Japan, and a technology had been developed for road construction, tree felling, and the dragging of logs along temporary trails. Levers began with trial shipments from government-owned forests on Ghizo, a raised coral island that had been completely depopulated in the late headhunting era and became the administrative headquarters of the Western Solomons. In 1968 Levers moved to Kolobangara (conventionally rendered "Kolombangara" among expatriates) to begin large-scale logging operations there from a base at Ringgi Cove (see Chapter 10).

Levers' initial objective was to log forests on alienated lands owned by government, the hard-won "forest estate" of the 1960s. However, from the outset the company's long-term objective was to gain access to customary land, so as to make the economics of the processing plant they had established at Ringgi more viable. Meanwhile their operation on Kolobangara flourished. By the mid-1970s Levers had become the biggest employer in the Western Solomons and contributed, in corporation tax, some

17% of the Protectorate's foreign exchange earnings (Bennett, in press, ch. 10). In 1978 they extended their logging to Barora, a strip of alienated land near the northern tip of New Georgia.

Despite this success, the forestry sector was still not taken very seriously by international experts. Their advice was that the large-scale production of timber and fish was not a sustainable source of export revenue, while restrictions on the further alienation of customary land meant that the plantation sector (coconuts, oil palm) had reached its ceiling. The future for the Solomons economy therefore lay in village agriculture, among small-holders whose energies needed to be channelled into more commercial forms of production (Jones, Muqtada and Ronnas, 1987). Hurricane damage to forests from Cyclone Namu in 1986, plus the withdrawal from the Solomons that year of the largest logging company, Levers Pacific Timbers, seemed to signal that forestry could not be relied upon as the engine of national economic growth.

The experts have been proved wrong: over the last ten years the forestry sector has taken off in spectacular fashion. While no one believes that the current rate of logging is sustainable, at least half of "the wealth of the Solomons" (depending on how such a thing is measured) now derives from the nation's forests. The late 1980s did indeed see a downturn in the industry, but in the 1990s output rose to extraordinary levels. After 1992, in particular, world market prices soared following the decision by the Malaysian government to ban log exports from Malaysia, and suddenly there were Asian logging companies queuing up to make deals with customary landowners in both Papua New Guinea and Solomon Islands.

Inroads into Marovo forests

The great Solomon Islands logging boom of the 1990s is reviewed in Chapter 11. Here we examine its local impact along the margins of Marovo Lagoon, where extensive logging has taken place on government-held and customary lands in Vangunu, Viru and North New Georgia. In 1996-97 there was much talk of further expansion into new areas of customary land. It is not uncommon in Marovo Lagoon today to see small groups of Asians and Europeans travelling to and from logging camps, or visiting the villages of **butubutu** who are flirting with the idea of selling logging concessions and thereby pursuing the goal of **va hore kabani**, 'make a company land [on one's beach]'. The foreigners usually arrive at the Seghe airstrip, and they are driven around the lagoon in company-owned aluminium dinghies with large outboard motors. This traffic is particularly noticeable and commented on in central Marovo, where villagers have a panoramic view of the main lagoon and where motorised sea travel tends to follow routes rather close to shore, but where few **butubutu** have dealings with logging companies (partly because most of them are 'coastal' with small, even negligible land holdings). Whenever some influential man of a 'bush' **butubutu** is sighted in a noisy, high-powered "company" boat together with some more or less well-known foreigner(s), the sea-holding 'coastal' people of central Marovo voice their opinion on where logging operations are going to 'land' (or, in a more active sense, 'be landed') next.

In mid-1996, when one of us travelled around to forty-five villages throughout Marovo in connection with a collaborative educational project involving the Marovo-wide distribution of two new books in the local languages (Hviding, 1995b, 1995c), quite a few elderly chiefs were not at home. They had travelled to Honiara by air or sea for one of two main purposes: either to be lavishly entertained at hotels and clubs as the guests of Asian logging companies, or to appear in High Court cases involving disputes over logging concessions. Some of these chiefs found themselves becoming regular commuters between Honiara, the Seghe airstrip (or Patutiva wharf) and their home villages.[5] Indeed, since arrival and departure times at Seghe are notoriously unreliable, and there is much waiting around, the Solomon Airlines office shed at the Seghe airstrip was in 1996 one of the best spots to pick up well-informed news and less reliable rumours about current developments in logging, conservation, tourism and politics on many levels.

The frequent Seghe trips and Honiara flights of chiefs were also motivated by the need for them to be present at several successive timber rights hearings held at the administrative headquarters, also at Seghe, where the Marovo Area Council heard arguments and evidence for and against applications from **butubutu** representatives and from enterprising individuals who wished to enter into negotiations with logging companies. **Va hore kabani** initiatives require endorsement or at least a non-objection declaration from the Area Council. Such hearings also mean hectic work for the severely understaffed archaeology unit of the Western Province Cultural Office, which tries to respond to most calls from **butubutu** for surveys of tabu sites and other important places in forest proposed for logging.

At the same time a number of younger men of influential descent were busy partying in town, spending tens of thousands of dollars from the very substantial advances they had received from logging companies for acting as their facilitators and mediators vis-à-vis the **butubutu** at home. These enterprising sons of chiefs were quickly and ironically dubbed 'L.O.'s (for Land Owners) by village commentators who know well that according to **kastom** (1) no single person owns the **puava**, (2) no individual person is empowered to sign off logging agreements on behalf of their **butubutu**, and (3) those who try are likely to meet with serious trouble when they return home. Yet the biting sarcasm of the L.O. designation could do little to restrain or diminish these men's enthusiasm at sudden wealth and spending power. Their free-spending habits, known in Marovo as **nabulu** ('showering others with favours to further one's own cause') – meant that of the thousands, ten thousands (and reputedly, in some cases, hundreds of thousands) of dollars they received little ever got back to family, village or **butubutu**. According to recent reports (cf. also Berg, 1999) this giddy cycle of interlinked fields of activity, in village, court, hotel bar and casino, has continued to unfold.

Meanwhile, on the ground actual logging activity is still quite piecemeal and far from sustained. By September 1997 the large-scale operation on government land on Vangunu by the Silvania company had ceased, and only a few new inroads were evident. Near Ketoketo on the eastern side of the Bareke peninsula, the long-surviving Allardyce company landed equipment in mid-1996 and since commenced logging on customary land up towards the valleys of the Kele river system (where, to complicate the picture, gold prospecting is a lively current issue). On the far eastern margin of the Marovo area, at Kavolavata on the weather coast of Gatokae, another operation was also established. But overall what may be seen as an in-built buffer of dispute potential from multiple claims to any land – owing not least to the uneasy relationship of clear-cut land rights to complicated structures of bilateral kinship whereby, as is often said in Marovo, 'everyone is some-how related to everyone else!' – still appears to slow down most company overtures. For example, quite unprecedented confrontations were seen during Area Council meetings in mid-1996 when spokesmen of non-land-holding 'coastal' **butubutu** emerged on the scene to recount genealogies and ancient histories of place and settlement so convincingly that they were recognised as indisputable decision-makers in matters pertaining to certain tracts of inland forest. What might be seen by some outsiders as esoteric knowledge was thus quickly transformed to acutely powerful words capable of blocking logging proposals. The complex cultural history of Marovo as a region, and the many twists and turns of the 'coastal'/'bush' equation, con-tinue to exert unexpected influences on today's politics.

Loggers, big and small

Multinational logging companies have been major actors in New Georgia over the last three decades: Levers Pacific Timbers Ltd., an offshoot of British-based Unilever; Kalena Timber Corporation (mainly Australian); Golden Springs International (Indonesian); Silvania Products (Malaysian); and Eagon Resources Development Co. Ltd. (Korean). In addition a number of smaller operations have been on the scene for varying periods of time since the 1960s. During that decade, a handful of mainly Australian forestry enterprises carried out rather small-scale logging of easily accessible land in the central to eastern lagoon. These operations were based on light machinery, employed largely local men and were usually limited in their duration. Some mid-sized lagoon islands which had not formerly been converted to coconut plantations, such as the Roromana islands southeast of Marovo Island itself, were selectively logged in this way. Such enterprises were based on close contact between the Australian "boss" in question (such as 'Mr. Cox' and 'Mr. Schenk' who are still remembered by name) and the relevant local chiefs and involved a flow of various services in cash and kind. In a few instances, 'help' was also enlisted from small logging operations like this by **butubutu** wishing to transform a lagoon island or a stretch of coastal land into coconut plantation. Logging was in effect a way of having that land cleared with the added bonus of local employment and of fees paid by the timber extractor.

Although logging in the decades since the 1960s has been mainly the domain of large transnational companies, recent years have also seen well-delimited "hit-and-run"-missions by certain smaller Solomon Islands enterprises. A joint venture in 1995 between an urban Marovo businessman and a Malaita-based company which removed most large trees (notably large numbers of the valuable **kivili** or Merbau, *Intsia bijuga*) from a long section of the double barrier islands chain bordering the eastern lagoon. Three quick shipments of logs reputedly earned SI\$ 2.7 million, but mainly to the Malaita company. The Marovo businessman was reputed to have received much less than expected, moreover also getting a court case on his hands raised by another prominent urban Marovo man claiming equally strong entitlements in the barrier island in question. Another quick attempt in early 1996 by the same joint venture to extract **kivili** from the uninhabited offshore island of Bulo got well under way despite protests from several elders connected to the customary "consortium" of Bulo owners, one of whom quickly put his complaint before the High Court. Operations were halted in May of that year following the High Court's finding that no licence to log had been issued, and the Court's interlocutory injunction that logging was to stop, that the accumulated logs could be sold "under the normal requirements of relevant authorities", and that the proceeds of the sale be deposited in court until questions of customary land rights were resolved (High Court of Solomon Islands, 1996).

If we compare these examples from the 1960s and the 1990s, we can see how the ethos surrounding Marovo logging has shifted from consensus to conflict. Instead of having chiefs acting according to local **kastom** through dealing with loggers on an agreed and reciprocal basis, in consultation with their **butubutu**, the situation has become one where town-based entrepreneurs mount hit-and-run operations on the basis of disputed claims to land rights. The inherent complexities of overlapping and cross-cutting relationships of bilateral kinship exacerbate the conflict. In the 1996 case just mentioned, it was notably stated that

> ... the plaintiff does not claim that he has rights over Bulo, to the exclusion of the defendants. It would appear that he will seek to establish his customary rights and in the meantime he would like, through court injunction, the operation of the defendants to be put on hold so that he is not left out in the event that he succeeds to establish his customary right over Bulo ... Defendants say in court that plaintiff is a relative though they contend that the relationship is too far removed to confer any customary land right ... As to whether [plaintiff] will succeed ... is too early to say and may well depend on whether the local court will find that he has customary right in Bulo Land. (Commissioner S. Awich, in High Court of Solomon Islands, 1996)

What has changed is not just the profitability of logging but also the level of distrust among all those concerned. To understand the roots of this change we need to uncover the turbulent history of large-scale logging by foreign interests, which has so far focussed on three major areas of Marovo: the Viru Harbour area, southeastern Vangunu, and North New Georgia.

Viru-Kalena: from logging to privatisation

Of the three major operations in the Marovo area in the recent decades, the logging at Viru is remembered locally as having been the least contentious. The block of land known in logging circles as the "Viru-Kalena" concession covers an area of 25,000 hectares on the southeastern coast of New Georgia. A wide coastal zone of raised coral terraces and sheer cliffs is overlain by a deep clay soil, and is crossed by valleys with freshwater swamp forest containing, even today, intact stands of the giant timber tree *Terminalia brassii* (**hoba**) (T.C. Whitmore, pers. comm.). Further inland are the foothills of the volcanic interior, with broad ridges and some quite steep slopes. In the 1960s neither coast nor hinterland were settled, and inland there were tall mixed stands of *Dillenia* spp. (**kapuchu**), *Campnosperma brevipetiolatum* (**olanga**), *Vitex cofassus* (**vasara**) plus many non-commercial timber species (cf. Wall and Hansell, 1975).

The Viru-Kalena area was regarded by the Forestry Department as being sufficiently "vacant" for it to be suitable for acquisition. In the 1960s the overall policy of the British Solomon Islands Protectorate was to establish a "Forest Estate", if possible on land owned by the government, as a way for forestry to "make a contribution towards economic development"

(BSIP 1963:30). The Viru acquisition, like the large block of land in south-eastern Vangunu (see below), is an example of this pro-active policy in operation. From 1965 onwards the Australian-based Kalena Timber Company (KTC) was granted logging rights there and began to exploit the large tract of coastal plain and lowland hills that lies inland from Viru Harbour. By the standards of the 1990s progress was slow: annual production was below the allowable 500,000 cubic feet (14,160 cubic metres, and roading could not keep up with logging (Bennett, in press, ch. 10). By comparison, in 1995 a single average shipment by the Eagon company from Choiseul to Japan contained a declared 150,000 cubic metres, and the actual (un-declared) volume was probably more (M. Iles, pers. comm.)

Eventually, apart from the freshwater swamp forests that grow in depressions near to the coast, most of the dryland forest at Viru was eventually logged by KTC. In the 1970s this logged-out area was clear-felled by the Forestry Department who then undertook a programme of reforestation. However, maintenance of the new plantations was minimal. T.C. Whitmore (pers. comm.) observed that many non-commercial species had invaded the plantations by 1995, and the replanted area had become a dense jungle in which it was not easy to make out the planted trees. Both logging and reforestation were blamed by Shield (1992) for the erosion which caused extensive sedimentation in the wide, almost landlocked cove of Viru Harbour into which three major rivers flow from the areas in question. Coastal sedimentation has also been reported from Kalena Bay to the west, where logging activity expanded in the early 1990s.

Despite these environmental impacts, up until the time of their withdrawal from Viru Harbour the Kalena Timber Company kept on reasonably good terms with the local **butubutu** (the Chuvilana and Libo groups, traditionally subsumed as 'Kalivarana people'). In a certain sense these groups still uphold customary claims to the government-held land and have a long-running interest in establishing their own small-scale commercial projects there. They also own adjacent areas to which logging has been extended. As argued elsewhere, these generally amicable relations resulted from the nature of the contact that KTC maintained with the originally land-holding **butubutu** (Hviding, 1996a:317). Back in the 1960s when the company began its operations the rights of local people at Viru were virtually disregarded by the Government, secure in their legal acquisition of a Forest Estate. But because the Kalena company adopted a pragmatic and direct approach towards ongoing negotiations, they conformed much better to local demands for mutual recognition and for the company side to be accountable in the conduct of its affairs. In addition, the company's large logging camp at Ilemi in the estuarine inner parts of Viru Harbour offered infrastructural opportunities (including medical facilities) for the people of two large villages of Tetemara and Tobe, which would otherwise have continued their relative isolation in the thinly populated area between the Marovo and Roviana lagoons. Undoubtedly, too, it has helped that the communities concerned are Seventh-day Adventists with a history of entrepreneurship and commercial orientation, and that most of the land logged is relatively unattractive as garden land, being in part water-logged and bordering crocodile-infested swamps.

Replanting the government's "forest estate" (including Viru) petered out in 1992 when overseas aid was no longer forthcoming to pay for this branch of government activity. At Viru some 11,000 hectares of the total of 25,000 had been replanted (Bennett, in press, Ch. 16). By 1995 the "loggers' government" of Solomon Mamaloni was in deep fiscal crisis, and privatisation of the forest estate was announced as one measure to raise cash and cut jobs. A valuation study of Viru was carried out by Kolombangara Forest Products Ltd. (KFPL, see Chapter 10), funded by EU aid money, and calculated that its value under a "logging/re-planting/sustainable forestry" regime amounted to about SI$ 46 millions (M. Iles, pers. comm.). Mamaloni used the KFPL report to negotiate with the Eagon company, by then well established in Choiseul, and agreed on a sale.[6] There was no process of competitive tendering or even consultation with the government's own Forestry Division. In November 1995 the Viru "forest estate" plantation passed into the hands of Eagon for SI$ 23 million, and Mamaloni's government was rescued from insolvency.[7]

A further cycle of logging thus began in Viru-Kalena. It was reported that trial shipments from Viru Harbour had already, by August 1996, delivered the company SI$ 17 millions worth of logs (A.V. Hughes, pers. comm.). It remains to be seen if the Korean company will avoid more adverse environmental impacts, and whether they can maintain the same good relations with local communities.[8]

Vangunu: raping the forest estate

Another large block of land that has been heavily affected by logging, in this case rather recently, is on the southeastern side of the large island of Vangunu. The block is known to the Lands Department as "Lot 16 of LR 515", and is today conventionally referred to also among modernist-oriented Marovo people as 'Lot 16'; an area subject of much rumours and myth-making. It consists of 10,299 hectares of "vacant land" which the colonial government somehow managed to acquire from its customary landowners in 1963 as part of its expanding "forest estate". The Vangunu block was alienated at a time of great expansion in government forestry. Its alienation was facilitated because most of the area was virtually uninhabited and of little immediate value to the local population. At this time the sparse coastal population of this part of Vangunu, as virtually everyone else throughout Marovo, was busy planting coastal land with coconuts, copra being the form of development so strongly encouraged in he late colonial era.

The Vangunu acquisition is a most interesting and well-documented example of the colonial government's assertive "forest estate" policy that was agreed in September 1962, which presupposed that the most rational and efficient way to manage forestry was to focus it on government-held lands. The history of Lot 16 can be examined using archival documents as well as oral history and personal recollections. In today's Vangunu, oral history of this period of colonial land acquisition amounts almost to a mythology of collective assertiveness (or, in the case of Lot 16, a lack of solidarity) in the face of colonialist ambitions.

The Vangunu case is a further example of how "colonialism", in this case negotiations between British officials and Vangunu leaders, should not be seen on either side as involving a set of predictable moves between actors motivated by homogeneous cultural values and stereotypical assumptions. Instead the colonial encounter was nuanced by cultural diversity, even idiosyncrasy, by agents on both sides. These agents were coming from different generations, different social groups and classes, and different religions.

On the Vangunu side, some leaders in 1963 were anxious to cooperate with government, while others fought off the administration all the way to the High Court. An example of the cooperative (or easily persuaded) was the Vura-Chakope community of Seventh-day Adventists, as represented by the two chiefs Kineo and Kuku. They decided after a meeting with the Forestry officer that they "agreed in principle to sell the land [Lot 16] to government – the price however to be negotiated with government after further discussion among themselves". Their only worries were that provision should be made for future garden expansion, that "only Vangunu people will be settled in these extentions as they become available", and that each community should be allowed "if they require it one free permit per year to cut one Goliti tree Gmelina salomonensis for canoe construction". On the other hand the representatives of Bopo, Saira [Zaira] and Nineveh (all Methodist villages) who were present at the same meeting "refused to negotiate for the sale of their land to Government on any terms".[9] David Livingstone Kavusu, a chiefly man of the "middle" generation (then around forty years old) and the spokesman of this group, remains a folk hero in Vangunu to this day because of his determined stance on behalf of his **butubutu**. Until then Kavusu had not been much involved with the outside world except for a period during World War II as a scout and barge pilot for American troops.

However, his persistent engagement during the land acquisition process and his legendary stand of **"dai, dai, dai meni dai!"** (*'no, no, no and finally no!'* in the Vangunu language) are fondly remembered among these groups as ultimate examples of the potency of the **kastom** of the south Vangunu people in the face of colonial greed and deception. Indeed, unlike their Seventh-day Adventist neighbours at Vura and Chakope, the Methodist villagers of southern Vangunu retain an old fame throughout Marovo for strong magical powers as well as determined political will, and it is sometimes commented that the colonial government at the time played with fire when they tried to 'trick' Kavusu and his **butubutu** into selling the land west of the Sagivi river.

Attitudes on the government side were equally diverse. On the one hand there was the colonial establishment, as represented by Chief Forestry Officer K.W. Trenaman. He instructed his field officer J.W.F. Chapman that Chapman should "try to leave the impression [in Vangunu] that ... Government is making a very reasonable offer such as is not likely to be substantially improved upon, [and] the people have nothing to lose and very much to gain by accepting this offer".[10] There was no need for him to specify that by saying "nothing to lose" he actually meant 10,299 hectares of land under tropical rainforest, and that by "very much to gain" he actually meant £ 800 in cash (for Lot 16) plus 10 per cent of any logging royalties.

On the other hand there were young district officers like A.V. Hughes in Gizo, whose job it was to arrange for the signature of papers and the handing over of the £ 800 payment. He reported back that the job had been completed, but that afterwards there were widespread feelings on Vangunu of "anxiety and dissatisfaction", for the following reasons:

(1) Loss of ground, the only form of security, for ever. Vendors are worried that they may have retained too little garden land ...

(2) Size of share. Vendors realize now that an individual's share of even £ 800 ... is a very few pounds when the line includes a hundred or more people. For these few pounds, the individual has sold – or has had sold for him – his main form of wealth and status ...

(3) Disproportionally small total price, compared to the profits likely to be shown by companies exploiting the timber ... [11]

Prophetic words, indeed. It is interesting to note that while K.W. Trenaman retired at the end of the 1960s and returned home to England, A.V. (Tony) Hughes married a woman from the Western Solomons, continued in government service, and finished his career as head of the Central Bank of Solomon Islands castigating the Mamaloni government in the 1990s for its lax fiscal policies, poor management of foreign logging companies, and failure to encourage small-scale sustainable alternatives to operations like the rape of Vangunu's Lot 16, which was then under way. Meanwhile David Livingstone Kavusu continued his career as a chief, Methodist lay preacher and widely travelling traditional healer of increasing fame, specialising in the curing of infertile couples. In the 1990s he has remained on the scene as an venerable spokesman of customary affairs and an opponent of unwise land deals on Vangunu, this time fending off the blandishments of some Asian logging companies while simultaneously conducting his very own effort at having part of the customary land on south Vangunu selectively logged through a deal conforming to his own specifications and with an Asian company of his own choice. Thus, in one of the ironies of post-colonialism, former protagonists found themselves united in the face of a new perceived threat.

Logging concessions were granted on Vangunu to local companies in the 1970s, but the block was only exploited on a very small scale. Not until the Malaysian company Silvania Products Ltd. was granted a lease in 1992 was the inland area opened up with roads, and log exports began quickly from a new port on customary land at Merusu, conveniently provided for by representatives of the generation whose fathers sold Lot 16. Large volumes have been exported, but Silvania have consistently declared very low values for their exported logs from Vangunu – the lowest values of any company operating in Solomon Islands. As a result its liability for export duty is of course reduced, and more than once Silvania has been required to halt exports to explain this anomaly. Their actual logging practices have also come under criticism from the Ministry of Forests, as detailed by Forests Monitor Ltd., an independent environmental consultancy based in the UK:

In November 1995 Silvania had their logging licence suspended for the fourth time since 1993. This most recent suspension was due to a number of factors, including excessive production of low grade logs and failure to construct roads in advance of felling operations to a satisfactory standard ... The National Forest Resources Inventory [funded by AusAid] found [that] 'the degree of canopy removal and soil disturbance was the most extensive seen by the authors in any logging operation in tropical rainforest in any country. It appears more like a clearfelling operation and bore little relation to any attempt at retaining even a token sample of future commercial crop on the site'.... In March 1994 a visit by representatives of the Ministry of Forests, Environment and Conservation [reported]... 'an immediate consequence of the logging operations is deposit of silt in Marovo Lagoon from rivers flowing down from the eastern slopes of Vangunu Island'. (Forests Monitor Ltd., 1996:6-7).

Because statistics are so sparse we do not know how much timber Silvania has exported altogether from Vangunu, but in the year 1995 the island was the third largest producer in Solomon Islands, producing 88,000 cubic metres of logs with a declared value of US$ 8,644,995 (nearly SI$ 30 millions).[12]

The logs exported from Vangunu derive not only from Silvania's own concession, which comes to an end in 1999, but also from an encroachment into adjacent areas. According to the Malaysians themselves, "SPL [Silvania] has extended its operations into surrounding customary lands either by way of entering into Standard Logging Agreements or Technology Agreements with the respective landowners" (Kumpulan Emas Berhad, 1996:2). According to leaders of the Tobakokorapa **butubutu** in Michi on the northwestern Vangunu coast, the expansion of logging at least on the northern lagoon-facing side was nothing more than an unauthorised robbery of timber from the lands of Tobakokorapa. Numerous cases for compensation have been held in the High Court in Honiara.

The future of southeastern Vangunu – Lot 16 – is now very uncertain. In 1996 the Solomon Islands government in received a proposal from Silvania's parent company in Malaysia for the existing 10,000 hectare lease on Vangunu, plus an additional 20,000 hectares to be acquired from adjacent landowners, to be completely cleared of trees and replanted as a gigantic oil-palm plantation. Further inroads into Vangunu's forests have been made since 1996 by several smaller logging companies that have reached agreements with the groups holding the customary lands around the Kele bay immediately north of Lot 16. And meanwhile, in 1999 Leigh Resource Corporation (of Australia) reports on the Internet to have found porphyry copper gold mineralisation in the Kele river catchment on Vangunu, and states that "currently logging operations on Vangunu Island are improving access with roads now being constructed to the edge of the defined area of mineralization". This extraordinary transformation in the landscapes and political economy of the Marovo Lagoon is a possible scenario that we review in more detail in Chapter 10.

North New Georgia: experiments in corporate logging

The third large area that has been logged in Marovo reveals the full potential for political complexity when large-scale logging takes place on customary land. Logging in North New Georgia has inspired much controversy and has been reported on, analysed and written about at some detail both by insiders and by outsiders with shorter- or longer-term involvements with the area (Rence, 1979; Tausinga, 1992; Cassells, 1995; Whitmore, pers. comm.;

Hviding, 1996a; Bennett, in press). What we attempt to provide here is a balanced overview of a situation which, as admitted by one of us elsewhere, has become "steadily more complicated" (Hviding, 1996a:319). Disputes and litigation have, in fact, marked every attempt to turn the northern New Georgia forests into a marketable commodity.'

The imposing volcanic slopes and wide coastal terraces of the North New Georgia area have been attractive to logging companies because they contain good stands of lowland rain forests, undisturbed since the rather sparse population moved to the coast about a century ago. The species composition of the forests is typical of the region, and includes *Calophyllum* spp. (**buni**), *Campnosperma brevipetiolatum* (**olanga**), *Dillenia salomon-ensis* (**kapuchu**) and *Pometia pinnata* (**meda**). Around the coast there are freshwater swamp forests which contain the commercially valuable species *Terminalia brassii* (**hoba**) which are still unlogged at the present time (T.C. Whitmore, pers. comm.).

As elsewhere, it was land alienation that provided the initial impulse for the commercial exploitation of these forests. The Barora land near the very northern tip of the island is a coastal strip 10 km wide and extending about 4 km inland, and it was acquired by Lever Brothers under a Protectorate law of 1900 entitled the "Solomon (Wastelands) Regulation". Then (as now) the Solomons government was extremely short of cash, and this law was an attempt to encourage the establishment of expatriate plantations on land made vacant by wars and depopulation. Levers was ultimately (in 1931) awarded a Certificate of Occupation in Barora, which represented less than a freehold title but sufficient, the government hoped, to provide an incentive for plantation development. In fact at Barora most of the land was never developed, and the certificate was transferred to a new company, Levers Pacific Timbers Limited (henceforth, "Levers"), when it was formed in 1963. Up to this point the history of Barora is identical to the much larger area of alienated land on the island of Kolobangara (see Chapter 10).

In 1972, when Levers – in need of expansion from logged-out lands on nearby Kolobangara – began to consider logging at Barora, it was clear to the company that profitability depended upon access to a much larger area on New Georgia. Such access required an agreement between the company and the customary landowners of the areas adjacent to Barora, and in retro-spect it is clear it would have been better for Levers if this had been achieved on a piecemeal basis through separate negotiations with one **butu-butu** after another. Instead, Levers appealed to the Lands Department to help them to achieve a regional agreement rather than a series of local deals. As the Government at this time was itself pro-active in land acquisition to achieve the establishment of the national Forest Estate, and because timber exports were seen as one of the few remaining options to diversify an economy desperately dependent on copra, the Lands Department were eager to help.

The Government's strategy for North New Georgia was, quite simply, to separate the trees from the land. For every tract of land they needed to specify a landowning group that could be considered as possessing the "timber rights", and someone to make decisions on behalf of the group. Immediately two problems emerged. No one could agree who should be the "trustees" to act legally on behalf of the **butubutu**, and secondly the boundaries of **butubutu** lands were often in long-running dispute. Resolving such disputes had not mattered when the forest was unused except for occasional visits to hunt pigs, find honey or fell a **goliti** tree for a new canoe or two, but now the ownership of trees suddenly meant money and power on a grand scale.

We are in the unusual position of having two accounts by insiders concerning the course of events in the alienation of timber rights from customary lands, written from two different points of view. The first account is by Gordon Rence (1979), a man with a substantial knowledge both of customary land tenure, colonial and national land legislation and the history of New Georgia. His own grandmother was taken captive from Kia on Santa Isabel by Gerasi headhunters around 1900; almost exactly 100 years later the descendants of those Gerasi warriors were burning the bulldozers of an Asian logging company operating in the northern hinterland of Marovo Lagoon, and were in open confrontation with the armed police who had been sent from Honiara to protect the loggers. Gordon Rence was actually born on Kolobangara but later moved to his home area in Gerasi, growing up in Ramata, an old barrier islands village of much fame from headhunting times. He received his secondary education at the Seventh-day Adventist school at Betikama near Honiara, and in the early 1970s he assisted the National Museum in Honiara with the identification of tabu sites threatened by logging operations in north New Georgia. In 1974 he had joined the government as an assistant lands officer, and by 1985, at the height of conflict involving LPTL operations in North New Georgia, Rence had become the Solomon Islands Commissioner of Lands. According to his account,

> The government officers wanted to find out who were owners of the land, then register their land for them, so the owners could grant a lease ... to cut the timber (....) Silas Eto [the Holy Mama, founder and leader of the Christian Fellowship Church, CFC] was elected (in 1972) to be trustee for all the land [in the] north-east and west of New Georgia. .... [M]any people in the area were not happy about Silas Eto, because he was the leader of their movement [the CFC] but not overall leader for their land. .... [P]eople felt that once the trustees' names were registered they would have more power, and the people

whose names were not registered would have less power, so they wanted the trustees to be the original owners of the land. (Rence, 1979:122-123)

From 1972, five years followed of prolonged and sometimes bitter negotiations, which served only to drive a wedge between the pro-logging faction (mostly Seventh-day Adventists [SDA]) and those who wished to control logging by means of a small-scale sawmilling operation (mostly CFC communities). In February 1977, with Independence just one year off, the Lands Department abandoned the attempt in North New Georgia to produce a register of customary land and a list of trustees with whom a logging company could negotiate.

It was perhaps one hundred years too late for a central government to have the power and charisma to impose order in this way. In Fiji a register of customary land had been produced in the 1880s, based on some rough justice and the drawing of fixed lines on maps where often such rigid lines had never existed on the ground (France, 1969). Whereas in Fiji the system imposed by the British took root and today is so "traditional" that it is never questioned, in Solomon Islands such a task was never undertaken. The twilight years of British colonial rule was not, perhaps, a good time to start.

Instead, in February 1977 there was a change of policy. The task of appointing "representatives" was delegated to an Area Committee, which was to be chaired by an SDA man who was also pro-Levers and pro-logging. There was the appearance of balance on the Area Committee, with some CFC members as well as representatives of SDA villages, but in fact it had a majority that favoured a deal with Levers. The Committee established, with government help, the North New Georgia Timber Corporation (NNGTC), and after several meetings with Levers (meetings which the CFC largely boycotted) an agreement was signed in June 1980. Levers had purchased the timber rights on 45,000 hectares of customary land, estimated to contain 3 million cubic metres of merchantable hardwoods. Royalties were to be paid at variable rates, averaging about 12.5%, for a period of fifteen years (Bennett, in press, ch. 10).

Meanwhile logging had already started. With Kolobangara by now logged-out, Levers extended operations in 1978 to the government-held land around Barora, where a camp was set up and an airstrip constructed. This initial stage was accompanied by considerable dispute between the two closely related villages of Kolobaghea (CFC) and Tusu Mine (SDA), immediately adjacent to the Barora lands. While the Tusu Mine people were eager to facilitate immediate expansion by Levers, the people of Kolobaghea were just as determined to oppose logging. A court case ensued, from which it was reported in villages that the magistrate in Gizo "managed to disentangle a tightly knit genealogy and then divide it into two!". Although the populations of both villages were, and are, regarded as inextricably linked to each other through generations of shared descent, the actual court case was lost by Kolobaghea, and the Tusu Mine community was defined as "owners" of the disputed area. A strong foothold was thereby established for Levers. From 1981 logging moved westwards in the Lupa area of the Kusaghe region to Jela (the northernmost village of the Marovo administrative sub-district), and beyond that to the important Kusaghe area of Mase. To the southeast, logging expanded into the long uninhabited old inland districts of Dekurana, Maqela (Magela) and Hoava and into the lowlands bordering the Gerasi Lagoon.

Quite a different perspective on the negotiations leading up to the formation of the NNGTC is provided by Job Dudley Tausinga, who is the son of CFC founder Silas Eto, and also a very influential elected politician with a distinguished career on provincial and national levels. A leader of the CFC faction which opposed the further expansion of logging by Levers (see below), Tausinga was elected to the Western Provincial Assembly in 1984 and simultaneously became the Provincial Premier. In 1988 he wrote an article reflecting on the logging experience of his area, entitled "Our land, our choice: development in North New Georgia" (Tausinga, 1992). In it he explained how the CFC's first line of attack was through the local courts, but how all of their court cases eventually were lost along the lines of the first one involving Kolobaghea:

> By virtue of the court's decision, the non-vendors [i.e. CFC communities] became landless. This was ridiculous ... From the traditional point of view, both factions ... should have equal rights of ownership, use, cultivation and occupation of disputed areas. The court's decision ... threw away customary ownership principles ... and destroyed Melanesian communalism as the basis of our societies. (Tausinga, 1992:56-57)

When the scale and impact of Levers' logging operations became clear, opposition to logging by Levers became more widespread. As on Kolobangara, the operations in North New Georgia were not very selective and often reminiscent of virtual clearfelling. Expanding still further to the southwest to set up a camp at Enoghae at the southern perimeter of Kusaghe lands, Levers increasingly met with dissatisfaction among the great variety of landholding groups and spokesmen who were all party to the agreements with the NNGTC over "timber rights" concessions. Complaints were voiced about an unexpected degree of clearfelling and about the random destruction of ancient and not-so ancient skull shrines and other tabu sites inland. For many grievants, it was as if the long and complicated cultural history of Kusaghe and the hinterlands of northern Marovo Lagoon, represented by a dense landscape of human-made stone structures – including a large number of **ruta** taro terraces (cf. M. Tedder, 1976; and Chapter 5) – was being violently wiped out on a regular day-to-day basis.

Conflict also escalated internally in the NNGTC, in part fuelled by the uneasy relationship within the Corporation of the two rather different SDA and CFC denominations, the latter developing a pattern of strong resistance unparallelled in later years. The Christian Fellowship Church was founded in the 1950s as a breakaway movement from the Methodist Church, and when logging by Levers began the CFC was still led by its charismatic founder Silas Eto, a prophetic leader also known as The Holy Mama. **Mama** is an affectionate term of address for 'father' in New Georgia, and aptly signifies Eto's benevolent yet all-powerful control over his followers both in life and death. Whereas the SDA communities from Gerasi in the east to Kusaghe in the west seemed overall to be relatively and pragmatically content with Levers operations and the ensuing royalties and other benefits (such as the construction of roads and other infrastructure), The Holy Mama and his followers grew increasingly dissatisfied. The CFC is notable for its very strong connections between religious worship (a synthesis of old-style Methodism and traditional New Georgia religion, expressed in liturgy and hymns written by the Holy Mama himself). Customary principles of land tenure, kinship and political leadership closely integrate an original number of 22 villages in northern, central and western New Georgia. Being the spiritual leader of the CFC, The Holy Mama was also a political leader in his own right with inherited chiefly powers bolstered by his spirituality and extending throughout the territory of the NNGTC and beyond.[13]

Let us note at this stage that the growing CFC dissatisfaction did not emerge from land disputes, denominational schisms, unexpected clearfelling and tabu site destruction alone. Nor was the involvement of the Rainforest Information Centre – an Australian conservationist organisation backed by the Friends of the Earth – decisive.[14] As much as anything, perhaps, it was the aloof style of the British company officials that angered and alarmed the people. Levers refused to deal with their opponents in a locally recognised respectful way over legitimate concerns such as environmental damage, and also refused to acknowledge any local 'sides' (Marovo **kale**; cf. Hviding, 1993a, 1996a) other than the group of "landowners" that had been identified in the NNGTC Act of 1979. A fundamental feeling developed in CFC communities of what may somewhat formally be termed "procedural breach". Levers Pacific Timbers saw itself as – and was – empowered by the colonial administration and later the national government to operate according to agreements reached, and the NNGTC for its part was to some degree exempt from government forestry policy, in its capacity as a registered association of customary land-holding groups.

In North New Georgia it is still commented how Levers executives – or 'chiefs' – did not play up to initiatives from certain NNGTC parties (notably The Holy Mama and his co-leaders) at ongoing processual modification of the regulatory framework for logging operations. The Levers leadership were seen as refusing to enter into new discussion about agreements. This amounted to a denial of customary New Georgian ways whereby any agreement is subject to continuous further discussion and adaptation to changing perceptions and circumstances – a process which is founded on the dualist Marovo concept of **vari kale** ('making sides'), implying that the involved parties relate to each other reciprocally and with full responsibility for their own doings. Levers, however, appeared unwilling to discuss such things with a plethora of disgruntled chiefs, let alone the "mysterious" Holy Mama, and instead referred to the national government as guarantor for the logging concessions in NNGTC's area. In the eyes of many villagers, Levers' approach was seen as arrogant and as a direct affront to established relational ways of developing reciprocal agreements with the full accountability of both involved parties. This contrasted sharply with the prevailing local opinion about the Viru operations of the Kalena Timber Company (Hviding 1996a:316-320).

In 1982, the Levers camp at Enoghae on the southern Kusaghe coast was burned down by local anti-logging activists. Workers in the camp were approached by men armed with bushknives, who told them to leave the camp unless they wanted to risk violent action. Violence did not ensue, the camp was abandoned, and buildings, bulldozers and other equipment were set fire to by the armed men. Let us quote a remark made by one such activist, who did not himself participate in the action at Enoghae but who was a main anti-logging spokesman during these years of conflict:

> We warned the company that this contract was not made up properly, and told them not to go on logging, certainly not as long as the contract had not been straightened out properly. But the company said that they had signed a contract with the government, not with us, and they went ahead. At that time, then, people came along and burned down that camp. (Cited by Hviding, 1996a:319)

After the burning of the Enoghae camp the conflict took on a sharper cast. Arrests were made by the police, and several activists were imprisoned. Internal dispute within the NNGTC escalated. A few threats were heard from independently operating activists of further action, this time possibly violent, against continuing logging operations. Several **butubutu** leaders refused to undertake any further negotiations with Levers, and the company no longer felt confident to expand their operations (as originally agreed) southwards into Gerasi lands.

On the formal political level times were hard for Levers as well, in that the Western Province Premier during this period was none other than Job Dudley Tausinga. With his elder brother Ikan Rove who took over the spiritual leadership of the CFC upon the death of the Holy Mama in 1984, the well-educated and internationally sophisticated Tausinga has emerged as a powerful leader of the pan-New Georgian CFC system. Tausinga is another important actor in New Georgia's recent history who does not fit into the pre-packaged categories of social science and who exemplifies the analytically challenging (cf. White and Lindstrom, 1998) nature of post-colonial Melanesian leadership. Is he big-man, priest or chief? In terms of NGO discourse: is he environmentalist or logger? Like his father, and his brother Ikan Rove, Tausinga has come to be seen as a somewhat of an enigmatic figure, and – even for informed Western observers like Frazer (1997:55-56) – a notoriously unpredictable force, sometimes strongly anti-logging and sometimes in favour of it. He has been a noted communicator of customary New Georgian views on the environment and its utility for the people, a message which he has fused with insights from his years as a student of political and environmental sciences at the University of the South Pacific (cf. Tausinga 1992, examined below).

Under Tausinga's leadership as Premier, and with important contributions from environmental scientist Graham Baines (one of his former university teachers whom Tausinga had invited for a post as provincial planner in Gizo), Western Province in 1985 launched a comprehensive plan and policy document entitled *Strategy for Development*. It was strongly based on small-scale, sustainable resource use alternatives yet informed by pragmatic insights into the local scene. An introductory "call to the people" from the Provincial Executive stated that "[w]e do not want to be dragged along a line of development which we inherited from the colonial government" (Western Province, 1985:2; see also Baines, 1989). In 1986-87, a visitor to Premier Tausinga's office in the provincial capital of Gizo would be met with a very large abstract oil painting, by Tausinga himself, covering most of the wall immediately behind the Premier's desk. The painting contained vibrantly colourful imagery of the forest, and in it the following was inscribed in large, stylised letters: **SAVE THE RAINFOREST – WOMB OF LIFE**. Assuming that Levers officials did have to travel to Gizo to meet with the provincial Premier from time to time, this must truly have been a discouraging signal to them, especially in the context of prevailing rhetoric in the province about "taking control over development" and about the merits of small-scale forestry.

After two years of uncertainty following the Enoghae incident, Levers closed its operations on North New Georgia. In 1986 the company announced its total withdrawal from Solomon Islands. National export earnings dropped sharply. A large collection of logging machinery and infrastructural equipment at the Levers township at Ringgi Cove on Kolobangara was auctioned off, and logging in the Western Solomons seemed to have come to an end. It was a triumph for the NGO workers which had collaborated with Tausinga and the CFC, among them Paul Scobie, a New South Wales-based conservationist with kinship ties to New Georgia. Scobie had written about the Enoghae incident in *Habitat*, an Australian conservation journal, in 1982, which led to the involvement of Friends of the Earth, campaigning also in Britain against Levers' activities. Unilever, the parent company, did not welcome this publicity (Bennett, in press, Ch. 10). All in all, the escalation of "global" critique and local resistance culminating in Levers' withdrawal seemed like a perfect picture of spiritual conservationist victory over the evils of multinational capitalism. However, the environmentalists' triumph was short lived. The actual rainforest managers in New Georgia, particularly the leadership, had surprises in store for them.

An environmentalist critique? Voice of the modern managing chief

Gordon Rence (1979) in his article suggests that in North New Georgia all disputes about whether or not to allow logging, about land boundaries, and about who should act as 'trustees' in negotiations between landowners and logging companies, are really disputes about who has the power to decide ownership. In his view "it should be the chief or council member, and not the Church, government officers or the Local Court" who has such power (Rence 1979:124).

Rence's opinion twenty years ago about what ought to be happening in New Georgia was in fact an accurate prediction about the dominant trend in rural politics in the following two decades. In New Georgia it is indeed the "chiefs" (in other words the **bangara**; hereditary **butubutu** leaders) and the "council members" (in other words modern-style power brokers who achieve elected office through local support) whose power is now recognised. Such men have been the ultimate beneficiaries of logging disputes, in the sense that it is their power that has been magnified. There is a contrast here to copra production, which in a sense "democratised" access to wealth and status earlier this century because there was no aspect of the copra industry that could be brought under the sole control of local leaders. The commodification of the forest, on the other hand, has so far had the opposite effect.

Not unexpectedly, one of the most powerful of these new leaders is still the aforementioned Job Dudley Tausinga. In his article "Our Land, Our Choice: Development of North New Georgia" (Tausinga 1992), already quoted above, he presented the CFC point of view. He argued that Solomon

Island Governments both before and after Independence had favoured the interests of Levers through the device of a pro-logging North New Georgia Timber Corporation, and that this policy was morally wrong as well as foolish. The original decision to log was based on unfair collusion between a government that was acting in favour of Levers, an Area Committee that was acting in favour of the SDA faction, and the courts which were biased in favour of the status quo. The effect was an unjust conspiracy which allowed Levers to "sneak in to 'steal' the people's logs" (Tausinga 1992:56-57). Tausinga went beyond the particular case to argue that any large-scale logging operation was the wrong option, for the following reasons:

(1) Levers' logging operation was multinational and only served the interests of foreign capital. It therefore did not meet the real needs of the people: "How long are we going to continue exporting raw logs to assist other countries to process and keep their industries steady, whilst we would soon face timber shortage and employment?" Furthermore, the government cannot be expected to act as a regulator: "It is just greedy for export duty dollars from logs. It thinks like a logging company" (Tausinga, 1992:57, 63).

(2) Large-scale logging is inevitably destructive of the environment. Tree seedlings are destroyed in addition to the mature trees which are taken. With only 20 per cent canopy retention, the land that has been logged becomes choked with vines. There is enormous disturbance to soils: "At Barora, where three bulldozers were working down hill, tons of soil were bladed". Streams are polluted, and eroded sediment ends up in coastal waters (Tausinga 1992:59). Independent recent observations by Tim Whitmore (pers. comm.), a leading international tropical forestry expert, confirms that the logging by Levers amounted virtually to clear-felling. They had developed a market for so-called "super smalls" (30 cm diameter logs) as well as for larger trees, and even fourteen years later the area logged had not recovered. It was covered with a carpet of *Merremia* vines through which the young trees were just starting to push.

(3) The dependence of rural people on natural forest products is jeopardised by large-scale logging. Fruit, honey and wild game disappear from logged forests. Wild pigs, instead of being an important resource for hunters, instead become a pest as they invade people's gardens in search of food. "Is it necessary to devastate the forest in return for short-term economic peanuts?" (Tausinga 1992:59-60).

(4) Finally, the social effects of large-scale logging are also mainly negative. The influx of "foreign" workers resulted in patterns of behaviour not in line with local practices. The seduction of young girls, laziness, drinking alcohol, gambling and fights are all mentioned. The young people start to misbehave in ways that challenge the authority of community chiefs

and religious leaders. "These influences deteriorated human relationships within the areas of logging operations" (Tausinga, 1992: 60-62).

When he was writing in this way about logging in 1988, Job Dudley Tausinga was still the Premier of Western Province, which at the time was working hard to increase its legitimacy and actual power as a provincial government (until then also under the administrative leadership of Sam Patavaqara, Tausinga's close relative from the Methodist community of One/Vakabo in north-central Marovo, as the Provincial Secretary). As one of the Holy Mama's sons Tausinga was also a prominent spiritual and political leader within the CFC faction that played a dominant role in the protest movement. Thus in 1988 the North New Georgia people, too, had every reason to feel triumphant. They had kicked out a powerful multinational company, despite logging agreements that had been signed by local people, and despite the opposition of a national government very anxious to encourage inward investment and to boost log exports.

If the world's media had been paying any attention to these events in the remote Solomon Islands, Tausinga could have become internationally famous in the mid-to-late 1980s as an environmental activist and a spokesman for indigenous peoples. The rhetoric of Tausinga's case against logging was primarily in terms of its social and environmental impact, which was just what the world expected to hear. His proposed alternative was a community-based timber industry, to produce sawn timber for home consumption and export. With greater "value-addition" the rate of logging could be diminished, and it could become more selective. With 80% canopy retention, rather than the 20% achieved by Levers, the forest would regenerate more quickly, and there would be less damage to topsoil. Zoning could be achieved, to safeguard rivers and forest reserves.

> In this way, the social and religious influences would be minimal. (....) Marketing of timber should be done by companies entirely owned by Solomon Islanders. When sufficient funds are accumulated from the sale of logs, they should be invested in establishing local saw mills. This should generate increased local employment and raise the total profit margin. (Tausinga, 1992:63-64)

This line of argument could well seem distilled from the Brundtland Report on sustainable development (WCED, 1987) or from the 1990s propaganda of western environmentalism (e.g. Greenpeace 1995). Tausinga's notion, often quoted around New Georgia, that "although we claim to own the land and the forest, in the final analysis we did not inherit the land and forest from our parents, rather we borrowed these from our children..." (Tausinga 1992:66), is consistent with global environmental rhetoric. What seems to be emerging here is a simultaneous commitment to sustainable development and

Melanesian communalism, under a dynamic leadership that has technical sophistication as well as spiritual charisma. The reality has turned out to be an even more complex version of Melanesian modernity.

Corporate logging continued: entry of an Asian tiger

Even though Levers Pacific Timbers had been defeated and were forced out of the area, the North New Georgia Timber Corporation was still in existence. The departure of Levers in 1986, the collapse of copra, and the lack of any clearcut alternative in this rather remote area seems to have resulted in some sort of crisis for North New Georgia. Talks soon began with Asian logging companies. In 1989 the NNGTC signed a new agreement with Golden Springs International Ltd., an Indonesian company, part of the Sumber Mas group, which subcontracts logging to a Malaysian Chinese firm. Job Dudley Tausinga led the negotiations, and in 1990 the Asians re-commenced operations from the old Levers camp at Enoghae. To Western observers who had followed the anti-logging movement of North New Georgia, this move by Tausinga was unexpected, to say the least. To them it appeared that he had somehow "changed his views" (Frazer 1997:56).

Meanwhile Tausinga's career in politics went from strength to strength. As a member of parliament several times re-elected, he has remained highly visible on the national public arena, serving for periods in the 1990s first as Minister of Foreign Affairs and then as Minister for Natural Resources, a capacity in which he presided over much of the great logging boom of those years. He has also, among other things, been the chairman of the board of both Solomon Airlines (the nation's flag carrier) and Solomon Taiyo (a joint venture between a Japanese fisheries giant and the Solomon Islands govern-ment, and the key actor in the national tuna export industry). Concurrent with this varied portfolio of influential business positions Tausinga has in more recent years been a key backbencher in parliament for the Mamaloni government (and similarly an important leader for the parliamentary opposition after the Ulufa'alu government took over in 1997).

The deal between NNGTC and Golden Springs is full of the rhetoric of a more sensitive form of logging, of local control being re-established, and of development benefits flowing to local communities. The reality may appear to be little different from the bad old days of Levers-style logging. Tim Whitmore (pers. comm.) visited NNGTC areas logged by Golden Springs in August 1995, and reported that all commercial stems over 50 cm diameter had been taken, with clearfelling in areas intended for camps. He notes that all vegetation has been removed in a wide swathe extending about 40 metres each side of the main logging road, and that beyond is a zone of almost total canopy clearance. However most trees have been taken from within 1-2 km of the main road and there seems to have been little interest in logging the forests beyond. Although locally devastating, the overall impact on the North New Georgia forests could have been worse: one should not invoke images of a totally treeless, scorched and barren land. Even those areas clearfelled by Levers 15 years previously were gradually starting to recover in 1995 (T.C. Whitmore, pers. comm.). As usual, though, through ignorance and carelessness shrines and other 'tabu sites' have been bull-dozed. The destruction of sacred sites in the Hoava area inland of Gerasi in northern Marovo led to a court injunction by the Western Provincial government.

Local discontent with Golden Springs operations took different forms than in the days of Levers. Yet in 1994 conflicts over new logging operations at Gerasi resulted in bulldozing equipment being burnt, followed by open confrontation between the CFC villagers of Keru and armed police of the Solomon Islands Field Force. In an interview the following year Tausinga admitted that "the intentions and purposes of NNGTC have not been well explained to the people so the level of understanding is not always very high. This needs to be improved" (Cassells, 1995:14). Tausinga's older brother Ikan Rove (the spiritual leader of the CFC) was also interviewed in 1995. He made a remark which hints at a common problem that has emerged all over the world as traditional leadership confronts forms of modernity: "The idea of NNGTC is good but the people working for it forget about village people" (Cassells, 1995: 13). The North New Georgia Timber Corporation was an attempt by government to dress up old forms of power and responsibility in modern clothes, to enable the customary leadership to deal effectively with the loggers. Has it failed?

Big-men and chiefs on the board of directors

Ross Cassells, a socio-economic consultant, visited practically every village in North New Georgia in the course of an investigation into attitudes towards reforestation (see Chapter 10). Everywhere it was the same story of dis-content with the NNGTC. In the SDA villages there was an low opinion of the Corporation, the common view being that "it wastes money and looks after its own interests". In the CFC villages of "the Kula Gulf" (more conventionally referred to as the Kusaghe area) there was "a very low opinion of NNGTC". In the CFC villages at the north end of Marovo Lagoon it was considered that NNGTC had not considered the needs of villagers, and ought to have carried out a survey to determine development projects that they could assist with. In some places there was a belief that timber royalties were not always transferred from the chiefs to villagers. Examples of NNGTC investing in Honiara property, rather than in village development, were cited. The directors were accused of wasting money on overhead costs such as travel and accommodation. The greatest irony was the adverse comparison that was drawn in the SDA villages between the tangible benefits derived from Levers timber royalties, which had been used to build permanent housing, and the non-existent benefits so far derived from NNGTC royalties, although Cassells points out that some communities have in fact been provided with a school or a clinic (Cassells, 1995:8-9, 19).

Cassells (1995:19) is careful to note that he made no attempt "to substantiate or disprove the comments made by villagers regarding the NNGTC", which he listed simply in order to illustrate their views. The same is true of our own account. However, the mismatch between the high ideals expressed by Job Dudley Tausinga ten years ago and today's reality cannot be ignored. What we are seeing here is the creation, through logging, of a new type of Melanesian political leader, a big-man/chief whose position is legitimated by **kastom** through inheritance but is cemented by elected office or by a directorship in a new town-based organisation like NNGTC. The corporate control of logging royalties in North New Georgia has thus been the main means to power of a class of "nouveau riche" who are bending and transforming the rules of **butubutu** leadership in order to establish their positions as new chiefs.

We believe that such new leaders are emerging almost everywhere in Melanesia where logging is taking place. In the particular case we have examined, the privileged status of the new Melanesian leadership is sanctified by the laws set up to facilitate logging deals. The *North New Georgia Timber Corporation Act 1979* spells out who should sit on the Board of Directors. For the seven **butubutu** (called "tribes") and associated "estates" (in Marovo, **puava**) that were identified, the Act names 28 persons (all men). The name Silas Eto/Holy Mama features as a representative of three different CFC "tribes", so in fact the list contains the names of 26 miscellaneous "chiefs". The Second Schedule, Appointment of Directors (Amendment 1984), also spells out the procedure for replacing "chiefs":

> Where the Tribal Chief specified (above) ceases to be such chief, his successor appointed in accordance with customary law applicable to his tribe shall have the authority to represent his tribe in the Corporation. Such successor shall have the power to nominate, from time to time, any one of the members of his tribe, to represent his tribe in the Corporation... (Cassells, 1995: 9)

In this imaginary well-ordered social landscape of tribes and chiefs, it is easy to see how the NNGTC could become a self-serving nepotistic body in which the twice-yearly meetings in Honiara hotels are thought by many a villager to absorb considerable amounts of Corporation revenue. Revenue is only available for distribution after such expenses have been paid and after the Reserve Fund – which also includes such worthy purposes as the provision of overseas scholarships for students from the NNGTC area – has been topped up. According to the Act, the revenue "shall be distributed to the Tribal Chiefs on behalf of the members of each tribe on whose land work is currently in progress under the terms of a felling licence granted by the Corporation ...". The directors are not liable to ensure that the money is actually distributed in the right way, or to the right people.

These apparently streamlined and exact rules assume the existence of a sociopolitical world of clearly defined "tribes" and undisputed "estates" that has never existed in the context of New Georgia's bilateral kin relations and cognatic descent reckoning, on which land tenure is based. Furthermore, the rules assume a degree of trust between nominated "chief" and those whose interests they are supposed to serve that is equally naive, and that does not reflect the customary practices whereby the whims of a hereditary chief may be countered by established co-leaderships that diffuse the powers of day-to-day decision-making and severely limit a **bangara**'s claim to absolute, hereditary power. The law-makers designing the NNGTC Act and associated legislation seem to have swallowed the a non-indigenous rhetoric of Melanesian "communalism", without examining the reality of how such apparent communalism works on the ground in contexts of customary hierarchies and countermeasures. In the circumstances the alternative proposed by one SDA village to Ross Cassells seems radical in its simpli-city: "One village (Jericho) considered timber royalties should be split equally between households in each community and deposited directly by NNGTC into individual household bank accounts" (Cassells 1995:19).

While discontent over NNGTC spreads around North New Georgia, Golden Springs are continuing the work that Levers began, and most lands of the Corporation are rapidly approaching the status of "logged-out" – but this time with considerably less canopy removal. Statistics are, as usual, very sparse, but according to Whitmore (pers. comm.) some 150-160,000 cubic metres of logs – worth at least SI$ 46 millions – have been removed each year since the 1990s boom began. At the local level, the average amount of log royalties paid by the NNGTC directly to villagers in 1995 was widely stated to be around SI$ 50 "per head" (i.e. each household member, young and old) per six months. This is a rather trivial sum compared to normal household expenses, for example school fees in SDA villages, which typically exceed SI$ 300 per child per year. It is certainly no different, and sometimes less, than the level of income provided by copra in the early 1980s.

A diverging social landscape

As late as the 1970s the almost unbroken inland forest extended on New Georgia from north to south and from lagoon to lagoon, and continued across to the adjoining islands of Vangunu and Gatokae. But its apparently unbroken canopy already obscured a complex social geography of land alienation and indigenous control. The three logged areas that we have examined in this chapter shows how the social landscapes of New Georgia are now following very divergent pathways. A complicated story of alienation versus customary land ownership and logging versus replanting is summarised in Figure 9.4.

Figure 9.4   The diverging history of three logged areas

AREA	Original status, c. 1960	British colonial intervention, 1960s	Outcome just before/after Independence	Fate in 1990s logging boom	Possible future
VIRU-KALENA	Customary land	Alienation to government, logging by Australian company	Reforestation by government	Sold to Korean company; re-logged	Korean-owned forestry plantation?
SOUTH-EAST VANGU-NU	Customary land	Alienation to government, no logging	Very limited logging by local companies	Logged by Malaysian company	Malaysian-run oil palm plantation?
NORTH NEW GEORGIA	Customary land	Failure to settle land disputes; no logging	Landowners organised as 'Corporation'; partial logging by British company	Logged by Indonesian company	Natural forest regeneration?

Logging in Marovo is therefore far from being a uniform and predictable package for the people either to adopt or reject. The three areas that so far have been affected have had such contrasting experiences that each one represents a radically different choice. Moreover it is also no longer a question of "to log or not to log?". The Marovo people, as their fellow New Georgians and many other Solomon Islands peoples, must also consider an even bigger, long-term question: what happens after logging? It is to this question that we turn in the next chapter.

10 After Logging:
Reforestation – or What?

Does logging destroy forests?
A set of perspectives

"Tropical rainforest destruction" is a slogan that has been repeated so often that there is a danger we believe that it is an inevitable and irreversible process. Does logging destroy forests? Logging may well be implicated in a process of destruction in areas where felling is followed by cattle ranching, which is what frequently occurs in Latin America, or when logging roads subsequently become the routes for settlement by peasant farmers, as in parts of Africa and Southeast Asia. In such cases the forest has no chance to recover, and logging is merely the most profitable stage in the conversion of forests to low-grade pasture or cultivation.

Neither scenario, cattle ranching or invasion by landless peasantry, is likely to be a consequence of logging in Solomon Islands (although real threats to forest regeneration in Marovo are posed by recent proposals for the development of oil palm plantations). Instead what is most often seen is the regrowth of secondary forest amidst the logged-over remains of what was there before, and given time there is no doubt that there would be an almost complete recovery. As discussed in Chapter 5, large areas in New Georgia and Vangunu supported substantial bush populations in the late 19th century, until the "great transformations" of the period 1880-1910. These inland areas, that once had villages, gardens and irrigated taro terraces, are now under dense forest. Some Marovo men who worked as bulldozer operators for Levers Pacific Timbers in the 1970s can tell stories of how they would be bulldozing access roads through apparently trackless forest, when suddenly their machines would break into almost-buried skull houses. These remote 'tabu sites' were not marked as places to avoid, unlike some well-known skull houses on ridge tops near to the coast. As the contents of these un-known historic shrines were spilt and crushed beneath the heavy machines, their hapless destroyers learnt a bitter lesson about the capacity of the

Marovo rain forest to engulf areas of former settlement, and a century later to produce a rich crop of valuable logs.

Such random destruction of very old skull houses played a part in the dissatisfaction with the Levers operations. Even in cases when the specific identity and location of such shrines is forgotten, they remain sacred sites whose presence signifies that the forest is a cultural landscape in which there is potential for future land claims. Thus their destruction was seen by many as an irreversible loss of such potential. But in addition to underpinning customary ownership of land, such sites are still regarded by many with awe and respect and as retaining their 'heat'. Being 'hot' (**reka**; often referred to by its Roviana equivalent **mangini**) in this respect is a local concept which implies that the ancestral powers embodied in the skulls of the shrine are still at work – being potentially beneficial to properly entitled, respectful users of the forest, but having an equally strong potential for interfering with the work and lives of destructive intruders. Certain recent events in Vangunu's Lot 16 have contributed towards an emergent theme in local oral histories, concerning dreadful things that reportedly have happened to some workers of the Silvania company. As in North New Georgia, the logging on Vangunu bulldozed many skull shrines. Customary landholding **butubutu** of southern Vangunu sent their own task forces up into the deep forest to identify sacred sites by painting red warning marks on adjacent trees, but this was mostly disregarded, not least by Malaysian bulldozer operators. Ancestral skulls and shell valuables, some hidden in the dark forest for centuries, were left scattered and broken. By 1995 **kastom** was said to be "on the loose" in Lot 16.

It remains well-known among New Georgian Methodists, Seventh-day Adventists and CFC followers alike that ancestral spirits (Marovo **poda**, Vangunu **savude**, Hoava **tomate**) are peaceful and potentially helpful in intact shrines, but may turn wild and roaming when their shrines are destroyed. Consequently, by 1995 Lot 16 was reported locally to be full of 'wild spirits' which posed dangers to all kinds of people moving about in the forest, and which caused several deaths among company employees. Experienced workers from other islands in the Solomons, who had been employed in several other operations, were not unfamiliar with crushed bodies and severed limbs caused by falling trees and the reckless handling of dangerous equipment, and several such accidents were not unexpected in the Silvania operations. But these old hands also told their South Vangunu colleagues about strange things happening in connection to accidents, and moreover, about unknown diseases coming from the wild forest. Reports had it that for several men small scratches on the skin developed into terrible boils (on the head of one and on the legs of others), which ultimately caused their death. The recognised shrine-keeper of the Vangunu people simply said that he could do nothing to appease the restless spirits, the damage being already done (although the company, worried over its employees' concerns, offered to transport him by truck into relevant but remote locations). It was at this stage that most South Vangunu Methodists who had sought company employment quit their jobs and returned home, feeling that Lot 16 was no longer safe even for them now that wild spirits were afoot. Not only was the forest being destroyed, but the land itself was being transformed into space not amenable to human movement or occupation.

Bulldozed shrines being thus connected to dangerous roaming spirits and to the broken bodies and deaths of transgressors, an image was constructed locally of the cultural landscape of the forest – with its resident spirits as agents – reaping its vengeance. In the eyes of the South Vangunu people, Lot 16 was transformed in the 1990s from forested ancestral lands (alienation notwith-standing) filled with cultural meaning and with the benevolent though basically slumbering presence of generalised guardian spirits to an unwieldy maze of useless, ragged remains of forest and desecrated shrines with non-controllable spirits going wild. From a certain point of view, this amounted to a worst-case scenario of total chaos unleashed in the land – with utterly destroyed forest and useless lands being the ultimate result.

However, from a very different, botanical point of view the logging in the Solomons – even that on Vangunu – is not clearfelling, and to some extent it therefore mimics a natural process of disturbance. The long-term studies of Tim Whitmore (e.g. 1990:130) in forest plots on Kolobangara island show that over the period 1964-85 the plots were affected by two episodes of canopy disturbance associated with tropical cyclones. At the six different sites that Whitmore has been monitoring, the effects of the first storm impacted between 1% and 25% of the canopy, while the second more severe hurricane damaged 47-96% of canopy area. Whitmore shows that for many so-called "climax" trees, for them to be able to regenerate they actual-ly require occasional gaps so that their seedlings or saplings can grow up to the canopy. For example, **olanga** (*Campnosperma brevipetiolatum*) is a tree important both for supplementary canoe-construction material and as com-mercial timber. It is a species that cannot replace itself unless severe canopy damage creates an opportunity for its regeneration. For this species to exist at high densities in a rainforest actually requires big hurricanes to happen about once every hundred years (Whitmore 1990:25). For the New Georgia area the dominant presence of *Campnosperma* in inland areas is also an indicator of intensive 19th-century use, presumably for extensive swidden agriculture and for settlements (see Chapter 5).

We therefore have three distinctive processes of disturbance: cyclone damage, long-term human usage for agriculture and settlement, and the recent phase of selective but widespread logging. It is possible that the forest will recover from each type of disturbance in a similar way. This argument is further substantiated by recent observations made by T.C. Whitmore in areas of North New Georgia which were virtually clearfelled in the early 1970 by Levers. Some fourteen years after felling, he found that the areas had abundant well-grown *Campnosperma* trees 13 metres tall plus some *Pometia* (**meda**, another prime commercial timber also of local significance), and that the new saplings were in the process of pushing through the carpet of *Merremia* vines (T.C. Whitmore, pers. comm.). Areas which, for more than a decade, offered the dreadful sight of treeless wastes that were, it seemed, permanently smothered by the omnipresent **kualeve** vine (*Merremia* sp., an archetypal Marovo invader of cleared but untended lands) may finally be regenerating to a significant degree.

The evidence from both forest ecology and recent history therefore suggests that the rainforests of Marovo will not necessarily be irreversibly damaged by logging. However, it is also clear that a long recovery period will be required, so that for the communities hoping to gain commercial value from their forests, logging is essentially a once-in-a-lifetime opportunity for wealth. As we have seen, when negotiations with the logging companies are managed within the structures of kinship and power that exist in Marovo, it is inevitable that the benefits of logging will be unequally shared while the costs (environmental and social) are borne more widely. For this reason, reforestation of logged-over land is encouraged in official rhetoric, but these days it seldom happens in practice. It should be possible to speed up the process of forest regeneration, and to "enrich" the forest with seedlings of commercially-valuable species. This policy was in fact carried out during the 1970s and early 1980s, during the late colonial era and in the early years after independence. At this time the Forestry Department claims to have planted 25,600 hectares of new forest on government land that had been logged, including 8,800 hectares at Viru Harbour (see Chapter 9) and 8,400 hectares on the large island of Kolobangara to the northwest (Aupai, 1994).

We begin this chapter narrowly outside Marovo, with a review of the reforestation programme on Kolobangara, and how it is managed today. As an apparently "sustainable" system of forestry that is now reaping large profits for the company that manages it, Kolobangara represents one option for the owners of a logged-over Marovo Lagoon in the future. The history of logging on Kolobangara was a 1970s phenomenon rather than one of the 1990s, and substantial parts of the island were clearfelled rather than being selectively logged. However, in other ways the two areas share some similar features. Like Marovo, Kolobangara is an area with a small and scattered indigenous population, all of them living in coastal settlements. Both areas have had a generally disappointing relationship with the market economy, apart from small-scale vegetable marketing and, in a few places, an ailing copra economy. But unlike Marovo, Kolobangara has seen a massive experiment in reforestation, made possible by its unusual history of land alienation.

Deforestation and reforestation on Kolobangara

"The population of Kolobangara island in 1894 was estimated to be only 150 people and that must be the main reason for its alienation" (Riogano, 1979:85). In his article which opens with these words, Josiah Riogano (later to hold the post of the Solomon Islands Commissioner of Lands) explores the history of land alienation on Kolobangara, which begins with competing land claims by a German company and a British company each anxious to establish plantations in Melanesia. In 1903 the Pacific Islands Company (London) was awarded a Certificate of Occupation under the Solomon Islands Wasteland laws, and this title was transferred to Lever Brothers two years later. There followed a long period of negotiation with the Protectorate government, which ended in 1931 when the Phillips Commission awarded Levers the title to a somewhat reduced area. In addition, the Kolobangara people were given access rights to settlements all around the north and east coasts (Riogano, 1979:87; Ruthven, 1979:244).

The island is a cone-shaped volcano 30 km across and almost circular in plan. Up until 1967 only about 1,000 hectares had been used by Levers, mostly for coconut plantations, out of the 46,000 hectares allowed to them by the Phillips Commission. As in New Georgia, the interior the island had once been cultivated for irrigated taro and there are traces of settlements on all the main ridge tops (Miller, 1979), but for almost a century most of the island was practically unused by anyone and magnificent forests extended from coast to coast. However in 1968 a newly-formed company, Levers Pacific Timbers Ltd., began operations on Kolobangara, shipping logs to the emerging market in Japan. By this time many of Levers' old claims to "wastelands" such as Kolobangara were under challenge, and the company agreed with government to surrender 36,000 hectares of the land it had been awarded by Certificate in 1931 in return for timber-cutting rights over the entire area (Bennett, 1987:332). The company's willingness to relinquish land rights shows how quickly the British company switched to a short-term, log-grabbing strategy, the same behaviour pattern that we see in the Asian companies that have dominated logging in Solomon Islands in recent years. Independence looming, Levers realised they had little prospect of retaining their title to unmanaged tracts of forest, and so moved towards the Asian strategy of seeking temporary logging concessions on land that otherwise remains under customary control.

The British colonial government was also pleased to have acquired more land for its Forest Estate (which by then also included Lot 16 in southeast Vangunu), at a time when "public ownership" (i.e. state control) of the means of production was unchallenged dogma for forestry both in UK and in the remaining British colonies. In 1975 the government's Forestry Department began to replant the area in the interior of Kolobangara that Levers had logged, while a strip around the north and the east coasts was, in effect, reserved for the coastal communities that had been colonising the area since 1931. By 1982 the island was almost logged out, and Levers shifted its operations some 20 km across the "Kula Gulf" to North New Georgia. Four years later, following setbacks there, Levers Pacific Timbers cut its losses and withdrew altogether from Solomon Islands (see Chapter 9).

While its early history of land alienation and coast-to-coast logging is very different, the current experience of Kolobangara could be quite relevant to Marovo Lagoon, or at least to those parts of Marovo that have been or are about to be logged. Kolombangara Forest Products Ltd., the company now operating on Kolobangara, is not exploiting so-called virgin rainforest, but instead is involved in sustainable timber plantations. It is also associated with an increasing number of local villagers ("outgrowers") who themselves hope to reap benefits from individually-managed plantations of commercially valuable trees, and this experiment in small-scale reforestation also has lessons for what might happen in future on New Georgia.

Kolombangara Forest Plantations Ltd. (KFPL) is today a successful company that is owned partly by the Commonwealth Development Corporation (CDC) in London and partly by the Solomon Islands Government. KFPL is using logged-over land and since 1989 has pioneered a system of large-scale plantation forestry which they claim is sustainable. The company has established more than 8,000 hectares of managed plantation, and the area is being increased by 500 hectares every year. The existing plantation is mainly *Gmelina arborea*, a fast-growing Southeast Asian species, but there have been increased plantings in recent years of *Eucalyptus*, *Acacia*, teak and mahogany. A network of 40 km of roads with permanent bridges has been established, as well as the sawmill, school and clinic at Ringgi (population 2,000). The KFPL workforce is 670 in permanent jobs, with 5-600 more employed in gangs as contract labour (KFPL, 1995; M. Iles, pers. comm.).

What lies behind this striking success story? Vital factors in the commercial success of KFPL are its resources of capital and expertise, its ruthlessly efficient management structure, and its access to freehold land. The earlier history of first logging and then reforestation on Kolobangara has also been a favourable factor, providing infrastructure (roads, the port at Ringgi Cove) and also existing plantations of commercial species that enabled KFPL to move quickly into round-log exports. Up until 1995 KFPL's operations were financed by new investment money supplied by CDC in London (Bennett, in press, Ch. 12). However, because the company has inherited not only the land logged-over by Levers but also all of the land previously replanted by the Forestry Department, since 1995 it has been able to fell and export some of these planted trees. The earliest of the Forestry Department's plantations are now, 17 years later, becoming mature, and the export of round-logs from Kolobangara now totals 50,000 cubic metres per year. The logs, which find a ready market in Japan, are mainly *Eucalyptus deglupta*, a species native to New Britain in Papua New Guinea. So although the company's ongoing investments are impressive, they are partly subsidised by the earlier plantations of the government's Forestry Department.

Can the experience of Kolobangara be transposed to Marovo Lagoon or to any other place where customary land tenure still prevails? This is the relevant question to ask, as there seems at present to be no prospect that customary land will ever again be alienated, either to government or to a private company, and certainly not on the scale that occurred a hundred years ago in places like Ghizo and Kolobangara, and more recently at (in the 1960s) Viru-Kalena on New Georgia and on Vangunu. In fact most Solomon Islanders have never fully acknowledged the legitimacy of these transfers of land ownership, and in many cases the customary landowners are reviving their own claims. For the foreseeable future, Solomon Islands forests must be used within the framework of customary land tenure.

If the KFPL model of reforestation is to be transposed, for example to Marovo, it must be adapted to some very different structures of land ownership and social organisation. As we saw in Chapter 9, each of the three large areas so far logged in the Marovo area has a different history of customary or alienated tenure and contested ownership.[1] The customary **puava** of North New Georgia **butubutu** are tied up by act of parliament into a corporation which has a strong organisation but a long history of internal dissent. Viru-Kalena land was alienated by government, then logged, then sold to the giant Eagon company of Korea, but meanwhile the two **butubutu** of the area have revived their claims. In southeast Vangunu the government's Lot 16 has now been logged by Silvania of Malaysia, and its alienated status is now under challenge by adjacent landowners who also contest each other's claims. In this atmosphere of political uncertainty, who is going to re-plant trees and manage the plantations in the hope of long-term benefits? And who will own those trees when they eventually reach maturity? The reaction of the Kolobangara people to what KFPL has achieved provide instructive insights.

Reforestation on Kolobangara: some local perspectives

The vast reforestation scheme on Kolobangara is now into its second phase. The land now being logged has *Eucalyptus deglupta* plantations dating from the late 1970s, replanted on a 12-year cycle with the Southeast Asian *Gmelina arborea.*[2] What has been the impact of this large-scale demonstration of sustainability on the local population? The islanders of Kolobangara have so far been rather passive bystanders, watching from their coastal villages[3] as the inland part of the eastern half of the island has undergone successive transformations.

First there was the original land alienation, which must have appeared to be a matter of little immediate concern when it was first announced by the British colonial government back in 1903. At that time the Kolobangara population had fallen to just 150 people living on the southwest coast as a relict population, following catastrophic losses in warfare and the exodus of major groups across to the islands of the Vonavona and Roviana lagoons. The Kolobangara forests were super-abundant, and in any case the only land with value then seemed to be those areas that were suitable for coconuts and were adjacent to coastal settlements where foreign ships could drop anchor for trade. As on New Georgia, following the move of the population to villages around the coasts of the island old ridge-top settlements were abandoned, and the irrigated taro plots along the valleys far inland also fell into disuse (Miller, 1979). The Kolobangara population became concentrated in a few coastal sites, allowing the forests inland to grow up and cover all traces of the pre-colonial settlement pattern and land use system. In any case, for a while the Kolobangara people retained access to the interior forests even if, according to the Protectorate government, they no longer owned them.

When Levers began logging in 1968 there were benefits for Kolobangarans: some jobs were available, and new roads provided access to areas hitherto inaccessible, while the migrant labour force at Ringgi constituted a large market for vegetables and other produce. On the other hand there were also costs: social disruption from the outsiders moving in to the logging camp at Ringgi, pollution of rivers, and a great reduction in access to forest products. Despite a number of tangible benefits, all this amounted to devastation, for a people whose lives had been devastated once before, at the turn of the century. Vaena Vigulu, a student later being sponsored by KFPL for forestry studies in PNG, provides a fair summary in his sociological survey of Kolobangara villages:

> Locals who own land in the customary area received royalty, employment, roads and clinic (Ghatere) as benefits during and after logging ... Logging made it easier to walk and make new gardens and start cash cropping but

harder to get building materials such as loya cane and wild betel, find wild game and get drinking water because it cleared the forest and destroyed the land. (Vigulu, 1992:7)

The coming of KFPL in 1989 unleashed a new form of development on Kolobangara – reforestation. Roads and bridges are now being built in more permanent materials, and new trees are being planted on logged-over land. These are exotic trees, mainly *Gmelina arborea*, which signal unmistakably the long-term right of ownership that the foreign company (KFPL) claims to the fruits of the land. The status of the land itself is still being debated, and a Kolombangara Landowners Trust Foundation has been formed which hopes to persuade Solomon Islands Government to transfer to it the government share of the ownership of KFPL. Politics will determine the ultimate outcome of this case, but meanwhile another interesting local response to reforestation has emerged. Kolobangara landowners are themselves planting blocks of exotic tree species, ostensibly as a way through which they can participate in this new and perhaps profitable form of forest management.

The Kolombangara outgrowers movement

The possibility that Kolobangara islanders might wish to participate in the reforestation scheme was recognised at an early stage by CDC. In 1991, at the time when *Gmelina* reforestation was already under way and a financial restructuring of the company was being negotiated with Solomon Islands Government, a report talked of the "considerable scope" that existed for outgrowers to be linked to the replanting activity of KFPL (CDC, 1991: 31). At the time, however, CDC in London was thinking of rather large-scale blocks:

> Financial analyses for projects using Gmelina, teak and mahogany show that projects of at least 50 ha and preferably of between 100 ha and 500 ha are desirable. However existing analyses do not take proximity to a processing site into account. Two of the landowning groups have prepared reforestation plans and submitted them to KFPL. Substantial land areas with a potentially productive area of 1200-1500 ha would be committed to plantation. (CDC, 1991: 31)

What has so far emerged on Kolobangara has been very different from what CDC envisaged back in 1991. Individuals, not groups, have come forward in quite large numbers with proposals, but the spatial scale of planting has so far been quite miniscule (Figure 10.1). The 135 hectares that had been planted by 106 outgrowers up to the end of 1995 compares to the 6,000 hectares planted by KFPL itself over the same period. The tree which almost all the outgrowers have planted is *Gmelina arborea*, the mainstay of the KFPL plantations. Clones of trees selected for fast growth and good form have been planted out by KFPL in a multiplication garden, from which cuttings are taken and rooted in plastic boxes, using growth hormones. These cuttings are available to outgrowers for SI$ 0.35 each. Within 12 years each cutting should produce a tree 30 m tall containing up to 7 m length of saw log. The rooted cuttings are planted at an initial density of 1000 stems per hectare, but this stand of saplings then needs to be thinned to produce an eventual density of about 500 trees per hectare.

Figure 10.1 Numbers of persons in the outgrowers movement on Kolobangara, and the area planted (in hectares)

Date	Numbers of persons	Area planted	Area proposed	Area potentially available
July 1993	23	13	not stated	not stated
November 1993	59	51.5	140	400
May 1994	83	86	141	586
December 1995	106	135.5	204	669

Source: KFPL News, Ringgi (mimeo.), 1993a, 1993b, 1994, 1996

For an outgrower the investment per hectare is therefore about SI$ 350 for cuttings, after which direct costs are zero unless he employs contract labour. However, although no further money needs to be spent, the out-grower must himself make a substantial investment of effort so as to carry out a series of tasks known as singling, pruning and thinning, as well as basic brushing to keep away the undergrowth (especially creepers). KFPL data for 1991 indicate that their own total labour requirements, for land that began as a logged-over secondary forest and ended up as a thinned *Gmelina* plantation three years later, amounted to 81.5 man-days per hectare (these are only the direct labour inputs). At the costs of labour prevailing in 1991 this represented an investment for KFPL of SI$ 1,478 per hectare in order to pay for at least 14 separate operations to be carried out. There are also in-direct costs. There is almost no likelihood that outgrowers could find this sort of money, and therefore these tasks are carried out by the person himself or are not done at all.

In 1996, when one of us (Bayliss-Smith) visited a number of outgrower plantations on the fringes of the KFPL land, it was clear that in at least half of the cases many of these 14 operations had not been done properly, particularly those that should have been carried out after the planting stage. Unless singling, pruning and later high pruning are done properly and promptly, *Gmelina* will not produce knot-free timber of saw-log quality, and unless the stems are thinned to about 500 per hectare the actual growth of the trees will be suppressed. The Extension Officer at KFPL, Eric Havea, estimated that about half of the 106 outgrowers that he is advising are, in his words, "genuine", that is to say they are outgrowers who are reasonably conscientious about the proper management of their plantations.

Why, in company terms, are at least 50 outgrowers "not genuine"? Why have so many islanders on Kolobangara sought "outgrower" status from KFPL, each spending at least SI\$ 300 per hectare on seedlings, but then neglecting their *Gmelina* trees to the point where, in extreme cases, a competing canopy of secondary forest trees threatens to shade out the struggling *Gmelina* trees altogether? There was insufficient time during fieldwork to locate and to question more than a few of these men, but from the information available there is a very strong suspicion that *Gmelina* is being treated on Kolobangara in the same way that coconuts have been treated for generations in Solomon Islands, as a means to establish a long-term claim on land.

On Kolobangara as elsewhere, customary land is under perpetual group (**butubutu**) ownership as "ancestral estate", but it remains the property of the individual for usufruct purposes for at least as long as the crop planted remains productive. For taro this productive period is less than one year, but for new tree crops the usufruct period is very much extended. Coconuts even had the advantage that they could be interplanted among taro or sweet potatoes in a normal garden for a few years, before the palms expanded to occupy all the space available. In this way coastal communities all over the Solomons have managed to establish more individual rights to areas of land devoted to copra production (see Chapter 7). However, this coconut option is no longer available. Declining prices have made copra such an unrewarding cash crop that in most cases the existing plantations are no longer maintained, and the planting of new coconuts is even being outlawed in some communities. Planting coconuts in a garden is now recognised as no more than a bid for privatisation, a means whereby an individual can achieve a private claim of ownership within public (**butubutu**) space.

Gmelina on Kolobangara may well be perceived as a new means to achieve the same purpose, on an island where, in the past six years, KFPL's extraordinarily rapid progress towards converting 8,000 hectares of logged-over rainforest and pasture into *Gmelina* plantation has provided an impressive spectacle of what privatisation can achieve. Almost anywhere in Melanesia the planting of thousands of exotic trees and the associated infrastructure of roads and bridges would be a fundamental challenge to the implicit notions of usufruct that still prevail. A logging lease merely removes the standing crop of the forest, leaving the status of the forest essentially unaltered in cultural as well as in ecological terms. In most places some sort of forest (even, rather rapidly, *Campnosperma* trees) will quickly re-establish itself, even though it may be a century before the valuable hardwood species (*Terminalia, Calophyllum, Vitex, Intsia*) recover to form significant stands. In contrast, if a logged-over forest is converted to plantation, which is then harvested and replanted indefinitely on a sustained basis, then the alienation of the Kolobangara "wasteland" that was announced by the colonial government in 1903 as an abstract concept, has finally become a harsh reality.

The Kolobangara outgrowers movement should perhaps be seen as an attempt by Kolobangara islanders to reassert their claims to some patches of land to which they want to obtain, and maintain, undisputed title in future. It is easier to assert these rights on an individual basis, by laying claim to an area of land that is not so much bigger than a normal agroforestry plot. The individual has to invest a non-trivial sum of money on seedlings, but in turn he hopes to benefit from whatever value the *Gmelina* stems may have when harvested. But that particular benefit is in the vague and uncertain future, and it does not constitute, for most outgrowers, the principal motive.

Reforestation on New Georgia?

KFPL has been hoping for years to extend its tree plantations to other sites in the Western Solomons. The logic for this expansion is strictly commercial. Early on in the project, a consultant's report to the World Bank suggested that even if KFPL were able to plant 13,600 hectares on Kolobangara, the volume of wood produced would still be relatively small compared to the fixed costs of any local saw mill or chip mill that the production must maintain. Kolobangara at present is still only one-third or one-quarter the size of comparable projects in other countries, for example Sabah Softwoods in Malaysia and the Fiji Pine Commission (Hunter, 1989:5). For this reason KFPL was extremely interested in acquiring Viru-Kalena, a government-owned block in west New Georgia totalling 25,015 hectares of which at least 8,800 hectares at Viru Harbour had been logged and replanted by the Forestry Department. In 1995 KFPL carried out an inventory for the government to assess how much loggable timber remained and what value to place on the area. KFPL's report revealed the potential of Viru to contribute usefully to the Kolobangara operation if managed for plantation forestry, and KFPL were therefore very disappointed when their own bid for Viru was rejected by Solomon Mamaloni's government. Instead, Viru was sold in early 1996 to Eagon for reasons which relate to the near-bankruptcy of the Solomon Islands Government and the skills of Asian businessmen in adjusting to Melanesian ways of conducting business (see Chapter 9).

An earlier opportunity for KFPL seemed to have emerged at the far north end of the Marovo Lagoon in 1993. This was the area where North New Georgia Timber Corporation, acting on behalf of customary land-owners, had awarded a logging concession first to Levers and then to Golden Springs International (see Chapter 9). In 1992 the directors of NNGTC (a group of **butubutu** and community leaders) were reported to have made the decision to replant 22,000 hectares of their logged-over land. This area would have been highly suitable for the kind of trees favoured by KFPL – *Gmelina* (on a 12-year cycle), mahogany (25-30 years) and *Acacia*. A trial area of 20 hectares was set aside at the logging camp at Enoghae, which KFPL planted in 1993 with a token demonstration plot of half a hectare of *Gmelina* (KFPL, 1993a:6). This expression of interest from NNGTC persuaded KFPL to carry out feasibility, environmental impact and social impact studies in 1995. Ross Cassells' (1995) report entitled "Social and land tenure assessment of Viru Harbour and north New Georgia villages" provides a fascinating window on to the confused state of North New Georgia in the aftermath of logging. Cassells held meetings in every village, including some in the far north of the Marovo Lagoon. These remote communities are Christian Fellowship Church villages, as well as some of the Seventh-day Adventist Church, with an economy based primarily on subsistence but with some cash income from copra, markets, bêche-de-mer and trochus.[4]

Cassells reported to KFPL that the Christian Fellowship Church villages did want a reforestation project, but with many caveats. If reforestation went ahead they would be concerned about a possible shortage of land for their gardens, for hunting, and for the gathering of forest products. They were also very concerned about the adverse social impact of outside labour. Among the Kusaghe-speaking Seventh-day Adventist villagers at Baini, on the northern arm of Marovo Lagoon, there were fears that during replanting the camps of contractors would pollute water sources, and that the labourers from outside the area would steal from gardens. They wanted no Malaitans who, they said, always start fights and then want compensation. In Keru, a Marovo-speaking CFC village in the barrier islands, the main worries were (mainland) water pollution and land disputes, while in "Kolobaghera" (the

Hoava-speaking CFC village of Kolobaghea, mentioned in Chapter 9) there was a fear that outsiders could be murdered (Cassells, 1995, Appendix 3).

Leadership in Keru and Kolobaghea is dominated by Ikan Rove, the elder son and spiritual successor of the Holy Mama, and by Job Dudley Tausinga, Ikan Rove's younger brother with a remarkable career as provincial Premier, businessman, cabinet minister and long-serving member of parliament for the area (see Chapter 9). Cassells felt that both men supported reforestation, but that Ikan Rove's preference was for small-scale reforestation that could be done by the villagers themselves rather than it being taken over by a company. Tausinga, on the other hand, favoured a large-scale reforestation scheme along the lines proposed by KFPL and – ostensibly – agreed to by the NNGTC (Cassells, 1995:8, 13-14).

In September 1995 Cassells was uncertain whose view would prevail in the CFC villages of North New Georgia – the spiritual leader's wish for small-scale reforestation, or the politician's desire to collaborate with KFPL to carry out a Kolobangara-scale operation. In the event neither option has been chosen. The NNGTC itself decided not to continue its talks with KFPL, and instead to enter into a final phase of logging with Golden Springs, mostly re-logging areas previously exploited less intensively. As at Viru, KFPL has been by-passed. The chosen solution will not achieve sustainable forestry for North New Georgia but, from the point of view of the local people, it will be less contentious than the unknown hazards of reforestation. Like the Viru sale, it also has the merit in the short term of putting a good deal of money into certain people's pockets.

In the light of what has happened so far in North New Georgia, one of the conclusions of Cassells' perceptive report deserves to be quoted:

> In the longer term diminishing indigenous timber reserves, both locally and globally, are likely to create an increasingly favourable economic and political climate for [sustainable forestry]... Notwithstanding this, deforestation [in Solomon Islands] is now largely confined to customary land. The disincentives for investing on customary land are well documented so until these are adequately overcome large-scale re-forestation is unlikely to occur. (Cassells, 1995:4)

The KFPL example, building upon the replanting work of the Forestry Department in the 1970s, shows what is technically feasible where large blocks of land can be centrally managed. At the present time the gulf is enormous between this working model of sustainable forest plantations, and what is actually feasible in the real world of Solomon Islands customary land tenure, social structure and realpolitik.

Reforestation as a local issue: North New Georgia, 1996

All the meetings and "fact-finding" concerning the prospect of reforestation by KFPL generated a lot of local discussion, and quite a few scenarios (including some explicit alternatives to the KFPL strategy) for 'replanting' (**choku pule**) were proposed by enterprising villagers. Aivin Kerovo of Keru, Area Council Member for the Gerasi part of the northern lagoon and an experienced participant in miscellaneous aid-funded "projects" over the years, is a good example of villagers who are ready to critically evaluate the possible implementation of new projects. In a discussion with one of us (Hviding) in August 1996 Kerovo pointed out that "The Forestry Department" (actually KFPL)[5] provides young trees of the non-local *Gmelina* to villages owning logged land, and that he himself had considered joining this – although he really did not see any need for the particular species offered beyond the nebulous promise of future timber export.

While initially offering the universal New Georgian saying that "**vahu** [fruit bats] are by far the best workers in replanting the forest", Kerovo admitted to a more-than-average interest in human intervention through the KFPL reforestation project, but added that he himself had a rather different opinion about suitable trees. He emphasised his own strong wish to try out the planting of the popular **chovuku** (*Burckella obovata*), which he personally considered to have a great potential for reforestation purposes on the type of land held by his group, judged on the basis of the known 'life requirements' of **chovuku**. In Marovo two varieties of **chovuku** are recognised; one growing in the coastal forest of the mainland and one in the barrier islands. Both are increasingly used for locally sawn timber, and the mainland variety has a nice edible fruit.[6] Kerovo also reported that some people of his **butubutu** had started to plant small **naginagi** (the valuable Kerosene wood, *Cordia subcordata*) in their plentiful good locations out in the barrier islands near their villages. Some of these areas (in which not a few **naginagi** trees had been growing naturally) had previously been cleared for coconut plantation purposes, but without any coconuts being planted. Several stands of up to 100 small **naginagi** trees were now reported to be growing surprisingly fast, and Gerasi people were becoming optimistic about the possibility of selling this wood to the carvers of the central lagoon. But related attempts at replanting the equally depleted **rihe** (ebony, *Diospyros* spp.), potentially much more profitable in this regard, had turned out to be less successful. Its seeds are hard to obtain, and it is extremely difficult to determine whether a growing tree is going to contain all-black wood ("King Ebony") or just become a **rihe kokojiolo**[7] ("Queen Ebony") with irregular black-and-brown grain, some of which cannot even be used for carving.

It is clear that local perspectives on reforestation focus on direct utility as well as on observations about different trees' suitability in terms of the land available for planting. This invariably results in a low priority for non-local, fast-growing timber trees such as offered by KFPL. However, another line of observation and reasoning also figures strongly in Marovo discussions about the future potential of logged lands – the perspective of natural regeneration. In an exchange of views following the above discussion, Aivin Kerovo and the prominent Marovo intellectual and activist Vincent Vaguni commented that, surprisingly, **bunibuniani** (pure stands of *Calophyllum* spp.) were reappearing in 1996 in the same coastal locations where large **buni rarusu** (*Calophyllum inophyllum*) had been logged in the 1960s by the operation of Mr. Cox (cf. Chapter 9). To both Kerovo and Vaguni it seemed clear that **buni** trees were now reclaiming their own areas and forcing older secondary growth into submission, and the plant associations and visual appearance of these new **bunibuniani** were becoming very similar to the conditions that reigned in the original ones.

They also observed that there is a successional stage that precedes these new **bunibuniani**, as exemplified in 1996 by the Ligutu Passage near Tamaneke village. Here large areas of barrier island forest were logged in 1993-94. Some of the seaside forest was left standing while substantial parts of the interior were clearfelled – ostensibly with a view to plant new coconuts (which was not done). Two to three years after, the cleared land had dense regrowth of **araruani** – pure stands of *Casuarina equisetifolia*. It is a recognised fact in Marovo that **aru** trees generally 'do not let' other trees grow with them, and **aru** are considered to 'do something with the soil'. But somehow, Kerovo and Vaguni concluded, **araruani** regrowth appears to prepare the ground for other trees, and from regular observation over the years it appeared clear that in time, the **araruani** of Ligutu were likely to be replaced by **bunibuniani**, if the developments in the areas that were cleared of **buni** during the 1960s is anything to go by.

This North New Georgian perspective of natural regeneration through successive stands of different species, culminating in an abundance of valuable local trees in areas where those trees used to grow before, is not locally unique but was encountered in 1996 in many other parts of the wider Marovo Lagoon area. It relates to a complex of beliefs about different trees leading their own 'lives' in their self-chosen locations and in the company of a specific repertoire of other trees, shrubs and vines (as examined in Chapter 3); certain repertoires replacing each other in time. On a less species-specific level the local regeneration perspective is also in several ways epistemologically convergent with the recent observations made in logged (even clearfelled) areas of North New Georgia by forest botanist Tim Whitmore (pers.

comm.) of vigorous, spontaneous re-growth of *Campnosperma* and *Pometia*. What is further notable about the "model" exemplified by Aivin Kerovo's and Vincent Vaguni's observations is that it is based on the ecological succession of one dominant tree species after another.

The "natural regeneration" approach bypasses the vexed question of who is to own replanted trees, since it implies a continuation of communal control by the **butubutu** of whatever grows on its land. Even the modest planting of stands of highly valuable trees for local markets (notably the carving woods) or of less coveted but still locally useful trees is likely to cause relatively little conflict. Located on communal land but planted and tended – and intended to be harvested and sold – mostly by individuals or families, ownership of these emerging local small-scale "plantations" will probably follow the established model of **hinoho**, modest tree groves (of coconuts, sago, *Canarium*, etc.) planted on communal land in small 'blocks' over which the planter and successive generations have rather permanent usufruct rights. The responses of Marovos's customary land managers cannot be as easily predicted when challenged by the long-term scenario of much larger stands of forest trees having enormous commercial value, which may, however, only be realised after a long period has elapsed during which there has been more or less active management of the growing trees. Few, if any, **butubutu** leaders would be eager to grant control to individual **butubutu** members over lands of the scale required for the type of forest plantation proposed by KFPL. One possible alternative is represented by the exceptionally large coconut plantations established by certain Christian Fellowship Church communities (such as Tamaneke). These plantations have been worked communally over several decades, the proceeds during times of copra profitability being shared within the involved **butubutu**. On a more general level, however, the question remains whether long-term commitment to the tending of alien tree species is an attractive prospect for most villagers. Experiences from other forms of "community-level" development projects in the Solomons involving long periods of managed growth, such as the mariculture of giant clams (Hviding, 1993a), indicate that the strong emphasis in household-level economies on flexibility, occupational multiplicity and the minimisation of risk mitigates against the eager adoption of new labour-demanding projects.

Thus there are diverse reasons for the luke-warm reaction in North New Georgia to KFPL's proposals for large-scale reforestation. On the other hand, that the future for some of the logged areas of Marovo may be characterised neither by slow regeneration with little or no human interference, nor by well-organised community-held plantations of forest trees, is signalled by certain far-ranging proposals that were coming into light just as

North New Georgians were discussing the merits of natural succession and selective replanting of locally important species. Let us return to the much-troubled Lot 16 on Vangunu.

Vangunu's "reforestation"? A Malaysian oil-palm proposal

The very latest reforestation scheme to impact upon Marovo Lagoon comes from a Malaysian company, Kumpulan Emas Berhad (1996), which proposes to plant oil palms on the logged-over land on Vangunu. To an even greater extent than the North New Georgia proposals of KFPL, the Emas scheme would impact directly on Marovo Lagoon, both environmentally and socially. As this book was being finalised for publication in August 1999, news emerged that the scheme had been accepted and agreed by the national government despite much local opposition (predictably, this time also being voiced via Internet) and well-formulated research-based intervention from the NGO sector (LaFranchi and Greenpeace Pacific, 1999). The government of Western Province was also quick to announce its disapproval at the way the deal had been arranged, as well as to add, on a pragmatic note, the firm condition that if the development should go ahead, employment must be restricted to people of the province.

The proposal derives from the parent company of Silvania Products (SI) Ltd., and builds upon the infrastructure, in particular roads, already established on Vangunu by Silvania in the course of their logging operations since 1992 on Lot 16 and adjacent customary land (see Chapter 9). In 1996, with the Mamaloni government so sympathetic to Asian capital, it was an opportune time for Silvania's parent company to consider the next step: re-planting with oil palms. In 1999 the Ulufa'alu government faced a sudden crisis with severe unrest on Guadalcanal, involving the large-scale exodus of Malaitan labour and the consequent collapse in oil palm exports; and the Emas proposal was quickly revived to help the situation.

Kumpulan Emas Berhad's proposal for Vangunu was available to certain Members of Parliament long before it was available to local people for discussion. An MP lent it to someone in a village in Marovo Lagoon, who in turn allowed one of us to see it – provided it was returned to him the next morning. Reading this leaked document by the flickering light of a hurricane lamp made for a sleepless night of revelations. Both the content of the document and the circumstances in which it was made available to us signal one possible future for land use in Marovo Lagoon: its transformation through shady deals made in faraway places, the deals then being legitimated locally through pseudo-democratic means.

In a sense, then, nothing has changed. As we have seen (Chapter 9), back in the 1960s the original plan to acquire Vangunu from its customary landowners was pushed through by a handful of enthusiastic British officials in the Forestry Department. The acquisition of "vacant" areas like Vangunu was justified by the dominant western ideology of "public ownership", and so that forestry could be seen to be making a useful contribution towards "economic development" (BSIP, 1963:30). Who doubts that such schemes were not devised by small groups of expatriates, probably over gin and tonic in the club in Gizo or Honiara? The strategic decision was then packaged and "negotiated" on Vangunu itself, by secret negotiations with "chiefs" who were cajoled or flattered into an agreement. Today a Malaysian company does its entertainment in the hotels and restaurants of Honiara, and a plan to take over Vangunu for an oil palm plantation is agreed. Those who will be most affected are the last to hear about this proposal, long after their elected representatives have been encouraged to be sympathetic to the new needs of "development". The sinister retracing of "global" colonial trajectories is graphically illustrated in an announcement posted on the World Wide Web on 2 August 1999 by the Board of Directors of Kumpulan Emas Berhad:

> We wish to inform that Kumpulan Emas Berhad (KEB) and through its wholly-owned subsidiary, Silvania Plantation Products (S.I.) Ltd had on 29 July 1999 entered into a Development Agreement with the Government of Solomon Islands to plant oil palm over a gross area of 10,299 hectares of logged-over forests in Vangunu Islands, Solomon Islands ("Development Area") with 75 years lease period. The project also involved value added downstream and related activities. KEB has been given attractive tax incentives and exemptions to undertake this long term investment. KEB also expects to enjoy attractive returns from its new investment in Solomon Islands. This project is also part of the Group's strategic plan to relocate oil palm business from high-cost area in Malaysia to low-cost areas like Solomon Islands and India. (www.klse.com.my/website/listing/lc./kemas.htm#Announcement)

Oil palm refineries and a new town?

In its 1996 report Kumpulan Emas Berhad had indeed recommended that the 10,000 hectare concession that Silvania had on Vangunu, which expired on 30 May 1999, should be transferred to them on a 75-year lease. In addition, it was proposed that, with government help, KEB should acquire a further 20,000 hectares of customary land adjacent to their original concession. They estimate that 23,000 hectares of this 30,000 hectare block ought to be suitable for planting with oil palm, and that the eventual production would make viable three palm oil refineries and a palm kernel mill, "thus taking Solomon Islands to yet another level of downstream industrial activity" (Kumpulan Emas Berhad, 1996:2). They estimate that total employment in the project would be 5,000-5,500 people, necessitating the construction of a new town with electricity, hospital, schools, churches and entertainment centres. Of these employees, up to 10% at any one time could be expatriates, implying the presence of at least five hundred Malaysians and other foreigners managing and running plantations, refineries, mill and town.

This astonishing vision of an alternative future for Marovo Lagoon has not really been discussed by anyone living in the area. The attractions to the Marovo **butubutu** of schemes of this kind is their combination of immediate gain plus the promise of employment and sustained revenue in the longer term. There would be an immediate windfall gain from the land being logged, with a proposed 10% royalty for round logs, followed by a continuing rental payment for the land in the form of a SI$ 3 per tonne royalty on the production of oil palm fresh-fruit bunches. It is estimated by KEB that if 23,000 hectares were to be planted with oil palm then production would peak at 575,000 tonnes in the year 2007, representing a SI$ 1.5 million royalty to be shared among **butubutu** members. In 1996 there were an estimated 2,200 people living on Vangunu, so in the unlikely event that the SI$ 1.5 millions would be equally divided, it would amount to SI$ 680 per person per annum, which is approximately ten times the 1996 per capita cash income.

The disadvantages of the scheme are also obvious, and include all those issues raised in North New Georgia in relation to the forest plantation proposals of KFPL: loss of agricultural land, loss of hunting and gathering in the forest, water pollution, and social disruption through internal disputes and the arrival of thousands of outsiders. Lack of agreement over such matters and over the distribution of royalties may well prevent the oil-palm scheme from proceeding very far – the agreement reached with the national government in 1999 only covers the already alienated and logged-over land of Lot 16. The Malaysians may have foreseen such problems, and are perhaps mostly interested anyway in the huge profit they have built into their scheme from the initial clearfelling of up to 20,000 hectares of intact forest on customary land. Their 1996 proposal assumes no restriction on log exports and full tax exemption, and is otherwise quite candid:

> To convert the land use the existing trees will be felled and the land cleared for the planting of oil palm. .... This will mean that trees of no commercial value will also be felled. .... Logs not exported shall not attract any royalty whatsoever to the landowners .... Trees normally prohibited from felling under normal logging practices, such as ebony, canoe trees and other nut trees, will have to be exempted from logging restrictions. (Kumpulan Emas Berhad, 1996:6)

Out of the 20,000 hectares of customary land requested from government, an estimated 7,000 hectares would not be planted with oil palm (but one suspects they might well be selectively logged anyway), "being either at too high an altitude, or too steep, or should be preserved as water catchment area" (Kumpulan Emas Berhad, 1996:11). The rest would be left in a state of total forest removal and broken ground not seen so far in New Georgia; awaiting the planting of oil palms. The present logged-over state of Lot 16 represents an almost intact forest in comparison. With the single exception of the above statement about catchment area preservation there is no mention in the entire proposal of environmental impacts such as sedimentation of the lagoon, water pollution and loss of garden land. Nor is there any consideration whatsoever of the social impacts envisaged by local people.

The government has already shown at Viru that it will ruthlessly privatise state assets where an opportunity arises. It can claim that its aspirations to develop rural areas, generate new jobs and boost export revenues will also be met by the Vangunu oil-palm scheme. And in the rhetoric of overseas consultants working for government ministries, the Agricultural Opportunity Area (AOA) approach used by land use planners in the 1960s has been re-cycled to identify Plantation Opportunity Areas (POAs) for the 1990s. The POA approach, say the planners, "... is a rigorous one, with a high probability of nominating superior sites. Such an approach is considered essential to select sites for capital intensive industrial plantations" (Shield, 1992:13).

Is this the Great Transformation of the 21st century through which the Marovo Lagoon will be changed forever? Throughout the 20th century outsiders in Solomon Islands have been relentless in their drive to re-organize land tenure to meet the preconditions of their production models. We have seen "waste lands" set aside as a means to stimulate the plantation sector and satisfy the laissez-faire ideals of classical economics. Then there were "vacant lands" added to the "forest estate" of public-interest forestry, to satisfy Keynesian interventionist ideas within a centrally planned colonial state. Now we see the privatisation of that estate, and the establishment of "corporations" like the North New Georgia Timber Corporation as legal entities, as a means through which customary land can be made available to foreign business, satisfying neo-liberal economic dogmas of the New World Order.

Could the situation be any different? Perhaps in Melanesia central governments have never had much freedom of action. The historian Judith Bennett has written that "[i]n the Solomons the dominant motivation behind all government policy decisions was the need for the islands to be self-supporting. The colony was run like a business and the revenue column had at least to balance with the expenditure column, if not to exceed it" (Bennett,

1987:149). She is talking about the year 1900, but as we approach the year 2000 almost nothing has changed other than a growing dependency upon foreign aid money. A bankrupt Solomon Islands government can offer nothing better to its people than privatisation and "business as usual" for the logging companies. It is only non-government organisations who offer any alternative vision. Unfortunately, in the past the NGOs have been willing to offer a new vision of heaven and hell, but have not been able to provide workable ways in which the common property resources of the people can be mobilised for the common good, rather than being sold cheap to Asian capitalists. Is there an alternative model?

A capitalist future?

There is now is a widening gap between what the agents of capitalism foresee as the next stage for Marovo Lagoon's incorporation into the global economy, and what the Marovo people themselves can achieve in the management of their own resources using their own social capital. Industrial logging, plantation-scale reforestation, and the production and processing of oil palms are all uses for the forest which, from the perspective of the outside world, seem logical forms of capitalist enterprise at the beginning of the 21st century. However, it seems to us that they offer local people little but cash handouts, the degradation of resources, social disruption, and a permanently menial role in the new world order.

Capitalism burst upon the island world of Melanesia almost 200 years ago with the captains of sailing ships bribing local chiefs in order to fill their holds with sandalwood logs for the China trade. It continued 100 years ago with the arrival of settlers uprooted from Europe, often social misfits living lonely and dangerous lives on small tracts of alienated coastal land where they hoped to establish plantations. The Marovo people were not troubled by the first wave, having no sandalwood trees, and they managed to adjust successfully to the challenge of the coconut planters by means of small-scale imitation. But the capitalist mode of production has itself made giant strides since those early colonial days, and it now faces the Marovo people with new challenges, large temptations, yet few real opportunities for meaningful participation. How can the scale of capitalist operations be diminished so as to provide for Marovo some degree of empowerment, a more meaningful role, and a more sustainable technology? In the next chapter we review the option of small-scale logging. If large is ugly and threatening, then perhaps small is beautiful?

11 Small is Beautiful? Steps Towards Sustainable Forestry

The beginnings of a national debate

In the last two chapters we discussed the history and social and environmental consequences of rainforest logging, with a focus on New Georgia and the adjacent islands of Kolobangara and Vangunu. These areas around and immediately beyond the Marovo Lagoon are microcosms of what is happening elsewhere in Solomon Islands and Papua New Guinea, where similar local resistance is matched by local advocacy of logging, and where events are also being manipulated by a new class of leaders – whether we call them "modern big-men", "today's chiefs" or "landowning corporate directors" – who see in logging an opportunity for the advancement of their own priorities and expansion into non-local spheres of political economy. But there is also a national debate about logging in the Solomons, and about the appropriate scale at which it should be carried out in order to minimise negative impacts and maximise benefits, national as well as local. In this chapter we examine this debate in the context of the great Solomon Islands logging boom of the 1990s.

The potential of logging to create as many problems as it solves has long been foreseen, and concern has been widely expressed also on the national level, not least by the Central Bank of the Solomon Islands. Over the past decade the Bank has taken upon itself the responsibility not only to manage the nation's money supply but also to serve as the nation's conscience in matters of economic policy. The Bank thus occupies a role that in more "developed" nation-states is usually filled by a coherent parliamentary opposition and by other sources of informed opinion in "civil society", such as religious leaders, the media, voluntary organisations, universities, or the business community. Of course such people do exist in Solomon Islands too, and sometimes their opinions on logging and other matters are freely expressed on the radio, in the newspapers and at public gatherings. There is also abundant discussion at the Area Council and Provincial levels of government, which have at least nominal constitutional rights to intervene. However, like the NGOs, churches and other bodies, most of these individuals and institutions cannot punch directly and hard in the national political arena. The Central Bank, on the other hand, exerts some leverage. In 1992 this is what the Bank had to say about the timber industry:

> Management of the nation's forest resources in 1991 continued to cause concern at many levels of the community. The government's demand for tax revenues was used to justify the granting of more logging licences, with apparently no assessment of the long-term economic and social costs of rapid deforestation. Improvements to the authorities' ability to police logging methods to minimise environmental damage have been painfully slow.
>
> And bitter divisions at village level continue between the advocates of selling the standing rainforest to logging companies, and those who want slower, higher-value-added methods of using the forest, based on small local sawmills. (Central Bank of Solomon Islands, 1992:14)

In this chapter we focus on this second option, the smaller-scale and more sustainable use of the forest based on local sawmills and chainsaws rather than industrial logging. Ecologically-minded Westerners with sympathy for the hardships of developing countries are accustomed to assuming that "small is beautiful", whereas the large-scale capitalist alternative is ugly in every way. Is this true?

Large is ugly?

In its 1991 report the Central Bank provided data on the various options for forest management, quoting prices for the end of that year. Figure 11.1 shows the average price that was then available for unprocessed roundlogs compared to sawn timber and "eco-timber". The relatively low value of roundlogs in 1991, despite price rises during the year, reflects in part the dishonest practices of some companies. As usual the Central Bank's report is couched in rather polite language: "There is much concern ... about the wide range of export prices reported by logging companies, for similar shipments to similar markets, leading to suspicions of transfer pricing". A headline in the Honiara newspaper *Solomon Star* was more forthright: "LARGE-SCALE LOGGING CHEATS VILLAGERS" (16 August 1991:9).

Figure 11.1 The price of logs and timber, 1991*

Product	Price per cubic metre of roundlog
Roundlogs that were exported unprocessed	SI$ 168
Sawn timber exports	SI$ 311
Eco-timber exported on behalf of the owners of 54 portable sawmills and chainsaws	SI$ 625

* In this table the volume of sawn timber exports is converted to an equivalent roundlog volume by assuming 48% utilisation, as cited by the Central Bank's 1991 report (1992:14). However, the data presented by Anonymous (1996:Table 1) show, for 1991, 6 200 cu. m of sawn timber exports in total rather than the 6 960 cu. m reported by the Bank. Anonymous (1996) converts this figure to roundlog equivalent by assuming only a 30% utilisation. The disparity is entirely characteristic of the statistical confusion and factual uncertainty that characterises the timber industry in Solomon Islands.

Considering the superior returns available from sawn timber and eco-timber, one might have expected the government to have pushed producers towards adopting the value-added option, but the production figures for 1991 (as estimated by Anonymous, 1996) did not show much movement in this direction (Figure 11.2). The vast majority (84 per cent) of the trees harvested ended up as roundlog exports, while the "value-added" options, either sawn timber exports or so-called eco-timber exports, accounted for only 6% and 0.2% respectively of total production. The eco-timber exports totalled a mere 270 cubic metres of sawn timber, which represented just four trial shipments, but they fetched a 3.5 times better price than the export of roundlogs. Even if the producer converts roundlog to ordinary sawn timber, he will almost double the value of the log.

From these figures the economic advantages of selling sawn timber (if possible, eco-timber) would appear to be obvious, but what about the costs of producing it? The case of New Georgia presented later in this chapter shows what a large gap there is between the gross and the net returns from small-scale timber milling. From the point of view of the foreign logging companies, the picture also looks quite different. We have to consider the total benefits to be derived from exporting unprocessed logs from a remote periphery (Solomon Islands) to places within the East Asian industrial centres of Taiwan, Korea and Japan. As the Bank admitted, "the profitability of exporting logs may significantly exceed that of sawn timber, because much higher utilisation of the log is achievable if it is sawn in the industrial market-place" (Central Bank of Solomon Islands, 1992:13).

Figure 11.2 The volume of production of logs and timber, 1991

Sector	Product	Volume (cubic metres)	Proportion of total log output
Commercial logging	Roundlog exports	302,600 cu. m were recorded; in addition, an estimated 30,260 cu.m were "under-recorded"	84%
	Sawn timber	20,100 cu. m of logs, generating 6,200 cu. m of exported sawn timber	6%
		560 cu. m of logs, generating 270 cu. m of exported eco-timber	0.2%
Subsistence logging	Local consumption	35,000 cu. m of logs (estimate) from over 100 portable sawmills and chainsaws, and serving local needs	10%
TOTAL LOG PRODUCTION		358,260 cu. m	100%

Sources: Anonymous (1996:Table 1); Central Bank of Solomon Islands (1992:24)

There is also the question of transfer pricing. How accurate was the declared 1991 price for roundlogs of SI$ 168, when the "sale" actually took place between an exporting company and a milling company both being under the same umbrella of ownership? We must recognise that the actual value of logs is somewhat higher than the declared prices, and the reluctance of logging companies to invest in sawmills must represent a rational decision on their part. These companies operate within a get-rich-quick culture and in a political climate in the Solomon Islands that threatens to impose more restrictive policies with every new government. Prime Minister Solomon Mamaloni never retracted a pledge to end roundlog exports in 1999, while the Ulufa'alu government that replaced him did impose a temporary embargo in 1998. "Sustainability" for a logging company means extracting value from forests as fast as possible while the logs remain available, and then re-investing the profit in some less rewarding but more sustainable enterprise such as agri-business, manufacturing or tourism.

What of the customary landowners, from whose forests most of these logs derive? As indicated in the preceding chapter, they do not, of course, receive anything like the full value of the roundlogs that are exported from their land. Many of the agreements made in the past were based not on a proportion of the value of the logs, but on a fixed royalty payment. If prices rise the companies have no incentive to pass on additional income to the owners of forests. On Choiseul, for example, the Eagon company was paying in 1991 SI\$ 5 per cubic metre to landowners, during a year when average roundlog prices rose from SI\$ 135 to SI\$ 174. With such boom prices the royalty paid on Choiseul amounts to less than 3% – a shocking throwback to the bad old days of frontier colonialism when resources were stolen from the "natives" for little more than beads and trinkets.

As log prices rose during the 1990s and as customary landowners in the Solomons became more knowledgeable about the value of their forests, so the new agreements with logging companies became slightly more generous. In 1996 typical levels of royalty paid to customary landowners varied between 5 and 15% of the declared export value of the log. Landowners had a choice, as they saw it, between selling their forests to Asian loggers for an immediate and apparently substantial lump sum, or earning money from sawn timber through some sort of portable sawmill or chainsaw operation. This latter option required investment and expertise; it was a way to earn money through hard work rather than from "free" handouts. Unfortunately, it could generate an annual income somewhat less than that immediately obtainable from the royalty option. However it could pay the producer 20-40 times more money per cubic metre of log – an estimate is based on the comparison between a 10% royalty payment on roundlog exports and the return from the same log exported as sawn timber.

At first sight it appears to be an unusually clearcut case of "large is ugly and small is beautiful", although the small-scale option is obviously not as profitable as the simple price comparison suggests. Do we have here a convergence between good conservation practice and sensible economics? In a climate where even a conservative business journal can refer to the Asian logging companies operating in the South Pacific as "the new colonialists" (*The Economist*, 6 August 1994), the political case for encouraging eco-timber would appear to be unquestionable.

The Solomon Islands logging boom

In fact, far from coming under political control, the logging industry in the Solomons enjoyed a period of almost unrestricted growth until the economic recession in Southeast Asia in 1998, in parallel with the boom in log prices. In international markets logs were worth on average US$ 177 per cubic metre in the 1980s, but after 1989 the price of logs rose year by year reaching a peak of US$ 500 in June 1993 and averaging US$ 386 for that year as a whole. Prices remained high for the rest of the decade, although after 1998 Asian markets lost their capacity to absorb logs on an almost unlimited scale.

The decade saw logging become a hot political issue in Solomon Islands, debate focusing on the issues of sustainability, the appropriate level for export duties, and the exemptions on duty offered to certain companies (including the logging company on Makira in which Prime Minister Solomon Mamaloni had a large stake). Accusations of bribery and corruption were made, and accurate information became harder and harder to find. In 1995 the Central Bank pointed out that several studies had highlighted the likelihood that the country was losing revenue through inefficient surveillance and inadequate monitoring of log export prices and volumes: "Given the scattered nature of Solomon Islands and the remoteness of some of the logging sites, it is possible that illicit activities and unrecorded shipments may be taking place all the time" (Central Bank of Solomon Islands, 1995: 17). The Bank emphasised again and again the dangers of economic dependence upon a short-term boom:

> The thrust of forest policy in Solomon Islands should be sustainability. This not only allows for the resource to regenerate and replace itself but will also allow future generations of Solomon Islanders to derive income and other benefits from the forest resource .... Sadly ... actual production levels are estimated to be three times greater than the sustainable levels... [However] the logging companies prefer to pay the high rates of duty rather than reduce production levels. (Central Bank of Solomon Islands, 1995:18)

A bleak situation has been compounded by a lack of information. The Statistics Division of the Ministry of Finance has not managed to publish any volume statistics on roundlogs since June 1994. Most of the forestry experts believe the resource has been "mined" by the companies in a way that will prevent the forest from ever recovering. Forestry advisers within one of the government ministries, frustrated and marginalised by their political superiors, wrote an anonymous and unpublished report that was leaked to us by an environmental activist in Honiara. Their conclusion was as follows:

> The estimate of 12.8 years of remaining resource is as good as can be achieved at present. The Solomons may face a decline in its forest industry far sooner than twelve years. .... No detailed studies of logging practices are available, however the general consensus appears to be that forest practices in many locations are amongst the worst in the world. Logging companies are interested in extracting the maximum resource at minimum cost, and therefore have no interest in ensuring that the forest is treated in such a way as to allow it to regenerate. (Anonymous, 1996:3)

It is not only expatriate advisers that have been driven to protest at what they see as an unfolding tragedy of laissez-faire economics and short-term expediency. Although the protest movement in Honiara against the logging boom is spearheaded by NGOs such as Greenpeace and WWF (Worldwide Fund for Nature), it covers a wide spectrum of opinion particularly within the Christian churches. The Solomon Islanders active in this movement find one focus in their newspaper journalism and in magazines such as *Link*, published by the well-established NGO Solomon Islands Development Trust (Figure 11.3.). There is a spiritual dimension to this protest which may have a stronger impact on public opinion than mere appeals to "sustainability".

Small is beautiful?

The small-scale alternative to industrial logging is to fell the trees on a more selective basis, using chainsaws and other methods that are more friendly to the forest. The product is sawn timber for local use, or for export – to take advantage of the higher prices available (see Figure 11.1). According to the environmentalists, forest-friendly methods can also generate higher, more sustainable incomes. So far the effect of this small-scale option on the volume of sawn timber exports has been modest. While total log production increased an astonishing 2.45 times between 1991 and 1995, 1995 figures still show an overwhelming dominance of roundlog exports, which accounted for 85% of all production. Sawn timber exports doubled in four years, but still only amounted to 5% of logs produced, despite the apparent attractions of small-scale forestry and its sustainability (Figure 11.4.).

Figure 11.3 Cover of the environmental magazine *Link*

Figure 11.4 The volume of production of logs and timber, 1995

Sector	Product	Volume (cubic metres)	Proportion of total log output
Commercial logging	Roundlog exports	701,360 cu.m were recorded; in addition, an esti-mated 35,070 cu. m were "under-recorded"	85%
	Plantation logs From KFPL	32,460 cu.m	4%
	Sawn timber and eco-timber exports	60,000 cu. m (log equivalent)	5%
Subsistence logging	Local consumption	50,000 cu. m (log equivalent)	6%
TOTAL LOG PRODUCTION		825,150 cu. m	100%

Source (for all data except sawn timber and eco-timber exports): Anonymous (1996:Table 1); the sawn/eco-timber figure derives from the 12,400 cu.m of exports reported by Central Bank of Solomon Islands (1996b:64)

One reason for the failure to shift from roundlogs to sawn timber is hinted at by the Central Bank in its 1995 report. It refers to the activities of small portable sawmills and chainsaw operators as being "encouraged and promoted with advice and technical assistance from local non-government agencies" (Central Bank of Solomon Islands, 1996a: 7). This points to a growing paralysis in the Solomon Islands government's capacity to act. Not only is it hand-in-glove with the big logging companies, it is also so strapped for cash that even normal expenditure cannot be maintained. For example the government was unable, in 1995 and early 1996, to keep up the payment to the National Provident Fund of the pension contributions of its own employees. The backlog of payments could only be met when the logged and partially reforested government lands at Viru Harbour was sold to Eagon for a reported cash payment of SI$ 23 millions (see Chapter 9). Neither the political will nor the funding exists to start new development projects in small-scale logging, so the only activities in this field are organised by NGOs such as SWIFT and Greenpeace.

To establish whether small-scale logging in Marovo Lagoon is potentially "beautiful", despite its lack of progress so far, we therefore need to look more closely at the rather disparate actors of the anti-logging movement. Some environmentalists are passionate promoters of the small-scale alternative, but others are deeply distrustful of logging in any shape or form. To understand this logging phobia requires us to deconstruct some of the values which underlie Western environmentalism, in particular its utopian vision of the tropical rainforest.

A vision of Utopia:
butterfly ranching, furniture making and bee keeping

As outlined in Chapter 1, Western perceptions of the rainforest have gone through many changes. A relevant early example already mentioned by us is the British naval lieutenant B.T. Somerville, who after eight months spent mainly on hydrographic surveying around New Georgia could see nothing of value in the rainforests of the islands, but instead looked forward to the day when these seemingly "fertile" lands might, through better management following colonisation by a "more industrious race", be transformed into plantations of useful cash crops (Somerville, 1897).

Today the perceptions of most educated westerners have been shaped by a dominant discourse that sees the forest in quite different terms. The environmental movement, which established strong roots in western Europe, North America and Australasia in the 1980s (and shallower roots in other regions), adopted the tropical rainforest as perhaps its most powerful symbol. The new role of the rainforests is summed up in the headline on the front cover of *The Ecologist* magazine for October 1987: "SAVE THE FOREST: SAVE THE PLANET". This slogan was superimposed on a dramatic photograph of a clearfelled rainforest, with blackened stumps and red, bleeding earth. The photograph may have been from Amazonia, or from Thailand, or – conceivably – from Vangunu in Marovo (except that logging did not begin there until 1992), but the picture's location was irrelevant to the potency of its symbolic message. It was the role of deforestation in exacerbating the greenhouse effect that underpinned this new, secular morality. A world without logging has become a new vision of Utopia.

In addition to a growing belief in the rainforest's global healing power, a new responsibility was being imposed upon rainforest peoples because of their perceived role as guardians of so much of the planet's genetic database. The rhetoric varies from romantic journalism to scientific jargon, but the underlying message – exemplified below by passages from an article in the Solomon Airlines in-flight magazine and a proposal for the conservation of Marovo forests, respectively – is the same:

> The seclusion of ... Marovo was invaded by missionaries in the early 1900's, but the customs and beliefs of the people have survived hand in hand with Christianity. Now the culture, developed over at least 7 000 years; the strange plants, animals and insects of the lush tropical jungle and sequestered waters, have attracted not only anthropologists and other scientists, but exploiters as well .... In the protection ... of universally important sites [like Marovo] ... the task includes introducing local landowners to the value of conservation and sustainable management, at the same time generating a steady income. (Evans, 1995:42)

> The wide variety of environments ... have created a region of great ecological diversity in the Marovo Lagoon and its forested catchments ... These features, particularly the presence of the world's finest example of a double barrier-island enclosed lagoon, give the Marovo Lagoon and environs exceptional ecological diversity and conservation values of outstanding international importance. (Lees et. al., 1991:95)

What gives urgency to this message is a perception that in the world as it now is, all change will be irreversible. For example, for Solomon Islands Annette Lees proposes that because of the rate of forest loss has become so rapid, "steps must be taken now to ensure that the best examples of the unique forests found in these islands are not lost forever" (Lees et.al., 1991: 1-2). A "protected forest system" for the country is therefore recommended, the costs of which should be shared with the international community, in recognition of the "international importance" of the forests. Funding, it is suggested, should come principally in the form of development aid programmes designed to benefit Solomon Islanders living in areas adjacent to protected forests to compensate them for being denied access to forest resources. To quote Lees' Maruia Society/Australian Parks and Wildlife Service report again, "if villagers are to be interested in participating in the protected forests system, development opportunities will need to be part of the reserves package" (Lees et.al., 1991:3).

There are many weaknesses in this approach. There is the assumption, firstly, that the Solomon Islands government takes seriously its obligation (under the SPREP Convention) to establish protected forests so as to preserve what conservationists call "the natural heritage". Second is the assumption that the government has the power and the will to take away from customary landowners their rights to the use of forests. There are echoes here of the top-down approach to resource management that was typical in late colonial times – for example, the designation for Marovo of Agricultural Opportunity Areas (Wall and Hansell, 1975) identified on aerial photographs and delimited on maps without any pretence at consultation or recognition of local reality (see Chapter 7). It was in this way that the Russian commissars in Moscow planned the development of Siberia – but in Marovo, unlike the USSR, the Agricultural Opportunity Areas could not subsequently be developed.

Another area of weakness in the environmentalists' approach is the benefit package that they offer, as a way, it is hoped, to compensate local people for the loss of their forest rights. This package is a miscellaneous shopping list that ranges from the mundane to the bizarre (Lees et.al., 1991; Evans, 1995; Greenaway, 1995): Village improvements such as better schools, health clinics, roads and bridges, piped water, and "other needs identified by villagers"; assistance in establishing what are termed "commercially viable, self-sustaining and environmentally sound village development projects" (the examples given are fishing ventures, crocodile or butterfly ranching, clam farming, furniture making, and bee keeping); nature tourism, which it is hoped will be attracted by the well-protected environment (projects in Marovo designed to promote tourism are the topic of Chapter 12).

What these "projects" all have in common (furniture making is a possible exception) is that none of them has any connection at all with forest exploitation. Sustainable use of the forest itself is not recommended – in fact it is not even mentioned except for the so-called exclusion zones. According to this vision of Utopia, the forest ecosystem is too fragile (or perhaps too sacred) for it be used for timber, or hunting and gathering, or even agroforestry. In the Lees model, villagers' agroforestry is to be restricted to the "Exclusion Zone" (the zone from which conservation is excluded?), which forms a buffer zone between the coastal settlements and the protected forest (Lees et.al., 1991:3).

An alternative vision: small-scale logging

It would be wrong to caricature all conservationists as new-wave missionaries who wish to place a permanent taboo on forest access. For example, other consultants employed by the New Zealand government have taken a more tolerant view. In 1992 Darby reported on the Solomon Islands World Heritage Programme, which by then had focussed on two promising candidates for World Heritage status: East Rennell and Marovo Lagoon. Although not as desirable as eco-tourism, Darby felt that local sawmilling was acceptable provided it was done properly. After what are he calls "disastrous experiences with uncontrolled projects" in Vanuatu and Papua New Guinea, village sawmilling or "walkabout sawmilling" had become "an emotive subject":

> On the one hand innumerable villages request aid to buy equipment to mill their own trees, and on the other hand resource sustainability interests usually oppose helping yet more rainforest logging. Small scale milling is not regarded as incompatible with World Heritage listing ... provided it is carried out in strict accordance with an appropriate management plan and monitoring procedures that ensure the conservation of all forest values in perpetuity, not just the timber values. (Darby, 1992: 5.3, 9.3)

This suggestion has not yet been followed by the New Zealand-funded World Heritage Programme (WHP) in Marovo Lagoon, which instead has focussed on eco-tourism as the main alternative option to logging (see Chapter 12). Bee keeping has also not been ruled out by these advisers provided the stores in Honiara can sell off the current glut of honey. However, so far they have done nothing to encourage small-scale logging. Indeed, it was startling to discover in August 1996 that the New Zealanders working for the WHP in Marovo and on Rennell had no knowledge of the existence of a sustainable forest management project (SWIFT) based at Munda further west in New Georgia, even though SWIFT was already recruiting and training some Marovo timber producers.

Thus we can see that the neo-utopian ideology is taking many forms. In Marovo in the 1990s the idea has been promoted by various external agencies that "small is beautiful" provided that what is "small" is also sustainable. In practice this means that the small must never be allowed to become too big. Some of these agencies are completely unaware of each other's existence. At an earlier stage in the 20th-century transformations of Marovo, the Christian religion was spread by a similar process, haphazardly and by trial and error, with mission rivalry and through often precarious relations with "target" communities whose social dynamics were little known by the purveyors of Christianity (Hviding, 1996a:118-124). Similarly, the people being missionised were for the most part quite unaware of the missionaries' self-ascribed agendas. The people we now categorise as "the missionaries" were no doubt as uncoordinated in their actions as the people that history will categorise as "the environmentalists".

However, Marovo history teaches us not to be too cynical. Those who wonder whether an ethic of sustainable forest management can ever take root in Marovo so that the allure of the logging company bonanza can be resisted, might consider the situation in Marovo Lagoon a hundred years ago. Would it have seemed likely then that more than half of the people of Marovo Lagoon would, within a generation, be converted to a cult which makes self-denial a religious duty? Despite the continuing syncretist cast of Marovo Christianity – God still has to compete with sorcerers and ancestral spirits for control over **mana** in quite a few present-day contexts and situations (Hviding, 1996a: 122-123) – the following remains solid and true: the Seventh-day Adventist Church removes 10 to 20% of each person's income as a tithe, forbids the eating of two of the main protein foods (pork and shellfish), and prohibits all stimulating or intoxicating beverages including betel nuts. The success of the Seventh-day Adventists in Marovo shows that the wilder dreams of environmentalism only need to be absorbed into certain influential social and political frameworks for the implausible to become reality, and then mere history.

The SWIFT project

It is in fact not the SDA Church but the United (formerly Methodist) Church which, in the 1990s, has become the spiritual home for a sustainable forest management project known as SWIFT (Solomon Western Islands Fair Trade). Conservation via eco-tourism, butterflies, bees, and so forth can be seen as one branch of the aspirations arising from 1980s environmentalism ("Save the forests: Save the planet"). Fair trade and sustainable development is the other branch, arising from the realisation that in an interdependent world the hand that drags the log from the forest is, in a sense, being guided by another hand which is bringing home tropical hardwoods from the suburban Do-It-Yourself supermarket. Those who own, but increasingly do not control, the shrinking area of the world's tropical rainforests are rather powerless to resist the approaches of foreign logging companies not merely because they are unaware of the value of what they are selling. They lack power also because they see no alternative ways of generating a cash income.

Consumers in the West have become aware that they are, in a sense, an integral part of this problem, since they constitute at least part of the market for tropical hardwoods. Perhaps if this market did not exist the pressures on the tropical rain forest would diminish? Convinced by the logic of this approach, Greenpeace, Friends of the Earth (FOE) and Worldwide Fund for Nature (WWF) all initiated campaigns to ban the use of tropical hardwoods. Although largely ineffective in slowing the rate of deforestation, these campaigns did result in the emergence, especially in western Europe, of a latent demand for tropical hardwoods that consumers believed came from genuinely sustainable sources. Unfortunately, up until the mid-1990s such sources were practically non-existent, despite many dubious and even fraudulent claims to the contrary by various timber merchants.

So it was that when WWF were asked in 1995 to provide sustainably managed tropical hardwoods for the interior furnishing of a prestigious new civic building in Rotterdam, they were at a loss to know how to provide this "eco-timber", despite their many years of campaigning on this issue. In desperation they turned to a Dutch group sponsored by the World Council of Churches and by ICCSU, the umbrella organisation for all NGOs in the Netherlands. This group was operating in New Georgia under the name of SWIFT (Solomon Western Islands Fair Trade), and rather rashly it promised that it could fulfil the Rotterdam contract, which required 150 cubic metres of eco-timber to be delivered by the end of the year.

Although its operation had only begun in 1994, SWIFT was happy to make this undertaking because of the project was reporting a great upsurge of interest in small-scale sustainable logging throughout the Western Solomons, including Marovo Lagoon. SWIFT's local connections are with the United Church headquarters in Munda (a church with a relatively strong record of resistance to large-scale logging). Its recent historical roots are in the United Church's "Integrated Human Development Programme" (IHDP) which was established in the 1980s to support "socio-economic projects" (the usual package of "piggery, poultry, cattle, cocoa, fishery and pineapples" [Schep, 1997:81]) in scattered locations throughout the influence sphere of the church in the Western Solomons.

In line with the general failures of such project activities in Solomon Islands, exacerbated by the range of "economic sectors" and the faraway locations involved plus a general lack of infrastructure and "know-how", the IHDP stopped this type of development work in 1993. This was a time when village people were asking the IHDP to help them in the marketing and production of timber (Schep, 1997:81-82). The SWIFT programme was launched in 1994, with emphasis on a form of "eco-timber" production that in fact attempts to achieve what has seldom been managed successfully anywhere in the world by Greenpeace, FOE or WWF: translating the ideals of ecological sustainability into terms that make sense to the owners of the rainforest resource, and providing for them a market for eco-timber. In this way, it is hoped, a more attractive option can be offered to the people than the alternative available from large-scale logging, and without the interests of future generations being sacrificed. The forest and its biodiversity will also be safeguarded.

The SWIFT Netherlands Foundation was set up in February 1995 "to find the best way to solve the problem of marketing SWIFT timber", aiming to revive the collapsed market for tropical timber in Europe by demonstrating "the differences between destructive harvesting of timber and SWIFT's sustainable way of timber production" (SWIFT Newsletter, 1996). The connection was made through the WWF with the civic building project in Rotterdam. In fact only 30% of the WWF order from Rotterdam was fulfilled through properly certified sustainable sources in the Western Solomons. The remainder came from small-scale, selective felling of trees from areas on New Georgia where the "stated intention" of landowners was to manage forests sustainably. The reason for this shortfall from 100% "genuine" eco-timber was that the certification of SWIFT's timber producers (which is required by WWF) has proved to be an elaborate, complicated and bureaucratic process, and therefore it has proceeded at a slow pace.

The standards for genuine sustainability are set by an organisation called the Forestry Stewardship Council (FSC) in London. FSC approval reassures the consumer, but carries with it many obligations for the producer, some of whom are visited in the field by FSC inspectors, a sort of Ecology Police. The FSC inspection (which is at SWIFT's expense) is to check the management plans for the producers' blocks, and to ensure that the plans are being followed. The plans are based on maps of one-hectare blocks of forest which enable the ultimate fate of every tree on the map to be determined. FSC investigates the legal as well as the ecological status of the land that is to be sustainably managed, and also demands assurances about the training available to those who are to be certificated. Training courses are provided in Munda by SWIFT volunteers from the Netherlands, using the medium of Solomon Islands Pijin.

The producers are mostly young New Georgia men who lack the education for them to have any job prospects in Gizo or Honiara, but who have access through **butubutu** membership to large areas of forest. Their main interest in eco-timber is as a means for them to gain some degree of personal control over a better source of income than copra, marine products or carvings. But to gain access, they must be prepared to undergo some indoctrination into the more "theological" aspects of sustainable forestry. To return to the missionary analogy, FSC surveillance exists in order to maintain theological purity, and to make sure that the organisers in the field do not make too many concessions to local conditions. In the period when the missionary churches were expanding in Melanesia, each church also had its procedures for the surveillance of missionaries. The role of the Bishop or his equivalent was to ensure that even on the frontier of darkness there was no compromise with dogma, and no decline in standards of behaviour. No missionary was allowed to "go native". The position of FSC in relation to SWIFT is not dissimilar.

The analogy also works quite well at the international scale, where the legitimacy of FSC itself is not unchallenged. Just as the Anglicans, Methodists and Roman Catholics in their home countries engaged in a strenuous and sometimes bitter theological debate, so FSC is under constant attack from "deep ecologists" and others who think that any relationship with the market will be damaging to the integrity of the forest, its wildlife and its indigenous communities. It is argued that participation in trade will erode the (assumed) self-sufficiency of forest peoples, and will undermine their cultural and spiritual values.

Sustainable forestry is also seen as dangerous because it provides the slippery slope towards large-scale commercial logging. The United Nations agencies are constantly being warned of the dangers of forest management projects like SWIFT that are established in the name of sustainability. The Intergovernmental Panel on Forests (IPF) is a good example. The 1992 UN Conference on Environment and Development (UNCED) at Rio set up a Commission on Sustainable Development (CSD), which in turn spawned the IFP. At its third meeting in Geneva in September 1996, the IFP was lobbied by, amongst others, the International Alliance of Indigenous-Tribal Peoples of the Tropical Forests. This organisation appears to be a front for a technical secretariat which is based in London, and its submission to IPF (published in collaboration with the Copenhagen-based International Work Group for Indigenous Affairs) contains the following statement about certification schemes like those that are authorised by FSC and put into practice by SWIFT:

> Processes of certification ... should ensure that companies respect the environment and deal openly and fairly with us [the indigenous peoples]. However, unless these measures are particularly stringent, their effect will be worse than useless. .... The discussion on ... sustainable forestry ... should not become simply a discussion on maximising logging within certain limits. ... We are very concerned that certification ... can be misused to promote the extraction of our resources. We therefore insist ... that certification is based on recognition of our rights and welfare. (International Alliance of Indigenous-Tribal Peoples of the Tropical Forest, and International Work Group for Indigenous Affairs, 1996:89)

In this way a politically correct concept of tropical rainforest "sustainability" is defined by self-styled experts in London, Geneva or Copenhagen. Without their approval the lucrative market for eco-timber would not be available to organisations like SWIFT. In response, in places like Marovo small forest plots are measured out by SWIFT and sustainable management plans are put into place, so that continued FSC certification can be guaranteed. Marovo knowledge finds no place in this grand scheme for global eco-Utopia.

It would be hard to find a clearer case of knowledge reinforcing power, in a way similar to power/knowledge relations in any field of specialist expertise. The classic case was analysed by Michel Foucault (1975) in his study of the growth of criminology and the practice of psychiatric medicine in the 19th century. Control is exerted over the lives of others by a group professing to know a higher truth, and the power that derives from this control serves to reinforce that "truth" by deepening its basis in new knowledge. It is for the readers of this book to decide whether or not our own efforts to reveal the "truth" about Marovo will escape from the Foucaultian knowledge/power nexus which currently has such a strong grip on Third World environmentalism.

The costs and benefits of SWIFT

The benefits to producers who are converted to a scheme such as SWIFT are not just sustainable, they are also very substantial if calculated per cubic metre of roundlog, and quite respectable as a gross return per hectare of rain forest, although few trees are felled on a per-hectare basis. The typical returns for a hectare under small-scale forestry compared to industrial logging is shown in Figure 11.5 (Figures 11.6-11.8 provide fuller details). What such a diagram does not reveal are the disadvantages of the small-scale: the fact that it requires considerable commitment, effort and investment by the landowner, whereas any logging royalty comes as a sudden rush of money which involves no direct cost – it is virtually a windfall profit.

Figures 11.6 and 11.7 provide a detailed comparison for a 1 hectare block of forest that is being managed by a typical New Georgia landowner in two different ways. The returns available to certified producers under the SWIFT scheme (Figure 11.6) are based on current SWIFT prices and permitted yield levels. The data are calculated for forests having different densities of the large, potentially harvestable trees, those in excess of 60 cm dbh (diameter at breast height), some of which will be commercially valuable species. We can take as an example land having 25 large trees per hectare (a fair average for North New Georgia).

According to the FSC rules which SWIFT was imposing by 1996-97, three trees can be removed from this hectare block by a certified producer during each five-year period, representing an annual yield of 0.6 trees. Each tree should yield a roundlog of 5 cubic metres, which when sawn will yield

A. If logged :

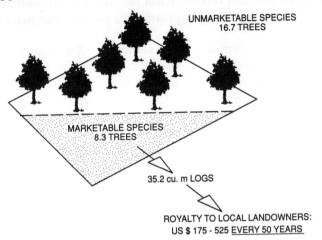

B. If managed by a Certified Producer and sold as ecotimber to SWIFT :

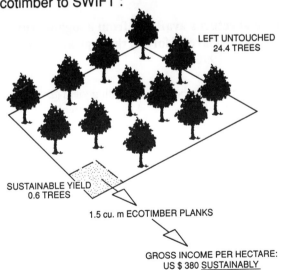

Figure 11.5 The royalty payment from a logging company, compared to the eco-timber alternative*

* Data relate to the situation in 1995, and refer to an average forest stand with 25 trees per hectare greater than 60 cm dbh (diameter at breast height).

Figure 11.6 Financial returns from the SWIFT alternative, per hectare of New Georgia forest: 1996 policies and prices

No. trees >60 cm dbh	No. of trees harvestable per 5-year period	No. of trees harvestable per year	Annual sawn timber yield @ 2.5 cu. m per tree*	Annual income @ SI$ 900 per cu. m
< 9	0	0	0	0
10-14	1	0.2	0.5	450
15-24	2	0.4	1.0	900
25-34	3	0.6	1.5	1,350
>35	4	0.8	2.0	1,800
Typical average 25	3	0.6	1.5	1,350

*The roundlog yield is 5 cu.m per tree (typical average for selected mature trees) which will produce 2.5 cu.m in sawn planks.

Source: SWIFT staff members, August 1996

Figure 11.7 Financial returns available from a logging royalty agreement, per hectare of forest: the typical Solomon Islands situation in 1996

Total number of trees > 60 cm dbh per hectare of forest	Average number of trees of commercial value (1/3 of total)	Roundlog yield @ 4 cu. m per tree*	Royalty paid @ SI$ 15-45 per cu. m
8	2.6	10.4	156-468
12.5	4.1	16.4	246-738
20	6.6	26.4	396-1,188
30	10	40.0	600-1,800
36	12	48.0	720-2,160
Typical average 25	8.3	33.2	623-1,868

* The roundlog yield per tree is a smaller figure than for SWIFT producers because loggers take all commercially valuable trees including some with defects, thus lowering the average.

Sources: Number of trees and yields, including typical average: A.V. Hughes (pers. comm.); range of royalty payments: SWIFT, and newspaper reports, Honiara

Figure 11.8 Examples of the SWIFT price for timber of different species[a]

Species	Marovo name	Per cu. m sawn timber (SI$) 52 x 130 mm	Per cu. m sawn timber (SI$) 52 x 205 mm	Per cu. m sawn timber (SI$) 104 x 155 mm
Calophyllum peekelii[b]	**buni vijolo**	850	900	870
Pometia pinnata	**meda**	900	970	950
Vitex cofassus	**vasara**	1,050	1,100	1,100
Intsia bijuga	**kivili**	1,050	1,100	1,100
Pterocarpus indicus[c]	**rigi**	1,150	1,200	1,300
Dillenia salomonensis	**kapuchu**	[d]	[d]	[d]

[a] Prices are those available to FSC-certified producers. The prices available to beneficiaries of SWIFT chainsaws who are not yet certified are lower by SI$ 200 per cu. m in each case.

[b] Formerly *Calophyllum kajewski*

[c] SWIFT's unit sizes for *Pterocarpus indicus* ("Rosewood") were different from other species. The prices shown are for pieces 52 x 155, 52 x 205 and 78 x 205 mm respectively. The top price of SI$ 1300 per cu. m was paid for pieces measuring 52 x 420 mm. The minimum acceptable length was 1.5 m.

[d] In 1996 no price was being quoted by SWIFT for *Dillenia*, as shipments had temporarily ceased while problems of the timber cracking while drying out were being investigated.

Sources: SWIFT

2-3 cubic metres of marketable timber – say 2.5 on average. This represents an average net yield of 1.5 cubic metres per hectare per year. Using the current SWIFT prices offered for good sawn timber planks (52 mm thick, 205 mm wide, and at least 2 m long), a certified producer will receive from SWIFT SI\$ 900 per cubic metre for the typical tall timber tree **buni vijolo** (*Calophyllum peekelii*), and rather more for other species (see Figure 11.6). Using the *Calophyllum* figure as a typical average for all timber sizes and all species, this hectare block will therefore yield to the producer 0.6 x 2.5 x 900, in other words SI\$ 1,350 every year in gross income from timber.

This can be compared with the alternative option, whereby the same stand of 25 trees is made available to a logging company like Golden Springs International (of Malaysia) or Eagon (of Korea), which has acquired logging rights over it. On poorer land only one-quarter of large trees have any commercial value but on better land about eight trees out of the 25 growing on the block can be logged, yielding for export around 33 cubic metres per hectare of round-logs. Typical logging agreements on New Georgia have varied between SI\$ 15-45 per cubic metre in royalty payments to landowners, which looks like a pathetic return compared to SWIFT's price of SI\$ 900. The logging companies are offering royalties which range from 2% to 5% of the eco-timber price. What they offer to the landowner is a once-and-for-all windfall payment of SI\$ 623-1,868 in the first year, and thereafter nothing at all, since in extracting these marketable logs the remaining two-thirds of the stand will be mostly destroyed. On the face of it the SWIFT alternative is exceedingly attractive, typically yielding SI\$ 1,350 per hectare per year on a sustained basis, year after year, whereas the logging alternative will generate at best around SI\$ 1,868 but usually less, and this on a once-only basis. However, the analysis disregards two vital elements: the costs to the landowner of choosing one or the other option, sustainable forestry or logging, and secondly the questionable relevance of assessing costs and benefits on a per-hectare basis.

The logging option: a lottery jackpot?

The landowner able to negotiate the logging royalty option does not have to bear any direct costs of any kind. The real costs are environmental – the likelihood that at least 20% of the land will be compacted by heavy machines and eroded by logging roads, and so will be permanently degraded, and secondly the loss of most of the value of the remaining 80% of the forest for at least a generation. If these costs can be disregarded – and quite a few of the Marovo **butubutu** that have a history connected to the hinterlands of the mainland bush do indeed have such extensive forests that their leaders appear to be willing to "write-off" the resource in this way – then the cash income can be thought of as essentially cost-free. The "costs" are more likely to be thought of in social, rather than environmental terms: logging royalties have to be shared with other members of the **butubutu**. This places a dangerous amount of power in the hands of the leading men of the **butu-butu** who undertake negotiations with logging companies, and requires that strict boundaries be drawn around the **butubutu** membership in ways quite alien to the usual more flexible practice (cf. Hviding, 1993b).

If these problems can be overcome, the windfall profits from logging can be substantial. The logging concession in North New Georgia that has been worked by the Malaysian company Golden Springs is a case in point. The land leased in 1989 consisted of 45,000 hectares, and the details of the deal with Golden Springs have not been made public. However, if a deal similar to this one were to be negotiated today, we can calculate the potential benefits by considering that today there are still only 1,460 people living in the relevant part of North New Georgia in about 760 households, so that an equitable distribution of forest would allocate 60 hectares to each household. The calculations in Figure 11.7 indicate that the 60 hectare block, if completely logged, should result in a royalty payment of at least SI$ 37,380, and possibly three times this amount, spread out over perhaps a five-year period of logging. In whatever way the figures are juggled, it is clear that this household will be receiving an income greatly in excess of anything normally experienced in the rural Solomon Islands – a lottery jackpot indeed. To point to the very meagre and unequally distributed benefits that actually did emerge from the 1989 agreement between Golden Springs and the North New Georgia Timber Corporation has certainly not been realistic in the late 1990s. Throughout this decade Solomon Islands has found itself in a situation of sky-high tropical timber prices, with a number of Asian logging companies actively competing with each other in their pursuit of deals with local communities about logging concessions on "unexploited" customary land.

Small is stupid

Contrast this logging jackpot with the situation of the certified SWIFT producer. He might earn more dollars in gross income on a per-hectare basis, but he must himself bear all the costs. These include marking the forest blocks, felling selected trees, slabbing and milling the logs in the forest, and then carrying the sawn planks to the coast where SWIFT will pay the producer for all his effort and investment. SWIFTS's boat picks up the timber and organises its export to Rotterdam, but even so the producer's costs are really quite substantial. The biggest item is the Stihl chainsaw needed for felling and the Alaska frame needed for slabbing and milling timber. In 1996 these items would involve each SWIFT producer in the following costs:

Stihl chainsaw	SI$ 11,000
Alaska milling frame	SI$ 6,000
Petrol, oil and spares for 3 years of operation	SI$ 1,000
TOTAL	**SI$ 18,000**

SWIFT themselves estimate that their chainsaws will depreciate by 40 % per year, representing a useful life of only 2.5 years. The Alaska frame may be more durable, but it seems reasonable to regard SI$ 18,000 as the necessary investment over a three-year period of sustainable logging.

It is immediately apparent that under these terms the "small-scale" character of the SWIFT alternative is something of an illusion. If their selective felling guidelines are strictly followed by the producer (and unless they are followed, SWIFT will no longer be available as a market outlet), and if we accept the estimates in Figure 11.6. which show that each hectare will only generate, on average, SI$ 1,350 in gross income, then the dilemma of the sustainable logger becomes apparent. He will need to sustainably manage between 4 and 5 hectares of forest just so he can break even on his direct costs, in other words in order to cover the operating and depreciation costs of his equipment. The analysis takes no account of the added burden of loan interest repayments, which up to now SWIFT has not imposed on the producers to whom equipment has been provided.

Five hectares of available land is actually the minimum level of land-holding which is required by SWIFT for a producer to be allowed in to the scheme. it is clear that this amount of forest is not sufficient for a producer to be financially viable. If each SWIFT producer went beyond the "small-is-beautiful" scenario and managed, say, eight 1 hectare blocks, then his net income could be as much as SI$ 4-5,000 per year on a sustained basis. This should be sufficient to pay for some hired labour, as well as constituting a reward to the producer for his and his family's own (substantial) efforts. Such an income would more than match the logging company's royalty jack-pot.

How does this 8 hectare target for viability accord with reality? In fact only nine producers were fully certified by SWIFT in August 1996, managing on average just 3 hectares each. Another six producers were in the final stages of training, land registration, block marking, and formulation of a forest management plan, in preparation of the final agreement (legally binding on both sides) due to be signed between them and SWIFT. Of these 15 producers, three were from Vella Lavella, three from Choiseul, and nine from New Georgia (seven of them from Roviana, two from Marovo). With only 3 hectares in production they are not financially viable unless they can discount the costs of the initial investment in some way.

This discounting was indeed what was happening. In 1995, in order to "kick-start" the option of sustainable forest management and establish it as a perceived alternative to the looming threat of logging, SWIFT held workshops and meetings to explain their proposals, and then distributed on loan almost 100 chainsaws to those who showed a genuine interest in participation. The initial selection of suitable people and their training were necessarily limited, by comparison with the more elaborate programme now seen as necessary for the select groups of those who are to be certified. As with every new idea brought in by outsiders, the initial "converts" in this initial group of SWIFT beneficiaries ("account-holders") included a fair number of opportunists. Small-scale and supposedly selective felling by these 97 account-holders provided the timber which fulfilled the bulk of the WWF order for Rotterdam, and SWIFT was left with the problem of clawing back from each man the SI$ 6,000 cost of the chainsaws. Their rule is to deduct 50% of the value of timber sold to SWIFT, giving the producers just half of the money they might hope to receive if and when their loans are fully repaid.

Unfortunately, while the machines are estimated to depreciate by 40% per year loan repayments are taking place at only 20% per year. There is obviously no prospect of these producers repaying the cost of their loaned equipment unless they can subsidise sustainable logging from external funds. Even the most fervent environmentalist could not hope for such a bizarre outcome. The best prospect for the 97 account-holders whose eco-forestry efforts provided Rotterdam's civic centre with its much-acclaimed eco-timber interior is that SWIFT will bow to the inevitable sooner rather than later. They must hope that SWIFT will write-off the 97 chainsaw loans (or the proportion of the loans still outstanding) as irrecoverable debts. Their only other chance is to log many more hectares of forest (probably non-selectively) and then persuade SWIFT to buy what they have produced despite its tainted origin.

Quest for the Green Umbrella

SWIFT is therefore torn between on the one hand wishing to help producers (and sustain their own accounts) by buying whatever timber is produced, and on the other hand needing to persuade the Forestry Stewardship Council in London that their Western Solomons operation is primarily (if not entirely) a sustainable one. Without FSC approval SWIFT will be denied use of the coveted "Green Umbrella" logo which is regarded as a necessity for opening up a large and lucrative European market for tropical hardwoods with the full blessing of Greenpeace, FOE and WWF. Although a total of only 36 SWIFT producers were FSC-certified and safely under the Green Umbrella in February 1998 (SWIFT, 1998b), many more were eager and willing to join at producers, but felt that there was simply too much certification to deal with. In the face of this challenge it has been observed by SWIFT that

> ... not all [SWIFT's] producer groups ... are able or willing to produce according to the strict and paper work demanding criteria of the ... FSC. Especially producers who are only milling one or two trees per year find it very difficult to set up the whole administration that is demanded when milling according to the FSC principles. SWIFT wants to offer the large group of producers which would drop out of the SWIFT-FSC scheme ... an alternative which enables them to sell their timber to SWIFT, but which also builds a minimum level of sustainability into the programme. This new system will be used next to the FSC standards and will not result in a lower priority to the FSC. (SWIFT, 1998a)

Whereas this new, pragmatic supplement to FSC-certified production is partly intended to offer an outlet for timber produced from trees felled in connection with the expansion of gardens (and which therefore cannot be sold as "FSC timber"), it will also include "the production of a Forest Management Plan ... as well as the commitment of the producer to sustainable forest management, low impact harvesting techniques and the compliance to the five year allowable cut" (SWIFT, 1998a). Thus even for those who mill only one tree per year there is no overall escape from the moral strictures under the Green Umbrella.

   It is too early to pass judgement on SWIFT as being altogether too ambitious an option at this stage of the evolving relationship between the Marovo people and global capitalism. There is a genuine interest in Marovo in the SWIFT alternative, and the SWIFT organisation has for its part shown a willingness to be pragmatic towards producers who are disinclined to engage in the green bureaucracy of certification. The people know that where logging is concerned, in lots of ways "big is ugly". There is anger at the excessive profits of the logging companies, concern for the environmental damage that they cause, and a fear of the social conflict that often follows from the distribution of logging royalties.

In practice, however, the Western Solomons experience of the small-scale alternative looks disappointing. However desirable it may seem in human terms, putting into practice Schumacher's (1973) vision that "small is beautiful" has never been easy. The desirability of "sustainable development" has been apparent at least since the Brundtland Report (WCED 1987), and the links between sustainability and smallness of scale seem obvious in theory. The SWIFT example shows that in practice, the likelihood of achieving sustainable development in Marovo Lagoon by means of a small-scale "certified-eco-timber" approach is extremely doubtful. The small scale seems to be successful in fulfilling the dreams of environmentalism, but cannot satisfy the aspirations of Solomon Islanders in relation to the harsh realities of forestry economics. SWIFT will probably have to become much bigger in order to survive. It actually began its operations in 1994 promoting medium-scale forest exploitation on a more-or-less sustainable basis, partly as a worthwhile strategic aim in itself, but also as a tactical anti-logging initiative. The intractable demands of WWF, Greenpeace *et alia* forced them to embrace FSC certification, and this has proved to be such a bureaucratic nightmare that it restricts their operation to the (very) small scale.

Certification also ties Solomon Islanders into an agreement so tight, legally binding, and financially threatening, that for these reasons too its appeal is likely to be limited. The current operation is only viable if combined with chainsaw give-away policies that only a heavily-subsidised NGO could afford. The intractable logistics and economics of forestry show that rather than "small is beautiful", the real situation for logging is that "small is stupid". A New Georgian eco-timber producer is forced towards a medium-scale of operation that conflicts not only with the ideals of environmentalists, but also with existing land tenure practices, the rules of **butubutu** organisation, and implicit Melanesian notions of equity.

Somewhat reluctantly, we are forced to conclude that SWIFT is a well-intentioned and admirable effort, but in its present form it is a top-down rather than a bottom-up form of development, unsustainable without Dutch money and expertise, and basically inappropriate in the present-day conditions of the Western Solomons. At the same time SWIFT is pioneering a new approach to forest management which, if and when the primary forests become a scarce resource, will become a much more relevant option for Solomon Islands.

There are in fact rather few examples in the world of parsimonious but sustainable forms of management emerging fully-fledged from a situation of resource abundance. In Marovo the rainforest still seems so limitless, but at the same time it has now become so valuable, that the temptation is almost irresistible to sell it to outsiders who have the ready means to exploit it. The history of other regions teaches us that, almost certainly, much of the Marovo area is now destined to undergo a phase of large-scale deforestation before what is left of the resource can be thought about in a different way. In a future situation of scarcity the commercially valuable trees will have to be conserved and probably replanted, but the remaining stands will also become more easily manageable with an infrastructure that includes a network of logging roads and facilities to service expensive items of machinery. In this way village-level chainsaw logging and local milling will become a more appropriate technology than at present. In addition, perhaps, these forest fragments will become the property of a social groups somewhat smaller and less amorphous that the typical Marovo **butubutu** organisation of today. Large is ugly, small is stupid, and medium is probably beautiful, but in Marovo Lagoon the time for the medium-scale solution has not yet arrived.

12 Rumours of Utopia:
Conservation and Eco-tourism

Marovo values in the age of "trousers and respectability"

One hundred years ago the first wave of missionaries in the Marovo Lagoon brought with them a vision of a new spiritual life for the Melanesian people, based on Christian ideals and practices. A surprising number of these men wrote books about themselves, and from such sources we can piece together the set of beliefs which motivated them. What of the "pagans" whose world view the missionaries had set out to transform? It is much more difficult to reconstruct the spiritual values of Marovo men and women in the first decades of this century, or to know how far, and in what ways, their beliefs were changed by the "great transformations" which we examined in Chapter 6. It seems likely that the changes in their outlook were much less funda-mental than some Western observers have supposed, but at the same time we should not imagine that Marovo **kastom** was or is fixed, timeless and unchangeable. It might be considered to be axiomatic (Hviding, 1996a: 80) that the "traditional system" of sociopolitical relationships in Marovo that we see today is actually an historical amalgamation of precolonial and colonial forms. The present pattern of relationships between and among groups (**butubutu**) and their territories (**puava**) has only therefore existed in something like its present form for seventy or eighty years. We should no doubt regard Marovo people's perceptions of and approaches to the environ-ment of lands and seas as having had a similar flexibility over the same time period.[1]

At the time of this initial transformation in values, European observers were convinced that its effects would encompass all aspects of Melanesian life. The missionaries all urged the necessity for schooling, improved housing, clothing and other forms of social hygiene: Christians should be clean in thought, word and deed. In 1911 the head of the administration, Charles Woodford, put together a *Handbook of the British Solomon Islands* (a kind of *Lonely Planet Guide* for prospective colonists) which provided a summary of these various assumptions. If Westerners continued to be so successful in imposing their cultural hegemony over Solomon Islands, Woodford suggested, then it would surely not be long before Melanesian culture was itself transformed: "the influence of trader and missionary [will] efface all trustworthy traditions and reduce the natives to the uninteresting dead level of trousers and respectability" (BSIP, 1911: 33).

Woodford's rhetoric of transformation did not include the management of gardens, forests and reefs, but the processes that he anticipated were bound to include a shift in what would in today's language be termed "environmental values". In order to buy the required trousers Solomon Islanders would need money, which in turn would involve them in an acceptance of new attitudes to labour and to the resources of their land and sea environments. Copra, trochus shells and timber needed to be commodified, and change was also needed in the social organisation of surplus so that the transactions with the market economy could take place. Money needed to be inserted into the value systems of Melanesian society, and the use of money had to be legitimised not only by trade but also by the consistent encouragement by the churches of material progress and "betterment of life".

In Marovo the Seventh-day Adventist Church in particular has encouraged a more individualist orientation towards both money-making and salvation (Hviding, 1996a:69). Their emphasis on the cash economy remains strongly linked to heavy tithe obligations, and not least to the financial requirements of a sectarian policy of running their own village primary schools. The SDA Church has thus been particularly successful in establishing and promoting social structures and strategies that permit men, and to a lesser extent women, to participate in the market economy with some success – and indeed spectacular success in the case of a few Honiara-based entrepreneurs. Six of the nine "recognised" tourist lodges operating in Marovo Lagoon in 1997 were managed by SDA families, and almost all the small guest houses not officially recognised were also SDA enterprises.

On the other hand it may well be that an active involvement in business is regarded by the participants as entirely compatible with attitudes that emphasise stewardship and sustainability. Christian values can imply not merely caring for God and for other people but also caring for the environment upon which we all depend. There is no doubt that in some cases a strong environmental ethic has taken root among Solomon Islands Christians. The environmental NGOs in Honiara provide a regular outlet for this new set of beliefs, as expressed for example in the artwork of Marcellin Maetarau (Figure 12.1) and the other contributors to *Link* magazine. What we see here is a new blend of Christian and environmental ethics.

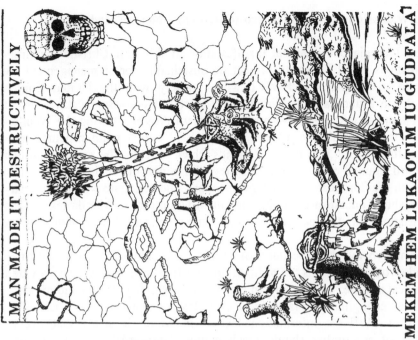

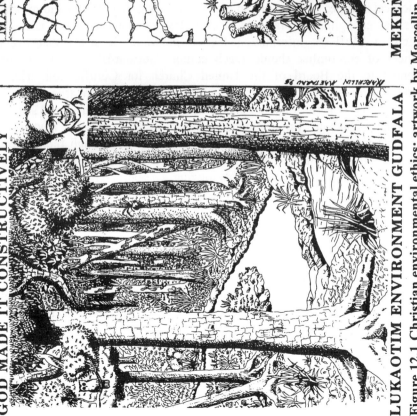

Figure 12.1 Christian environmental ethics: artwork by Marcellin Maetarau

The new mission: eco-timber, eco-tourism and local precedents

In New Georgia one practical manifestation of this new Christian environmentalism is SWIFT, whose project on sustainable forest management we reviewed in Chapter 11. SWIFT works closely with the United Church hierarchy in Munda and its Director is a Marovo man – Sam Patavaqara, of former fame as administrative head of Western Province during the Premiership of Job Dudley Tausinga (see Chapter 9-10) – but the main impetus comes from a Dutch NGO. It is the Netherlands which provides the funding through the World Council of Churches. It is they who import the chainsaws, maintain links with the European market for eco-timber, and negotiate with the Forestry Stewardship Council in London. The Dutch volunteers in Munda take a lead in translating Christian environmentalism into practical rules for managing the forests.

In many ways the procedures of SWIFT parallel those of early missionary endeavour: strong links to militant organisations overseas, which provide ideological muscle; and locally an emphasis on winning "hearts and minds" as well as changing the practices of everyday life. This approach is made explicit in SWIFT's information leaflet, in which it states that every producer of eco-timber should reach certain "standards" in order to be presented to the Board of the United Church for Certification. These standards include a requirement that each person "should show true commitment to the SWIFT Sustainable Forest Management Philosophy", and should be willing to make an "Environmental Pledge". In this way SWIFT hopes to spread the word about sustainable forest management through their select band of certified producers, who in turn will convert others towards a new and more enlightened attitude towards logging.

At the same time as this revival of Christian missionary activity in a new form (eco-timber rather than trousers), the Western Solomons has also fallen under the influence of a different and more secular form of environmentalism. The new wave is led by outsiders who perceive the value of conservation to lie in preserving nature, landscape and biodiversity. The two movements, the Christian and the secular, are not easy to separate, since both the expatriate "eco-missionaries" and the Solomon Islander "converts" find their motivation in an intermingling of the spiritual and the scientific/ materialistic values of nature.

The complete absence of nature reserves and national parks in Solomon Islands, yet the presence there of spectacular coral reefs, volcanoes, rain forests and atolls, and a fauna rich in endemic species especially birds, began to attract a particular set of outsiders in the 1980s. Environmental activists from Australia and New Zealand began to target Solomon Islands and in particular Marovo Lagoon, as an environmental cause of more than local significance. Still, a baseline review of conservation needs in Oceania published by The International Union for Conservation of Nature and Natural Resources (IUCN) in 1986 offered little promise that the Marovo Lagoon area should become such a hot-spot for conservation interests a few years later.[2]

It is important to note that much of the original impetus for suggested UNESCO World Heritage Listing of Marovo Lagoon (examined in a later section of this chapter) came from anti-logging-oriented chiefs and politicians around this time (mid-1980s) and not initially from foreign consultants. The "ouster" of Levers Pacific Timbers in 1986 (see Chapter 9), and the associated impression among foreign NGOs that here was an indigenous population eager to repel capitalist resource grabbers and enlist in the noble cause of conservation (to the degree of offering their lands and lagoon to UNESCO), placed Marovo on the map of the global environmental movement. This impression was further strengthened by the Marovo Lagoon Resource Management Project, a joint effort from 1985 by the Marovo Area Council and Western Province. At that time, with logging and mining looming on the horizon and with conflict over the tuna industry's increasing use of the Marovo Lagoon as a source for live for baitfish, grave concerns over the future well-being of the Marovo environment were expressed by villagers, urban Marovo elite and politicians on local, provincial and national levels alike. A uniquely strong political-administrative set-up provided for some pioneering attempts at integrating "useful" research by invited foreigners with the needs for a rapid building-up of knowledge about the marine and terrestrial environments of Marovo and the human practices that depend on and transform these environments (see Baines and Hviding, 1992, 1993, for details on the structure, history and practical approaches of the project).

In the mid-1980s the influential Marovo men Job Dudley Tausinga (CFC) and Sam Patavaqara (United Church) were the political and administrative leaders of Western Province. The Marovo Member of Parliament Christopher Columbus Abe (United Church), then in his first elected period, was a vocal spokesman for pragmatic development appropriate to local needs. From his position as Provincial Assembly Member for north-central Marovo, Vincent Vaguni (CFC), a former teacher then of recent "anti-Levers" fame, infused his brilliant rhetorical powers and dedication to environmental matters into any conceivable context in villages, at Area Council Meetings, and at provincial level. Furthermore, Seri Hite (United Church), the administrative officer in charge of the Marovo sub-division and himself a man of central Marovo, commanded Area Council headquarters at Seghe with great attention to what was not yet beginning to be called "sustainable development". All of these men have since pursued remarkable careers in national politics or in the conservationist-oriented NGO sector that has flourished through the 1990s. But in 1985 their insistence on the need to take charge in development matters produced an outcome that was neither national nor non-governmental. Through the international brokerage and village-level meeting activity of Graham Baines, the aforementioned planning officer of Western Province, the Marovo Lagoon Resource Management Project saw light as a practical implementation of Western Province's new *Strategy for Development* (Western Province, 1985), with funding from the Commonwealth Science Council as part of a coastal zone management programme for the Pacific Islands (CSC, 1986). In 1985, 1986 and 1987 CSC-funded "community workshops" were held at Seghe with delegates from nearly every village of the Marovo area. This pan-Marovo institutionalisation of local concerns about appropriate development and autonomous control over resources has waxed and waned and reappeared in various permutations right up to the present, when a "Marovo Butubutu Development Foundation", fronted in the media by Seri Hite, opposes the oil palm development plans for Vangunu's Lot 16 (Chapter 10)

During the active phase of the Marovo Lagoon Resource Management project (1985-1988) about fifteen researchers (among them the two present authors) were invited to carry out longer or shorter periods of fieldwork in Marovo. They were asked to address questions that ranged from broad ethnographic and human-ecological perspectives on the long-term uses of the Marovo Lagoon (e.g., Hviding, 1988, 1996a), via intensive surveys of village economy and environmental attitudes (Bayliss-Smith, 1987, 1993; Juvik 1993), to specific studies of important fields of "traditional ecological knowledge" (e.g., Johannes, 1988; Johannes and Hviding, 1987). Over these years the Area Council office, as well as a large number of villages (a few **butubutu** devised task-specific "environmental associations" and some even devised conservation-oriented "village community" statutes), built up considerable expertise in dealing with foreign research workers, which prepared Marovo Lagoon for the next wave of "experts": the conservation consultants. In Honiara, a support group for the Marovo Lagoon Resource Management Project was active with members from the urban Marovo elite of government employees and businessmen from all three church denominations (the engagement of SDA communities in the project had at first been more modest).

When CSC funding ended rather abruptly in 1989, the "Marovo Project" had already diversified beyond coherence and had spawned a range of separate initiatives within "business", cocoa-farming, "development" more generally, and miscellaneous issues of local but not pan-Marovo interest (such as negotiation committees dealing with mining and logging proposals for specific sites). But long-term relationships with certain researchers have continued and resulted in further collaborative work (see Hviding, 1995b, 1995c), and the active years of the project have left a significant stamp on the local preparedness for taking on large questions posed by new foreign arrivals. As the global environmental movement intensified its gaze at the Solomons, the Marovo Lagoon was probably the only place in the country that had the infrastructure needed to whisk environmentalists into action in a new round of community workshops – this time not devised by Marovo people them-selves but mediated through their recent experience from "workshopping" and such activities.

When the South Pacific Conservation Programme of the WWF (World Wide Fund for Nature) arrived on the scene in 1990, its agents were quickly incorporated into this existing infrastructure, to the extent of employing former local coordinators of the "Marovo Project" (including Vincent Vaguni and Seri Hite) in their service. The still-evolving World Heritage issue was meanwhile being navigated around the Honiara bureaucracy and in diplomatic circles by the former support group of the Marovo Project, and it caught the attention of the New Zealand government, which has since built up a Marovo presence that competes for attention with the work of the WWF. In many ways the World Heritage Programme and the WWF are like the rival missions of eighty years ago; in competition over turf and converts while being obliged to follow existing social and political channels of expanding influence in a bewildering place where they know little in the way of language and "local customs". Postcolonial encounters these may well be in the current parlance of cultural studies, but for those involved they are uncertain situations and scenes lacking the "moral certainties" (Thomas, 1997:23) of colonial times and being more reminiscent of the preceding frontier phase of the late 19th century (Hviding, 1998a).

A landmark in the intensifying campaign for the Solomon Islands environment was the report entitled *A Protected Forests System for the Solomon Islands* (Lees et.al., 1991) that was commissioned by the Australian National Parks and Wildlife Service, partly paid for international organi-sations concerned with bird conservation, and written by a group of New Zealand environmentalists called the Maruia Society. As described in Chapter 11, their report recommends the establishment of over twenty forest reserves in order to conserve Solomon Islands biodiversity. There is some justification provided for this extraordinary proposal, in a section of the report which argues for the value of forests to Solomon Islanders, but this consists of little more than a listing of the customary uses of trees (house timbers, thatch, hunting, nuts, medicines and so forth), alongside an expla-nation of the value of forests in soil conservation so that downstream the lagoons and coral reefs can remain unpolluted. The commercial value of forests to those who own them is covered in one sentence (Lees et.al., 1991:28), while the fact that almost all forests are the property of Solomon Islanders is hardly even mentioned. The conservation proposals are well meaning, but are obviously driven by the habitat needs of the endemic bird species. The report may have had some influence in Canberra, but it seems remote from the human and political realities of forest management in Solomon Islands.

While conservation undoubtedly provides the main motivation for groups like the Maruia Society and Worldwide Fund for Nature (WWF), eco-tourism is one of their chosen weapons to withstand the forces of neo-colonial commodification. In Marovo, as Chapters 9 and 10 have shown, logging is undoubtedly a threat to both the forests and, indirectly, the lagoon itself. The people of Marovo Lagoon are being offered what appears to them to be a lot of money, in return for the sale of their trees and the significant modification of their land. Everyone seems to recognise that areas adjacent to villages that are regularly used for agroforestry are not for sale, but there remain large tracts that in some areas are little used except for occasional visits to hunt feral pigs, to gather fruits and nuts, or to fell particular trees for canoes, house timbers or carvings. If the outside world wishes to place a different (and even higher) value on the tropical rain forest than the loggers, how can this value be translated into effective conservation? How can the value of the forest cover be translated into a form which will provide landowners with a realistic alternative to logging? In Marovo Lagoon eco-tourism is at present the alternative being most widely debated, and is the focus for a number of initiatives by outside bodies.

The ultimate goal: World Heritage status

It is important to realise that for most of the outsiders who are promoting eco-tourism in Solomon Islands, it is seen not as an end in itself but rather as an incentive for environmental protection. It is part of a strategy that, in the case of Marovo Lagoon and East Rennell, might ultimately enable these two areas to be included on the World Heritage List of UNESCO. The Solomon Islands Government has signed UNESCO's "Convention Concerning the Protection of the World Cultural and Natural Heritage", and so is pledged to conserve listed sites situated on its territory. At the end of 1996 the World Heritage List comprised 506 sites worldwide, of which 380 were cultural sites, 107 were natural and 19 were so-called mixed sites with both natural and cultural values. East Rennell, part of a remote "Polynesian outlier" island located some 250 kilometres south of Guadalcanal, was put forward for listing in June 1997, and was accepted by UNESCO in 1998. Moves towards full enlistment have since proceeded. The Rennell case was argued on the basis of the area's outstanding natural values (raised atoll, undisturbed forests, inland lake with unique wildlife, endemic bird species, etc.), and the fact that these values were not significantly jeopardised by the activities of the 500 Rennellese people who own the area and use its resources (Wingham, 1997).

The case for Marovo Lagoon is rather more complicated than for the small Polynesian outlier of Rennell. The area is far from being an isolated wilderness, it supports a population of more than 10,000 people, and has long ago lost some of its most "pristine" qualities. To qualify for UNESCO listing it would necessarily be a mixed site, and UNESCO would need to be convinced that its lagoon, reefs and rainforests were being managed in a non-destructive way. It is in the context of a sustainable management plan that eco-tourism in Marovo finds its intended niche. The logic for eco-tourism was summarised as follows by one of the New Zealand consultants who has been advising Solomon Islands Government, in an article that he wrote for the Solomon Airlines in-flight magazine:

> It would be impossible for Marovo or Rennell to receive World Heritage status without recognition of the unique cultures of both sites. The people of the Solomon Islands consider themselves as one with the land, so preservation of their natural resources can only succeed if the culture which has governed their interaction with the environment for thousands of years is also protected .... The task includes introducing local landowners to the value of conservation and sustainable management, at the same time generating a steady income. The income counters the temptation of fast cash in return for exploitation of the land, and it can be derived without damaging the environment through activities such as eco-tourism, butterfly ranching, handicrafts, even bee keeping. (Evans, 1995:42)

This is not the place to comment on the naive view exposed in this article, that Marovo (or anywhere else in Solomons) has, at the very end of the 20th century, some kind of pristine "culture" which is in need of "protection". It is equally foolish to imply that Marovo culture has never generated, or has not preserved, its own knowledge of the value of "conservation and sustainable management". As has already been indicated, the Marovo people have a long and significant experience in dealing with imported ideas about "conservation" and "sustainability". Rather than deconstructing the naivety of statements by external consultants, let us examine the viability of the eco-tourism option. Is there any conflict between the environmental and cultural values that Evans is so enthusiastic about, and which might merit international recognition through World Heritage status, and the business activities that are envisaged as compensating the Marovo people for not receiving "fast cash" such as from logging royalties?

There is one contradiction that Evans himself is uneasy about:

> The prestige [that World Heritage status] ... would bring could, of course, be a mixed blessing. While protecting the area from the depredations of logging and unsustainable development and maintaining the ecology and life styles of the people, it would probably attract tourists and investors like moths to a candle. (Evans, 1995:42)

This negative attitude towards tourism echoes in an eerie way the worries of the Resident Commissioner of the British Solomon Islands Protectorate, Charles Woodford, 90 years ago. Like Evans, Woodford was not keen on attracting conventional tourists, but he recognised that there was much on offer for the visiting botanist, zoologist or student of exotic cultures. Woodford wrote in the official *BSIP Handbook* that for such people "there are many problems of interest awaiting solution" before it was too late (BSIP, 1911:33).

According to this persistent Western stereotype, places like Rennell Island or Marovo Lagoon are mainly interesting because they are exotic, and this exoticism is the result of the prolonged isolation of their flora, fauna and inhabitants. When exposed to the outside world these island ecosystems and cultures are liable to collapse. Nature and culture are conflated into a single, fragile "Other", which needs protection through a special type of intervention – although in fact continuing isolation would be preferable. "Ecotourism" is the current term for one of these new forms of measured and restricted intervention.

Tourism in Solomon Islands

In 1995 a "Tourism Resource Consultant", Rob Greenaway, made a study for the New Zealand Government's World Heritage Programme in Solomon Islands. The report indicated that tourism as an industry was almost undeveloped in the Solomons and, moreover, showed almost no signs of growth. Whereas the official Tourism Development Plan envisaged steady growth in the 1990s, with the number of visitors expanding from 10,000 in 1990 to more than 50,000 in the year 2000, the actual numbers arriving had not risen above 12,000 visitors per year, and of these by no means all were genuine tourists. One reason Greenaway identified for the stagnant situation was the lack of accommodation and the few activities available for tourists. He suggests that these things need to be expanded first, "although the risk of focussing on product development before considering market growth and needs is evident". When translated from the arcane language of consultant-ese, "product development" means places for visitors to stay. Greenaway gives as an example the large number of eco-tourist lodges being developed in Marovo Lagoon, well in advance of any obvious demand for accommodation of this type (Greenaway, 1995:9).

In addition it has become obvious that Solomon Islands remains an undeveloped "product" because it remains a little-known destination, so far off the beaten track that it was only added to the *Lonely Planet Guide* series in 1988. In *Solomon Islands: a Travel Survival Kit* the country is described as "the third largest archipelago in the South Pacific", yet at the same time a place where "you'll often have to make your own arrangements, but if you don't mind that you can get to a long list of ultra-remote places". The Travel Survival Kit continues:

> You really will have beaches all to yourself, need guides and maybe even bearers to climb rainforest-covered volcanoes. You'll take long canoe journeys from village to village, explore natural coastlines by foot and stay in small villages with traditional leaf huts. (Harcombe, 1988:7)

Despite the international sales of Lonely Planet Guides and the seemingly irresistible appeal of this image of the islands as an unspoilt frontier of adventure tourism, the numbers visiting Solomon Islands remain small. Probably, given the circumstances of a little-developed "tourism product" and the risk of catching malaria even in the capital, Solomon Islands will remain a "niche" destination for adventurous travellers – some of whom spend a lot on diving tourism (paid, however, in foreign currency outside of the Solomon Islands economy), but most of whom belong to the low-spending categories of "backpackers" and "anti-tourists". For the latter, the Solomons is but one of increasingly few "unspoilt" destinations, possibly soon to be "spoilt" – the Lonely Planet Guide appears to be popular since it is already in its third update edition (Honan and Harcombe, 1997), and the Lonely Planet site on the World Wide Web (www.lonelyplanet.com) has begun receiving postings concerning "greed" and "ripoff" experienced by poor backpackers venturing out into the rural Solomons.

In any event, the question remains: can Marovo Lagoon attract a larger slice of the 12,000 or so foreigners who currently visit the country each year, and perhaps bring in a new wave of international eco-tourists? There are currently three types of tourist "product" in the Marovo Lagoon: private enterprise, WWF-sponsored eco-tourism, and World Heritage Programme-sponsored eco-tourism. We will review these developments before making an overall assessment of whether eco-tourism can provide a new way for the Marovo people to gain value from their land and sea.

Private enterprise tourism: the foreigners

If we discount the interaction which took place with Japanese and American soldiers during the war, we can date the first engagement of the Marovo people with tourism to the 1960s. It was then that some of the wood carvers discovered a sales outlet in Honiara for their polished and pearlshell-decorated bowls, **toto isu** war canoe figureheads (more widely known under their Roviana name **nguzunguzu**), sharks and crocodiles. The SDA church assisted with technical training (at its vocational school at Batuna and at its secondary school at Betikama outside Honiara) and with marketing, and for some households the sale of handicrafts became the main source of income. However, few tourists ever visited the places that produced these much-admired wooden carvings. Indeed if they had visited Marovo there would have been practically nowhere for them to stay. Most "tourists" visiting Marovo until the 1990s have in fact been passing through on board yachts that have the lagoon as one well-known port-of-call in the long route around the world.[3] Up until ten years ago tourist accommodation in Marovo Lagoon was dominated by just one place: Uepi Island Resort, an Australian-run scuba-diving centre located on the alienated barrier island of Uipi in the central lagoon. The pioneering first edition of the Lonely Planet Guide reported that "the resort is exclusive and so are the prices", but was enthusiastic about the diving, snorkelling and "the magnificent meals". Other activities on offer included fishing, windsurfing, bushwalking and canoe trips (Harcombe, 1988:133). An agency in Queensland, Australia, handled the bookings, and this link enabled the resort staff to meet incoming flights at Seghe and to transport the divers direct from Seghe to Uepi.

Today Uepi continues to thrive, and if anything it has gone even further up-market. Guests are housed in eight bungalows. There is an electricity supply and a fully-equipped dive shop. Apart from the purchases of fresh fruit, handicrafts and carvings, interaction between Uepi and the rest of Marovo is limited. Chubikopi on Marovo Island is one place that has established strong links with Uepi (many resort employees are from this village), and the villages on and near Marovo Island are usually chosen by the resort as places to visit when the tourists grow tired of diving and want to look at a local village and perhaps buy handicrafts. Greenaway (1995:49) reported that Chubikopi had developed "a half-day cultural experience package", which included custom dancing, a paddle in a war canoe, and handicraft sales. The clients are mostly from Uepi, or from the Honiara-based Bilikiki Cruises company whose exclusive live-aboard" dive ships have the Marovo Lagoon on their itineraries, and the "cultural experience" at Chubikopi is not intended by the organisers to extend beyond the "package" itself. One reason, according to Greenaway (1995:49), is that "no accommodation or toilets are available at the village".

Back in the mid-1980s another small and very exclusive enterprise was established by an expatriate on Tenggomo Island in the lagoon near Gatokae, in a attempt to exploit a lesser-known niche offered by the seas of Marovo. Even ten years ago Jake's Sport & Game Fishing could charge SI$ 650 for a full day's offshore fishing trip for marlin, tuna or sailfish, but in 1996 the operation was closed following the suicide of the owner. Today the Bililiki Cruises company continues to exploit Marovo Lagoon as an up-market destination for serious divers intent on the ultimate reef experience, but the tourists view the villages mainly through the glass windows of the boat as they sit back in air-conditioned comfort, experiencing the Marovo landscape as if it were a non-interactive video. Interaction with the Marovo people is limited to the boat's stopping places, where the passengers of the *Bililiki* have some contact with villagers as they buy handicrafts or view a pro-gramme of entertainment's at selected villages. A similar pattern applies to a few other up-market "cruising" operations whose ships visit the Marovo Lagoon less regularly.

Local private enterprise

Until recently tourism in Marovo was dominated by these foreign-owned enterprises, and independent tourists disembarking from a flight to Seghe or an inter-island ship to Patutiva met with an absolute lack of accommodation. The 1980s, however, also saw the beginning of locally-organised projects aimed at the cheaper end of the tourist market. These took the form of small "tourist lodges", and by 1988 several had been established (although not at Seghe, the airstrip where most visitors to Marovo Lagoon arrive). Those visitors who were going on to Uepi were whisked away from Seghe by motorised canoe, but for the others there was nowhere to stay. Yet the *Lonely Planet Guide* was reassuring: "The local Area Officer may be able to help you find somewhere if you give him due warning. Otherwise just ask to camp by the airfield" (Harcombe, 1988:132). Not until 1995 was the Seghe Lodge established by a local family (six beds, self-catering, SI$ 20 per night in 1997).

The 1988 *Lonely Planet Guide* did note, however, that not far away from Seghe there were the beginnings of some small-scale alternatives to Uepi. Around Vangunu, for example, there were small resorts on Matikuri and Telina Islands, houses for visitors at Batuna and Chemoho, "rest houses" at Kopinae Island, Cheke and Kichombelo Point, and empty houses available here and there on the lagoon shores of Vangunu Island itself. Some of these places were described as "rather basic", for example the tiny island of Kopinae where a leaf hut for two people complete with showers, toilet and cooking equipment cost SI$ 35 per night with no charge for any children (Harcombe, 1988:175).

The largest of these projects was Matikuri Island, with four leaf houses and a communal dining hall, operated by the same extended family that runs the Seghe Lodge: "Ask around at Seghe airport and local people will direct you, though you should send a message in advance" (Harcombe, 1988:176). The business is today the largest and most flourishing of the locally-owned tourist lodges. The owner-operator family set it up with some friendly assistance from a medical doctor from Brisbane. Greenaway (1995) analysed the Visitor Book kept at Matikuri for the period 1986-94, and in Figure 12.2 this record is updated to September 1996. It shows rapid growth in visitor numbers from 1988 to 1992, then a more stable period as Matikuri stopped expanding and had to compete with the various other tourist lodges that opened, followed by more recent growth. Dominating the list of visitors are local expatriates on holiday from Honiara or Gizo, visiting Australians (especially from Brisbane), and visiting New Zealanders, but the resort can also claim a truly international clientele. There are currently eighteen beds, and it was estimated in 1995 that Matikuri earned in that year SI$ 45-50,000 for the family that runs it (World Heritage Programme consultants, pers. comm.).

The Matikuri Visitors Book provides many clues as to why the place is appreciated by the type of tourist who have "discovered" it:

Incredible place – hope it won't be spoiled in the future. Second time here – I will come back (woman, Florence, Italy)

Caught kingfish, coral trout, barracuda, and fat trevally. God, this is heaven. (man, Sydney, Australia)

An idyllic blissful tranquillity – good for the soul. May the beast of greed and materialism never rear its ugly head in your lagoon. Thanks for sharing your world! (woman, New York, USA)

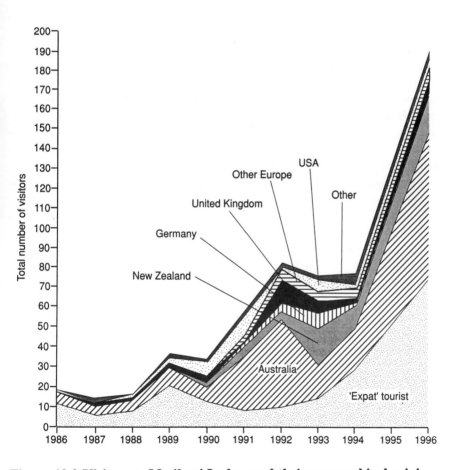

Figure 12.2 Visitors to Matikuri Lodge, and their geographical origin (1986-1996)

Source: Annual totals compiled from entries in the visitors book, as analysed by Greenawy (1995:45) for the period 1986-1994 and Bayliss-Smith (fieldwork) for the period August 1995-July 1996.

Leana uka, Benjamin and Peter, for sharing Marovo with us – beautiful underwater sea creatures including sharks, wonderful food. Exotic custom dancing, even dolphins! Cherished memories for snow and storm in Canada's winter time ... (woman, Saskatchewan, Canada)

Appropriate tourism can be forever, logging is a smash and grab exercise ... (man, Townsville, Queensland)

En oplevelse for livet!! Og vi er udhvilet. (couple, Aarhus, Denmark)

Occasionally we can find more critical comments ("incredible amounts of rain", "it would be great to have a dugout and a compost"). But negative remarks are greatly outnumbered by litanies of praise. Many visitors do not hesitate to use terms such as "paradise" and "soul" which one suspects do not exist in their everyday conversation, and many show that they regard Marovo society (or what little they see of during their stay on otherwise uninhabited Matikuri Island) as a paragon of peace, serenity, contentment, harmony with nature and an uncomplicated lifestyle – notions which seem to derive almost directly from Jean-Jacques Rousseau's construction of the Noble Savage two hundred years ago.

The success of Matikuri as a business has stimulated other Marovo entrepreneurs to establish their own tourist lodges. Greenaway (1995) listed eight already in operation and another two under construction. In addition he reported that informal accommodation was available in several other villages, and even in some quite remote places there were plans underway for new tourist projects. In southern Gatokae, for example, Biche village was considering the construction of a lodge not far from the village even though it had received fewer than one party of visitors per year over the past decade (Greenaway, 1995:46-48).

Two years later all those places mentioned by Greenaway were still in business, and three others had opened. There were nine lodges officially recognised by the Visitors Bureau in Honiara, and it was possible to make advance bookings through the network of radio telephones that had been provided by the World Heritage Programme (WHP) of the New Zealand Government. It has been this programme and the parallel but separate activities of the Worldwide Fund for Nature (WWF) that has stimulated an explosive growth in tourist accommodation. These interventions can all be seen as a knock-on effect of Annette Lees' (1991) report, which set the tone for all the subsequent eco-missionaries, in recommending small-scale tourism as the solution to the perceived problem of Marovo Lagoon. But what is the Marovo "problem"? The desperate need of the Marovo people to safeguard their future, by finding a viable and dependable replacement for copra, the main income source from around 1904 to 1984, is never mentioned. The perceived evil is deforestation, loss of biodiversity, and the erosion of Marovo Lagoon's unique, semi-wilderness status.

Can tourism keep the loggers at bay? In 1997 the situation in Marovo seemed at first glance to be highly promising. Those visitors wishing to experience the attractions of the area now have on offer a wide range of accommodation, some luxurious and some simple, some bookable through the Internet and some totally informal. Not only can Marovo Lagoon claim to be able to accommodate all types of tourist, it can also offer a wide range of attractions to visitors, including handicrafts, fishing, bush walks, sea kayaking, diving at Uepi, snorkelling, cultural shows and village visits, river trips, World War II debris, flora and fauna, or just "tropical relaxation". Moreover, local enterprise is emerging in a variety of forms:

> The skills to deliver good interpretive talks and guiding services exist in many locations, including Mbiche with its stone carving, John Wayne's with wood carvings near the village of Telina, Rukutu where bukaware is made, and at the Lagoon Lodge where a range of activities including guided walks and fishing trips are available. (Greenaway, 1995:49)

Only the small number of visitors threatens the viability of this new source of livelihood. Some reasons for this are hinted in an account by Chris Ladner, a Canadian kayaker, which he published on the Internet in the *Wave-Length Paddling Magazine* (December-January 1996, Vancouver, BC). Some brief excerpts from a rich catalogue of imagined threats and real disasters serve as a useful antidote to the relentless praise of the Matikuri Visitors Book:

FAR FROM PARADISE: SONG OF THE SOLOMON ISLANDS...

We were lured to Marovo Lagoon for what we envisioned as a tropical paradise with white sand beaches and relaxing sun. What was in store was far more of an adventure... Each day was intensely hot for us. The rain would come down so hard you could shower in it and even finish the cream rinse! ... Being in the chief's house made us feel like we were imposing. Faces would appear through the bushes checking us out constantly. We never seemed to escape the local natives' curiosity. Although the open windows were a welcome respite from the heat and humidity, the threat of malaria hummed close to our ears each night.... Strange bugs and animals were everywhere. Walks through the jungle revealed a long history of headhunting and strict tribal rituals. There were certain areas where women were not allowed to go. This included the particular areas for meeting nature's call. Everyone did it in the ocean so discreetly we never saw them...

Wherever we camped we had visitors who seemed to uncannily know we were coming. They wanted to know if we were coming to claim the land, I suppose. We kept dreaming of that secluded spot we could lounge about undisturbed...

Stories of crocodiles eating villagers the previous week kept going through my mind... As we meandered through the coral heads the waves had their way with us and deposited us on top of a particularly sharp coral head. We thought nothing of it until I asked Chris if she felt water in the boat. Sure enough we had a hole, and nowhere to land. I have never felt so close to being in a desperate situation...

With information like this on the Internet (where, in September 1999, a simple AltaVista search for web pages on which "Marovo" is mentioned gave no less than 232 hits, mostly to tourism- and diving-related pages), and with cheaper and more relaxing tropical island destinations available, it is perhaps not surprising that tourists fail to arrive in the Solomons in the numbers anticipated. We now examine in more detail some of the eco-tourist lodges, and demonstrate that a range of problems are emerging.

Michi: an eco-tourism flagship

The tourist lodge known as Vanua Rapita (a local pun meaning 'a house which I searched for [and found]') at Michi in central Marovo is regarded by environmentalists as such an international success story that details of it are widely available on the World Wide Web. Yet locally it is regarded by many as a bizarre and lavish experiment, and as a business enterprise that may collapse in the near future. The reasons for this mismatch between alternative versions of reality tell us much about the politics and ideology of rainforest conservation.

It would be easy to view the Michi project as something imposed on the community by outsiders, in this case by the Wordwide Fund for Nature (WWF), producing in Michi the victims of an eco-tourism experiment. Have the people of Michi been sold an idea which serves the needs of environmentalists for a flagship project in Marovo Lagoon, but which does nothing to meet their own needs? Such a view would be simplistic. It is by no means clear in this case, as in so many cases of dealings between Marovo and the outside world, exactly who has been manipulated by whom. Nor is it clear that "manipulation" is the right word for a project which has been mutually beneficial both for WWF and for certain Michi villagers.

Michi (see also Chapter 8) is a United Church village whose resident **butubutu**, despite being of a coastal historical origin, holds considerable tracts of land on the north side of Vangunu island. Magnificent mature rainforests extend inland from the shoreline, so far unlogged and not needed for gardens in the foreseeable future. The area is adjacent to the northwestern perimeter of Lot 16, the logging concession on Vangunu granted to the Silvania company and possibly the site of a future oil palm plantation (see Chapters 9-10). Michi's agroforestry takes place much closer to the village, and examples of the gardens are shown in Figures 4.3 and 8.6. The community's subsistence resources are rich, but since the collapse in copra prices the Michi people have had few sources of income other than intermittent marketing of fish, shellfish and vegetables at Patutiva and Seghe. In 1986 Seri Hite, an influential chiefly son of Michi, was working in Seghe as a government officer and was closely involved in the research carried out by ourselves and others under the Marovo Lagoon Resource Management Programme. During the 1990s he has worked mainly in Gizo as an employee of WWF, and has used his influence to steer WWF towards an eco-tourism pilot project in Michi.

Vanua Rapita is built on the tiny island of Michi about 100 metres offshore of the village. This was in fact the old village site from about 1900 until an earthquake in 1939 when it was abandoned. It has an area of less than one hectare, and now has three accommodation buildings (14 beds altogether), a communal dining room the roof of which serves as a water catchment, a kitchen, showers and toilet. There is a canoe anchorage with the two fibreglass canoes of the lodge, each with an outboard engine. The kitchen has a gas fridge and kerosene cookers, but open fires are often used instead for cooking. WWF originally proposed a composting toilet but the villagers preferred a septic tank system, which is what has now been installed. The buildings are beautifully constructed out of local materials including sago-leaf thatched roofs, planked floors covered in mats, windows all around on the sea side, and beds. Other materials have had to be purchased. Each bed has a mattress, sheets, pillows and mosquito nets brought in from Honiara, and there is also some imported furniture – coffee tables, bedside tables and easy chairs. Each house is provided with a vacuum flask containing hot water, and coffee, tea, Milo, milk and sugar are freely available. However, self-catering is not encouraged. All meals are provided, for an all-inclusive charge of SI$ 85 per night, plus SI$ 20 transfer fee to and from Seghe. Snorkelling equipment is available for hire, and fishing trips, bush walks, visits to Uepi Island Resort, or evenings of "custom dancing" in Michi village can all be arranged at extra cost (about SI$ 60 per person per day is the figure quoted).

The Vanua Rapita resort was constructed using largely unpaid village labour, including relatives of the Michi people from nearby villages who also contributed sago leaves and other building materials. Compared to other tourist lodges which tend to be family businesses and often are tied to the process of "hamletisation" examined in Chapter 8, the Michi project seems at first sight to be more "traditional" in its organisation, with communal labour under the leadership of the chief. This form of organisation, which in fact is fairly typical of community projects of all kinds in United Church and SDA villages, is now being modified. After the first six months of operation profits of SI$ 16,000 were paid by the Vanua Rapita project to the village, but money for reinvestment in the project was not retained. There is now a new management plan with monthly accounts. The Plan envisages that payments to individuals or groups be related to workload and the project's profit margin. For example, the women's group that is sub-contracted to do the catering work was originally paid wages at the flat rate of SI$ 100 per week, irrespective of the number of paying guests requiring meals. This payment has now been changed to 4% of the monthly profits, for the women to distribute among themselves as they see fit. An overall manager (a man from Tikopia) is employed, and he now receives 20% of monthly profits as his salary. There are smaller payments made on the same basis for the deputy manager, the two boatmen and for activity groups (for example the young people who put on custom dancing). It is intended that money will be set aside to replace indispensable capital assets such an outboard engines.

There are various rumours about the scale of the initial funding that the Michi project received from WWF, but a figure of A$ 140,000 (about SI$ 250,000) is reliably quoted by New Zealand consultants, and seems plausible. The community stated their preference initially for large groups of guests, ten or twelve people for a whole week, with one group arriving about every two months. This sounds like any hotel manager's dream: full occupancy for brief periods followed by a total layoff of staff. After the first experimental year of operation (1995-96) the management at Michi realised that it is unrealistic to expect only the intermittent group bookings. A constant but erratic level of activity is what can be expected. In order for the resort to break even, the aim is to have an average of at least four guests in residence; with six guests the project would be profitable. All the indications are that neither target has yet been reached.

Since the lodge opened a Visitors Book has been maintained, but there are gaps in the record. For a period totalling 333 days when names were recorded between June 1995 and August 1996, exactly 100 persons are listed (mostly adults – children's names may have been omitted). Sixty were men and forty were women, and they came from all over the world but especially from Australia (Figure 12.3). As for the Matikuri Visitors Book, the comments of the guests written in Vanua Rapita's book are almost embarrassingly enthusiastic, as the following almost random selection demonstrates:

> We would like to thank Michi and Chea villages and Talina for the most friendliest and contented people on Earth. I admire you for your great character. Stan [the manager] is a great host. Harold [deputy manager] made our stay much

more fun. We had a wonderful relaxing time at Rapita. We would never forget it (couple, Queensland, Australia)

Exquisite service, great food, dolphins and peaceful (man, Italy)

The most wonderful place in the world. I look forward to returning. I hope the people, trees, reefs, islands and waters remain the same. "Leana via" (man, Queensland, Australia)

An education of the uncomplicated life style. Best accommodation in the Solomons! (couple, USA)

Vanua Rapita is the placidness of a Kashmiri lake combined with the strength and constantness of the South Pacific. It is a chance to really experience, all too briefly, a people and a culture where life is lived – rather than merely being grasped at (man, New South Wales, Australia)

Truly without parallel. Marovo Lagoon is pristine and untouched at the moment, and truly deserves its title 'The Eighth Wonder of the World'. And Rapita is the only true way to really experience the village lifestyle and lagoon together. The people are marvellous and come from their heart; the activities are great; and the food is wonderfully traditional and copious in quantity... It's a much more 'real' experience than staying at Uepi (European man, Honiara)

Keep this a secret – let's keep Paradise (couple, USA)

In the circumstances, perhaps, negative remarks are not to be expected. The staff at Vanua Rapita, in the normal Marovo way, deal with their guests by trying to establish with them a personal (rather than a formal) relationship of good company. The guests respond with gratitude, and probably find it difficult to write comments that might hurt anyone's feelings. The closest the remarks in the Visitors Book come to criticism are the suggestion that "the girls need to be involved more in the activities" (Queensland woman), and the enigmatic comment that "not even 24 hours of continuous rain could dampen the Rapita spirit!" (New South Wales man). But in general a cynical deconstruction of the Visitors Book seems churlish and unnecessary: from the point of view of the visitors it is clear that Vanua Rapita has worked well, providing experiences that the tourists find acceptable and even pleasurable.

Paying for eco-tourism: the Plan

From the point of view of the WWF, however, Vanua Rapita is not to be judged according to the level of happiness of those involved. Ultimately it must be financially viable, but in any case it is just one component of an overall Resource Management Plan for the **butubutu** Tobakokorapa of Michi. Discussions have taken place and maps have been prepared showing what uses will be allowed the **puava** in future, divided into four categories:

1. "Normal uses to continue": areas of lagoon, mangrove and forest where customary activities will continue unchanged, for example agroforestry, cutting of timber, fishing and shellfish gathering.

2. "Butubutu Nature Reserves": for long-term protection from any exploitation, with ownership shared by the community as a whole. The five areas selected as reserves are a barrier island, a reef in the lagoon, an inshore area adjacent to Vanua Rapita where tourists like to snorkel, and two areas of rainforest on Vangunu.

3. "Conservation Sites" that have resource or custom value, to remain under **butubutu** ownership but to be protected by special rules. These include an island of nesting birds (**kurukuru**, fruit doves), an area where no collecting of **riki** shellfish is allowed, an area of mangrove where no collection of timber, shellfish, **puhaka** (bêche-de-mer, "sea slug") or finfish is allowed, and several major rivers which are to be protected from pollution and damage.

4. "Repair Areas": temporarily closed from exploitation so that resource numbers can increase. The two areas specified are small islands where **tupe** (coconut crab) have been overexploited.

In 1996, one year after this Plan was adopted by Michi, it was unclear whether or not it could work. Some pressures from outside were already apparent. The Jalire river catchment, a designated "Butubutu Nature Reserve", had been somewhat degraded by the activities of the Silvania logging company, whose concession extends to the watershed of the Jalire and even includes some of its headwaters (although the Lands Department boundaries are disputed by the Michi people, who seem unaware of the full extent of the area alienated as Forest Estate [see Chapter 9] and being logged by Silvania). As a result, the Jalire river is polluted with red topsoil eroding from the headwaters, where the ground has been severely impacted by wide logging roads and deep skid trails. In 1996 the Michi community attempted to start a court case against Silvania for compensation, but did so without any support from WWF which refused to get involved. Pressures from within the community for the Resource Management Plan to be disregarded were not yet strong. Continuing WWF interest in Vanua Rapita meant that the Michi community still believed strongly in the eco-tourism alternative to logging, even though the benefits were not yet on the scale that some people had anticipated. It was said that only three families in Michi were lukewarm in their support for the WWF project.

However, even if the rhetoric of sustainable development is still strong in Michi, it has to be acknowledged that the logging option is not going to disappear. A section of the community began secret negotiations with the Eagon company in mid-1996, not over logging but merely to hire a bulldozer from Viru Harbour in order to build a new road from the shoreline up to the top of a ridge about 1 km away from Michi. Eagon were happy to oblige, no doubt sensing future possibilities. The idea was to level the ridge for a new village site, away from the existing site which is built on muddy reclaimed mangrove swamp. This all took place without the knowledge of the recognised community leader Seri Hite, who lived and worked (for WWF) in Gizo – the old men of chiefly status were few and ailing. When he learned of the deal with Eagon, a furious row broke out. Re-locating Michi would remove the workforce from its easy access to Vanua Rapita, and this might jeopardise the eco-tourism project. Meanwhile the bulldozer arrived, and many fine *Canarium* trees were knocked down in constructing the new road (Eagon took away the logs), but the community leader vetoed further progress by threatening that he himself would burn Vanua Rapita to the ground if the village re-location proposal continued.

It is not an intended part of the eco-tourism agenda to create social divisions within the communities that are selected for projects, but such an outcome seems inevitable unless everyone can be persuaded that conservation is worthwhile. By committing themselves to a strict policy of forest protection, the leadership in Michi have been antagonising those who have seen few if any benefits, and who therefore wish to reach a compromise agreement with the timber industry. As WWF themselves suggest on their World Wide Web site ("Community Eco-Tourism Takes Off"), through working on the project "the people in Michi now have greater confidence in dealing with outsiders". Sooner or later those "outsiders" will start to include the logging industry, whether small-scale/local or large-scale/multinational. Unless there are tangible and widely distributed benefits from conserving the forests, it is difficult to see how (or why) such opportunities to sell timber will be resisted.

World Heritage Programme: projects galore

There was an early phase when many WWF workshops were held in villages distributed throughout the Marovo area, but later relations with a number of initially interested **butubutu** soured – especially after one promising group of south Vangunu demanded chainsaws for sawing their own timber. Ultimately

Vanua Rapita became the only project of the Worldwide Fund for Nature in Marovo Lagoon, although in fact, apart from its lavish WWF subsidy, Vanua Rapita is indistinguishable from a number of other tourist lodges that are being established with the help of the World Heritage Programme (WHP) of the New Zealand government. WHP operates quite independently from WWF, but has also decided to focus mainly on eco-tourism (there are also bee-keeping and paper-making projects). Incidentally both WWF and WHP refuse to have any dealings with SWIFT, apparently regarding the chainsaw in any form as the work of the devil. This refusal of the NGOs to cooperate or co-ordinate their activities, and the competition that exists for hearts and minds, continues to be very reminiscent of the rivalry which permeated the activities of the various missionary churches in Solomon Islands in days gone by. It also inhibits the emergence of a convincing alternative to logging and oil palm development.

To discuss fully the operations of World Heritage in Solomons is beyond the scope of this chapter, and would be an extremely intricate story which began around 1987 and involved a sundry cast of UNESCO bureaucrats, expatriate diplomats, Solomon Islands politicians, New Zealand consultants, and Marovo chiefs, entrepreneurs and rogues. Some of this was touched on earlier in this chapter. There are, finally, a number of local communities who have been willingly enlisted in an elaborate programme of projects. For several years New Zealand has been the prime mover, with a programme that has the hidden agenda of doing nothing which might facilitate logging, and doing everything which might promote conservation and sustainable development. Both strands are seen as necessary preconditions for Marovo Lagoon to meet the standards for it to be recognised by UNESCO as worthy of being added to the list as a World Heritage Area.

Since 1994 eco-tourism has been the main hope of the WHP, and this emphasis has the support both of Western Province and local communities. Money that was made available by the Solomon Islands Government in earlier years was all spent on small business projects, mostly connected with chainsaw logging. For reasons which SWIFT in Munda are now rediscovering (see chapter 11), chainsaws are not a very sustainable technology in the circumstances of Marovo Lagoon. The New Zealand Government hopes that small tourist lodges will be more successful, and to this end it established a bilateral aid project through the Ministry of Culture and Tourism.

There was no shortage of Marovo communities wishing to participate. WHP preferred to deal with individuals rather than whole communities, sensing that the Matikuri model was easier for them to handle than the Michi one. In reality, most of the projects that they have funded were either existing lodges that needed upgrading (in particular, by the provision of toilets), or they are new projects approved by villages but in most cases taken over by the sons of chiefs. To gain the support of the political hierarchy in Marovo is always a sound tactic, but if no benefits from eco-tourism trickle down to the rest of the community, the programme will surely fail to win hearts and minds as constituting an adequate alternative to logging. But the main problem that has emerged is not the tactical one of who gains the benefits, but rather the strategic issue: is eco-tourism itself a viable strategy?

In 1997 seven lodges were receiving financial support from WHP. Michi was separately funded by WWF, while Matikuri was already well established as a successful business. But where were the customers? Fieldwork in September of that year showed that the main problem was still lack of visitors. In the three lodges for which data were available, visitors stayed for the longest time – on average, for just under three days – in Vanua Rapita, where the original intention was that each guest would stay for a week. The average stay was 2.5 days in the case of Ropiko Lodge, and only 1.5 days for Lagoon Lodge which tends to be used by tourists who are in transit to somewhere else (Figure 12.3).

Occupancy rates were also low. Vanua Rapita was the busiest, improving over a two-year period from 7% of full capacity in its first full year of operation (1995-96) to 13% in its second year, and in the latest two months of data (August-September 1997) almost 26% of capacity. July 1997 was Rapita's busiest month ever with 38 visitors, and the lodge appears to be approaching its break-even point of 25% occupancy. The other lodges were operating at extremely low levels of occupancy: about 5% for Ropiko and 3% for Lagoon Lodge.

The origins of the visitors to these three lodges show some interesting patterns (Figure 12.4). Rapita Lodge, reflecting its high-profile publicity including the WWF website, had the most cosmopolitan clientele. More than a quarter of visitors to Rapita came from Europe and there were signicant numbers from North America, although, as in Matikuri (see Figure 12.2), Australians were still the largest category. The more obscure and remote lodges (Lagoon and Ropiko) depend on Australia and New Zealand for half of their visitors, and visitors giving their address as Solomon Islands -- mainly Honiara expatriates -- make up most of the rest.

For the eco-tourist lodges of Marovo Lagoon to attract larger numbers depends upon them becoming better known through more effective publicity, to reach the rather specialised worldwide market that exists for this kind of tourism. The Lonely Planet Guide must help enormously, but obviously it reaches mainly an English-language audience, as do the increasing numbers of references to Marovo tourism on the Internet. When we look at the breakdown of visitors from Europe (Figure 12.5), it is clear that the United Kingdom and, surprisingly, Switzerland are the major countries of origin. Germany and Italy are under-represented, and no visitors were recorded from France or Spain.

Figure 12.3 Occupancy rates at three eco-tourist lodges in Marovo Lagoon

Lodge (number of beds)	Period	Capacity (person-nights)	Number of guests	Average length of stay (days)	Occupancy (person-nights)	Rate of occupancy
Vanua Rapita (12)	July 1995 - June 1996	4,280	108	2.93	316	7.2%
	July 1996 – June 1997	4,380	195	2.93	571	13.0%
	mid-August - September 1997	924	81	2.93	237	25.6%
Lagoon Lodge (15)	January - mid-September 1997	3,180	59	1.54	91	2.9%
Ropiko Lodge (14)	mid-September 1996 - mid- September 1997	5,110	116	2.50	253	5.0%

Source: Fieldwork by Tim Bayliss-Smith, 1996 and 1997

Figure 12.4 Geographical origin of the visitors to three Marovo Lagoon eco-tourist lodges, 1995-1997 (% of all visitors)*

Lodge	Dates	Solomon Islands	Australia	New Zealand	North America	Europe	Japan, Pacific Is.	Unstated	Total
Vanua Rapita	June 1995 - September 1997	13	29	15	7	27	3	6	100
Lagoon Lodge	January 1997 - September 1997	25	41	12	0	22	0	0	100
Ropiko Lodge	January 1996 - September 1997	42	25	24	2	6	0	1	100

* Sample size (total number of visitors to each lodge):
Vanua Rapita: 289 (185 women, 204 men)
Lagoon Lodge: 59 (22 women, 37 men)
Ropiko Lodge (65 (44 women, 21 men)

Source: Fieldwork by Tim Bayliss-Smith, 1996 and 1997

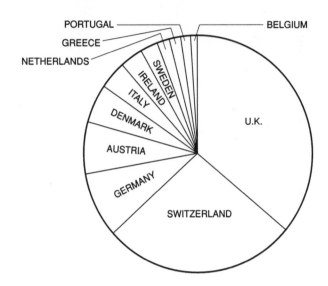

Figure 12.5 Visitors from Europe to three Marovo Lagoon eco-tourist lodges: Vanua Rapita, Lagoon Lodge and Ropiko Lodge, 1995-1997

Tourism: a sustainable future?

In 1960, when Marovo was embarking on its optimistic phase of agricultural development based on copra from smallholdings, there were 60 million tourist "arrivals" worldwide. In 1990, when copra had virtually collapsed and the Marovo people were being courted by Asian logging companies, the global figure had reached 450 million. Only about one-millionth of these tourists reached Marovo Lagoon. By the year 2000 Marovo's market share is hardly likely to have increased, even though tourism is now being described as the world's largest and most fast-growing industry (Survival International, 1994).[4]

Mass tourism has been subjected to much criticism concerning its social, cultural and environmental impacts. In the Third World most of the profits leak away from the areas that are being exploited, while local people are employed only in menial jobs as drivers, cleaners or garbage disposers. At best there is a market for local handicrafts, at worst there emerges a sub-culture of drugs and prostitution. Eco-tourism hopes to change the unequal relationships of conventional tourism, by encouraging the use of local guides and locally-produced housing and food. "Ethical tours" claim to combine environmental education with a more "simple" life style, providing access for the tourist to remote landscapes, cultures, flora and fauna. All this, it is hoped, will provide local people with economic incentives to protect their environment.

According to the dogma of the environmentalists, if eco-tourism in Marovo is to succeed there can be no commercial uses of the forest or lagoon. The two alternatives are seen as utterly incompatible, or at least they must be held separate until World Heritage listing by UNESCO is achieved. It is assumed that when this point is reached the stream of wealthy (presumably not backpacker-dominated) eco-tourists coming to Marovo will spread such obvious benefits that the Marovo people would stop the logging of their forests just as Egyptians prevent the demolition of their pyramids. This argument is based on a fragile web of assumptions, but also depends on a rather fundamentalist position in relation to the concept of "World Heritage". The initial emphasis in UNESCO was to sanctify buildings and monuments (Stonehenge, the Pyramids, Macchu Picchu), and in this context Bernd von Droste, chief of UNESCO's World Heritage Centre, regarded it as crucially important that "each property should meet the test of authenticity" both in an historical and a material sense (von Droste, 1995:22). No copies or reconstructions would be allowed. The result was a substantial imbalance in the World Heritage List: a bias towards European cultural properties, historic urban centres, and Christian religious sites, and an under-representation of the non-monumental, the non-religious and in fact the whole world outside Europe, particularly in regions of what UNESCO calls "the non-monumental cultures". Until East Rennell (in 1998) there was, for example, nothing at all listed from the Melanesian region.

In 1994 UNESCO therefore shifted its criteria towards the recognition of "cultural landscapes" as a legitimate form of World Heritage. The main architect of this new policy, Bernd von Droste, saw this shift as representing "a new and multicultural concept of the World Heritage with composite authentic elements". He looked forward to a new concept of authenticity that would encompass both the monumental and the vernacular, constructions "built not only of stone but also of wood, earth and straw or other materials", and including not just authentic materials and techniques but also "the context and spirit of the original building or culture" (von Droste, 1995:23).

Translated into Marovo terms it would seem that an authentic cultural landscape can include the villages, even though the sites of these settlements do not in most cases pre-date the 20th century, provided the houses are made of timber and thatch. Any place where the people are prosperous enough to build houses out of concrete and roofing iron would appear to be excluded. Are churches to be included, if made of traditional materials? Dugout canoes constructed using steel axes and adzes are probably authentic, but fibreglass ones presumably are not. Above all there seems to be no place in an authentic Marovo cultural landscape for a logging camp, even though the forests are at present the only means whereby the Marovo people can enjoy a 20th-century living standard, rather than 19th-century subsistence. Presumably, in the 21st century, World Heritage-seeking tourists will spend enough nights in thatched cottages and will buy enough handicrafts for Marovo living standards to improve. However, even this rumour of Utopia will be denied to Marovo if the rainforests are seen to be desecrated by means other than "acceptably tradition-al" swidden cultivation. According to the bureaucrats in Geneva (WWF), Paris (UNESCO) and Wellington (the WHP eco-tourism programme), the designated future role for Marovo will be as Guardians of World Heritage. Not only is this a far cry from being Guardians of the Marovo Lagoon (an emic concept reflected in the title of Hviding's 1996 book), but also it is a role that only makes sense if we accept the rhetoric of globalisation, threatened biodiversity, and a crisis of cultural authenticity.

The Marovo people have always shown an open-minded response to new things coming to them from the outside world, such as those selling steel axes or promoting the Bible, or others buying copra, trochus shells, baitfish, logs or merely accommodation in a tourist lodge. The Marovo people listen politely to each new wave of missionaries, and their response is pragmatic and ambi-valent. Like the authors of this book, they cannot envisage Marovo Lagoon becoming a museum of either culture or nature, and they cannot understand why a cultural landscape cannot accommodate new as well as old features.

Our conclusion is that tourism does have a future in Marovo Lagoon, but it need not be restricted to some theologically correct version of eco-tourism. The wider world needs to recognise that rainforest logging is as "authentic" as comparable practices in, for example, the forests of Switzerland or Norway. Forest management there has generated cultural landscapes that are widely regarded as part of Europe's cultural heritage, as well a providing a standard of living that in Solomon Islands is only enjoyed by corrupt politicians. A focus on eco-tourism can only serve to distract the Marovo people from confronting their real problems, which in the 21st century will be centred more and more on rain forest management for the market economy. In Amazonia, in Congo, in Borneo and in Solomon Islands it is the same fundamental question: what social institutions can be devised by indigenous people, so they can incorporate on more satisfactory terms the commodification of their main resource, the rainforest?

13 Epilogue: Rainforest Narratives

We conclude this book where it began, with the "globalisation" of the tropical rainforests. We have seen that places once regarded as small and obscure corners of the world, such as Marovo Lagoon, have now become centres of a bitter struggle for their resources, involving a myriad of local and non-local perspectives. The forests of these places are the object of radically alternative visions for the future. It is no longer a dialogue between indigenous rainforest owners and colonial masters, or, in Marxian terms, a conflict between use value and exchange value. These black and white images do not capture the full complexity of what is happening in Marovo Lagoon, and the same problem would no doubt arise almost anywhere else in the world. Viewed from Marovo Lagoon, or from Cambridge, or from Bergen, the clearance of the Amazonian rainforests may look like a simple struggle between insiders and outsiders, small and big, goodies and baddies. No doubt in close up the situation there is just as complicated as the one we have described in Solomon Islands. Yet in a world that sees itself as being progressively globalised, there is an overwhelming temptation to see small corners of the world in terms of the big picture, draw conclusions on the basis of a satellite image, ignore culturally and socially complex encounters and situations "on the ground", and so reduce problems into slogans.

Globalisation is indeed a "narrative" that we wish very strongly to avoid. By narrative we mean, in this context, a story about the world that seems to encapsulate "truth" (Roe, 1991, 1996). Narratives in this sense are ways in which problems can be standardised, and are the means towards a justification of equally standardised solutions. For example, in relation to environment and development in tropical Africa, the extraordinary and persistent power of certain narratives or "landscape discourses" (deforestation, desertification, tragedies of the commons) result in this vast region being intellectually absorbed, or globalised, in ways which seem to make local fieldwork redundant (Fairhead and Leach, 1996; Leach and Mearns, 1996; Cline-Cole, 1998). Arguing from a critical anthropological perspective, Jonathan Friedman (1994, 1997) sees "global narratives" as belonging to a distinctive category of ideas. Globalisation is not a system in itself whereby ideas, concepts and cultures flow (from some source) and mix. Rather than being (in a neo-diffusionist way) about the "flow or movement of culture", globalisation is to be understood as an aspect of social processes through which "meaning is attributed in specific social contexts distributed in the global arena" (Friedman, 1997:270).

An important dimension in such processes is that of power. We can find examples from both economics and environmental studies where the narrative of globalisation attains power by seeming to achieve interpretation and by legitimating political action. Kelly (1997) illustrates this through the writings of Kenichi Ohmae, futurologist and business consultant. In a recent article in the *Harvard Business Review* Ohmae urges the necessity for successful business-men "to put global logic first", and to target the "natural economic zones in a borderless world" (Ohmae, 1995:122). Global forces are inexorable, according to this view: "No more than Canute's soldiers can we oppose the tides of the borderless world's ebb and flow of economic activity" (Ohmae, 1995:125). Let us be a bit more explicit: it is a short step from this logic to consider places like Solomon Islands as the "natural" source area to feed the economic centres of East and Southeast Asia. Kelly (1997) shows how this narrative is used in the Philippines by political and business interests to extend their control over land and resources. While the desire for personal gain might underlie the actions of local politicians, in their rhetoric they appeal to the narrative of the global in order to legitimise their local actions.

The globalisation narrative of the conservationists is fundamentally not so different, but here the narrative emphasises the fragility of the biosphere, the threat of global warming, an ongoing wave of extinctions that justifies urgent actions to conserve wildlife, and in general a "plundering of Paradise" (cf. Broad and Cavanagh, 1993). Increasing human populations, the indirect effects of habitat degradation and the direct impacts of harvesting plants and animals are used to construct an image of the world on the verge of an ecological crisis. According to the "biosphere crisis" narrative local people do not value wildlife, so the "solution" is to remove certain areas from extractive use by creating nature reserves, national parks and World Heritage areas. As Campbell (1997: 3) has shown in the case of marine turtles in Costa Rica, "the extent of the crisis is determined by wildlife biologists, and protection is enforced by the state". Local people who do not conform to this narrative are labelled as "poachers" and "encroachers". Their very existence confirms beliefs about the source of the crisis, and because they are breaking the law the logical "solution" becomes more and better enforcement. A cynical interpretation would be that the ortho-dox "fences and fines" approach to rainforest management is something main-tained by actors (administrators and politicians as well as scientists) because they have an interest in perpetuating the biosphere crisis narrative (Campbell, 1997:4; Leach and Mearns, 1996:19).

Paradoxically, then, we have two distinct outcomes of globalisation for tropical rainforests, either *open-market access* (freedom of use) as the outcome of a global market narrative, or *zero access* (non-use) as the outcome of the global biosphere crisis narrative. What these narratives have in common is the way in which they empower those who wish to use their logic in order to pursue a certain course of action. Globalisation is therefore a social construction which has power relationships embedded within it, as well as being a source of powerful metaphors which have the capacity to legitimise actions. These might include, for example, the commercial use or alternatively the non-use of the forest, pursued in each case without reference to national, regional or local interests.

The case of Marovo Lagoon shows that the narratives of environmentalism have now diversified, in line with worldwide developments (cf. Escobar, 1999), and a particular new turn is emerging. Alongside continuing pleas for non-use of the forests and reefs we have what Campbell (1997) calls the "counter-narrative of sustainable use" of these resources. The "traditional" conservation narrative makes little sense in nations of the South where neither international experts nor national governments have the means to enforce a "fences and fines" approach to non-use, in the face of local opposition and local need. Small-scale logging and eco-tourism can be seen as constituting new narratives which have hidden roots in the metaphor of biosphere crisis but find a more immediate justification in the metaphor of sustainable development. Through the compromise solution of *acceptable use*, the environmentalists hope that forests and wildlife will be given an economic value which generates for the locals an incentive for their conservation (Adams, 1990).

However, the narrative of sustainable use of the rainforest is far from uniform and monolithic. As we have seen in Marovo, the "eco-missionaries" and their local followers are not all using the same version of the sustainable use narrative. Just as an earlier wave of Christian missionaries waged bitter disputes over theological truth, so the adherents of non-consumptive use of the forest (eco-tourism) and consumptive use (eco-timber) are presenting alternative versions of ecological truth. The NGOs which spearhead these initiatives seem incapable of co-operating or agreeing with each other, even though they have the same goal of presenting to the Marovo people (and to those funding their operations) a viable and sustainable alternative to logging. Thus logging and even more drastic modifications to Marovo lands continue into the 21ˢᵗ century, since the counter-narrative that is presented by the NGOs is not seen locally as providing a coherent alternative. Instead, what is presented by one group one week as "environmentally sound" is often rejected the following week by another group as being "unsustainable". Some Marovo villages have been subjected to literally dozens of different "community workshops", "structured group interviews" and questionnaire surveys. A recent Greenpeace study of Marovo (LaFranchi and Greenpeace Pacific, 1999) strongly supports small-scale alternatives to oil palm and logging, but it invokes the magic of a cost-benefit methodology that is unlikely to convince the Marovo people themselves, whose "rational decision-making" is the ultimate NGO target.

What guidance can be expected from government? In relation to rainforest management, the ideological position of both local and national governments can be confusing. The Solomon Islands government has inherited from the British colonial system an economy based on the export of commodities, and more than a few politicians are driven by their own free-spending impulses to boost export revenues in the quickest and easiest way. In colonial days it was expedient to encourage the coconut overlay and the production of copra, which was exported in unprocessed form and so had the bonus (in the globalised system of imperial commerce) of providing jobs and profits for factories in Britain. Unilever's soap factories on Merseyside belonged to the same company that was investing in Solomon Islands plantations.

The independent government did not need to approach economic policy in the same way, but it has been easily suborned by its external advisers, by its own fiscal crisis and by the blandishments and bribes of Asian logging companies. A neo-colonial relationship of primary production (for example from the forests of New Georgia) linked to remote consumption (for example in the cities of Japan) is thus being very precisely reproduced. It is beyond the scope of this book to analyse the *economic development* narrative which justifies the policy of large-scale logging, but it is worth pointing out that although "development" has been predominant in all government discourse in the Solomons since at least the 1960s, it must now co-exist uneasily with other narratives. These include the encouragement of tourism and the signing of conventions which commit the Solomon Islands government to respect World Heritage areas. Politicians and civil servants in Honiara and at provincial level in Gizo must therefore contend with a situation where alternative and contradictory narratives are competing to reach the top of the political agenda. In other contexts this is described as one of the conditions of post-modernity, a line of argument which we decline to pursue.

Instead, let us in conclusion return to the local level. This book could be seen as a sustained plea for what we call the *indigenous use* narrative to be given more attention. In an attempt to throw a much-needed light on processes of change in the colonial and post-colonial existence of Melanesian peoples, we have pursued an ethnographically-based analysis that draws on insights from many other disciplines and whose historical-anthropological approach also tries to grasp certain pre-colonial dynamics. We have traced the changes that have happened over the past 150 years in the various categories of indigenous use of the rainforest environments of the Marovo Lagoon. Just as the Marovo agro-forestry system has undergone a series of adjustments and innovations, so we believe the local narrative which explained, modified or perpetuated the pattern of land use must have been equally dynamic. It remains "indigenous" in the sense that it springs from the Marovo people and by definition is part of "Marovo culture", and also conforms to the local rhetoric about the uniqueness of Marovo **kastom**. However it is clear that this local narrative cannot be analysed as a monolithic entity – Marovo thought and practice has indeed always remained in a dynamic relationship with other worlds beyond the lagoon, and today's **kastom** is by its very definition a transcultural pheno-menon with its own history.

As our analysis of post-colonial scenes of logging, conservation and eco-tourism has shown, cracks are appearing in the indigenous use narrative along various fault lines, as individuals and communities respond to the apparent chaos that surrounds them by absorbing and modifying new narratives in various ways. We have pointed out how long-established differences between 'bush' and 'coastal' groups now effects quite dramatically their respective access to and attitude to logging opportunities. Then there is the religious split between Methodists, SDAs and CFC adherents, which gives rise to increasing differences in the approach to money in different communities. Because of other sources of inequality, there are contrasted opinions being expressed about all the new narratives. There are some who support non-use of the forest (an uneasy coalition of cultural conservatives and World Heritage enthusiasts); others promote its free-market use (logging), or alternatively its sustainable management through consumptive use (eco-timber) or non-consumptive use (eco-tourism). No doubt some gender-based and age-based divisions could also be identified.

All this has implications for how we set about trying to understand such a reality and the language that we use in order to summarise our understanding. One of the most irritating metaphors of the globalisation narrative is its construction of "complexity". Local cultures, it suggests, are simple, especially those small-scale societies of technologically unsophisticated people who only now, at this late stage in world history, are "emerging" into the complex world of the global system. It is hard not to see this latest conceit of Western knowledge as anything more than yet another resurgence of the old racist assumptions of social darwinism, but we would insist also on the simple fact that it is wrong. Social life in Marovo was never "small-scale" (not even in the cartographic sense), and nor was it ever "simple". Deciding whether or not Marovo has become a more or less "complex" place in which to live and work is a futile value judgement, but what we can point to today is the co-existence in Marovo of an increasing number of competing narratives, none of which has the power of absolute hegemony over how to interpret the world. In relation to the use of forests, adoption of any one rather than another of these alternatives would orient future actions in a radically different direction.

By comparison, the cultural world of a logger or a conservationist or even a university academic looks rather straightforward. The farflung, global activity field of these various rainforest actors obscures the fact that their singleminded pursuit of a single narrative greatly simplifies their task. By comparison those who actually live in the rainforest operate in a local activity field of multiple choice. If we are interested in the future of the tropical rainforest, then we must understand the outcome of these various competing narratives. We must examine, in a grounded ethnographic sense that takes into account the perspectives of the protagonists of the different narratives, what goes on in encounters between them as socially positioned "real people". Ultimately, this book is a plea for approaching the continuities and disjunctures of the pre-colonial/colonial/post-colonial world through a narrative of localisation rather than globalisation.

Plate 1: Islands of rainforest. Panoramic view of Marovo Lagoon showing the complex mosaic of lagoon, reef and island habitats. The lagoon is far from being the "pristine wilderness" that some eco-tourists have imagined. The entire marine area is subdivided among kin-based groups (**butubutu**) under the authority of chiefs (**bangara**), in a way that mirrors the tenurial system that regulates the agroforestry resources of the mainland. (EH, 1994)

Plate 2: Land use zonation. Chubikopi village on Marovo Island, showing zones of coastal settlement, coconut palms, gardens and Canarium groves (**buruburuani**). (EH, 1992)

Plate 3: Housing and settlement. Family subdivision of Chea village, showing a typical house (centre), attached kitchen (left), a former main house (right), and a canoe landing. Walls and roofs are of sago leaf, while floors are made of sawn planks or split black-palm trunks. Behind are *Canarium* trees rising above the "coconut overlay" that spread around every Marovo village since the beginning of the copra trade after 1900. (EH, 1987)

Plate 4: Acquiring basic skills. The skilful use of knives is something that children pick up at an early age through play. Most of people's knowledge of gardening and the forest is gained by experience, and is as much skill as concept. (EH, 1991)

Plate 5: Three forest experts. From the left, Ezekiel Mateni (Marovo), Nicolas Kwate'ana (Kwara'ae) and Tena Baketi (Vahole/Hoava). Their species identifications and knowledge of plant uses provided a crosscultural basis for the overview in Figure 3.2. (EH, 1989)

Plate 6: Vincent Vaguni, famous anti-Levers activist, wearing his Marovo Project T-shirt. Opposition to logging was straightforwardly voiced by Vaguni and his associates in the 1980s, but today the number of conflicting "rainforest narratives" has increased. (EH, 1989)

Plate 7: Canoes from the forest. A 20-metre dugout canoe from Chea is used for communal fishing. Most of the 2,500 canoes in Marovo are dugouts made from **goliti** (*Gmelina moluccana*). Some logging agreements specify the conservation of these trees. (EH, 1986)

Plate 8: A virgin forest? An aerial view of northwest Vangunu Island showing unbroken forest extending from volcano rim towards the coastal mangroves. The forest's appearance as "wilderness" is deceptive: it is full of trees such as *Campnosperma* which indicate a history of disturbance. More than a century ago this area supported a large population cultivating swiddens and irrigated taro terraces (**ruta**). (EH, 1996)

Plate 9: Guardians of a cultural landscape. In the forest are skull shrines that embody ancestral powers. Their destruction by loggers has let loose restless spirits that now terrorise those who dare to enter this spiritual wilderness. (EH, 1994)

Plate 10: The swidden cycle, I. A new garden near Bareho, where a coastal **butubutu** is short of garden land. The cycle begins with clearing and burning a 3-4 year old growth of grass, gingers (**piropiro**) and small trees. After 2-3 sweet potato crops there will be 1-2 crops of cassava, before the garden reverts to fallow. (TBS, 1986)

Plate 11: The swidden cycle, II. Planting a new swidden creates a chaotic mosaic: patches of sweet potato, vegetables, bananas and trees like coconuts are planted among the debris of the cleared forest where old *Canarium* trees remain. On good soils, as here on Marovo Island, cultivation may continue for over 5 years before the fallow begins. (EH, 1996)

Plate 12: The swidden cycle, III. A more communal organisation of labour in the CFC village of Tamaneke creates large-scale blocks of land use. Here a large sweet potato garden has been established below the village's huge coconut plantation. (EH, 1986)

Plate 13: Logging landscapes. A road, recently abandoned, which allowed loggers of the Malaysian Silvania company to penetrate deep into Lot 16 on Vangunu. The logged-over forest has lost more than half of its canopy, and *Merremia* creeper is invading. (TBS, 1996)

Plate 14: Forest recovery. By the side of the abandoned logging road on Vangunu, a 2-metre sapling of **olanga** (*Campnosperma*) signals the beginning of the forest's recovery. Mature stands of this tree mark areas of 19th century settlement and cultivation. (TBS, 1996)

Plate 15: Eco-timber, I. A log is dragged to a river on Gatokae, prior to being towed to the sawmill at Batuna. Small-scale logging operations of this kind are organised by family groups, but without bureaucratic assistance from an organisation like SWIFT the product does not qualify as genuine "eco-timber" in European markets. (EH, 1987)

Plate 16. Eco-timber, II. A log of **kapuchu** (*Dillenia*) being sawn in a sago swamp near Chea, for use in the construction of a new church. With increased access to the technologies that allow hardwoods like *Dillenia* to be exploited, there is now real competition between local needs and the demands of the logging companies. (EH, 1996)

Plate 17: Eco-timber, III. Planks for the new church at Chea, produced by chainsaw from one *Dillenia* tree. By exploiting forests in this way ecological damage is minimised because of the absence of roading, the small size of gaps in the canopy, and the large proportion of nutrients that are not exported from the forest. (EH, 1996)

Plate 18: Eco-timber, IV. The Director of SWIFT, Sam Patavaqara (right), and an employee, at SWIFT's main timber yard in Munda. Here planks of eco-timber are sorted and dried prior to being shipped in containers to Rotterdam, where Dutch NGO workers organise the selling of the timber in European markets. (TBS, 1996)

Plate 19: Eco-tourism. Ropiko Lodge near Sobiro on Gatokae, which was established as a family business by a local customary leader using funds supplied by New Zealand's World Heritage Programme (WHP). The intention of WHP is that the stream of benefits from tourism will compensate local communities for not logging the forests. (TBS, 1997)

Plate 20: Urban attractions. The bottle shop, supermarket and casino on Mendana Avenue, Honiara, show three of the ways in which payments from logging companies are spent by those men who have managed to claim "landowner" status. The "rural development" benefits of logging royalties are less apparent than this hectic urban expenditure. (TBS, 1997)

Plate 21: The future? A new oil palm plantation at Kimbe, West New Britain, Papua New Guinea, signals a possible future for the lands of Marovo. In 1999 the Solomon Islands government signed an agreement with Silvania to plant oil palms on Vangunu. (TBS, 1999)

Notes to Chapters

Marovo garden maps were surveyed by Tim Bayliss-Smith and produced by the Department of Geography, University of Cambridge.

Notes to Chapter 1

1. In this scheme of food classification Marovo views are informed by some basic ideas of dualism and complementarity that are widespread in Oceania and the wider Austronesian realm (see, e.g., Pollock, 1992, concerning food; and Blust, 1981, for a general Austronesian perspective).

2. See also Parmentier (1987) and Myers (1991) for comparable examples from Palauan fishers-and-agriculturalists and Australian hunter-gatherers; Tilley (1994) for general phenomenological approaches to "landscape"; and Bender (1993) for a collection of case studies of the "spatiotemporal subjectivities" of landscapes.

Note to Chapter 2

1. Wall and Hansell (1975, Map 4h East) describes these singular grasslands as having the plant composition mentioned. The northeastern slopes of Gatokae are said to have been off-limits to all human settlement for more than two hundred years because of the strong presence on the land of malevolent spiritual powers. It is interesting to note that the grassland patches are in an area with much volcanic activity, including hot springs still active today. Thus it is possible that the Gatokae grasslands are not a result of human activity after all, but rather of volcanic gases or other influences killing the forest and driving away the human population.

Notes to Chapter 3

1. "Non-unilineal descent" prevails in many parts of the Solomon Islands, and the patterns outlined here are not unique for Marovo. For further analysis of the Marovo **butubutu** in a comparative perspective and in the light of general anthropological theory, see Hviding (nd b, 1996a, ch. 4). For detailed analysis of similar situations elsewhere in the Solomons, see Scheffler (1965) for the Varisi of Choiseul and Keesing (e.g. 1968, 1971) for the Kwaio of Malaita. A lack of easily identifiable unilineal kin reckoning caused frequent consternation among British colonial officers seeking to identify more clearcut principles of customary land ownership. This discrepancy between local social realities and colonial views of "customary law" concerning who owned which land was demonstrated in many land disputes that were taken to court, and notably influenced the comprehensive *Report of the Special Lands Commission*

(Allan, 1957). The discrepancy has also left a certain legacy in that many Solomon Islanders appear to believe that "Europeans" are more easily convinced about the legitimacy of a group's title to a certain territory when presented with a simple, matri- or patrilineal genealogical depiction of the longevity of the relationship in question (Hviding, 1993b; see also Tiffany, 1983, for analysis of court cases).

2. The forests of Marovo contains a number of other larger animals that are not eaten for reasons of preference, largely based on traditional ideology. These include the remarkable prehensile-tailed skink *Corucia zebrata* (which was, however, a rare delicacy reserved for chiefs during olden times), certain large tree rats reported to be roaming the interiors of the islands, and snakes, of which the Marovo forest contains few species, notably **noki rou** (the brown tree snake, *Boiga irregularis*), **noki charava** (the tree snake *Dendrelapsis calligaster*), the ground-living **noki oreke** (Pacific boa, *Candoia carinata*); and the venomous but rare **noki picha** (*Salomonelaps par*).

3. In the Marovo language, nouns and verbs are commonly reduplicated with a locative suffix added to refer to repeated occurrence or action in a certain place. In this sense, **chigochigoani** would refer to a tract or zone of land where swidden garden occurs with frequency and abundance. In a parallel manner (as shown in a range of examples in the present discussion), the name of a tree such as **buni** (*Calophyllum* spp.) may be subject to the same transformation resulting in **bunibuniani**, 'grove of *Calophyllum* trees' or (more in line with a Marovo perception of the lives of trees) 'place where *Calophyllum* trees thrive'. Another, very prominent example, is **buruburuani**, 'grove of *Canarium* nut trees'. This transforms the forest into a detailed mosaic of small and large patches where different phenomena occur and different plants lead their preferred lives.

4. In Marovo and elsewhere in the Solomons, this internationally-driven demise of turtle shell as a local export commodity has a parallel in the somewhat earlier decline and final demise of the crocodile skin trade. From the 1950s into the early 1980s crocodile hunting contributed significantly to village economies in the lagoon. This benefit coincided neatly with a rather universal wish among Marovo villagers to get rid of, or at least decimate, the much-feared saltwater crocodile (*Crocodylus porosus*) which up until intensive hunting started was a deadly scourge of estuaries, mangrove shores and lower rivers. More recently the trade in crocodile skins was banned, and by the mid-1990s saltwater crocodiles appeared to be thriving once again in many parts of Marovo, to the consternation of villagers who have to travel through the domains of the crocodile on the way to and from their gardens.

5. See Hviding (1996a, chapter 4 and Appendix 1) for further detail on the structure and demography of present-day Marovo settlement; Bayliss-Smith (1993) for details on household expenditures and consumption; and Leivestad (nd) and Hviding (1996a, esp. ch. 2) for more details on food practices, household economies and village life in general.

Notes to Chapter 4

1. Bayliss-Smith (1993); an aggregate estimate based on official map data and on boundaries of the five wards of the Marovo administrative sub-area.

2. The overall resource potential of reefs and lagoon may be considered in the light that the average annual yield from intensive reef-and-lagoon fisheries – for finfish only, excluding shellfish – lies between one and five tons per square kilometre (Johannes, 1981; Munro, 1983). We recall here that the total expanse of lagoon and barrier reef is about 700 km². In addition the lagoon holds the added resource potential of baitfish (small herrings and anchovies) for the tuna industry. These small fish, not eaten locally, are exploited in the lagoon sections held by certain **butubutu** that have signed "royalty"-yielding agreements with the part-nationally owned tuna companies, and *de facto* provide substantial cash income on the community level. See Hviding (1996a:314-315, 321-325) for further details on tuna baitfishing in Marovo Lagoon.

3. Such larger extended-family subdivisions of agricultural land held by adult sibling (and cousin) groups whose parents are dead are talked about as being associated with the recently deceased and thus constitutes "ancestral estate" on the micro-level.

4. In Marovo as elsewhere in these parts of Melanesia, **mana** is a stative verb – implying a state of efficacy and success to be obtained – rather than the objectification as noun implied in the classic analysis by Codrington (1891). For details on **mana** in Marovo and elsewhere in the Solomons, see Hviding (1996a:89-91) and Keesing (1982, 1984).

5. With the transitive verb **choku** as a root, several additional forms denote aspects of the Marovo relationship between people and plants: the plural noun construct **chinokudi** means 'cultivated plants' in general; and the sometimes-used qualifier **ta choku** means 'planted' and is added to the name of a plant normally growing in the forest to distinguish its cultivated variety from its wild predecessor or "companion". When a cultivated variety is conspicuously different from the wild plant, distinction is stronger than that implied by the act of planting and cultivating; and the qualifiers **manavasa** and **piru** ('domesticated' and 'wild', respectively) are used instead to refer to stable states of difference.

6. In timber-rich Marovo, **goliti** is considered to be the only proper wood for making dugout canoes. There is estimated to be one canoe for every four or five persons in Marovo (Hviding, 1995a), i.e. not much less than 2,500 canoes – of which some 98% are small and large dugouts. With an average lifespan for a dugout canoe of less than ten years, considerable numbers of **goliti** trees are needed each year for making new ones. Population growth, plus the added demand for large motorised dugouts of 10 metres or more, intensify the quest for large **goliti** trees. There is no indication that the canoe builders of Marovo will start to consider other woods for their craft.

7. A comprehensive inventory with information on usages, cultivation methods and wider significance is provided in the Marovo/English dictionary of the marine and terrestrial environments of Marovo published by Hviding (1995b).

8. Tony Crook (1998:62) makes much the same point as Sillitoe in his discussion of the role of language in structuring knowledge of taro cultivation among the Angkaiyakmin of Bolivip, Papua New Guinea. In Crook's account "The end of knowing for Angkaiyakmin is neither the satisfaction of some intellectual curiosity, not finally cutting through so much falsification until the truth is

approached. These are Euro-American concerns. Angkaiyakmin are not pursuing knowledge for its own sake, but for its value as the demonstrated fecundity of a renowned man.... In a sense the taro garden is the tribunal of knowledge: not 'truth' but efficacy is manifested in the good shape and quality of the plants."

Notes to Chapter 5

1. The scarcity of archaeological work in New Georgia has been in stark contrast to the central role of these islands in the cultural history of Melanesia. See, however, the surveys by Miller (1979) and Reeve (1989), the latter containing identifications of Lapita pottery sites in New Georgia. Since 1996 researchers from the University of Auckland have been engaged (in collaboration with the Western Province Cultural Affairs Division) in more comprehensive, longer-term archaeological investigations in the Roviana Lagoon area, and results of this work are bound to improve the situation significantly.

2. There appear to be two quite different types of dog in New Georgia. One is the common domestic dog (*Canis familiaris*) which occurs in all villages in many different varieties, is reckoned to have come with the Europeans, and is often regarded mainly as a nuisance . The other type, said to have been present already in the distant past, is found today among people who hunt regularly for feral pigs. These hunting dogs are usually taken as puppies from the bush lairs of feral dogs (which abound throughout Marovo) and are of a rather uniform type. They have a reddish-brown colour, a pointed nose and prominent ears and shares attributes with the Pacific dog described generally for Oceania by Titcomb and Pukui (1969). In Waterhouse's early Roviana dictionary (Waterhouse 1929) the "local" New Georgian dog is referred to as **kakaula**, as a dog altogether different from the European one (**siki** in Roviana, **chie** in Marovo), and described thus: " ... the indigenous dog, like a dingo. Generally a reddish-brown colour. Always howls – never barks". Recent observations and examination of dog's teeth from New Ireland (Roy Wagner, pers. comm.) indicate tentatively that "local" hunting dogs there and in historically related New Georgia may possibly be an old form of Southeast Asian "dholes" (*Cuon alpinus*), of ancient introduction to Melanesia. Dholes hunt in packs and most notably lack a flight response when attacked by their prey – a behaviour perfectly in line with the much-desired attributes of the typical hunting dogs of Marovo.

3. See also Tedder (1974), who from a brief visual survey of old village sites on Marovo Island concludes that "food gardens must have been small".

4. In two of the three villages on Marovo Island a piped water supply from rivers on the adjacent mainland was established in 1995, through Seventh-day Adventist church development funds.

5. We know that the groups who maintained a stronghold at the Mategele mountain on Gatokae's top were not just mountain dwellers but also coastal marauders and avid seafarers who kept their war canoes by a sheltered reef-enclosed bay at Peava on the island's east coast. Linguistic clues to Gatokae's cultural history point to ancient relationships with the taro-cultivating people of Kalikolo. For example, the name Gatokae is itself an expression from the northern bush language

of Vahole meaning 'treeless', possibly referring to the island's old hill patches of bare grassland. The Gatokae people of old, who spoke a Marovo-related language called Chipuru which was replaced by Marovo after immigrations by war leaders from the Kalivarana area (traditionally regarded as a source of the Marovo language), may well have constituted an organisation of closely related **butubutu** all subsumed under one basic economic and political system that combined elements both from 'bush' groups (taro irrigation) and 'coastal' groups (maritime warfare).

6. In these inland areas, two parallel mountain ridges (with elevations up to 600 metres) are separated by wide, rather gently sloping river valleys quite far inland from the coast. In the far upper reaches of the Piongo Lavata river (approximately the southern perimeter of the Hoeze-Hoava districts), beyond a succession of shallow stony rapids, the terrain is wide and relatively flat. The Piongo Lavata there forms a series of long, wide clearwater 'pools' (**kopi**) reported to be quite deep – and, notably, to be the haunt of a special freshwater crocodile quite dissimilar to the feared estuarine species (**vua**, *Crocodylus porosus*) but apparently not described biologically for the Solomons. The freshwater crocodile of the inland rivers is called **kapakale** by the Vahole people, a name that refers to its habit of laying alongside · stones near the shore. It is not regarded by them as nearly as dangerous as the estuarine crocodile. 'Coastal' elders of Marovo Island also report the existence of this special crocodile far into bush country, but they call it **vua varane**, 'warrior crocodile', claiming that it has a reputation for absolute and outright ferocity as opposed to the saltwater crocodile's somewhat more predictable habit of killing by stealth and deception. Possibly, this perception held among coastal people reflects a fear among their former generations (still partly in evidence today) for phenomena and beings of the inner lands. In this sense the freshwater crocodiles remain as much a mystery to them as to Western biology.

7. The important association between arboriculture and a steady supply of fruit bats has been noted for other Pacific Islands agroforestry systems as well (e.g. Falanruw, 1989, for Yap).

Notes to Chapter 7

1. Nicholas Thomas (1989a, 1991) makes a case for the potential contribution to anthropological discourses of non-anthropological accounts written by European protagonists in events of early colonial entanglement with the remote worlds of Oceania. Also of interest is the observation made by A.P. Elkin in a rather obscure 1950s review of anthropological research needs in Melanesia that, despite the "inadequate interpreting facilities" of European explorers and navigators in the region, certain accounts by such early colonial (or, maybe, incipiently colonial) travellers do in fact provide useful information. As Elkin (1953:5) expresses it, such accounts "tend to give actual examples of cultural behaviour, and not merely to describe behaviour in general terms. This enhances their contribution." (Elkin 1953:5).

2. Although a few intrepid female North American travellers did find their way to Marovo and other parts of the Solomons in the 1920s and 1930s. Their rather lurid recollections, acutely aware of the perceived tribulations of a white woman in

these savage places – but as acutely ignorant of the lives led by local women – were published as books with telltale titles: the sensationalist and at times racist *Bride in the Solomons* by Osa Johnson (the wife of explorer-photographer Martin Johnson) and the rather more humorous, sympathetic and fact-oriented *Headhunting in the Solomon Islands* by amateur portrait painter Carolyne Mytinger (Johnson, 1945; Mytinger, 1942). Being women did not prevent these travellers from insisting on the privileges of a male colonial sphere, although Mytinger on occasion throws a questioning, ironic light on the attitudes and approaches of colonial officers and planters, as well as local headmen and chiefs.

3. The "trouble-spots" of New Georgia (most notably the Roviana and Marovo lagoons) with their reputation for large-scale headhunting had been of interest for quite some time to the rapidly expanding mission activity which was encouraged by the establishment in 1893 of the British Solomon Islands Protectorate. However, local reception had not been too warm, despite the lagoon dwellers' long record of good trading relations with Europeans. Violent colonial retaliation after the murders of traders, as well as the active encouragement from certain traders of long-term residence with solid local credibility, finally facilitated the arrival of the Australian Methodist Mission. Established in Roviana in 1902, the Methodists expanded to Marovo in 1912 and set up a station in what rapidly became the large new "mission" village of Patutiva at the southwestern entrance to the lagoon. Further trader rivalry opened up for the arrival in 1914 of Seventh-day Adventist missionaries, also Australian, at Viru Harbour, from where they expanded into central Marovo through establishing a school at Sasaghana, at the relict coastal stronghold of Marovo Island. See Hviding (1996a, Ch. 3) for details on mission arrivals and rivalries in Marovo Lagoon, and Bennett (1987) for general historical perspectives on the relationship between mission activity and commerce in the Protectorate.

4. Kennedy's coastwatching activities relayed information on Japanese sea and air movements to the Americans. He also organised espionage (and sometimes attacks) on Japanese camps by local guerrilla soldiers, and a network of lookout posts on the hills facing the lagoon, where men from nearby deserted villages were stationed on a rotational basis with the order to light a beacon fire as soon as an intruding vessel was sighted. It seems clear from recollection of Marovo elders that Kennedy's success as a coastwatcher was in large measure based on his repressive, even idiosyncratically violent, attitude towards the people of the lagoon – all in the name of wartime military requirements. See also Boutilier (1989) for a historian's perspective.

5. The urban scene of late-1990s Honiara has seen conspicuous consumption of extraordinary royalty sums from logging companies. Royalties have on the one hand been spent at casinos and nightclubs and on other features of "globalised modernity" only very recently arrived in the Solomons, and on the other, diverted into customary channels of reciprocity and gift-giving on levels sometimes approaching a "potlatch" condition. This intense flow of activity has so far received little research attention, with the notable exception of a pioneering anthropological study by Cato Berg (1999) of "**kastom** in the urban swirl", based on a year of fieldwork in Honiara during the logging boom.

6. Figure 7.1 combines information from a number of sources, including Levers Pacific Timbers (1969), Burslem and Whitmore (1996), Hviding (1995b), and information leaflets and newsletters produced by SWIFT (see Chapter 11).

Notes to Chapter 8

1. For some families, however, other sites must be found in the long run. In the 1970s a prominent segment of the Luga **butubutu** left Vakabo to establish a new village at One, an abandoned turn-of-the-century settlement site on the mainland to the south, where land (and freshwater) is plentiful. The majority who remained at Vakabo have also established gardens on the adjacent barrier islands, rather close to the village here in the narrowest parts of Marovo Lagoon. The two long barrier islands of Tatama and Avavasa were alienated land from 1914, though little developed for plantation purposes by the companies that originally bought them (for £80.00, according to local history). In 1966 the title over Tatama and Avavasa reverted to certain influential people of the Tamaneke and Vakabo groups (among them the Holy Mama, founder of the Christian Fellowship Church) after negotiation ` with, and subsequent purchase from, the colonial government. Unlike the mainland, these barrier islands were for a long time not informally subdivided among Vakabo families, and in 1986 seemed to be occupied only in a very patchy manner and on a first-come, first-served basis. Patches cleared from the tall and tangled barrier island forest were planted with sweet potato as a short-term crop, and with coconuts to ensure that long-term use rights evolved and persisted.

2. By 1986 the coconut had reverted in most parts of Marovo Lagoon to its traditional subsistence role. After rather reliable copra shipping services in the 1970s, partly run by the indigenous Christian Fellowship Church whose stronghold is in the nearby village of Tamaneke, Vakabo has seldom been visited by ships, and it is too remote for copra marketing by canoe to be a profitable option.

3. The Bisuana headland is not far from the stone ruins at Vavae where their own ancestors had had a powerful presence long ago. According to stylised oral tradition Vavae had a population of 7,000 people, later suppressed by expansionist saltwater people.

4. The pattern whereby men of the 'coastal' **butubutu** of central Marovo marry women from the land-rich bush groups of Bareke (cf. Chapter 6, and Hviding, 1996a:373-374) on a systematic **butubutu**-to-**butubutu** basis continues today, and is reinforced by the pronounced endogamy of Seventh-day Adventists. In effect, such marriages (for example between men of Chea and Telina and women of Bisuana and nearby villages) now replicate in the fifth or sixth generation what was established in the days of combined warfare and bush-sea barter. This pattern also contributes to putting some pressure on the immediately available garden land on the lower slopes of Bareke.

5. Although it has been commented recently by some people of the SDA villages of Bareke that they might consider getting guns to shoot foraging pigs anyway.

6. By 1996 many families of Tamaneke were quite regularly spending several days on end in makeshift huts, working with their new riverside gardens (many of

which are several hours' paddling upriver). The soil along the banks of the Piongo Lavata is rich and fertile, and there is much evidence of old gardens and settlements along the middle-to-upper reaches of the river. There are also a considerable number of stone terraces and other signs of taro irrigation on the slopes along smaller tributaries of the upper river. Vahole people were the last ones to abandon taro irrigation in Marovo, and although large-scale irrigation ceased by 1940, some smaller, less complicated irrigated fields of Vahole were actually tended into the late 1980s. In 1996 one elderly couple was said to be still growing their taro in a small pond system by a remote tributary of the Piongo Lavata.

7. In 1996 Michi village, one of the four case studies in this chapter, was divided in two by the establishment of a new village site several hundred metres inland on a low hill. The majority of the Michi people, who continued as dedicated United Church followers, thus moved away from an extended family cluster whose younger leaders had converted to a new evangelist church – and the Tobakokorapa **butubutu** was split along lines not unlike the intense mission competition 80-90 years ago. The people who remained in the old village also run the Vanua Rapita eco-tourism enterprise and exemplify a rather intense modern involvement, with several of their traditionally influential men also employed by conservationist organisations (see Chapter 12).

8. Some of the hamlet entrepreneurs of today's Marovo echo similar market-oriented operations established on areas of logged-over land in the island of Kolobangara (cf. Chapter 10) and servicing the new township around the tuna cannery at Noro.

Notes to Chapter 9

1. Campbell was the co-ordinator of the National Forestry Action Plan (NFAP) of the Ministry of Forests. This was an ill-fated attempt by experts funded from Australian aid to impose on the logging industry tighter monitoring and control, as part of a hidden agenda to reduce log production to a more sustainable level. Such actions represented a threat to powerful political interests in the government, and the NFAP was terminated in 1996. This is in line with other government responses to Australian-funded forestry management projects; for example, the numerous reports and papers arising in the early 1990s from the so-called National Forest Resource Inventory Project have remained "non-accepted" by relevant government ministries (T.C. Whitmore, pers. comm.).

2. A forestry expert, F.S. Walker, wrote a report for the British Government in 1948 which indicated that there existed about 80 square miles of "accessible" forest, of which 30 square miles were on New Georgia. However, the vast majority of Solomons forests (10,230 square miles) were considered by Walker to be inaccessible and too expensive to exploit, and he therefore he classified them as "unproductive" (Walker, 1948, cited by Allen, 1957:6).

3. In the mid-1950s Colin Allen (1957:7) estimated these costs of forest clearance to be A$ 40 per acre, while constructing roads into the forest cost A$ 5-6,000 per mile (an unskilled plantation labourer at this time cost an employer A$ 6

per month in wages). Most forests were therefore regarded as hopelessly in-accessible and too expensive to exploit.

4. In Marovo, the Batuna sawmill continued (although through many ups and downs) to process timber from local suppliers up into the 1990s, when operations ceased.

5. The national carrier Solomon Airlines flies at least daily into Seghe to and from Honiara, Munda and Gizo, and less frequently to Viru and to Ramata in northern Marovo. Until their operations were cancelled in 1998, the Seventh-day Adventist free-lance aviators Western Pacific Air Services had frequent scheduled flights to Batuna and Sobiro (in Gatokae) and could be chartered to most other strips around the New Georgia islands, thereby providing a much-needed supplement. A steady increase in Seghe flights by Solomon Airlines during the mid-1990s at first glance appeared to reflect accelerating tourism (i.e., divers to the resort at Uipi in central Marovo and a few "eco-tourists" to many small lodges – see Chapter 12), but logging-related traffic – as well as frequent visits by representatives of conservation-ist organisations – surely contributed almost as much to the brisk business on the Seghe-Honiara sector.

6. During its operations in Choiseul since 1989, Eagon has strived to maintain a projected image of near altruism and as a direct benefactor for the Choiseulese. Internet surfers in the world beyond Choiseul can access the company's presentation page on the World Wide Web (www.eagon.co.kr), which states the main business of the company as being "Reforestation, Logging (sustained yield system), Saw-milling", and presents the purpose of the "Eagon Foundation" as being "To promote economic, social and cultural development for the people of Choiseul Island". The basis for all this is a declared forest area (on customary land) of 300,000 hectares with a total harvestable volume of 13 million cubic metres.

7. These events are covered more fully by Judith Bennett (in press, ch. 16). The fiscal crisis came to a head in April 1996, when the commercial banks grew tired of accepting delayed repayments on loans of A\$ 3 million, and confronted Mamaloni with the possibility of legal action and the collapse of the economy. But in May "Eagon's deposit of SI\$ 20 million for the Viru plantation along with substantial yet decreased revenues from logging rescued the government from insolvency". Bennett quotes an even higher valuation for Viru ("said to be worth around SI\$ 80 million"). She points out that in Viru Eagon are under none of the restraints which, at least on paper, regulate logging practice on customary land. For example, one of their first acts was to log the research plots established by Forestry Division botanists. Nor was the former land-holding **butubutu** given any opportunity to assert claims concerning the land.

8. This time of reorientation and recommenced logging in Viru also saw an intensification of organised movements among some groups of customary land-owners, some of whom moved to register themselves and their remaining customary land as "community development projects", with a view to bolstering claims to former "forest estate". This reflects the relatively long history in the Viru area of local attempts to enhance the benefits from logged-out land handed back for village-level plantation purposes.

9. "Report - Mr JWF Chapman, visit to Vangunu Feb 1963". Copy provided by G.B.K. Baines, from files relating to Vangunu Land Purchase 1963.

10. "April 16th -63, Ref No. 171, K.W. Trenaman (Chief Forestry Officer) to Mr. Chapman (Forestry Officer), 3rd Vangunu visit – leaving Honiara 170463". Copy provided by G.B.K. Baines, from files relating to Vangunu Land Purchase 1963.

11. "District Commissioner Western, Gizo, to Commissioner of Lands, Honiara. Vangunu Forest Purchase. (AV Hughes for DCW)." Copy provided by G.B.K. Baines, from files relating to Vangunu Land Purchase 1963.

12. The Silvania company paid taxes in 1995 of SI$ 7,984,335, but for some reason it has been granted exemption from timber levy, and in 1995 this exemption cost Solomon Islands Government SI$ 2,235,775 in lost revenues (Anonymous 1996, Table 3). One can speculate whether there is any connection with the substantial bribes which, it was alleged by the newspaper *Solomon Star*, had been paid by Integrated Forest Industries (IFI) to three government ministers in November 1995 (Bennett, in press, Ch. 16). Both Silvania and IFI are owned 100% by a parent company, Kumpulan Emas Berhad of Malaysia.

13. Silas Eto died in 1984, but in line with the emphasis given in CFC doctrines to the ancestral worship on which pre-Christian religious beliefs in New Georgia are based, the Holy Mama remains an influential person. Enshrined in his home village of Tamaneke in northern Marovo, the Holy Mama still has a strong presence in the everyday and ritual lives of CFC followers, and his continuing powers (**minana**) manifest themselves regularly by the vibration of the 'prayer ropes' – a few metres of traditional bark-fibre string tautly suspended between two tall poles – which are present in all CFC communities and are approached at certain stages of church service and before any large work effort is started. His eldest son, Ikan Rove, has taken over as spiritual head of the CFC and appears to have attained an awe-inspiring, prophetic status (of a somewhat lesser degree than his father). Ikan Rove is very traditionalist-oriented and even declines to speak Pijin, but together with an impressive collection of well-educated 'left-and-right hand men' (**hedematao**), of whom the most powerful is his brother Job Dudley Tausinga, he wields significant power on behalf of the CFC in any field of contemporary politics. In this sense the CFC collective figures on the wider New Georgian arena as something of a super-**butubutu**, to a degree not remotely reached by neither SDAs nor Methodists. In the world of the CFC, the **butubutu** and **puava** of its followers form a pool, so to speak, of combined people, lands and seas crosscutting sub-regional and inter-**butubutu** differences.

14. The Rainforest Information Centre established a foothold in certain CFC villages in the early 1980s, under the motto "Stop The Killing – Save Our Trees". The RIC's stated aim, as reported by Vincent Vaguni (an important RIC contact in the CFC centre at Tamaneke and later a powerful resource management activist in his own right), was to stop logging by Levers through peaceful means through spreading information about the importance of the rainforest to people's lives. In the early 1980s Vaguni (Provincial Assembly Member for north-central Marovo throughout most of the decade) and Job Dudley Tausinga (Provincial Premier in the same period) were both vocal spokesmen for RIC initiatives and ran its branch at the

provincial capital of Gizo. The RIC was probably the first foreign activist NGO of its kind ever to enter the Marovo area. Seen on the background of the complex recent history of such NGO involvement in Marovo, the RICs brief success in the early 1980s stands out for its attainment of an exceptionally strong degree of collaboration with, and commitment by, powerful politicians on local, provincial and national levels.

Notes to Chapter 10

1. In this Marovo-oriented perspective on New Georgia it should be made clear that spatial and cultural boundaries between the Marovo, Roviana and Kusaghe are to some degree overlapping and fluid (see Chapter 3). We may repeat here that the area referred to as "North New Georgia" extends beyond the present-day administrative boundaries of "Marovo" into "Kusaghe" proper, which falls under "Roviana" in modern administrative terms. In a different manner, the "Viru-Kalena" area connects partly to other, more recently logged areas in the far eastern parts of the Roviana Lagoon, but is wholly contained within the wards of "Marovo". Language-wise, Marovo words for concepts related to land tenure are mainly used in this book, for reasons of clarity, and because their close cognates in the Kusaghe and Hoava languages (cf. Chapter 3) show a complete correspondence in terms of meaning. While **butubutu** is a universal term throughout the New Georgia islands (with the exception of the non-Austronesian speaking peoples of Vella Lavella and southern Rendova), the Marovo **puava** is **pepeha** in Hoava and **pepeso** in Kusaghe (and Roviana).

2. A tree recognised by New Georgians as being related to the 'canoe tree' – the Marovo **goliti** (*Gmelina moluccana*) – but regarded as completely useless for any local purpose, because its wood is so different from that of the **goliti**.

3. The villages of some influential groups are actually located not on Kolobangara but on the opposite side of the Blackett Strait, on the barrier islands bordering the island of Kohigo in Vonavona Lagoon.

4. The Kusaghe-speaking SDA villages of Baini and Hovoro, located by rivers on the mainland, are recent offshoots from the old village at Tusu Mine, a small coral island located at the northernmost passage into the Marovo Lagoon. Baini and Hovoro, as well as Jela further north (outside the lagoon) are dominated by rather large, prefabricated wooden houses complete with screened windows and iron roofs with rainwater tanks connected to them. This modernist building spree was financed by logging royalties from Levers operations and was strongly in line with an SDA emphasis on "improving" the material qualities of life in a manner approaching "European" standards. Despite the comparative luxury of their dwellings, however, these people have had few economic opportunities during the 1990s as they live in a backwater lacking transport facilities.

5. That KFPL should be labelled "Forestry Department" by Solomon Islanders with long experience also from the urban sector exemplifies a more general pheno-menon discussed earlier by one of us (Hviding, 1996a:320-321). Basically, a history of much collaboration between colonial and later national governments and private resource extraction companies seems to have fostered a conception in Marovo, at

least, whereby the names of relevant past and present government departments (Forestry, Fisheries, Geology) are applied metonymically for any form of joint venture between the government and a company. "Forestry" has tended to be synonymous with large-scale logging and to express local awareness of the close association between government authorities and foreign capital, and thus seems logically extendable to, for example, KFPL which even operates on government land at Kolobangara.

6. **Chovuku** as well as several other popular wild and semi-domesticated fruit trees of today's Marovo – such as **opiti** (*Spondias dulcis*, "Vi Apple") and **apuchu** (*Syzygium malaccense*, "Malay Apple") – form part of the ancient repertoire of Lapita-related, "Proto-Oceanic" food plants (see Kirch, 1997:205-208). Quite a few other fruit trees of this repertoire are not, however, regarded as such in Marovo today and appear to have had little significance also in former times. These include breadfruit (*Artocarpus altilis*, **omo** or **omo vaka** [see Chapters 4 and 5]), all types of pandanus (**ramoso**), and the large tree *Pometia pinnata* (**meda**), an important export timber. It appears that Marovo arboriculture has long been biased towards nut trees in favour of fruit trees.

7. Named after the small skinks (*Emoia* spp.) which are abundant in any seaside or village location in Marovo. Many of these lizards have striped patterns in black and contrasting bright colours, not unlike the undulating patterns of irregular contrasting stripes characteristic of nice wood from the "Queen ebony". While good pieces of this form of ebony is certainly popular among Marovo's carvers, it is the all-black "King Ebony" that fetches the highest prices for those who sell the wood, and subsequently for the carvers who sell their products in the tourist sector.

Notes to Chapter 12

1. For example, on a certain level of belief God is now regarded as holding His hand over most things – including forest and seas and everything therein. Many people of Marovo also regard Him as being a guiding force – a form of powerful **bangara** ('chief') – in the lives of both people, fish, animals and plants, although in this He has to compete with a varied repertoire of ancestral spirits ('kept warm' in well-maintained skull shrines in forests and on reefs) and more freely roaming spiritual presences of land and sea. In issues of environmental management, such as the depletion of fish stocks or the degradation of land, human agency is often down-played with reference to the more powerful agency believed to be possessed in this regard by spirits – and by God (cf. Hviding, 1996a, ch. 5).

2. The International Union for Conservation of Nature and Natural Resources (IUCN) in 1986 published a review (in collaboration with the United Nations Environment Programme [UNEP] and prepared by consultant Arthur L. Dahl) of biodiversity and perceived conservation needs in Oceania, with the aim to provide a framework for a "protected areas system" for the region. Solomon Islands receives considerable attention (IUCN 1986:73-90), and among the things we learn from the review is that "[t]he present protected area situation in the Solomon Islands is very weak, with much of the park on Guadalcanal degraded by subsistence gardens, and the Kolombangara forest reserve a 500 metre wide strip which may be unsustainable

ecologically. Major protected areas should be considered for Rennell, San Cristobal [Makira], Guadalcanal, Malaita and Vanikolo, with smaller areas to protect interesting sites and species on other islands" (IUCN 1986:16). The interesting features mentioned for New Georgia and Vangunu range from "6 species of frogs" to "rainforest including <u>Dillenia/Calophyllum/Campnosperma</u> type" and "best-defined double barrier reef in the world at Marovo Lagoon", but the area receives overall low rankings both concerning "Conservation Importance" and, significantly, "Practicality of conservation action". We also note that in terms of "reliability of data" New Georgia is ranked at zero ("no reliable data" and Vangunu at 1 ("poor data [both partial and out of date]").

3. Hviding (1996a:332-339) provides an analysis of Marovo perceptions of, and relationships with, yacht crews. This is a field of interaction tinged by the Marovo classification of such visitors as a version of the 'ship people' (**tinoni vaka**, also the general term for 'white people') who came on the sailing ships of the 19th century.

4. Ngaire Douglas, one of the few researchers to have focussed critically on tourism development in Melanesia, concludes her analysis by pointing to the vague, unattainable promise of this "sector", thereby highlighting some of the stark dilemmas represented by what we analyse here primarily from a local perspective: "… as long as leisure, pleasure and recreation are high priorities in the industrialized nations and foreign experts can access high consultancy fees to promote and develop the infrastructure required to satisfy these needs, then many small and rather vulnerable governments struggling to meet the expectations and priorities of their own populations will be seduced by the short term promises of tourism with little time or encouragement to determine the colour of the long term balance sheet" (Douglas, 1996:266-267). For Marovo Lagoon, we wish to add, it is an open question whether tourism will ever reach the level where actual balance sheets demand attention.

Glossary of Marovo Words

This glossary includes Marovo terms and concepts which have some frequency of occurrence in the text or which are otherwise significant for the analysis. Plant names are not generally included beyond a selection of important species mentioned in several different contexts. Therefore, reference is made to Figure 3.2 and to vernacular name and scientific identifications given throughout the text, particularly in association with the garden maps. Where necessary, (M) denotes Marovo language, (H) denotes Hoava language, and (E) denotes derivation from English.

apuchu a tree; *Syzygium malaccense*, Malay apple
are wind; weather
bangara 'chief'
batia bananas and plantains, *Musa* spp.
binalabala 'consciousness'; 'mind'
binaso 'that which is eaten with food'; protein food
boboro traditional leaf parcel of processed *Canarium* nut kernels
boku 'block' of land allocated to household/individual; specifically agricultural
bokuboku boundary marker
bolivi a yam, probably *Dioscorea pentaphylla*; wild and cultivated varieties
botu umalau sweet potato mound
bukulu a large tree lizard; *Corucia zebrata*, the "prehensile-tailed skink"
bulaeri a dark purple-to-black colour
buma green-and-blue
buni a group of trees, *Calophyllum* spp.
bunibuniani stand of *Calophyllum* trees
bupara brown
burongo a small tree, *Euodia hortensis*
buruburu *Canarium* nut tree; 'year'

buruburuani planted grove of *Canarium* nut trees
butubutu kin group, defined by cognatic descent and having corporate control over **puava**
butubutu koina resident core of **b.**
butubutu maena segment of **b.** with imigrant origins
chakei to look after, to care for, to manage
chevara 'to work in the garden'
chiama pre-Christian priest
chichiogo tall, mature secondary forest, showing signs of previous cultivation and habitation
chigo 'garden' (especially swidden)
chigo lavata 'great garden'; communally cultivated feast garden
chigo pa goana 'bush garden' located in old forest
chigo pa kavo 'garden by the river'
chigochigoani 'area of habitual, extensive garden cultivation'; agro-forestry zone
chinoko black; dark-coloured
chochoho a flowering shrub, *Hibiscus rosa-sinensis*

340

chochore a wild yam, *Dioscorea* sp.
choku 1. to plant, to cultivate; 2. dibble or digging stick, cf. **heuku** (H)
chovuku a fruit tree, *Burckella* sp.
chubina tree trunk; 'basis, 'foundation'
deana 'fat', 'greasy'
dekuru log; trunk of felled tree
edeve sago palm, *Metroxylon salomonense*
eruku mango tree, *Mangifera indica*
gete large
ghinerigheri building materials gathered from the forest
ghohere giant swamp taro, *Cyrtosperma chamissonis*
goana forest, 'bush'
goana pa nura forest type in valleys and depressions; **nura** = valley
goana pa taba forest type on hillsides and slopes; **taba** = slope
goana pa togere hilltop forest
goana piru 'wild forest'; remote inner forest with little disturbance
goliti *Gmelina moluccana*, the dugout canoe tree
habichi "elephant ear" taro, *Alocasia macrorrhiza*
habu to harvest
hae tree, wood
hecha southeasterly tradewind; tradewind season
heli to dig; to harvest by digging
heru to carry something in a specific direction
heva white; light-coloured
hinage nipa palm, *Nypa fruticans*
hiniva 'desire', strong preference
hinoho 'property'; use right in **puava**; ownership in planted trees
hirama to fell large trees
hirata a climber, *Piper betle*; leaves chewed with *Areca* nuts
hoba a large tree, *Terminalia brassii*
hoho to own; to possess, cf. **hinoho**
hope sacred; taboo; prohibition; sacred place; shrine; pan-Oceanic **tapu**
horevura 18th- and 19th-century migrations of Marovo's inland people to the coast
huba string bag

ihana fish
ijoko a large flowering ginger, ritually important
jajala "Croton", *Codiaeum variegatum*
jemijemiani freshwater swamp, lit. 'area of wet mud'
jipolo a shrub, *Cordyline terminalis*; essential for protective ritual
kabani 'company', capitalist enterprise; **kabani dekuru** logging company
kalala banyan trees, *Ficus* sp.
kale 'side'; important dualist concept referring to complementarity, symmetry, group-territory collectivity, etc.
kalekogu lagoon-facing zone (marine and terrestrial) of the barrier islands
kalelupa ocean-facing zone (marine and terrestrial) of the barrier islands
kapuchu a tree, *Dillenia salomonensis*
karuvera "Hong Kong taro", *Xanthosoma sagittifolium*
kavo river; freshwater
kererao a yellow coconut variety
keru (H) to dig, to harvest; cf. **heli** (M)
kiki small
kiko young taro sprouts
kino 'way of life'; mode of existence of living beings
kinovuru offspring, descendants
kinudu 'leafy greens'; edible leaves and shoots picked off growing plants
kivili a tree, *Intsia bijuga*
kogu lagoon
kolo ocean
kolokolo time; season; 'when ...'
kotukotuani fallow; secondary forest under regrowth
kotukotuani porana mature secondary forest (after 10-20 years)
kualeve creepers, *Merremia* spp.
kudu ngache to harvest **ngache** and other leafy greens (cf. **kinudu**)
kupati talo to replant taro tops after harvesting the corm
kurukuru grey fruit dove, *Ducula pistrinaria*
kuruvete a small, ritually important ginger
leboto 'bush knife' (machete)
lavata great
leana good, useful, pleasant

leru a coastal tree, *Hibiscus tiliaceus*

lipa a group of fishes; mullets, *Mugil* spp.

lolomo sea passage through reef; valley; 'space'

luju lesser yam, *Dioscorea esculenta*

malanga 'poor'; impoverished, in need

mana state of efficacy and success to be obtained; **minana** = 'blessing'

manavasa tame, 'domesticated'

manemaneke woman

manioko papaya, *Carica papaya*

maria a nut tree, *Canarium salomonense*

mati dry land; shallow reefs exposed at low tide; low tide

mati ipu low tide in nighttime; coincides with **mohu** season

mati rane low tide in daytime; coincides with **hecha** season

minila ginger, *Zingiber officinale*; also 'medicine' generally

mohu 'wet', 'fecund'; northwesterly monsoon winds; season of north-westerly winds

mudu a tree; *Cananga odorata* ("perfume tree", Ylang-Ylang)

nabo turmeric, *Curcuma domestica*

naginagi a tree; *Cordia subcordata*, "kerosene wood"

ngache an important garden shrub; *Hibiscus manihot*, "bush cabbage"

ngicha 'commoners'; traditionally the non-enslaved "workers" of a **butubutu**

nginira 'strength'; inalienable ancestral rights of ownership over **puava**

nginongo 'food'; carbohydrate staple

ngochara coconut tree, *Cocos nucifera*

ngochangocharaini coconut grove

ngoete nut tree, *Canarium indicum*

nura valley bottom

oha yellow

olanga a large tree, *Campnosperma breviopetiolatum*

orava red

paju batia to harvest bananas and plantains

palavanua village; any place of permanent human habitation

petu mangrove trees; mangrove zone

petu ta ngo *Bruguiera gymnorhiza*, mangrove tree with edible seeds

petupetuani mangrove forest

pijaka betel-nut palm, *Areca catechu*

pinausu pet animal, slave

piropiro a ginger shrub, *Alpinia* sp.

piropiroani areas with dense stands of **piropiro**, prototypical recent fallow

piru wild; uncontrollable

poata money; covering both modern cash and traditional shell valuables

poda ancestral spirit; dead person; corpse

poki to clear away lower layer of undisturbed forest

pokipoki to weed regularly

popa dry, 'poor'

pora mature, ripe

puava earth, soil; defined land-sea territory, ancestral estate of **butubutu**

puava chinoko black, fertile volcanic soil

puava bupara 'brown soil'; red-to-brown clay soil with greasy quality

puava gegha infertile soil, overgrown with bush after initial gardening attempts

puava hokara 'proper soil'; stony, brown, coral-based soil of the barrier islands

puava kolipi brown, rather infertile soil with stones

puava noti black clay

puava orava 'red soil'; alternative name for **puava bupara**

puava ruta waterlogged soils in places suitable for taro irrigation

puava ruvao hard, rocky soil that looks like stone

puava toba 'barrier islands soil'; alternative name of **puava hokara**

puava votu muddy soil, mixed with leaves, found close to river and on river banks

puhaka sea slugs, "bêche-de-mer"

pusi a climbing vine whose bark fibres are used for plaited string

rakoto to cut up and collect logs, branches, roots, shrubs etc. in heaps around big trees

ramoso 1. *Pandanus* spp. cultivated for their leaves; 2. pineapple, *Ananas comosus*

rarusu beach; seashore nearest to water

rekiti *Imperata* grass
regocho to destroy by non-magical means (cf. **ruasai**)
rejo hearth; stone oven
reka hot, warm
rigi a tree, *Pterocarpus indicus*, "rosewood"
rihe a tree, *Diospyros* sp.; ebony
riki ark shells, *Anadara* spp.
ropaini new, prospective garden site where clearing (**ropa**) is under way
roroto affinal relative, in-law
ruasai to perform malevolent magic
ruasai chigo to destroy gardens by magic
ruja pudding made from pounded root crops
ruta irrigated, usually terraced taro pondfields
saghabu (H) cloud forest (from **ghabu**, 'fog')
sangava wide navigable sea passage through reef leading from lagoon to ocean
sera beach landing; inhabited seashore
sinare guardian spirits of tree-climbing
singi tide; high tide (cf. **mati**)
sinoto 'filiative link'; parent-child link connecting a person with genealogical 'line'
sinu a ginger shrub, *Guillainia purpurata*
sinusinuani stands of **sinu** in waterlogged areas, sometimes planted
soloso large main islands [cf. **tusu**]; interior of large islands; the world
sulu to burn; in agriculture, to burn collected litter and the large trees
taba slope
tabaika (E) tobacco, *Nicotiana tabacum*
tagala *Polyscias* spp. , woody shrubs
talise a coastal tree, *Terminalia catappa*

talo taro, *Colocasia esculenta*
tavete to work; to make; to create; to accomplish
tina one thousand
tinamanae an act of making efficacious; that which confers blessing
tinavete work, end result of productive activity; **tavete** = to work, to produce
tingitonga leadi 'good things'; 'resources'
tinoni man; person; people
tinoni pa goana 'people of the bush'
tinoni pa sera 'people of the coast'
tinoni ruasai 'sorcerer'
tita "putty nut" tree, *Parinari glaberrima*
toba elevated barrier reef islands
togere mountain
tovu sugar cane, *Saccharum officinale*
tupe coconut crab, *Birgus latro*
tusu smaller island, lagoon island
ugulu cloud forest on mountain tops and ridges
ulu upwards; **pa uluna** = 'above'
umalau sweet potato, *Ipomoea batatas*
uvi greater yam, *Dioscorea alata*
uvikola cassava, *Manihot esculentum*
vaho a leafy shrub, *Heliconia solomonensis*
vahu fruit bats, fam. Pteropodidae
vaka non-local water craft; ship
vanua house
varane warrior
vasara a large tree, *Vitex cofassus*
vilaka 'row'; demarcated, parallel (mono-crop) divisions of cultivated garden
vinaritokae reciprocal help
voloso boundary; land or sea contained within a set of boundaries
vuro ten thousand

Bibliography

Adams, William M.
1990a *Green Development: Environment and Sustainability in the Third World.*
       London: Routledge.
Allen, Colin H.
1957   *Customary Land tenure in the British Solomon Islands Protectorate.* Report
       of the Special Lands Commission. Honiara: Western Pacific High Commis-
       sion.
Allen, J., C. Gosden and J.P. White
1989   Human Pleistocene adaptations in the tropical island Pacific: recent
       evidence from New Ireland. *Antiquity*, 63:548-561.
Amherst, Lord, of Hackney and Basil Thomson
1901   *The discovery of the Solomon Islands by Alvaro de Mendaña in 1568:*
       translated from the original Spanish manuscripts, edited with an intro-
       duction and notes by Lord Amherst of Hackney and Basil Thomson, 2 Vols.
       London: Bedford Press by permission of the Hakluyt Society.
Anonymous
1996   *1995 Forestry Review.* Unpublished report by Advisers in the Ministry of
       Finance, Honiara.
Aupai, T.
1994   Forest plantations on government land, in *Solomon Islands Forest Action*
       Plan: Proceedings of a Conference on Forest Policy and Law, 55-58. Honi-
       ara: Ministry of Forests, Environment and Conservation.
Baines, Graham B.K.
1989   Traditional resource management in the Melanesian South Pacific: A
       development dilemma. In *Common Property Resources: Ecology and Com-*
       munity-based Sustainable Development, F. Berkes (ed.), 273-295. London:
       Belhaven Press.
Baines, Graham B.K. and Edvard Hviding
1992   Traditional environmental knowledge from the Marovo area of the Solo-
       mon Islands. In *Lore: Capturing Traditional Environmental Knowledge*, M.
       Johnson (ed.), 91-110. Ottawa: International Development Research Centre.
1993   Traditional ecological knowledge for resource management in Marovo,
       Solomon Islands. In *Traditional Ecological Knowledge: Wisdom for Su-*
       stainable Development, Nancy M. Williams and Graham Baines (eds.), 56-
       65. Canberra: CRES, Australian National University.

Bank of Hawaii
1994   *An Economic Assessment of the Solomon Islands.* Honolulu: Bank of
        Hawaii.
Barlow, Kathy and Stephen Winduo (eds.)
1997   *Logging the Western Pacific: Perspectives from Papua New Guinea, Solo-
        mon Islands, and Vanuatu. The Contemporary Pacific,* Special Issue, 9(1).
Barrau, Jacques
1958   *Subsistence Agriculture in Melanesia.* Bulletin 219. Honolulu: Bernice P.
        Bishop Museum.
1965   L'Humide et le Sec. *Journal of the Polynesian Society,* 74:329-346.
Barth, Fredrik
1975   *Ritual and Knowledge among the Baktaman of New Guinea.* Oslo / New
        Haven: Norwegian University Press / Yale University Press.
Bayliss-Smith, Tim
1974   Constraints on population growth: the case of the Polynesian outlier atolls
        in the pre-contact period. *Human Ecology,* 2:259-295.
1977   Energy use and economic development in Pacific Islands communities. In
        Subsistence and Survival, T. Bayliss-Smith and R. Feachem, (eds.), 317-
        359. London: Academic Press.
1982   *The Ecology of Agricultural Systems.* Cambridge: Cambridge University
        Press.
1987   Population and Environment in the Marovo Lagoon, Solomon Islands.
        Marovo Lagoon Resource Management Project: Report presented to the
        Marovo community and to the Commonwealth Science Council. Mimeo.
1993   *Time, food and money in the Marovo Lagoon, Solomon Islands: village sur-
        veys in a proposed World Heritage Site.* London: Commonwealth Science
        Council.
Bayliss-Smith, Tim, R. Bedford, H. Brookfield and M. Latham
1988   *Islands, Islanders and the World: The colonial and post-colonial experi-
        ence of Eastern Fiji.* Cambridge: Cambridge University Press.
Bayliss-Smith, Tim and Jack Golson
1992   Wetland agriculture in New Guinea Highlands prehistory. In *The Wetland
        Revolution in Prehistory,* B. Coles (ed.), 15-27. Exeter: The Prehistoric So-
        ciety.
Bender, Barbara (ed.)
1993   *Landscape: Politics and Perspectives.* Oxford: Berg.
Bennett, Judith A.
1987   *Wealth of the Solomons. A History of a Pacific Archipelago, 1800-1978.*
        Pacific Islands Monograph Series, 3. Honolulu: University of Hawaii Press.
1995   Forestry, public land, and the colonial legacy in Solomon Islands. *The
        Contemporary Pacific,* 7:243-275.
In press *Pacific Forest: A history of resource control and contest in Solomon
        Islands, c. 1800-1997.* Cambridge: White Horse Press.
Berg, Cato
1999   Managing Difference: Kinship, Exchange and Urban Boundaries in
        Honiara, Solomon Islands. Thesis (anthropology), University of Bergen.

Blust, Robert
1981   Dual Divisions in Oceania: Innovation or Retention? *Oceania*, 52:66-79.
Boserup, Esther
1965   *The Conditions of Agricultural Growth: The Economics of Agrarian Change under Population Pressure*. London: Allen & Unwin.
Boutilier, James A.
1989   Kennedy's "Army": Solomon Islanders at War, 1942-1943. In *The Pacific Theater: Island Representations of World War II*, G. M. White and L. Lindstrom (eds.), 329-352. Pacific Islands Monograph Series, 8. Honolulu: University of Hawai'i Press.
Bradley, Joseph
c1860   *A Nine Months' Cruise in the 'Ariel' Schooner from San Francisco, in Company with the 'Wanderer' of the Royal Yacht Squadron, belonging to Benjamin Boyd, Esq*. First published by J.J. Beukers, General Printer, Church Street, Parramatta, New South Wales.
Broad, Robin with John Cavanagh
1993   *Plundering Paradise: the struggle for the environment in the Philippines*. Berkeley: University of California Press.
Brookfield, Harold C.
1972   Intensification and disintensification in Pacific agriculture: a theoretical approach. *Pacific Viewpoint*, 13:30-48.
1973   Full circle in Chimbu: a study of trends and cycles. In *The Pacific in Transition: Geographical Perspectives on Adaptation and Change*, H.C. Brookfield (ed.), 127-160. London: Edward Arnold.
1984   Intensification revisited. *Pacific Viewpoint*, 25:15-44.
1986   Intensification intensified. *Archaeology in Oceania*, 31:177-180.
1988   Fijian farmers each on their own land: the triumph of experience over hope. *Journal of Pacific History*, 23:15-35.
Brookfield, Harold C. et.al.
1977   *Population, Resources and Development in the Eastern Islands of Fiji: Information for Decision-making*. Canberra: Australian National University for UNESCO.
BSIP (British Solomon Islands Protectorate)
1911   *Handbook of the British Solomon Islands Protectorate*. Tulagi: Government of the British Solomon Islands Protectorate.
1963   *British Solomon Islands. Report for the years 1961 and 1962*. Honiara: Government of the British Solomon Islands Protectorate.
1965   *British Solomon Islands. Report for the years 1963 and 1964*. Honiara: Government of the British Solomon Islands Protectorate.
Burman, Rickie
1981   Time and socioeconomic change on Simbo, Solomon Islands. *Man* (n.s.), 16:251-267.
Burslem, D.F.R.P. and T.C. Whitmore
1996   *Silvics and wood properties of the common timber species on Kolombangara*. Solomon Islands Forest Record, 7. Oxford: Oxford Forestry Institute, Department of Plant Sciences, University of Oxford.

Campbell, K. (ed.)
1994   *Solomon Islands National Forest Action Plan. Conference on Forest Policy and Law.* Honiara: Ministry of Forests, Environment and Conservation.
Campbell, L.M.
1997   International conservation and local development: the sustainable use of marine turtles in Costa Rica. Unpublished Ph.D dissertation, University of Cambridge.
Cassells, R.M.
1995   Social and land tenure assessment of Viru Harbour and north New Georgia villages, Solomon Islands. Report to the Commonwealth Development Corporation, London (unpublished).
CDC (Commonwealth Development Corporation)
1991   Kolombangara Forest Products Limited Solomon Islands, Forestry VA Report No. 2. Commonwealth Development Corporation, London (unpublished).
Central Bank of Solomon Islands
1992   *Annual Report 1991.* Honiara.
1995   *Annual Report 1994.* Honiara.
1996a *Annual Report 1995.* Honiara.
1996b *Quarterly Review March 1996,* Vol. 7(1). Honiara.
Cheyne, Andrew
1971   *The Trading Voyages of Andrew Cheyne, 1841-1844,* edited by Dorothy Shineberg. Canberra: Australian National University Press.
Christiansen, Sofus
1975   *Subsistence on Bellona Island (Mungiki): A Study of the Cultural Ecology of a Polynesian Outlier in the British Solomon Islands Protectorate.* Language and Culture of Rennell and Bellona Islands, V. Copenhagen: National Museum of Denmark in cooperation with the Royal Danish Geographical Society.
Clarke, William C.
1971   *People and Place: An Ecology of a New Guinean Community.* Berkeley: University of California Press.
Clarke, W.C. and R.R. Thaman (eds.)
1993   *Agroforestry in the Pacific Islands: Systems for Sustainability.* Tokyo, London, Paris: United Nations University Press.
Clay, Jason W.
1987   *Indigenous Peoples and Tropical Forests.* Cambridge, Mass.: Cultural Survival Inc.
Cline-Cole, R.
1998   Knowledge claims and landscape: alternative views of the fuelwood-degradation nexus in northern Nigeria. *Environment and Planning, D. Society and Space,* 16:311-346.
Codrington, R.H.
1891   *The Melanesians: Studies in their anthropology and folk-lore.* Oxford: at the Clarendon Press.

CSC (Commonwealth Science Council)

1986 *SOPACOAST: The South Pacific Coastal Zone Management Programme.* CSC Technical Publications Series No. 204. London: Commonwealth Science Council.

Conklin, Harold C.

1957 *Hanunóo agriculture: a report on an integral system of shifting cultivation in the Philippines.* Rome: Food and Agriculture Organization of the United Nations (FAO).

Crook, Tony

1998 Growing knowledge in Bolivip, Papua New Guinea. *Cambridge Anthropology* 20 (3): 45-65.

Darby, d'E. Charles

1992 Solomon Islands World Heritage Programme. Consultant's report to Solomon Islands Ministry of Tourism and Aviation and New Zealand Ministry of External Relations and Trade, by Conservation Development Services, Auckland, New Zealand.

Darwin, Charles

1839 *Narrative of the Surveying Voyages of Her Majesty's Ships 'Adventure' and 'Beagle' between the years 1826 and 1836.* London. Reprinted as *The Voyage of the Beagle.* London: Dent, 1959.

DCW (District Commissioner, Western)

1950 Report on a tour of Marovo sub-district by District Commissioner from 28th August to 12th September. 33/4/5, Solomon Islands National Archives.'

Denoon, Donald and Catherine Snowden (eds.)

c1982 *A time to plant and a time to uproot: a history of agriculture in Papua New Guinea.* Port Moresby: Department of Primary Industries/Institute of Papua New Guinea Studies.

Denslow, J.S. and C. Padoch

1988 *People of the Tropical Rain Forest.* Berkeley: University of California Press, and Washington: DC: Smithsonian Institution.

Douglas, Ngaire

1996 *They Came for Savages: 100 Years of Tourism in Melanesia.* Lismore, NSW: Southern Cross University Press.

Elkin, A.P.

1953 *Social anthropology in Melanesia: a review of research.* Published under the auspices of the South Pacific Commission. London: Oxford University Press.

Ellen, Roy F.

1982 *Environment, Subsistence and System: The Ecology of Small-Scale Social Formations.* Cambridge: Cambridge University Press.

Errington, Frederick and Deborah Gewertz

1995 *Articulating change in the "Last Unknown".* Boulder: Westview Press.

Escobar, Arturo

1999 After Nature: Steps to an Antiessentialist Political Ecology. *Current Anthropology,* 40:1-29.

Evans, B.
1994   World Heritage Sites? Marovo, Rennell. *Solomons: The Airline Magazine of the Solomon Islands*, 14.
Fairhead, J. and M. Leach
1996   *Misreading the African Landscape: Society and Ecology in a Forest-Savanna Mosaic.* Cambridge: Cambridge University Press.
Falanruw, Marjorie V.C.
1989   Nature intensive agriculture: The food production system of Yap islands. In *Traditional Ecological Knowledge: A Collection of Essays*, R.E. Johannes (ed.), 43-50. Gland, Switzerland and Cambridge, UK: IUCN (The World Conservation Union).
Findlay, A.G.
1877   *A Directory for the navigation of the South Pacific Ocean: with descriptions of its coasts, islands, etc., from the Strait of Magalhaens to Panama, and those of New Zealand, Australia, etc.: its winds, currents and passages.* 4th Edition. London: Published for Richard Holmes Laurie.
Forests Monitor Ltd.
1996   Kumpulan Emas Berhad and it's involvement in the Solomon Islands. Draft briefing document, 22nd April 1996. Ely: Forests Monitor Ltd.
Foster, Robert J.
1995   *Social reproduction and history in Melanesia: mortuary ritual, gift exchange, and custom in the Tanga Islands.* Cambridge: Cambridge University Press.
Foucault, Michel
1975   *Surveiller et punir: Naissance de la prison.* Editions Gallimard, Paris. Translated as *To Discipline and to Punish: the Birth of the Prison.* London: Penguin.
France, Peter
1969   *The Charter of the Land: Custom and Colonisation in Fiji.* Melbourne: Oxford University Press.
Frazer, Ian
1987   *Growth and change in village agriculture: Manakwai, North Malaita.* South Pacific Smallholder Project Occasional Paper, 11. Armidale, NSW: University of New England.
1996   The struggle for control of Solomon Islands forests. In *Logging the Western Pacific*, K. Barlow and S. Winduo (eds.), 39-72. Special issue, *The Contemporary Pacific*, 9(1).
Friedman, Jonathan
1994   *Cultural Identity and Global Process.* London: Sage.
1997   Simplifying complexity: assimilating the global in a small paradise. In *Siting Culture: The Shifting Anthropological Object*, K.F. Olwig and K. Hastrup (eds.), 268-291. London: Routledge.
Geertz, Clifford
1963   *Agricultural involution: the process of ecological change in Indonesia.* Berkeley: University of California Press.

Gewertz, Deborah and Frederick Errington
1997   Why we return to Papua New Guinea. *Anthropological Quarterly*, 70:127-135.

Goldie, J.F.
1909   The people of New Georgia. Their manners and customs and religious beliefs. *Proceedings of the Royal Society of Queensland* 22(1): 23-30.

Golson, Jack
1981   The Ipomoean revolution revisited: society and the sweet potato in the upper Wahgi valley. In *Inequality in New Guinea Highlands Societies*, A. Strathern (ed.), 109-136. Cambridge: Cambridge University Press.

Goodenough, Ward H.
1955   A problem in Malayo-Polynesian social organization. *American Anthropologist*, 57:71-83.

Gosden, C. et.al.
1989   Lapita sites of the Bismarck Archipelago. *Antiquity*, 63:561-582.

Gourou, P.
1947   *Les Pays Tropicaux. Principes d'une géographie humaine et économique.* Paris: Presses Universitaires de France. Translated as *The Tropical World*, London: Longman (5th edition) 1980.

Greenaway, R.
1995   Ecotourism planning for Marovo Lagoon and Rennell Island, Solomon Islands. Draft Ecotourism Plan. Consultant's report for World Heritage Programme, UNESCO, by Rob Greenaway Tourism Resource Consultants, Wellington, New Zealand.

Groube, Leslie
1989   The taming of the rain forests: a model for Late Pleistocene forest exploitation in New Guinea. In *Foraging and Farming: the Evolution of Plant Exploitation*, D.R. Harris and G.C. Hillman (eds.), 292-304. London: Unwin Hyman.

Grünnadier Blahe to Admiral Maitland
1839   European and American seasmen are domiciled on [New Georgia]. (Despatches) - A 1282, p. 825. The Mitchell Library, Sydney.

Hancock, I.R. and C.P. Henderson
1988   *Flora of the Solomon Islands*. Research Bulletin No. 7, Dodo Creek Research Station. Honiara: Research Department, Ministry of Agriculture and Lands.

Hands, M., A.F. Harrison and T. Bayliss-Smith
1995   Phosphorus dynamics in slash-and-burn and alley cropping on ultisols of the humid tropics. In H. Tiessen (ed.) *Phosphorus in the Global Environment: Transfers, Cycles and Management*, 155-170. Chichester and New York: Wiley.

Hansell, J.R.F., J.R.D. Wall, I.S. Webb and P.G. Ash
1974   *Soil descriptions and analyses from New Georgia and Russell Islands, Solomon Islands*. Land Resources Study Supplementary Report 9. Tolworth Tower, Surbiton, Surrey: Land Resources Division.

Harcombe, David
1988   *Solomon Islands: A Travel Survival Kit.* South Yarra, Vic.: Lonely Planet Publications.
Henderson, C.P. and I.R. Hancock
1988   *A Guide to the Useful Plants of Solomon Islands.* Honiara: Research Department, Ministry of Agriculture and Lands.
High Court of Solomon Islands
1996   Billy Boy Kioto v. Presley Watts and Another, Interlocutory Judgment by Sam Awich (Commissioner).
Hocart, A.M.
1922   The cult of the dead in Eddystone of the Solomons. *Journal of the Royal Anthropological Institute of Great Britain and Ireland,* 52:71-112, 259-305.
1935   The canoe and the bonito in Eddystone. *Journal of the Royal Anthropological Institute of Great Britain and Ireland,* 65: 97-11.
nd   Manuscripts and field notes on Eddystone and New Georgia, on deposit at the Turnbull Library, Wellington, New Zealand.
Honan, Mark and David Harcombe
1997   *Solomon Islands.* Third edition. Hawthorne, Vic.: Lonely Planet Publications.
Hunter, L.A.J.
1989   Market prospects for Gmelina arborea and alternatives from Kolombangara, Solomon Islands. Report by ANUTECH consultants, Jamison, ACT, Australia for World Bank (21 pp., unpublished).
Hviding, Edvard
1988   *Marine Tenure and Resource Development in Marovo Lagoon, Solomon Islands.* Honiara, Solomon Islands: South Pacific Forum Fisheries Agency, FFA Reports 88/71.
1993a   *The Rural Context of Giant Clam Mariculture in Solomon Islands: An Anthropological Study.* ICLARM Technical Report, 19. Manila: International Center for Living Aquatic Resources Management.
1993b   Indigenous essentialism? "Simplifying" customary land ownership in New Georgia, Solomon Islands. *Bijdragen tot de Taal-, Land- en Volkenkunde,* 149:802-824.
1995a   Maritime travel, present and past, in Marovo, Western Solomon Islands. In *Seafaring in the Contemporary Pacific Islands: Studies in Continuity and Change,* R. Feinberg (ed.), 90-113. DeKalb, Ill.: Northern Illinois University Press.
1995b   *Of Reef and Rainforest: A Dictionary of Environment and Resources in Marovo Lagoon.* Bergen: Centre for Development Studies, University of Bergen, in collaboration with Western Province Division of Culture.
1995c   *Custom Stories of the Marovo Area.* E. Hviding, ed. and trans. Bergen: Centre for Development Studies, University of Bergen, in collaboration with Western Province Division of Culture.
1996a   *Guardians of Marovo Lagoon: Practice, Place, and Politics in Maritime Melanesia.* Pacific Islands Monograph Series, 14. Honolulu: University of Hawai'i Press.

1996b Nature, culture, magic, science: on meta-languages for comparison in cultural ecology. In *Nature and Society: A Contested Interface*, P. Descola and G. Pálsson (eds.), 165-184. London: Routledge.

1998a Western movements in non-Western worlds: towards an anthropology of uncertain encounters. *Suomen Antropologi (Journal of the Finnish Anthropological Society)*, 23(3):30-51.

1998b Contextual flexibility: present status and future of customary marine tenure in Solomon Islands. *Ocean & Coastal Management*, 40:253-269.

nd a The beaten and the dead: historical ethnography of headhunting in Marovo Lagoon. *Journal of the Polynesian Society* (Special Issue on headhunting in the Western Solomon Islands), forthcoming, 2000.

nd b Disentangling the *butubutu* of New Georgia: cognatic kinship in thought and practice. In *Oceanic Socialities: Ethnographies of Experience*, I. Hoëm and S. Roalkvam (eds.). Oxford: Berg (forthcoming).

Hviding, Edvard and Graham B.K. Baines

1992 *Fisheries Management in the Pacific: Tradition and the Challenges of Development in Marovo, Solomon Islands.* UNRISD Discussion Paper, 32. Geneva: United Nations Research Institute for Social Development.

1994 Community-based fisheries management, tradition and the challenges of development in Marovo, Solomon Islands. *Development and Change*, 25(1):13-39.

Ingold, Tim

1992 Culture and the perception of the environment. In *Bush Base: Forest Farm. Culture, Environment and Development*, E. Croll and D. Parkin (eds.), 39-56. London: Routledge.

International Alliance of Indigenous-Tribal Peoples of the Tropical Forest, and International Work Group for Indigenous Affairs

1996 Indigenous Peoples, Forest, and Biodiversity: Indigenous Peoples and the Global Environmental Dilemma. IAITPTF International Secretariat, 14 Rudolf Place, London SW8 1RP, with IWGIA, Copenhagen.

IUCN (International Union for Conservation of Nature and Natural Resources

1986 *Review of the Protected Areas System in Oceania.* Cland and Cambridge: IUCN in collaboration with the United Nations Environment Programme (UNEP).

Jackson, K.B.

1978 **Tie hokara, tie vaka**: Black Man, White Man. A study of the New Georgia Group to 1930. Unpublished doctoral thesis, Australian National University, Canberra.

Johannes, R.E.

1981 *Words of the Lagoon: Fishing and Marine Lore in the Palau District of Micronesia.* Berkeley: University of California Press.

1989 A spawning aggregation of the grouper, *Plectropomus areolatus* (Rüppel) in the Solomon Islands. In *Proceedings of the 8th International Coral Reef Symposium*, Townsville, Australia, Vol. 2:751-755.

Johannes, R.E. and Edvard Hviding
1987   Traditional knowledge of Marovo Lagoon fishermen concerning their marine resources, with notes on marine conservation. Technical report presented to the Marovo community and to Commonwealth Science Council.

Jones, S., M. Muqtada and Per Ronnas
1987   *Solomon Islands: Towards a Strategy for Rural Employment.* Asian Employment Programme Working Paper. New Delhi: ILO-ARTEP

Johnson, Osa
1945   *Bride in the Solomons.* London: George G. Harrap.

Juvik, Sonia P.
1993   Christian denominational influences on attitudes toward resources development, Marovo Lagoon, Solomon Islands. In *Ethics, Religion, and Biodiversity: Relations Between Conservation and Cultural Values*, L.S. Hamilton (ed.), 147-175. Cambridge, UK: White Horse Press.

Josephides, Lisette
1991   Metaphors, metathemes, and the construction of sociality: a critique of the new Melanesian ethnography. *Man* (n.s.), 26:145-161.

Kahn, Miriam
1984   Taro irrigation: a descriptive account from Wamira, Papua New Guinea. *Oceania* 54:204-223.
1986   *Always hungry, never greedy: Food and the expression of gender in a Melanesian society.* Cambridge: Cambridge University Press.

Keesing, Roger M.
1968   Nonunilineal descent and the contextual definition of status. *American Anthropologist*, 70:82-84.
1971   Descent, residence and cultural codes. In *Anthropology in Oceania: Essays Presented to Ian Hogbin*, L. Hiatt and C. Jayawardena (eds.), 121-128. Sydney: Angus & Robertson.
1982   *Kwaio Religion: The Living and the Dead in a Solomon Island Society.* New York: Columbia University Press.
1984   Rethinking Mana. *Journal of Anthropological Research*, 40:137-156.
1985   Killers, Big Men and Priests on Malaita: Reflections on a Melanesian Troika System. *Ethnology*, 24:237-252.
1988   *Melanesian Pidgin and the Oceanic Substrate.* Stanford, CA: Stanford University Press.
1992   *Custom and confrontation: the Kwaio struggle for cultural autonomy.* Chicago: University of Chicago Press.
1993   Kastom re-examined. *Anthropological Forum*, 6(4): 587-596.
1994   Theories of culture revisited. In *Assessing Cultural Anthropology*, R. Borofsky (ed.), 301-310. New York: McGraw-Hill Inc.

Keesing, Roger M. and Robert Tonkinson (eds.)
1982   Reinventing traditional culture: the politics of *Kastom* in Island Melanesia. *Mankind* (Special Issue), 13(4).

Kelly, P.
1997   Globalization, power and the politics of scale in the Philippines. *Geoforum*, 28(2):151-171.

KFPL (Kolombangara Forest Products Limited)
1995 *Facts about Kolombangara Forest Products Ltd. -- the nation's largest sustainable forestry company.* Ringgi Cove, Solomon Islands: KFPL, publicity leaflet.
1993a *KFPL News.* Issue 1 (July 1993). Mimeographed newsletter, Kolombangara Forest Products Ltd., Ringgi Cove, Solomon Islands.
1993b *KFPL News.* Issue 2 (November 1993).
1994 *KFPL News.* Issue 3 (1994).
1995 *KFPL News.* Issue 4 (1995).
1996 *KFPL News.* Issue 5 (1995).
Kirch, Patrick Vinton
1984 *The Evolution of the Polynesian Chiefdoms.* New Studies in Archaeology Series. Cambridge: Cambridge University Press.
1985 *Feathered Gods and Fishhooks: An introduction to Hawaiian archaeology and prehistory.* Honolulu: University of Hawaii Press.
1994 *The Wet and the Dry: Irrigation and Agricultural Intensification in Polynesia.* Chicago: University of Chicago Press.
1997 *The Lapita Peoples: Ancestors of the Oceanic World.* Oxford: Blackwell Publishers.
Kirch, Patrick Vinton and Marshall D. Sahlins
1992 *Anahulu: The Anthropology of History in the Kingdom of Hawaii.* Vol. 1, *Historical Ethnography* (M. Sahlins). Vol. 2, *The Archaeology of History* (P. Kirch). Chicago: University of Chicago Press.
Kirch, Patrick Vinton and Douglas Yen
1982 *Tikopia: The Prehistory and Ecology of a Polynesian Outlier.* Bernice P. Bishop Museum Bulletin 238. Honolulu: Bishop Museum.
Knauft, Bruce M.
1998 *From Primitive to Postcolonial in Melanesia and Anthropology.* Ann Arbor: University of Michigan Press.
Kumpulan Emas Berhad
1996 Proposal on the Development of an Integrated Oil Palm Project on Vangunu Island, Western Province (unpublished).
LaFranchi, Christopher and Greenpeace Pacific
1999 Islands Adrift? Comparing Industrial and Small-Scale Economic Options for Marovo Lagoon Region of Solomon Islands. Suva: Greenpeace Pacific.
Latour, Bruno
1983 *Science in Action.* Cambridge, Mass.: Harvard University Press.
1993 *We Have Never Been Modern.* Translated by C. Porter. New York: Harvester Wheatsheaf.
Leach, Helen M.
2000 Intensification in the Pacific: a critique of the archaeological criteria and their application. *Current Anthropology*, 40:311-340.
Leach, M. and R. Mearns
1997 *The Lie of the Land: Challenging Received Wisdom on the African Environment.* International African Institute. London: James Currey.

Lees, Annette with M. Garnett and S. Wright
1991   *A Representative Protected Forests System for the Solomon Islands.* Nelson, New Zealand: Maruia Society, for Australian Parks and Wildlife Service.

Leivestad, Karen
1995   Fra en ring av steiner: en etnografisk studie av matpraksis og mening i Marovo (New Georgia, Solomon Islands). [From a ring of stones: an ethnographic study of food practice and meaning in Marovo, New Georgia, Solomon Islands]). Thesis, Department of Social Anthropology, University of Bergen. (In Norwegian; pending translation)

nd   Food and food preparation in the Western Solomons: everyday life in past and present. In *Cultural History of Western Province*, Catherine Cole and Jully Makini (eds.). Gizo and Honiara: Western Province Divison of Culture and University of the South Pacific Solomon Islands Centre. (forthcoming)

Levers Pacific Timbers Ltd.
1969   *Timbers of the British Solomon Islands.* Kolombangara: Levers Pacific Timbers Limited.

Liligeto, Wilson Gia
1997   *Babata: My Land, My Tribe, My People. A Historical Account and Tradition of Butubutu Babata of Patu Laiti, Marovo Island. With recollections from the Tribe's Patriarchs* .... Chea Village, Marovo Lagoon, Western Province.

Lingenfelter, Sherwood G.
1975   *Yap: Political Leadership and Culture Change in an Island Society.* Honolulu: University of Hawaii Press.

Loy, T.H., M. Spriggs and S. Wickler
1992   Direct evidence for human use of plants 28,000 years ago: starch residues on stone artefacts from the northern Solomon Islands. *Antiquity*, 66: 898-912.

McCoy, Michael
1980   *Reptiles of the Solomon Islands.* Handbook No. 7. Wau, Papua New Guinea: Wau Ecology Institute.

MacKenzie, Maureen A.
1991   *Androgynous Objects: String bags and gender in central New Guinea.* Studies in Anthropology and History, 2. Chur: Harwood Academic Publishers.

McKinnon, John M.
1975   Tomahawks, turtles and traders: A reconstruction in the circular causation of warfare in the New Georgia Group. *Oceania*, 45:290-307.

McNabb, A.R.
1949   Appendix ["Taro varieties in Wana Wana Lagoon"] to Memorandum of 3 May 1967 from Agricultural Officer, Central, to Deputy Director of Agriculture, Honiara. BSIP CR/66/1241, Public Records Office, London.

Malinowski, Bronislaw
1922   *Argonauts of the Western Pacific.* London: Routledge and Kegan Paul.

1935   *Coral Gardens and their Magic.* 2 Vols. London: George Allen & Unwin.

Meller, Norman and Robert H. Horwitz

1987   Hawaii: themes in land monopoly. In *Land Tenure in the Pacific*, 3rd edition, R.G. Crocombe (ed.), 25-44. Suva: University of the South Pacific.

Miller, Daniel

1979   *Report of the National Sites Survey 1976-1978.* Honiara: National Museum.

Ministry of Forests

1994   *Solomon Islands Forest Action Plan: Proceedings of the Conference on Forest Law and Policy.* Honiara: Ministry of Forests, Environment and Conservation.

Moorehead, Alan

1968   *The Fatal Impact.* Harmondsworth: Penguin Books.

Mueller-Dombois, Dieter and F. Raymond Fosberg

1998   *Vegetation of the Tropical Pacific Islands.* New York: Springer.

Munro, John L.

1983   Coral reef fish and fisheries of the Caribbean Sea. In *Caribbean Coral Reef Fishery Resources*, J.L. Munro (ed.), 1-9. ICLARM Studies and Reviews, 7. Manila: International Center for Living Aqatic Resources Management.

Myers, Fred R.

1991   *Pintupi country, Pintupi self: Sentiment, Place, and Politics among Western Desert Aborigines.* Berkeley: University of California Press.

Mytinger, Carolyn

1942   *Headhunting in the Solomon Islands: Around the Coral Sea.* New York: The MacMillan Company.

Nankivell, P.

1991   *The Solomon Islands Economy: Prospects for stabilisation and sustainable growth.* PDP Australia Ltd. for Australian International Development Assistance Bureau. Fyshwick, ACT: Australian Government Publishing Service.

Nye, P. and D.J. Greenland

1960   *The Soil under Shifting Cultivation.* Harpenden: Commonwealth Agricultural Bureau.

Ohmae, Kenichi

1995   Putting global logic first. *Harvard Business Review* Jan.-Feb. 1995, 119-125.

Oliver, Douglas L.

1955   *A Solomon Island Society: Kinship and Leadership among the Siuai of Bougainville.* Cambridge, Mass.: Harvard University Press.

Paijmans, K.

1975   Vegetation. In *New Guinea Vegetation*, K. Paijmans (ed.), 23-105. Canberra: Australian National University Press.

Pálsson, Gísli

1998   The "Charm and Terror" of human ecology: nature and society in the age of postmodernity. Paper presented at the 96th Annual Meetings of the American Anthropological Association, Washington, DC.

Pana, B.
c1965 How Pastor and Mrs. G.F. Jones came to Sasaghana in the Marovo Lagoon
       in 1915. Typescript, in files of the Seventh-day Adventist Church, Honiara.
Paravicini, Eugen
1931   *Reisen in den Britischen Salomonen*. Frauenfeld: Leipzig, Hüber.
1932   Die Maravolagune. *Der Schweizer Geograph*, 6:1-5.
Parmentier, Richard
1987   *The Sacred Remains: Myth, History and Polity in Belau*. Chicago: Univer-
       sity of Chicago Press.
Pollock, Nancy
1992   *These Roots Remain: Food habits in the islands of the central and eastern
       Pacific since Western contact*. Honolulu: University of Hawaiii Press/Laie,
       Hawai'i: The Institute for Polynesian Studies.
Powell, J.M.
1976   Ethnobotany. In *New Guinea Vegetation*, K. Paijmans (ed.), 106-184.
       Canberra: Australian National University Press.
Rappaport, Roy A.
1968   *Pigs for the Ancestors: Ritual in the Ecology of a New Guinea People*. New
       Haven: Yale University Press.
1979   *Ecology, Meaning, and Religion*. Berkeley: North Atlantic Books.
Ravuvu, Asesela
1983   *Vaka i Taukei: The Fijian Way of Life*. Suva: Institute of Pacific Studies,
       University of the South Pacific.
Reeve, Rowland
1989   Recent work on the prehistory of the Western Solomons, Melanesia.
       Bulletin of the Indo-Pacific Prehistory Association, 9:46-67.
Rence, Gordon
1979   Timber and religion of north New Georgia. In *Land in Solomon Islands*, P.
       Larmour (ed.), 119-124. Institute of Pacific Studies, University of the South
       Pacific, and Ministry of Agriculture and Lands, Honiara.
Richards, P.W.
1952   *The Tropical Rain Forest: An Ecological Study*. Cambridge: Cambridge
       University Press.
Riogano, Josiah
1979   Kolombangara. In *Land in Solomon Islands*, P. Larmour (ed.), 85-89.
       Institute of Pacific Studies, University of the South Pacific, Suva, Fiji and
       Ministry of Agriculture and Lands, Honiara.
Roe, E.
1991   Development narratives, or making the best of blueprint development.
       World Development, 19:287-300.
1996   Sustainable development and cultural theory. *International Journal of
       Sustainable Development and World Ecology*, 3:1-14.
Ross, Harold M.
1973   *Baegu: Social and Ecological Organization in Malaita, Solomon Islands*.
       Urbana: University of Illinois Press.

Ross, Malcolm
1985   A genetic grouping of Oceanic languages in Bougainville and the Western Solomons. In *Focal II: Papers from the Fourth International Conference on Austronesian Linguistics*, P. Geraghty, L. Carrington and S. Wurm (eds.), 175-200. Pacific Linguistics C-94. Canberra: Australian National University.

Russell, Tom
1948a   The culture of Marovo, British Solomon Islands. *Journal of the Polynesian Society*, 57:306-329.
1948b   District of New Georgia. District Officer's Tour report for sub-district of Marovo. 18/8/48. 33/4/1, Solomon Islands National Archives.

Ruthven, David
1979   Land legislation from the Protectorate to Independence. In *Land in Solomon Islands*, P. Larmour (ed.), 238-248. Institute of Pacific Studies, University of the South Pacific, Suva, Fiji and Ministry of Agriculture and Lands, Honiara.

Sahlins, Marshall
1963   Poor man, Rich man, Big man, Chief: Political types in Melanesia and Polynesia. *Comparative Studies in Society and History*, 5:285-303.
1985   *Islands of History*. Chicago: University of Chicago Press.
1993   Goodbye to Tristes Tropes: Ethnography in the Context of Modern World History. *Journal of Modern History*, 65:1-25.

Salisbury, Richard
1962   *From stone to steel: economic consequences of a technological change in Papua New Guinea*. Melbourne: Melboure University Press.

Schama, Simon
1995   *Landscape and Memory*. London: Harper Collins.

Scheffler, Harold W.
1965   *Choiseul Island Social Structure*. Berkeley: University of California Press.

Schep, Jaap
1997   International trade for local development: the case of western Solomon Islands fair trade. In *Environment and Development in the Pacific Islands*, B. Burt and C. Clerk (eds.), 78-90. Canberra: National Centre for Development Studies, Australian National University.

Schneider, Gerhard
1996   Land dispute and Tradition in Munda, Roviana Lagoon, Solomon Islands: From Headhunting to the Quest for the Control of Land. Unpublished doctoral thesis, University of Cambridge, UK.
1998   Reinventing identities: redefining cultural concepts in the struggle between villagers in Munda, Roviana Lagoon, New Georgia Island, Solomon Islands, for the control of land. In *Pacific Answers to Western Hegemony: Cultural Practices of Identity Construction*, J. Wassmann (ed.), 191-211. Oxford: Berg.

Schumacher, E.F.
1973   *Small is Beautiful*. New York: Harper & Row.

Serpenti, L.M.
1965   *Cultivators in the Swamps: Social Structure and Horticulture in a New Guinea Society.* Assen, Netherlands: Van Gorcum.
Shield, E.D.
1992   *Plantation Opportunity Areas in the Solomon Islands.* Solomon Islands National Forest Inventory, Project Working Paper 13. ACIL, International Forest Environment Research and Management, and ERSIS Australia, for AIDAB and Ministry of Natural Resources, Solomon Islands.
Sillitoe, Paul
1979   *Give and take: Exchange in Wola Society.* New York: St. Martin's Press.
1984   *Roots of the Earth: Crops in the Highlands of Papua New Guinea.* Manchester: Manchester University Press.
1988   *Made in Niugini: technology in the Highlands of Papua New Guinea.* London: British Museum Publications.
1996   *A Place against Time: Land and Environment in the Papua New Guinea Highlands.* Amsterdam: Harwood Academic Publishers.
Somerville, H.B.T.
1897   Ethnographical notes in New Georgia, Solomon Islands. *Journal of the Royal Anthropological Institute of Great Britain and Ireland,* 26:357-413.
nd   Notebook. Original kept in files of the Royal Anthropological Institute of Great Britain and Ireland, London.
Spriggs, Matthew
1981   Vegetable Kingdoms: Taro irrigation and Pacific pre-history. Doctoral thesis, Research School of Pacific Studies, Australian National University. ·
1982   Irrigation in Melanesia: formative adaptation and intensification. In *Melanesia: Beyond Diversity,* R.J. May and H. Nelson (eds.), 309-324. Canberra: Research School of Pacific Studies, Australian National University.
1985   Taro irrigation techniques in the Pacific. In *Edible Aroids,* S. Chandra (ed.), 123-135. Oxford: Oxford University Press.
1990   Why irrigation matters in Pacific prehistory. In *Pacific Production Systems: Approaches to Prehistory,* D.E. Yen and J.M.J. Mummery (eds.), 174-189. Canberra: RSPS, Australian National University.
1996   Early agriculture and what went before in Island Melanesia: continuity or intrusion? In *The origins and spread of agriculture and pastoralism in Eurasia,* D.R. Harris (ed.), 524-537. London: UCL Press.
1997   *The Island Melanesians.* Oxford: Blackwell Publishers.
Statistical Office
1971   *Annual Abstract of Statistics 1971.* Honiara: Statistical Office.
Statistics Office
1985   *Primary Production.* Statistical Bulletin No.9/85. Honiara: Statistics Office.
1995   *Solomon Islands 1993 Statistical Yearbook.* Bulletin No. 16/95. Honiara: Statistics Office, Ministry of Finance.
Stoddart, David R.
1969   Geomorphology of the Marovo elevated barrier reef, New Georgia. *Philosophical Transactions of the Royal Society,* B 255:388-402.

360 *Islands of Rainforest*

Strathern, Marilyn
1988   *The Gender of the Gift: Problems with Women and Problems with Society in Melanesia.* Berkeley: University of California Press.
1992   The decomposition of an event. *Cultural Anthropology*, 7:245-254.
Survival International
1994   *Tourism and Tribal Peoples: The 'New Imperialism'.* Factsheet published by Survival International, London.
SWIFT (Solomon Western Islands Fair Trade)
1996   *SWIFT Newsletter.* Mimeo.
1998a   *SWIFT Newsletter.* Mimeo.
1998b   *SWIFT Newsletter.* Mimeo.
Tausinga, Job D.
1992   Our Land, Our Choice: Development of North New Georgia. In *Independence, Dependence, Interdependence: The First 10 Years of Solomon Islands Independence*, Ron Crocombe and Esau Tuza (eds.), 55-66. Honiara: University of the South Pacific / Solomon Islands College of Higher Education.
Tedder, James L.O.
1974   Notes on old village sites on Marovo Island, New Georgia. *Journal of the Solomon Islands Museum Association*, 2:12-21.
Tedder, Margaret M.
1976   Old Kusaghe. With additional field notes by Susan Barrus. *Journal of the Cultural Association of the Solomon Islands*, 4:41-95.
Thomas, Nicholas
1989a   *Out of Time: History and Evolution in Anthropological Discourse.* Cambridge: Cambridge University Press.
1989b   The force of ethnology: origins and significance of the Melanesia/Polynesia division. *Current Anthropology*, 30:27-42.
1991   *Entangled Objects: Exchange, Material Culture, and Colonialism in the Pacific.* Cambridge, MA: Harvard University Press.
1997   *In Oceania: Visions, Artifacts, Histories.* Durham: Duke University Press.
Tiffany, Sharon W.
1983   Customary land disputes, courts, and African models in the Solomon Islands. *Oceania*, 53: 277-290.
Tilley, Christopher
1992   *A Phenomenology of Landscape: Places, Paths and Monuments.* Oxford: Berg.
Titcomb, Margaret with M.K. Pukui
1968   *Dog and Man in the Ancient Pacific.* Honolulu: Bishop Museum Special Publication No. 59.
Tryon, Darrell T.
1981   Map 15: Solomon Islands and Bougainville. In *Language Atlas of the Pacific Area*, S.A. Wurm and S. Hattori (eds.). Canberra: Australian Academy of the Humanities.

Tryon, Darrell and Brian Hackman
1983   *Solomon Islands Languages: An Internal Classification.* Pacific Linguistics C-72. Canberra: Australian National University.

Tsing, Anna Lowenhaupt
1993   *In the Realm of the Diamond Queen: Marginality in an Out-of-the-Way Place.* Princeton, NJ: Princeton University Press.

USP (University of the South Pacific)
1988   *The Big Death: Solomon Islanders Remember World War II.* Honiara: University of the South Pacific Extension Centre and Solomon Islands College of Higher Education / Suva: Institute of Pacific Studies, University of the South Pacific.

Vigulu, Vaena
1995   Sociological survey of villages in the study area Kolombangara. Mimeographed report, KFPL, Ringgi Cove (unpublished).

von Droste, B.
1995   Cultural landscapes in a global World Heritage strategy. In *Cultural landscapes of universal value*, B. von Droste, H. Plachter and M. Rössler (eds.), 20-24. Stuttgart / New York: Gustav Fischer Verlag Jena, with UNESCO.

Vudere, George
c1975   Saikile. Typescript from interview. Rev. G.C. Carter MSS, Mitchell Library, Sydney.

Wall, J.R.D. and J.R.F. Hansell
1975   *Land resources of the Solomon Islands. Volume 4, New Georgia Group and the Russell Islands.* Land Resources Study 18. Tolworth, England: Land Resources Division, Ministry of Overseas Development.

Wall, J.D., J.R.F. Hansell, J.A. Catt, E.C. Ormrod, J.A. Varley and I.S. Webb
1979   *The Soils of Solomon Islands.* 2 Vols. Technical Bulletin, Land Resources Development Centre, Ministry of Overseas Development, Surbiton, Surrey.

Waterhouse, J.H.L.
1928   *A Roviana and English Dictionary, with English-Roviana Index and List of Natural History Objects.* Guadalcanar: Melanesian Mission Press.
1949   *A Roviana and English Dictionary, with English-Roviana Index and List of Natural History Objects and Appendix of Old Customs,* revised and enlarged by L.M. Jones. Sydney: Epworth Printing & Publishing House.

WCED (The World Commission on Environment and Development)
1987   *Our Common Future.* Oxford, New York: Oxford University Press.

Western Province
1985   *Strategy for Development: the resource development approach and policies of the Western provincial government of the Solomon Islands.* Gizo: Western Provincial Government.

White, Geoffrey M. and Lamont Lindstrom (eds.)
1989   *The Pacific Theater: Island Representations of World War II.* Pacific Islands Monograph Series, 8. Honolulu: University of Hawai'i Press.
1993   Custom Today. *Anthropological Forum* (Special Issue), 6(4).
1998   *Chiefs Today: Traditional Pacific Leadership and the Postcolonial State.* Stanford: Stanford University Press.

Whitmore, T.C.
1965   *Guide to the Forests of the British Solomon Islands.* London: Oxford University Press.
1969   The vegetation of the Solomon Islands. *Philosophical Transactions of the Royal Society,* B 255:259-270.
1984   *Tropical Rain Forests of the Far East.* Second edition, with a chapter on soils by C.P. Burnham. Oxford: Clarendon Press.
1990   *An Introduction to Tropical Rain Forests.* Oxford: Clarendon Press.
1998   *An Introduction to Tropical Rain Forests.* Second Edition. Oxford: Oxford University Press.
Whittaker, R.H. and G.E. Likens
1975   The biosphere and man. In Lieth, H. and R.H. Whittaker (eds.) *Primary Production of the Biosphere,* 305-328. Berlin, Heidelberg and New York: Springer-Verlag.
Williams, Nancy
1986   *The Yolngu and their land: A system of land tenure and the fight for its recognition.* Canberra: Australian Institute of Aboriginal Studies.
Wingham, Elspeth
1997   *Nomination of Esat Rennell, Solomon Islands, for inclusion in the World Heritage List, Natural Sites.* Christchurch: Larcombe Print Ltd.
Wittfogel, Karl A.
1957   *Oriental Despotism: A Comparative Study of Total Power.* New Haven: Yale University Press.
Wolf, Eric R.
1982   *Europe and the People Without History.* Berkeley: University of California Press.
Woodford, Charles M.
1888   Exploration of the Solomon Islands. *Proceedings of the Royal Geographical Society,* 10:351-376.
1890   Further explorations in the Solomon Islands. *Proceedings of the Royal Geographical Society,* 12:393-418.
Worsley, Peter
1997   *Knowledges: What Different Peoples Make of the World.* London: Profile Books.
Wurm, S.A. and Shiro Hattori (eds.)
1981   *Language Atlas of the Pacific Area.* Canberra: Australian Academy of the Humanities.
Yen, Douglas
1973   Agriculture in Anutan subsistence. In *Anuta: A Polynesian Outlier in the Solomon Islands,* D.E. Yen and J. Gordon (eds.), 112-155. Pacific Anthropological Records No. 21. Honolulu: Bernice P. Bishop Museum.
1974a   *The Sweet Potato and Oceania: An Essay in Ethnobotany.* Bernice P. Bishop Museum Bulletin 236. Honolulu.
1974b   Arboriculture in the subsistence of Santa Cruz, Solomon Islands. *Economic Botany* 28(3):247-286.

1976   Agricultural systems and prehistory in the Solomon Islands. In *Southeast Solomon Islands Cultural History*, R.C. Green and M.M. Cresswell (eds.), 61-74. Wellington: Royal Society of New Zealand.

1982   The history of cultivated plants. In *Melanesia: Beyond Diversity*, R.J. May and H. Nelson (eds.), 281-296. Canberra: Research School of Pacific Studies, Australian National University.

Index

Abe, Christopher Colombus, 295
Acacia, 246, 247, 248
agricultural intensification, 26, 119, 152
Agricultural Opportunity Areas, 167, 201, 274
agroforestry in general, 17-19, 26, 49, 77, 130, 144, 176; *see also particular trees and crops*
agroforestry in Solomon Islands, *see* gardens; *and names of crops, islands, tree species*
air travel, 205, 278, 314
Allardyce company, 216
alley cropping, 18
Alocasia taro, 65, 104, 161
Alpinia, see gingers
Alstonia, 59, 61, 168, 171, 173
Americans, 158-9
Aneityum, 151
Annona, see soursop
anthropology, 5, 7, 321; *see also* ethnography
Anuta, 22
arboriculture, 19, 21, 26, 99, 127-8, 129, 144, 388; *see also* agroforestry; *Canarium; and other trees*
archaeology, 5, 21, 131-5, 330
Areca, see betel nut
Artocarpus, see breadfruit
Asia, Southeast, 166, 265, 268, 322
Asians, 6
Australia, 207, 209, 304, 315
Austronesian languages, 21, 24, 33, 113
Avavasa island, 186, 333
axes, 123, 130-1, 149, 170

bags, 97-8
bats, 75, 117, 128, 144
Baines, Graham, xv, 132-5, 139, 231, 296
Baini village, 253, 337
baitfish, 41, 329

Baktaman, 143
bananas, cultivation, 65, 102. 106; in diet, 156, 180; history, 123-5, 146, 161; and prehistory, 21
bangara, 39-40, 151, 215, 231, 232
banking, *see* National Bank
Bareho, 177-82, 193-9
Bareke, 33, 37, 88, 90, 149, 150, 189; language, xvi, 33, 113-5; soils, 106, 108, 187
Barora, 225, 233
Barringtonia asiatica, 50, 63
Barringtonia edulis, 59, 66, 67, 104, 142, 144, 200
Barringtonia spp., 59, 142, 144
Barrus, Susan, 132
barter, *see* exchange; trade, early European
baskets, 96-7
Batuna, 75, 172, 213, 302, 304
beans, 65, 90, 161
bêche-de-mer, 28, 53, 75, 123, 165, 312
Bennett, Judith, 153, 261, 335
betel nut, 35, 49, 67, 84, 105, 183, 200
Betikama, 302
Biche village, 305, 307
big-man, 151, 231, 237, 263
Bili , 109
biodiversity, 2, 10, 35, 54, 176, 277, 320
birds, 88, 144, 163, 312
Bisuana village, 91, 116-20, 177-82, 186-90
Bolivip, 120, 143, 329
Bougainville, 22, 125
Bradley, Joseph, 124
breadfruit, 65, 104, 125, 144, 146, 338
British approaches, 227, 229; *see also* Land Resources Study; Levers company
British Solomon Islands Protectorate, 6, 164, 166, 213, 218